Trends in Chinese Education

This book considers a wide range of key developments and key areas of debate in China's education system. They include, but are not limited to, marketization; quality assurance; economic and gender inequality; expansion in the primary, secondary, and tertiary sectors; the impact of globalization; and the influence of education on China's economic growth. The book, which comprises contributions from many leading authorities, will be of great interest both to comparative education specialists and to all those interested in China's rise and development.

Chen Hongjie is a Professor at the Institute of Higher Education in the Graduate School of Education, Peking University. He is also the Director of the Center for Doctoral Education at Peking University, Editor-in-Chief of the *Peking University Education Review*, and Vice-President of the Higher Education Committee of the Chinese Higher Education Association.

W. James Jacob is an Associate Professor of Higher Education Leadership at the University of Pittsburgh, USA. His research and leadership interests include higher education strategic planning; academic affairs; quality assurance; organizational development; organizational effectiveness; and indigenous education issues of culture, language, and identity as they relate to post-secondary education.

Comparative Development and Policy in Asia

Series Editors
Ka Ho Mok (Hong Kong Institute of Education, China)
Rachel Murphy (Oxford University, UK)
Misa Izuhara (University of Bristol, UK)

Welfare Reform in East Asia
Towards workfare?
Edited by Chak Kwan Chan and Kinglun Ngok

China's Assimilationist Language Policy
Impact on indigenous/minority literacy and Social harmony
Edited by Gulbahar H. Beckett and Gerard A. Postiglione

The Emergent Knowledge Society and the Future of Higher Education
Asian perspectives
Deane E. Neubauer

China's Civil Service Reform
Wang Xiaoqi

Towards a New Development Paradigm in Twenty-First Century China
Economy, society and politics
Edited by Eric Florence and Pierre Defraigne

Public Policymaking in Hong Kong
Civic engagement and state-society relations in a semi-democracy
Eliza W. Y. Lee, Elaine Y. M. Chan, Joseph C. W. Chan, Peter T. Y. Cheung, Wai Fung Lam and Wai Man Lam

Nations, National Narratives and Communities in the Asia-Pacific
Edited by Norman Vasu, Yolanda Chin and Kam-yee Law

The Changing Policy-Making Process in Greater China
Case research from mainland China, Taiwan and Hong Kong
Edited by Bennis Wai Yip So and Yuang-kuang Kao

China's Social Policy
Transformation and c
Edited by Kinglun Ngok and Chak Kwan Chan

New Life Courses, Social Risks and Social Policy in East Asia
Edited by Raymond K H Chan, Jens O Zinn, and Lih-rong Wang

Trends in Chinese Education
Edited by Hongjie Chen and W. James Jacob

Hong Kong's Global Financial Centre and China's Development
Changing roles and future prospects
Edited by Yan-leung Cheung, Yuk-shing Cheng and Chi-keung Woo

Trends in Chinese Education

Edited by
Chen Hongjie and W. James Jacob

Routledge
Taylor & Francis Group
LONDON AND NEW YORK

First published 2017
by Routledge
2 Park Square, Milton Park, Abingdon, Oxon OX14 4RN

and by Routledge
711 Third Avenue, New York, NY 10017

First issued in paperback 2018

Routledge is an imprint of the Taylor & Francis Group, an informa business

© 2017 Chen Hongjie and W. James Jacob

The right of Chen Hongjie and W. James Jacob to be identified as the authors of the editorial material, and of the authors for their individual chapters, has been asserted in accordance with sections 77 and 78 of the Copyright, Designs and Patents Act 1988.

All rights reserved. No part of this book may be reprinted or reproduced or utilised in any form or by any electronic, mechanical, or other means, now known or hereafter invented, including photocopying and recording, or in any information storage or retrieval system, without permission in writing from the publishers.

Trademark notice: Product or corporate names may be trademarks or registered trademarks, and are used only for identification and explanation without intent to infringe.

British Library Cataloguing in Publication Data
A catalogue record for this book is available from the British Library

Library of Congress Cataloging in Publication Data
Names: Chen, Hongjie, 1959- editor.
Title: Trends in Chinese education / edited by Hongjie Chen and W. James Jacob.
Description: New York : Routledge, 2017. | Series: Comparative development and policy in Asia series | Includes bibliographical references and index.
Identifiers: LCCN 2016010730| ISBN 9781138902725 (hardback) | ISBN 9781315697291 (e-book)
Subjects: LCSH: Education–China.
Classification: LCC LA1131.82 .T74 2017 | DDC 370.951–dc23
LC record available at http://lccn.loc.gov/2016010730

ISBN 13: 978-1-138-59565-1 (pbk)
ISBN 13: 978-1-138-90272-5 (hbk)

Typeset in Times New Roman
by Taylor & Francis Books

Contents

List of illustrations	vii
List of contributors	x
List of acronyms and abbreviations	xvi

1 A review of key trends in Chinese education   1
CHEN HONGJIE AND W. JAMES JACOB

2 Research on returns on education at all levels and changes for urban residents in China: 2002–2009   17
DING XIAOHAO, YU HONGXIA AND YU QIUMEI

3 Analysis of factors affecting Chinese higher education graduates' employment satisfaction   32
YUE CHANGJUN

4 Studying abroad or internationalizing on campus: university students' global competence training   51
WEN DONGMAO, LU JIAO AND WANG YOUHANG

5 The influence of higher education on student development   67
LI WENLI

6 Decontextualization and recontextualization: understanding reform practice through teacher discourse   86
YANG FAN AND CHEN XIANGMING

7 State and public education: a new analytical framework   104
WANG RONG

8 Technology in the development of education   123
GUO WENGE

9 Education's role in economic growth patterns   155
MIN WEIFANG

10 The political logic of non-government/private education (NGPE) in rural China: Evidence from a northern county 169
YAN FENGQIAO

11 Shaking off adaptation theory, a historical misconception in higher education 192
ZHAN LIXIN AND CHEN XUEFEI

12 Donor behavior, donation income, and Chinese higher education institutions 229
CHEN XIAOYU AND FENG QIANQIAN

13 Changes in knowledge production and diversified models of academic research within world-class universities 250
MA WANHUA

14 Loan financing behaviors and financial operation characteristics of Chinese higher education institutions after enrollment expansion 261
BAO WEI

15 An examination of the "engineer of human souls" metaphor 289
LIU YUNSHAN

Index 306

List of illustrations

Figures

2.1	Time trend of returns on education at all levels (1991–2009) (%)	29
5.1	Explanation of the function of education according to human capital theory	68
5.2	Explanation of personal abilities and income according to the selection hypothesis	68
5.3	Explanation of the relationship between education, abilities, and income according to job characteristics theory	69
5.4	College students' academic achievements, cognitive ability development, and influencing factors	71
5.5	Dynamic model of college students' capacity and career development	71
5.6	Factors that influence graduates' career development in the order of their importance	83
6.1	Divergence process of the local "tradition and legacy foremost" discourse	96
6.2	Reform practice goes through the process of recontextualization	98
9.1	Significant positive correlation between human capital stock and per capita GDP	158
9.2	Relations between human capital and industrial structure improvement in different countries	160
9.3	Changes in income and quantity of a well-educated population	163
9.4	Change in income and quantity of a low-income-educated population	164
12.1	Lorenz curve on distribution of HEI donation income	234
13.1	Messier's S-curve model.	256
14.1	Analytical framework	265
14.2	Factors that led HEIs to borrow money from banks	269
14.3	Average loan per student for different types of HEIs (Unit: RMB)	273
14.4	Classification for HEIs	275

viii List of tables

14.5	Diversification of funding sources for different types of HEIs (Unit: %)	276
14.6	Financial stability of different types of HEIs	278
14.7	Fund sufficiency of different types of HEIs (Unit: RMB)	280

Tables

1.1	Student enrollment trends in basic, secondary, and higher education, 1949–2014	2
1.2	PISA exam results for Hong Kong, Shanghai, and other East Asian neighbors, 2000–2012	4
1.3	Comparison of ranked HEIs in BRICS countries, 2015	5
1.4	Study abroad numbers, 1949–2014	5
1.5	Citable documents by BRICS countries, 1999–2014	6
2.1	Estimated returns on education at various levels (using the ordinary Mincer equation)	24
2.2	Gross returns on education at various levels (%)	25
2.3	Estimated returns on education at various levels (using the extended Mincer equation)	26
2.4	Net returns on education at various levels (%)	28
3.1	Explanatory variables description	38
3.2	Regression analysis results of factors affecting employment satisfaction	40
3.3	Regression results of factors affecting employment	46
4.1	Participation of Chinese students at Peking University in international communication on campus (%)	57
4.2	Comparison between the benefits of using campus resources and studying abroad	60
4.3	Correlation between the use of campus resources and the development of students' global competence	62
5.1	Statistics of basic characteristics for effective samples of the survey	75
5.2	Basic statistics of college students' cognitive abilities and social skills	76
5.3	Results of multivariate regression analysis of factors influencing basic cognitive abilities	76
5.4	Results of multivariate regression analysis of factors influencing expanded cognitive abilities	77
5.5	Results of multivariate regression analysis of factors influencing social skills	78
5.6	Basic statistics of graduates' career development indicators	79
5.7	Results of regression analysis of factors that influence income (logarithm used for income)	80
5.8	Results of regression analysis of factors that influence the average annual number of promotions	81

6.1	Corresponding relationships between Tian Tian's explanation and the teacher group's native discourse	97
8.1	History of media technology development	130
8.2	Technology in the development of education	135
12.1	Total incomes and donated and raised incomes of Chinese HEIs from 1993 to 2006	231
12.2	Frequency distribution of sample HEIs and total donation income of various HEIs from 2005 to 2008	233
12.3	Frequency distribution of donations received by local HEIs from 2005 to 2008 and donation amounts	236
12.4	Regression coefficients of factors influencing HEI donation income	238
12.5	Logistic regression results on tendencies of donations to different HEIs by different types of donors	241
12.6	Logistic regression results on use tendencies of donations by different donors	242
12.7	Summary of relative behavioral preferences of donation subjects	243
12.S1	Donations by administrative type of institution	246
12.S2	Cross-tabulation for donors' natures and donation uses	247
12.S3	Results of variance analysis of donation income logarithm ANOVAa, b, c	248
13.1	Spectrum of traditional academic research disciplines	253
13.2	Spectrum of applied professional disciplines corresponding to the research disciplines	253
13.3	Example of possible change for each component of the framework	255
14.1	Specification for analysis indicators of higher education financial operations	274
14.2	Fund use efficiency of different types of HEIs	280
14.3	Score for the sound level of financial operation for different types of HEIs	281
14.4	Multiple linear regression analysis on the factors affecting HEI loan size	283
14.5	Financial operation characteristics and financing behavior for different types of HEIs	285

Contributors

Bao Wei is an Associate Professor and Chair of the Department of Education Leadership and Policy at the Graduate School of Education, Peking University. She has served as a Visiting Fellow at the Center for National University Finance and Management of Japan and as an Evaluator at Hokkaido University. She has also served as a Visiting Scholar at the Pennsylvania State University. She holds a bachelor's degree from Kyushu University and a master's degree and a PhD in Education from the University of Tokyo.

Chen Hongjie is a Professor at the Institute of Higher Education in the Graduate School of Education, Peking University. He is also the Director of the Center for Doctoral Education at Peking University, Editor-in-Chief of the *Peking University Education Review*, and Vice-President of the Higher Education Committee of the Chinese Higher Education Association. He served as the Director of the German Study Center at Peking University from 2002 to 2013. He has also been a Visiting Scholar at the Free University of Berlin, the Humboldt University of Berlin (as *Humboldt-Stipendiat*), the University of Eichstätt, the University of Kassel, the Max Planck Institute of History at the University of Göttingen, and the Max Weber Center for Advanced Cultural and Social Studies at the University of Erfurt.

Chen Xiangming is a Professor and former Chair of the Department of Education and Human Development at the Graduate School of Education, Peking University. She is a Council Member of the Chinese Society of Education, an Executive Council Member of the Pedagogy Branch of the Chinese Society of Education, and Editor of the *Peking University Education Review*. She has been a Visiting Scholar at the University of Oxford, Nagoya University, and Nanyang Technological University, Singapore. She holds a bachelor's degree from Hunan Normal University and a master's degree and a PhD in Education from Harvard University.

Chen Xiaoyu is a Professor in the Department of Economics of Education at the Graduate School of Education, Peking University. He is the Dean of

List of contributors xi

the Graduate School of Education and has been the Associate Director of the Office of Finance at Peking University since 2000. He is also the Executive Vice-President of the Economics of Education Branch of the Chinese Society of Education. He served as the Party Committee Secretary of the Graduate School of Education from 2002 to 2013 and as the Associate Dean from 2006 to 2009. He has been a Visiting Scholar at the University of Minnesota and a Visiting Research Fellow at the National Institute of Multimedia Education in Japan.

Chen Xuefei is a Professor in the Department of Education Leadership and Policy at the Graduate School of Education, Peking University. He has served as a Member of the Discipline Appraisal Group of the State Council Degree Committee, a Consultant for the Beijing Government, Vice-President of the Higher Education Committee of the China Association of Higher Education, Vice-President of the Institutional Research Committee of the China Association of Higher Education, and a Member of the Comparative Education Group in China's National Office for Education Sciences Planning. He has also served as a Visiting Scholar at Harvard University, the University of Michigan, Nagoya University, Hiroshima University, and Tamkang University.

Ding Xiaohao is a Professor in the Department of Economics of Education at the Graduate School of Education, Peking University. She is currently serving as an Associate Director of the Institute of the Economics of Education at Peking University. She is also the Chair of the Academic Committee of the Graduate School of Education. She has been a Visiting Scholar at the University of Michigan, the Free University of Berlin, the National Institute of Multimedia Education of Japan, Aarhus University, and the University College London (UCL) Institute of Education. She holds a bachelor's degree in Mathematics from Beijing Normal University and a master's degree in Applied Mathematics and a PhD in Education from Peking University.

Feng Qianqian is a staff member in the Office of Educational Administration at Peking University.

Guo Wenge is an Associate Professor in the Department of Educational Technology at the Graduate School of Education, Peking University. She is currently serving as a Member of the Chinese Teacher Network Platform Expert Group and as a Member of the Peking University Informational Development and Planning Expert Group. She has also served as a Program Committee Member for international conferences such as the Global Chinese Conference on Computers in Education (2010) and the International Conference on Hybrid Learning (2010). She has been a Visiting Scholar at the State University of New York and the Chinese University of Hong Kong. She holds a bachelor's degree and a master's degree in Computer Science and a PhD in Higher Education from Peking University.

W. James Jacob is an Associate Professor of International Higher Education in the School of Education at the University of Pittsburgh. Since 2007, he has served as the Director of the Institute for International Studies in Education at the University of Pittsburgh. His research interests include higher education management; HIV/AIDS multisectoral prevention, capacity-building, and principles of good governance; indigenous education issues of culture, language, and identity as they relate to post-secondary education; quality assurance; organizational development; higher education strategic planning; and organizational effectiveness. He is the co-editor of two book series related to the development of comparative, international, and development education scholarship: *International and Development Education* (Palgrave Macmillan) and *Pittsburgh Studies in Comparative and International Education* (Sense Publishers). He has written extensively on comparative, international, and development education topics with an emphasis on higher education. He holds master's degrees in Organizational Behavior (Marriott School of Management) and International Development (Kennedy Center for International Studies) from Brigham Young University and a PhD in Education from the University of California, Los Angeles (UCLA).

Li Wenli passed away in 2015. Prior to her passing, she was a Professor in the Department of Economics of Education at the Graduate School of Education, Peking University. She served in many leadership positions, having been the Associate Dean of the Graduate School of Education and a Council Member of the Economics of Education Branch of the Chinese Society of Education. She was also a Visiting Scholar at Stanford University and Columbia University. She received a bachelor's degree in Psychology, a master's degree in Education, and PhD in Economics and Education Management from Peking University.

Liu Yunshan is a Professor in the Department of Education and Human Development at the Graduate School of Education, Peking University. She is the Associate Dean of the Graduate School of Education. She is also currently serving as the Vice-President of China's National Council on the Sociology of Education, an Executive Member of China's National Council on the Anthropology of Education, and a Member of the Chinese Society of Education. She holds a PhD in Education from Nanjing Normal University.

Lu Jiao is a Program Coordinator in the Office of International Relations at Peking University.

Ma Wanhua holds three distinguished positions at Peking University: She is a professor in the Department of Education and Human Development at the Graduate School of Education; she is the Director of the Center for International Higher Education; and she is the Director of the Educational Policy Advisory Center in Internationalization of Higher Education. She has extensive experience in the field of international education, having been a Visiting Professor, an Erasmus Mundus Professor and a Fulbright New Century Scholar in Denmark, Belgium, Finland, Germany, England, and Canada as well as at Michigan State University, the University of Vermont, the University of Virginia, the University of California, Los Angeles (UCLA), the California State University at Sacramento, and the University of Pittsburgh. Her current research focuses on the institutional internationalization of the universities in Beijing. She has been an Education Consultant for the World Bank (on access and equity in higher education), for the Beijing Academy of Educational Sciences, and for the United Nations Educational, Scientific, and Cultural Organization (UNESCO). She is a Member of the Editorial Board of the *Journal of World Education*. She holds a bachelor's degree from Jilin University and a master's degree and a PhD from Cornell University.

Min Weifang is a Professor at the Institute of the Economics of Education at the Graduate School of Education, Peking University. He is currently serving as an Honorary Dean of the Graduate School of Education. He is also the Convener of the Public Management Discipline Appraisal Group of the State Council Degree Committee, Chair of the China Institute for Educational Finance Research, Chair of an Expert Panel of the World Bank Education Development Project in Poor Provinces of China, Executive Vice-President of the Western Returned Scholars Association, and Director of Editing of the *Peking University Education Review*. He is also a former Chair of the Peking University Council. He holds a bachelor's degree from Beijing Normal University, and master's degrees in Organizational Sociology and Educational Administration and Policy Analysis, and a PhD in the Economics of Education from Stanford University.

Wang Rong is a Professor at the China Institute for Educational Finance Research at Peking University. She has served as the Director of the China Institute for Educational Finance Research since 2005. She is now serving as the Vice-President of the Economics of Education Branch of the Chinese Society of Education, the Vice-President of the Educational Finance Committee of the Chinese Society of Educational Development Strategy, and an Educational Consultant for the World Bank, the United Nations Educational, Scientific, and Cultural Organization (UNESCO), the European Union, and the United States Agency for International Development (USAID). She holds a bachelor's degree and a master's degree in Education from Peking University and a PhD in the Economics of Education from the University of California, Berkeley.

Wang Youhang is a PhD Student in Public Policy in the Graduate School of Education at Peking University.

Wen Dongmao is a Professor in the Department of Education Leadership and Policy at the Graduate School of Education, Peking University. He currently serves as Vice-President of the Chinese Society of Educational Development Strategy and is an Executive Council Member of the China Association of Higher Education. He is the former Dean of the Graduate School of Education, Peking University, and he has been a Visiting Scholar at Columbia University, the University of Pennsylvania, and the East-West Center in Honolulu, Hawaii. He holds a bachelor's degree and a master's degree in Education from Hunan Normal University and a PhD in Education from Peking University.

Yan Fengqiao is a Professor in the Department of Education Leadership and Policy at the Graduate School of Education, Peking University. He is currently serving as the Vice-President of the Chinese Higher Education Management Association, a Council Member of the Institutional Study Committee of the China Association of Higher Education, and an Executive Council Member and Deputy Secretary-General of the Chinese Society of Educational Development Strategy. He has been a Visiting Scholar at Lancaster University and the State University of New York. He holds a bachelor's degree in Engineering from the University of Science and Technology Beijing and a PhD in Education from Peking University.

Yang Fan is an Associate Professor in the College of Education, Shanghai Normal University. He holds a bachelor's degree and a master's degree in Education from East China Normal University and a PhD in Education from Peking University.

Yu Hongxia is a Lecturer in the College of Education Administration at Beijing Normal University. She holds a PhD in Management from Peking University.

Yu Qiumei is the Director of the Consumer Price Division of the Department of Rural Surveys at the National Bureau of Statistics of the People's Republic of China. She holds a bachelor's degree and a master's degree from Beijing Normal University and is currently a PhD Student at Huazhong University of Science and Technology.

Yue Changjun is a Professor in the Department of Economics of Education at the Graduate School of Education, Peking University. He is serving as the Associate Dean of the Graduate School of Education and as Associate Director of the Institute of the Economics of Education. He is also serving as Vice-President of the Economics of Education Branch of the Chinese Society of Education and as a Council Member of the China Society of World Economics. He has been a Visiting Scholar at the University of California, Santa Barbara, the University of California, Davis, and the Chinese University of Hong Kong. He holds a bachelor's degree in Mathematics from Fudan University and a PhD in Economics from Peking University.

Zhan Lixin is an Associate Professor in the Department of Education and Human Development at the Graduate School of Education, Peking University. His research interests focus on the philosophy of higher education and adjustment theory as it applies to higher education. He holds a PhD from Peking University.

List of acronyms and abbreviations

BC	Before Christ
BRICS	Brazil, Russia, India, China, and South Africa
CAFSA	China Association for International Education
CAHE	China Association of Higher Education
Caltech	California Institute of Technology
CBN	China Business Network
CCDCP	Chinese Center for Disease Control and Prevention
CCDIC	China Charity and Donation Information Center
CCP	Chinese Communist Party
CCTV	China Central Television
CD	Compact disc
CEDF	China Education Development Foundation
CGSS	Chinese General Social Survey
CHEERS	Career after Higher Education: A European Research Study
CHIP	China Household Income Project
CHNS	China Health and Nutrition Survey
CPI	Consumer Price Index
CSC	China Scholarship Council
CSHE	Center for Studies in Higher Education
CT	Computed Tomography
DVD	Digital video disc
GDP	Gross domestic product
HEI	Higher education institution
IS	Information Science
IT	Information Technology
JPL	Jet Propulsion Laboratory
km2	Square kilometer
MIT	Massachusetts Institute of Technology
NACE	National Association of Colleges and Employers
NBS	National Bureau of Statistics
NSF	National Science Foundation
OECD	Organisation for Economic Co-operation and Development
OLS	Ordinary least squares

PhD	Doctor of Philosophy
PISA	Programme for International Student Assessment
PRC	People's Republic of China
R&D	Research and development
RMB	Renminbi
ROC	Republic of China
SCI	Science Citation Index
TV	Television
UK	United Kingdom
UNDP	United Nations Development Programme
UK	United Kingdom
US	United States
VIF	Variance inflation factor

1 A review of key trends in Chinese education

Chen Hongjie and W. James Jacob

The world's largest education system stems from millennia-old traditions that place great value and emphasis on learning, teaching, and the central role that institutions of learning at all levels should and do play in the education process. Parents and grandparents teach children from very early ages to cherish opportunities to learn. Chinese children in rural and urban settings dream of completing their basic and secondary education and performing well on the national higher education entrance exam (*Gaokao*, 高考). As it was in ancient times, economic opportunities in China tend to increase with the more education individuals attain (Jiang 2014).

In China, basic education comprises pre-school education, primary education and junior secondary education (nine-year compulsory education), senior secondary education, and special education. To remain consistent with the historical data, secondary education in this chapter refers to specialized secondary education, regular secondary education, and secondary vocational education (see Table 1.1). Given the state of the education system that the PRC inherited in a postwar context in 1949, the government has made tremendous progress in terms of reducing its national illiteracy rate and providing basic education opportunities to the masses. Yet even with all of this progress, several social justice issues remain (Jacob 2006; Jacob et al. 2015). A large percentage of eligible cohort students are unable to continue on with secondary and higher education schooling. Roughly 42% of all eligible students move on to attend secondary education, and only 30% of secondary students move on to pursue a higher education degree (Ministry of Education 2015).

Ethnic minority students struggle with issues of language, culture, and identity. Local, national, and increasingly global environmental push and pull factors create a perfect storm context that often prevents ethnic minority students from wanting to learn and use their indigenous languages and cultures in daily life, let alone in school and employment settings (Jacob 2015; Jacob et al. 2015).

Gender disparities still remain, with females having fewer mean years of schooling than males (UNDP 2014). There are also regional disparities, where the vast majority of the top schools and HEIs are located in the eastern region, and especially in major urban centers like Beijing, Guangzhou, and

Table 1.1 Student enrollment trends in basic, secondary, and higher education, 1949–2014

Year	Basic Education	Secondary Education	Higher Education		
			Total Students	Minority Students	Faculty Members
1949	25,430,000	1,268,000	117,000	2,900†	16,000
1954	55,294,000	4,246,000	253,000	NA	39,000
1959	122,097,000	12,903,000	812,000	16,100‡	100,000
1964	103,095,000	10,195,000	685,000	21,900§	135,000
1969	120,883,000	20,253,000	109,000	NA	137,000
1974	183,981,000	37,137,000	501,000	NA	148,000
1979	214,503,000	60,249,000	1,020,000	21,900**	237,000
1984	194,096,000	48,609,000	1,396,000	69,300	315,000
1989	187,812,000	50,540,000	2,082,000	132,000	397,000
1994	204,557,000	57,071,000	2,799,000	178,000	396,000
1999	226,828,000	80,027,000	4,134,000	247,700	426,000
2004	220,682,000	87,479,000	13,335,000	774,300	858,000
2009	206,400,000	100,704,000	21,447,000	1,410,500	1,295,000
2014	203,256,000	85,880,000	25,477,000	1,992,400	1,535,000

Sources: NBS (2005, 2015), Ministry of Education (2015), and State Ethnic Affairs Commission and NBS (2012).
Notes: †1952 data. ‡1957 data. §1965 data. **1978 data.

Shanghai. Since education is largely funded at the local level, wealthy cities and provinces tend to offer greater education opportunities than what is offered in rural and remote locations. Students of all ages from rural and remote regions of the country are at an added disadvantage due to geography (Fleischer et al. 2011; Hansen 2013; Heckman & Yi 2012; Jacob 2004). Other trends include an increase in the number of migrant children attending school in locations where their parents are working.[1] Schools have the potential to provide safe havens for these migrant children (Gao et al. 2015). But seasonal jobs and other life-changing events make it difficult for migrant children to maintain steady enrollment over long periods of time in any one school (Liu & Jacob 2013). While some urban centers open up public schools to migrant children, others do not. Migrant students are often forced to enrol late and endure frequent moves that are often in the middle of the school year, which puts them at a significant disadvantage compared to their local peer counterparts. Curricula also vary from province to province, so changing schools is often difficult for many migrant children in terms of being able to remain current with differing curricular requirements and teaching styles. Chen Yuanyuan and Shuaizhang Feng (2013) also note how many migrant children are prohibited from attending public schools because they do not have local household registration status. Many migrant children are forced to enrol in schools established specifically for migrant children (Lu & Zhou 2013). Being able to meet the continuing needs of migrant children with regard to basic, secondary, and higher education will be an ongoing challenge the country will face for many years to come.

While it is impossible to determine how the entire country would fare on the global stage on the Programme for International Student Assessment (PISA) in the areas of math, science, and reading, we do have a snapshot from two of China's largest cities – Hong Kong and Shanghai. Both consistently score among the top five participating countries and economies, and in 2012 Shanghai led all countries and economies in all three categories (see Table 1.2).[2]

Based on global rankings of HEIs, China leads the other BRICS nations with several world-class universities and thirty other national universities that have established international renown (Table 1.3).[3] In recent years, China has risen to become a top destination for foreign students studying abroad (Table 1.4). Higher education students from every major global region study in China, with the top ten origin countries in 2014 being South Korea, the United States, Thailand, Russia, Japan, Indonesia, India, Pakistan, Kazakhstan, and France. In 2013, the top seven destination countries for Chinese students studying abroad were the United States, Australia, the United Kingdom, Canada, Japan, Singapore, and South Korea.

Three animals – dragons, tigers, and turtles – in Chinese culture serve as appropriate analogies to the important role that Chinese students studying abroad play in the future development of the nation's economic and cultural development. The dragon is a leading figure in Chinese history and

Table 1.2 PISA exam results for Hong Kong, Shanghai, and other East Asian neighbors, 2000–2012

	Math					Science					Reading				
	2000	2003	2006	2009	2012	2000	2003	2006	2009	2012	2000	2003	2006	2009	2012
Hong Kong	560	550	547	555	561	541	539	542	549	555	525	510	536	533	545
Shanghai	NA	NA	NA	600	613	NA	NA	NA	575	580	NA	NA	NA	556	570
Macao	NA	527	525	525	538	NA	525	511	511	521	NA	498	492	487	509
Taiwan	NA	NA	549	543	560	NA	NA	532	520	523	NA	NA	496	495	523
Japan	557	534	523	529	536	550	548	531	539	547	522	498	498	520	538
South Korea	547	542	547	546	554	552	538	522	538	538	525	534	556	539	536
Vietnam	NA	NA	NA	NA	511	NA	NA	NA	NA	528	NA	NA	NA	NA	508
Brazil	334	377	370	386	391	375	390	390	478	405	396	403	393	412	410
Russia	478	468	476	468	482	460	489	479	405	486	462	442	440	459	475

Sources: OECD (2000, 2003, 2006, 2009, 2012).

Table 1.3 Comparison of ranked HEIs in BRICS countries, 2015

	Shanghai Jiao Tong University		Times Higher Education		QS	
	Top 100	Top 500	Top 100	Top 400	Top 100	Top 500
Brazil	0	6	0	2	0	7
Russia	0	2	0	2	0	9
India	0	1	0	4	0	7
China	0	32	2	11	4	25
South Africa	0	4	0	3	0	3

Sources: Shanghai Jiao Tong University (2015), *THE* (2015), and QS (2015).

Table 1.4 Study abroad numbers, 1949–2014

Year	Chinese Students Studying Abroad	Foreign Students Studying in China
1949	35*	33*
1954	1,518	324
1959	576	259
1964	650	229
1969	NA	NA
1974	180	378
1979	1,777	440
1984	3,073	1,293
1989	3,329	1,854†
1994	19,071	43,712‡
1999	23,749	44,711
2004	114,682	110,844
2009	229,300	238,184
2014	459,800	377,054

Sources: China Association for International Education (2015), NBS (2005), Ernst & Young (2014), Li (2000), and Yu (2009).

Notes: *1950 data, †1988 data, and ‡1997 data.

symbolizes royalty, power, and eternal progress. When children perform well on the *Gaokao* and gain admittance into a prestigious university, they are often referred to afterwards as a dragon in the family. Tigers are also important in Chinese culture and symbolize potential for growth, learning, and progress. Children and students of all ages are often viewed as crouching tigers with hidden talents and latent potential. *Hǎiguī* (海归) or the metaphor "sea turtles" (*hǎiguī*, 海龟) is a colloquial term often used in China and in the literature to refer to those who return to China after having studied abroad.

6 *A review of key trends in Chinese education*

Table 1.5 Citable documents by BRICS countries, 1999–2014

	1999	*2004*	*2009*	*2014*
Brazil	12,582	21,935	43,959	56,368
Russia	31,036	35,997	37,487	49,018
India	22,776	32,948	62,976	106,078
China	39,037	107,509	296,050	438,601
South Africa	4,626	6,397	10,242	16,215

Sources: SCImago Lab (1999, 2004, 2009, 2014).

The many thousands of Chinese who return to China after studying abroad help build local and national businesses and contribute to their communities through service and employment (Jacob et al. 2015).

SCImago first began collecting national citation data in 1996, when China ranked ninth overall with 28,630 citable documents (Table 1.5). In 1996, Russia led the BRICS countries with 31,425 citable documents. Since 1997, China has remained the clear leader among BRICS countries and ranks second only to the United States as of 2014. The dramatic growth China has experienced has remained significant from 1999 to 2014. Based on the most recent growth data available on academic publications as portrayed in Table 1.5, China will soon overtake the United States as the leading nation in academic knowledge production.

An introduction to this volume

This edited volume treats many key trends in Chinese education that are of significance for the discourse on comparative, international, and development education. These trends often shape how education institutions at all levels adapt to dynamic local and global forces. By understanding these trends and their influences, we hope to shed some light on possible future directions for education in China and the significance thereof for comparative education.

Key education trends that will be covered include issues relating to social justice, curriculum content, teacher preparation (both pre- and in-service teaching), administration, infrastructure development, quality, and governance. This volume is structured around current education trends at the national and local levels. The broad themes contained in the following fourteen chapters are as follows:

- Historical overview of education policy debates
- Marketization policy trends of education
- Quality assurance of higher education
- Study abroad experiences of Chinese higher education students
- Globalization's impact on adult education policies
- Education's influence on economic growth patterns
- Inequity in educational attainment

- Theoretical influences on education
- Expansion policies of primary, secondary, and higher education subsectors
- Gender policies and educational reform trends
- History of technology education shifts

This volume is timely in that it provides contributions from leading scholars and practitioners in the field of Chinese education. Many of the topics covered in this volume are relevant for anyone interested in learning about current trends in the world's largest education system. The following chapters provide important insights into furthering policy debates and education reform planning initiatives.

In Chapter 2, Ding Xiaohao, Yu Hongxia, and Yu Qiumei discuss the returns on education of all levels and their changes for urban residents in China from 2002 to 2009. The analysis is based on the statistics of household survey data provided by the National Bureau of Statistics (NBS). The returns were calculated using the ordinary least squares (OLS) method, which includes three empirical analyses: (1) the ordinary Mincer equation, (2) the extended Mincer equation, and (3) the time trend of education returns variation. Generally, the findings show that the returns on education during this period failed to show an increase and gradually flattened out with very little fluctuation. The authors argue that the returns on the next level of education became an important motivation to pursue further education. However, over time the returns failed to keep an upward trend; even that of senior high school to technical college levels declined during the 2002–2009 time period, while the returns on bachelor's and master's degrees remained flat. Similarly, the results of the extended Mincer equation showed that only the net returns on junior high school climbed from 2002 to 2008, but they then declined in 2009 while the net returns of other levels fluctuated or fell slightly. The results of time trend analysis also show a similar tendency. Only the returns from completing junior high school showed a steady increase, while returns from the other education levels remained constant or even fell slightly. From one perspective, the slow growth of returns on education can raise the alarm for education institutions in China. On the other hand, these findings may motivate people to pursue higher education or improve the quality of their skills and overall returns on their education investment. The authors also conclude that technology will be an important factor when it comes to helping reduce the costs of education at all levels, and that it will thus improve returns on education.

In Chapter 3, Yue Changjun discusses the factors that influence the satisfaction of higher education graduates in China. The analysis derived from a survey done by Peking University in 2011. The survey covered thirty higher education institutions (HEIs) in eight provinces in the eastern, central, and western regions of China. The factors of employment satisfaction were categorized into two main groups: job-related factors and non-job-related factors. The job-related factors included eight variables: monthly income, job location, geographic region, organization type, business type, job role, fit between major and job, and employment status. Among these eight variables, it is only geographic region that had no significant impact on employment satisfaction. Employees will have greater satisfaction when they have higher income working at state-owned companies in large and medium-sized cities rather than at private companies in small towns. Employees working for the Chinese Communist Party (CCP) or for government institutions, or those working in finance, information technology (IT), education, science, health, and culture felt more satisfied than those working for manufacturing companies. The fit between the graduate's major and type of job also had a significant impact on employment satisfaction. The higher the major matching is, the higher the employment satisfaction will be. Those with permanent status also felt more satisfied. Meanwhile, the non-job-related factors that influenced satisfaction included five variables: demographic characteristics, human capital characteristics, social capital characteristics, HEI characteristics, and job search status. Of these five variables, demographic characteristics had no significant impact on employment satisfaction. Graduates with student leadership experience and wider family and social relations felt more satisfied with their employment. Those who also felt satisfied were graduates who found a job through the Internet or after attending career guidance courses. The findings imply that graduates' employment satisfaction can be improved by establishing an equitable, just, and competitive labor market, narrowing the income gap, and providing career guidance. Another implication is that some measures should be taken to improve the opportunities for those who have difficulty finding satisfactory jobs, such as those from minority groups, from junior or less prestigious colleges, and those with poor academic performances, poor English fluency, and no student leadership experience.

In Chapter 4, Wen Dongmao, Lu Jiao, and Wang Youhang report the findings of their study on the strategies of improving students' global competence. They surveyed 800 domestic students and 600 international students at four schools or departments at Peking University, with the following three objectives: to identify the differences between students studying abroad and those studying locally but who use international resources; to explore the influences of studying abroad on the development of students' global competence; and to identify how students choose between studying abroad and internationalizing on campus. International resources here include studying abroad and such on-campus facilities as foreign language specialists, exchange scholars, access to information databases and literature, and an internationalized environment (like conferences, student apartments, and other international activities). The findings show that the number of Peking University students studying abroad is very small and that they only go for a short term (less than a year). Although they live abroad, they do not live in international environments, which is mostly due to the language barrier. The international students at Peking University also do the same. They rarely communicate with their Chinese teachers and peers during and after school or in daily life. Most of them also do not live with local residents, reducing the opportunity for developing close mutual communication between foreign and Chinese students. They also rarely take part in international conferences or courses delivered by foreign language teachers. Their use of the international campus resources is highly influenced by their majors and their degrees. Students from science departments use the resources more than those from social sciences and humanities departments. Thus, the higher the education level is, the higher the utilization degree of the international campus resources. The study also finds that taking part in international conferences and utilizing international resources result in positive impacts on the development of students' competence. However, students studying abroad rarely use these facilities. Responding to the findings, the chapter ends with recommendations. First, HEIs are recommended to not only expand opportunities for studying abroad, but also improve the quality of communication skills of domestic students so that they get more opportunities to have more international communication through visiting scholars, foreign language teachers, and international students. Second, campuses should provide an internationalized culture and improved infrastructure to create more opportunities for internationalization on campus. Finally, campuses should also develop a more strategic focus and systematic processes to help faculty members and students to be able to benefit from internationalization efforts.

Chapter 5 is a report of Li Wenli's study on how higher education influences students' development before they enter the labor market. The discussion is based on a sample survey, conducted in 2006, of college graduates at their workplaces. The study adopted the approach of human capital theory, together with job characteristic theory and labor market theory. These theories are based on the belief that both personal abilities and education determine what people do for a living. Students' development is then influenced by the characteristics of their education institutions, the environment of their education institutions, their personal characteristics, their curricular and extracurricular activities, and their relationships with their peers and with their teachers. The findings show that higher education has a positive role in improving students' cognitive abilities. Although yielding no significant impact on cognitive development, internships influence the development of social skills because students are given a more realistic view of the job market. Further, internships allow students to build up their communication skills, helping them more easily relate to and work with other people. As far as income is concerned, the influential factors are age, level of education, abilities, job stability, and participation in decision-making. As far as graduate career development is concerned, the influential factors are personality, collaborative skills, work experience, good basic knowledge, and good technical knowledge. All these factors support human capital theory.

In Chapter 6, Yang Fan and Chen Xiangming present their investigation of how a reform practice through thematic teaching takes place in an elementary school in Beijing. The discussion is mainly based on their discourse analysis of teacher dialogues at elementary schools that have introduced a theme-based pedagogy. The study is motivated by the enactment of a specific curriculum and teaching method in China known as "thematic teaching." It turns out that teachers have different understandings from one another about thematic teaching. Although they understand the forms of thematic teaching, they do not really pay attention to qualitative issues such as human dynamics, inquiry, transcending the classroom, and language proficiency. In addition, existing traditional teaching and faculty member behaviors sometimes hinder the practice of thematic teaching because they are indeed difficult to integrate into it. The case will be even worse if the paradigm is introduced only through class observations. Although the observing teachers may get new insights from their observations, they will likely run into difficulty when they have to transfer the results of their observations into their own teaching practices. Therefore, to successfully achieve the goals of the reform, recontextualization of the new paradigm should be done by considering the existing cultural contexts of the school and expanding the boundaries of school discourses – and one way to do this is by adopting new content and teaching materials. Further, schools should also increase the quantity and the quality of teacher discussions. Such peer discussions can lead teachers to a better understanding of the new concept and to better teaching practices.

In Chapter 7, Wang Rong proposes a new approach to educational economic research: a *new* human capital theory. This proposal is rooted in the fact that current human capital theory is limited to productive capital and private objectified capital, while in reality public education centers on distributive capital to transfer collectively objectified capital. The chapter starts with an overview of three prototypes of education systems in China and in Western countries: the church-based system, the guild-based system, and the imperial exam system. The discussion continues with the new concept of human capital theory. The highlight of this discussion is the claim that public education and the state should be seen not only in their productive and privately objectified capacity, but also in their distributive capacity and collectively objectified capacity. Taking this issue into account, the state can then choose whether to monopolize public education or to allow the development of private education. The state should be very careful because a failure in education means the failure of the state. Education should allow people to get a return on their investment by teaching practical knowledge and skills required for productive activities.

In Chapter 8, Guo Wenge presents a historical approach to media to explore how it has influenced education. First, the article proposes a definition of "media technology" by looking at four of its aspects: symbols, carriers, copying methods, and dissemination characteristics. It then continues with an analysis of five historical stages of media development – oral dissemination, manual transcribing, printing, electronic dissemination, and digital technology. While new media technology has developed and replaced old media technologies, the content of knowledge is merely the same. That is to say, it is highly possible that in the future there will be a technology that will create a new knowledge expression system and knowledge organization structure against the predominant technology currently available today. This will bring with it a fundamental change in how knowledge is stored and transferred.

In Chapter 9, Min Weifang presents three ways in which education transforms economic growth patterns. First, the development of education and the improvement of the overall national education level will see the economy grow according to an innovation-driven pattern. Second, the rise of investment in education will lay a firm foundation for upgrading China's industrial structure. Third, the provision of equal access to education will lay a foundation for accelerating economic growth through expanding domestic consumer demand. This chapter stresses that improving the quality of education in China, which is facing multiple challenges in its economic progress, is the key to realizing the role of education in the transformation of economic growth patterns. Higher education in China should also focus on ways to improve the overall higher education system, strengthen innovative education, and cultivate innovative ability through systematic innovation, and cultivate a large number of top graduates and faculty members who will strive to achieve innovation-driven growth. To improve its industrial structure, China must understand the development trends of the global revolution in science and technology and the industrial revolution, and develop strategically emerging industries with features that will produce long-term growth. To meet rising domestic consumer demand, the Chinese government needs to develop a better education system, increase investment in human capital, and promote the equitable distribution of education resources. Further, universities should make science fields a priority and forge ahead with a pioneering spirit, focusing not only on the quantity, but also on the quality, of academic publishing. As a field of study, comparative, international, and development education should also pay attention to students' development without giving less priority to their individualities, for a society without individuality has no vitality or creativity.

Chapter 10 by Yan Fengqiao discusses the actual operational status of private education in a county in northern China from an anthropological and a political point of view. He highlights the fact that local governments' fair treatment of the public and non-government/private education in rural China is still debatable. This case study, however, finds that a school needs to find sponsors so that it can maintain students' achievement and quality academic performance. A school should recruit the best students and best teachers, and implement vigorous management in order to advance its admissions goals. The study also finds that institutional factors render local government more favorable to public education, but the gap left by institutional restrictions in fact allows private education to develop. When private education is in its early development and does not influence government performance, the government adopts a free-market policy toward private education. When private education matures and has a positive influence on achieving government-set educational objectives and elevating political performance, the local government encourages and supports private education. This leads to a competition not only between private and public schools, but between local governments – that want to provide better service to attract more people – and between local governments and the schools in their territory.

In Chapter 11, Zhan Lixin and Chen Xuefei criticize the perspective of adjustment theory on education, which stipulates that higher education should adapt to the needs of social development. They argue that adjustment theory would restrict the development of China's higher education system. First, the theory reverses the relationships between cognitive rationality and many practical rationalities. The theory also tries to change the core of education from cognitive rationality to instrumental rationality, political rationality, and traditional practical rationality. In turn, this will hinder the development of Chinese education. Therefore, the authors recommend getting back to cognitive rationality and establishing a sound domestic academic market. While practical rationality may be seen as the application of cognitive rationality, it is restricted by certain values and may sometimes be inconsistent with or even contradictory to cognitive rationality. It is natural that the development of higher education is required to adapt to meet expected economic and social development goals. However, if the logic of adjustment theory is to be followed, these multiple functions of higher education will not be adequately protected and may be marginalized, perhaps even lost. By means of power over the academic system, the academic market can significantly guide and normalize the development of higher education by maintaining the persistence of specialized training to secure the growth of specialized knowledge; improving the efficiency and quality of teaching; and providing the best institutional environment for the separation of academic schools, so as to foster free competition among them. Academic market construction is able to emancipate the productive forces of knowledge production. The proposal brought forth in this chapter, to revisit the rationality that grounds the whole education system, should be considered by those in comparative, international, and development education.

In Chapter 12, Chen Xiaoyu and Feng Qianqian present a discussion of donor behavior and donation income in Chinese HEIs. Social donation is a significant potential income source for Chinese HEIs. Based on HEI donation income data and on data relating to the donations made to local HEIs from 2005 to 2008, this article analyzes the distribution features and factors that influence donation income at Chinese HEIs. The discussion also covers the behavioral characteristics of different types of donors. The findings show that the distribution of donation income to different HEIs in China is quite uneven: an HEI's donation income will depend on its popularity, rank, and geographic location. Furthermore, different donation subjects have different donation preferences, and each institution chooses its donation receptors based on the subjects and the rank of each HEI. In addition, enterprises, administrative institutions, non-profit organizations, and individuals show different donation tendencies. What's more, donation behaviors are also influenced by the levels of HEIs' teaching and scientific research and fundraising efforts. The authors identify four main tendencies when it comes to donation behaviors. First, the distribution of donation income is uneven, influencing the income rate of HEIs, as HEIs with less donation income will have significantly lower overall income. Second, the donations are highly concentrated in a few well-known HEIs with high rankings. Third, the donation income of HEIs with independent foundations is much higher than the donation income of those that do not have independent foundations. Finally, the donation motives and behavioral characteristics of donation groups are also different, thus determining potential donors for HEIs. Therefore, HEIs need to design fundraising projects to attract donors. The results of this study will certainly be valuable for those involved in HEI fundraising, and they may even influence relevant HEI donation policies.

In Chapter 13, Ma Wanhua highlights the changes in the ways Chinese universities produce knowledge and conduct research. This study discusses the ways in which world-class research universities are able to meet changing knowledge production needs while, at the same time, being able to maintain their academic traditions. It seems that knowledge production in universities should attend to theory building while stressing the real issues facing economic construction and social development. Furthermore, academic institutions in Chinese universities are still classified by discipline, which may weaken knowledge integration. With the changes in knowledge production that are emerging in large numbers of applied professional disciplines, research universities have turned to diversified models of academic development, such as the formation of interdisciplinary or cross-disciplinary research units; the formation of a variety of applied professional colleges or departments; the development of the case study model; and the formation of teaching and practice systems. Positive models that China can use to build its world-class universities include the formulation of knowledge production that tackles significant social and economic issues; the enhancement of linkages between basic disciplines and applied professional disciplines to integrate theoretical research and practical application; the initiation of systematic innovation to upgrade university-based research and development centers' comprehensive research competence; and the establishment of cooperative partnerships with outside laboratories.

In Chapter 14, Bao Wei presents a thorough discussion on financing behaviors of HEIs in China, especially after recent enrollment policy shifts. The chapter starts with a discussion of the institutional finance characteristics of Chinese HEIs and then continues with a deeper analysis of financing selection mechanisms and loan financing behaviors. HEI financing in China has several main characteristics. First, since the 1990s HEIs in China have actually been given greater autonomy, so that they can employ cost-sharing methods. However, the government-funded financing of education has continued to rise even as the proportion of HEIs that self-finance through tuition is also rising.

Second, Chinese HEIs are generally well-supported in terms of the public funding they receive from the government. Government funds are based on competitive grants, which can lead to a funding gap among many HEIs. The gap is widening because of the differences in the development of regional economies and the financing abilities of each HEI. And third, due to enrollment policy restrictions, many Chinese HEIs are forced to rely on bank loans for additional financing. Many of them, however, fail to use these loans appropriately, which leads them into a debt crisis. The loan-based funding of operations is actually a result of several factors. First, this practice actually started in the 1990s when the government released a series of educational reform and development guidelines, allowing HEIs to expand their enrollments. With higher enrollments, HEIs had to provide more infrastructure, the cost of which was financed by bank loans. In 2002, the government even formulated a policy that encouraged financial institutions to enhance credit support for HEIs. Banks took this opportunity to expand their businesses by offering increased credit. Since HEIs had limited extra financing channels when they needed to invest more because of enrollment expansion, they took on more bank loans. As a result, many HEIs are now facing a debt crisis. Although the amount of loans taken on by HEIs varies, the average size of the loans is on the rise and has even exceeded the growth rate of HEI revenues. Some HEIs have indeed made some efforts to diversify their sources of funding, trying to find alternatives to raising tuition. This has been achieved through the provision of training services, through research collaboration with third parties, and through HEI-run corporations. HEIs that have alternative financing channels generally borrow less money from the banks. In the case of some HEIs, however, the asset-liability ratio is still quite high, which indicates that the condition of their finances is highly unstable. This is probably due to the insufficient and inefficient use of funds. To overcome these financial problems, according to the author, the government and the HEIs should redefine their responsibilities. First, the government should increase investment in HEIs to alleviate their debt issues. Second, there should be better resource allocation to narrow the gap among HEIs. And third, there is a need to monitor the financial mechanisms of HEIs so as to improve their fiscal health. To overcome their debt crises, HEIs are encouraged to oversee their own management and strategic financial operations more closely.

In Chapter 15, Liu Yunshan analyzes the political and philosophical contexts of the "engineer of human souls" metaphors for teachers. This chapter starts with a discussion of how teachers are engineers who should be able to mold new generations of students by selecting teaching materials and teaching strategies. The use of "engineer" as a metaphor indicates that schools are likened to factories in a market-dominant economy. When the school is running well and economic returns are sufficient, there is nothing to worry about. Teachers tend to focus more on cultivating personal emotions, physical development, vocational skills, and adaptability than on students' souls and spirits. Teachers are transformed into "masters of specialists." The discussion then shifts to the way individuality is replaced with normality; the way norms become the core of education; the origin of political education in remolding new generations of students; and the way powerful forces are shaping Chinese education. Teachers are responsible for social enlightenment and liberation, and they should therefore become role models for students to imitate. This will not only shape new generations of students, but also elevate the transcendence of souls. An education that is focused on behavioral norms and intrinsic spirit is able to produce bright individuals with diverse identities.

Notes

1 On any day, there are over 150 million migrant workers in one of China's many urban areas. Many of these workers bring along their spouses and their children, who often attend public school.
2 We recognize that it is impossible to compare single urban centers, like Hong Kong and Shanghai, to entire country samples such as Japan, South Korea, and the United States. Regardless, it is clear that at least in these Chinese urban locations, students are performing well in the areas of math, science, and reading.
3 Peking University, Tsinghua University, and Shanghai Jiao Tong University consistently rank among the top universities worldwide.

References

Chen, Y. & F. Shuaizhang. 2013. "Access to Public Schools and the Education of Migrant Children in China." *China Economic Review* 26: 75–88.
China Association for International Education (CAFSA). 2015. *Statistics for Students Studying in China*. Beijing: CAFSA. Available online at: http://www.cafsa.org.cn/research/72/2.html. Accessed on October 12, 2015.
Ernst & Young. 2014. *Overseas Study Market Analysis Report 2014*. Beijing: Ernst & Young.
Fleischer, B., H. Li & M. Q. Zhao. 2011. "Human Capital, Economic Growth, and Regional Inequality in China." *Journal of Development Economics* 92(2): 215–231.
Gao, Q., H. Li, H. Zou, W. Cross, R. Bian & Y. Liu. 2015. "The Mental Health of Children of Migrant Workers in Beijing: The Protective Role of Public School Attendance." *Scandinavian Journal of Psychology* 56(4): 384–390.
Hansen, M. H. 2013. "Recent Trends in Chinese Rural Education: The Disturbing Rural-Urban Disparities and the Measures to Meet Them." In Eric Florence and Pierre Defraigne, eds, *Towards a New Development Paradigm in Twenty-First Century China: Economy, Society and Politics*, 165–178. New York: Routledge.
Heckman, J. & J. Yi. 2012. *Human Capital, Economic Growth, and Inequality in China*. National Bureau of Economic Research (NBER). Cambridge, MA: NBER.
Jacob, W. James. 2004. *Marketization, Demarketization, and Remarketization: The Role of the Economic Market on Chinese Higher Education*. PhD dissertation. Graduate School of Education and Information Studies, University of California, Los Angeles.
Jacob, W. James. 2006. "Social Justice in Chinese Higher Education: Issues of Equity and Access." *International Review of Education* 52(1): 149–169.

Jacob, W. James, Sheng Yao Cheng & Maureen K. Porter. (eds). 2015. *Indigenous Education: Language, Culture, and Identity*. Dordrecht: Springer.

Jacob, W. James, Xi Wang & Weiyan Xiong. 2015. "Dragons, Tigers and Turtles in International Contexts: The Cultural Background and Rising Role Chinese Students Play in U.S. Higher Education." Paper presented at a professional development workshop at Westmoreland County Community College, Youngwood, PA, on October 6, 2015.

Jiang, Y. 2014. "Interregional Disparity and Convergence Tendency: An Empirical Study of TFP Growth in China." *Applied Economics and Finance* 1(2): 1–10.

Li, T. (ed.). 2000. *History of Chinese Overseas Education: After 1949*. Beijing: Higher Education Press.

Liu, J. & W. James Jacob. 2013. "From Access to Quality: Migrant Children's Education in Urban China." *Educational Research for Policy and Practice* 12(3): 177–191.

Lu, Y. & H. Zhou. 2013. "Academic Achievement and Loneliness of Migrant Children in China: School Segregation and Segmented Assimilation." *Comparative Education Review* 57(1): 85–116.

Ministry of Education. 2015. *Educational Statistics*. Beijing: Ministry of Education. Available online at: http://www.moe.gov.cn/s78/A03/moe_560/jytjsj_2014/. Accessed on October 12, 2015.

National Bureau of Statistics of China (NBS). 2005. *China Compendium of Statistics, 1949–2004*. Beijing: China Statistics Press.

NBS. 2015. *China Statistical Abstract, 2015*. Beijing: China Statistics Press.

Organisation for Economic Co-operation and Development (OECD). 2000. *Literacy Skills for the World of Tomorrow: Further Results from PISA 2000*. Paris: OECD.

OECD. 2003. *Learning for Tomorrow's World: First Results from PISA 2003*. Paris: OECD.

OECD. 2006. *PISA 2006: Science Competencies for Tomorrow's World*. Paris: OECD.

OECD. 2009. *PISA 2009 Results: What Students Know and Can Do*. Paris: OECD.

OECD. 2012. *PISA 2012 Results: What Students Know and Can Do*. Paris: OECD.

Quacquarelli Symonds (QS). 2015. *QS World University Rankings 2014/15*. London: QS.

SCImagoLab. 1999. *SCImago Journal & Country Rank*. Amsterdam: Elsevier.

SCImagoLab. 2004. *SCImago Journal & Country Rank*. Amsterdam: Elsevier.

SCImagoLab. 2009. *SCImago Journal & Country Rank*. Amsterdam: Elsevier.

SCImagoLab. 2014. *SCImago Journal & Country Rank*. Amsterdam: Elsevier.

Shanghai Jiao Tong University. 2015. *Academic Ranking of World Universities, 2015*. Shanghai: Shanghai Jiao Tong University.

State Ethnic Affairs Commission & NBS. 2012. *China's Ethnic Statistical Yearbook 2012*. Beijing: China Statistics Press.

Times Higher Education (THE). 2015. *World University Rankings, 2014–15*. London: THE.

United Nations Development Programme (UNDP). 2004. *Human Development Report: 2004. Cultural Liberty in Today's Diverse World*. New York: UNDP.

UNDP. 2014. *Human Development Report: 2014. Sustaining Human Progress: Reducing Vulnerabilities and Building Resilience*. New York: UNDP.

Yu, F. 2009. *Chinese Overseas Education since the Opening Policy*. Beijing: Beijing Language and Culture University Press.

2 Research on returns on education at all levels and changes for urban residents in China
2002–2009

Ding Xiaohao, Yu Hongxia and Yu Qiumei

Since China launched the Reform and Opening-Up Policy, the distribution of educational opportunities and the distribution of income have changed immensely. The empirical study of the relationship between education and income, especially the evolution of this relationship, has important theoretical and practical value when it comes to understanding the role of education in the economy and improving education, employment, and income distribution policies.

Recent research by Ding et al. (2012) estimated the returns on education for the period from 2002 to 2009 and how they changed over time using the urban household survey data provided by the National Bureau of Statistics (NBS). The research results showed that in recent years returns on education did not maintain sustained accelerated growth as was experienced during the period from the late 1980s to the first five years of the twenty-first century, but rather gradually flattened out. After taking variables such as industry, employer type, and geographic region into account, returns on education show a slight decline. Until now, research reports have rarely been able to identify time change trends in returns on education in China. Since this research used years of education as a proxy variable, the estimated coefficient obtained therefrom actually indicated the average annual returns on education at all levels. However, education at different levels likely had distinct returns. It is difficult to identify structural differences between returns on education at different levels if the research does not distinguish between the levels. Recognizing the structural differences is significant when it comes to deciding whether the investment in educational resources is reasonable, whether the scale of education is proper, and why a certain group of students do or do not continue receiving education. Based on the above-mentioned survey data, this chapter analyzes the returns on education at all levels (i.e. distinguishing between the levels) and their development trends between 2002 and 2009.

Literature review

Studying returns on education is a major part of determining the relationship between the distribution of educational opportunities and the distribution of income. This research is therefore a major focus of both domestic and foreign institutions. Among this research, there are many empirical studies on the returns on education. According to our analysis of the relevant literature, however, there are four sources that are vital to the comprehensive and systematic research on the levels of returns on education and their changes over time in China.

The first source is the China Household Income Project (CHIP) database. This study that gave rise to the database was carried out between 1988 and 2007 with different geographic locations each year. It included more than 6,000 urban households each year in eleven or twelve provinces and municipalities, and over 20,000 individual participants. A research group that comprised domestic and foreign members and that was chosen by the investigation division of NBS designed the study questionnaire. Respondents were chosen from NBS' general household survey sampling frame. Research based on the database indicated that between 1990 and 1999 the returns on education at all levels increased significantly (Li and Ding 2003).

The second source is the database from the China Health and Nutrition Survey (CHNS), which the University of North Carolina in the US and the Chinese Center for Disease Control and Prevention (CCDCP) jointly established. A series of surveys was conducted in 1989, 1991, 1993, 1997, 2000, 2004, and 2006 that covered family members from 4,000 to 6,000 households in nine provinces and municipalities in each year. While research based on the survey data showed that the returns on education at all levels had improved, the income gap and the disparity in returns on education became wider between people with different education levels (Zhong & Liu 2011).

The third source is the database from the Chinese General Social Survey (CGSS) conducted by the Department of Sociology – along with other academic departments – at Renmin University of China. The survey was carried out in 2003, 2005, 2006, and 2008, and it covered more than 40,000 households in twenty-eight Chinese provinces and municipalities. Based on the data, the research indicated that from 2003 to 2008 the returns on primary education declined dramatically compared with a noticeable increase for junior high school education and no appreciable change for senior high school education. Also, the returns on three-year college, four-year university, and graduate education showed an upward trend (Fan 2011).

The fourth and final source is the Urban Household Survey carried out by NBS. As the data was collected (in part) through account-keeping, the data could accurately reflect residents' income and expenditure levels, and serve as a vital source of information for studying returns on education. The research based on the collected data showed that from 1991 to 2000 the returns on education at all levels improved considerably with time and that students at higher educational levels would gain increasing marginal earnings for each additional year of education than those at lower educational levels (Chen et al. 2003).

Through an in-depth literature review, we discovered that the research on returns on education for certain years and the research over time and disparity between different periods yielded three conclusions: (1) generally, from the late 1980s to the first five years of the twenty-first century, the returns on education at all levels were positive; that is, the higher the level of education that people received, the higher salary they earned; (2) returns on education generally showed upward movement from the late 1980s to the first five years of the twenty-first century (but this is based on a few comparative studies on development trends); and (3) the latest research was based primarily on NBS data from 2004, CHNS data from 2006, and CGSS data from 2008. The studies on the returns on education, especially those looking at trends, rarely used the most recent data to reflect real situations accurately.

Currently, there are two methods one can use to estimate returns on education, namely, parameter estimation and semi-parameter estimation. Parameter estimation can be further subdivided into such methods as ordinary least squares (OLS), instrumental variable, matching, and fixed-effects. The traditional OLS method may be biased in estimating education returns, as education and income are interrelated and endogenous. Researchers have tried to adopt new methods in an attempt to overcome this weakness. However, each method is somewhat limited. The instrumental variable method contains two flaws. First, it is difficult to find the proper exogenous variables, such as instrumental variables, that affect education levels instead of income levels. Second, even if exogenous variables are available, they affect only a limited population, so it is impossible to ensure that the education returns of the entire population is reflected (Card 1999). The conditions for which the matching method is applicable are limited, as the "experimental group" and "control group" must be random in terms of whether the samples are educated in the first place. Furthermore, deviations are more likely to occur during the matching process (Navarro-Lozano 2002). The fixed-effects method involves using twins as research samples and assumes that the selected twins have the same personal talents and family background, and that they share other income-level-determining features, so that the impact of unobservable factors can be removed and the education returns of the twins can be calculated (Chamberlain & Griliches 1975). However, such assumptions may prove dubious, and research samples for this method are not easily found.

In terms of the semi-parameter method, some researchers introduced the second-order curve of working experience into non-parametric form. It turned out that, while the results had a significant impact on working age, it was difficult to determine the influence on the estimated coefficient of education (Wang & Chen 2008). Lastly, studies on the comparisons of parameter methods and semi-parameter methods have shown that the former were more efficient while the latter generated consistent estimations, which means that each method has its advantages and disadvantages (Qian & Yi 2009).

Data and model selection

This chapter analyzes the returns on education at all levels and their variation trends using data generated by NBS' Urban Household Survey. NBS used permanent households in urban areas as survey samples and used the housing frame to select survey samples. Urban areas, as we defined them, include cities and towns meeting the *Regulations on Statistically Divided Cities and Towns* approved by the State Council. The NBS data had some unique advantages over other datasets applicable to education return analysis: (a) samples covered wide regions; (b) the data volume was large; (c) the data were collected over a long period of time; (d) statistical indices on income were rich against the same system of standards; and (e) the database required sampled households to record individuals' information through account-keeping rather than through a review. The five features of the database ensured the reliability, validity, and accuracy of the research on the returns on education. These features facilitated a comparative trend analysis over time.

We used the 2002, 2004, 2006, 2008, and 2009 data, and our sample size ranged from 70,000 to 100,000 households every year, with the total number of samples being around 430,000. The data contained an abundant amount of personal information, including education level, initial work year, gender, industry category, employer type, and geographic region. The education level category was broken down into the following subcategories, so as to lay a solid foundation for more detailed research in the future: illiterate, semi-illiterate, primary school graduate, junior high school graduate, senior high school graduate, secondary-level technical college graduate, technical college graduate, bachelor's degree, and master's degree. These subcategories were to indicate the highest level of education achieved. Previous research on this subject has jointly termed bachelor's and master's degrees as "bachelor's degree and above," which limited the research knowledge on the returns on graduate education. In addition, the rapid expansion of China's graduate education infrastructure made related education return research quite meaningful from a policy perspective.

As we have already mentioned, every estimation method has its own advantages and disadvantages. In our study, we use the traditional OLS method for three reasons. First, we found that the OLS method was acceptable after conducting comparative analyses on various estimation methods. Second, there were data restrictions – the absence of proper instrumental variables, sample features that did not meet the fixed-effects method requirements, and no method to meaningfully compare the data – associated with the other methods, which made the OLS method the only viable option. Third, OLS was the general method used in recent studies, and the derived estimation results were of greater reference value when compared with the results of studies that employed other research methods.

The empirical analyses used in this study include: (1) ordinary Mincer equation; (2) extended Mincer equation; and (3) time trend of education return variation.

The first part of our study applied the ordinary Mincer equation:

ln (income) = $\beta_0 + \beta_1 edu + \beta_2 exp + \beta_3 exp^2 + \varepsilon$ Model (1)

"ln" denotes the aggregation of salary income and business income, and was adjusted according to the consumer price index (CPI); related calculations used 2002 prices. "Edu" is the virtual variable of an individual's highest level of education completed: primary school graduate and below, junior high school graduate, senior high school graduate, technical college graduate, college graduate, bachelor's degree, and master's degree; primary school graduate and below was set as the control group. "Exp" is short for "working experience." Exp^2 is the square of working experience, and the variable actually refers to the year when data was collected minus the year when participants began working. β_0 is the constant, β_1 is the coefficient to be estimated, a vector is the coefficient to be estimated when the variables are virtual, and ε is a residual.

Many other factors may have the same impact on the income and education levels of individuals, and this may bias the results. To eliminate bias, we controlled for the individual's gender, industry category, employer type, and geographic region based on the ordinary Mincer equation of Model (1). Meanwhile, we included the annual virtual variable in the model to control for factors that change with time, one of which is the impact of macroeconomic shock. This resulted in the extended Mincer equation:

ln (income) = $\beta_0 + \beta_1 edu + \beta_2 exp + \beta_3 exp^2 + \beta_4 female + \beta_5 ind + \beta_6 org + \beta_7 reg + \beta_8 year + \varepsilon$ Model (2)

"Female" is the gender virtual variable: "male" is valued at 0 and "female" is valued at 1. "Ind" is the virtual variable of industry and is divided into five categories based on similarities between industries. The first category groups together the primary industries: agriculture, forestry, animal husbandry, and fishing. The second category groups together the more competitive secondary industries, which include manufacturing. The third category groups together the secondary industries that are monopolistic and depend on natural resources: mining, electricity, gas, water production and supply, and construction. The fourth category groups together the tertiary industries with low added value, such as wholesaling and retailing, hospitality, catering, leasing and commercial services, and resident services. The final industry category groups together the tertiary industries with high added value, such as transportation, storage and postal communication services, information transmission, computer services and software, finance, real estate, scientific research and comprehensive technological services, water conservancy, environment and utilities management, education, health, social security and social welfare, culture, sports and entertainment, public management and social organization management, and international organization management.

22 Research on returns on education at all levels

The first category was set as the control group. "Org" stands for the divisions of the surveyed population in terms of employer type, which includes employees of state-owned economic entities, employees of collective economic entities in urban areas, employees of other economic entities, urban self-employed and private enterprise owners, urban self-employed and private enterprise employees, re-employed retirees, and other employees. Employees of state-owned economic entities were set as the control group. "Reg" refers to the regional locations, which include the eastern, central, and western regions, with the western region being set as the reference region. "Year" is the annual virtual variable, and 2002 was set as the reference year. Other variables were consistent with Model (1). The study selected population samples between the ages 16 and 60 to remove abnormal values in the estimation of results.

Estimated results

Estimated results of the ordinary Mincer equation

The estimated results of the ordinary Mincer equation are shown in Table 2.1. By applying a logarithmic transformation to the mixed data's estimated results, we concluded that, compared to the salaries of primary school graduates and below, the salaries of junior high school graduates, senior high school graduates, technical college graduates, college graduates, those with bachelor's degrees, and those with master's degrees were 32.2%, 53.2%, 81.0%, 125.2%, 203.3%, and 339.8% higher, respectively. Using the primary school graduates and below as the control group, we found that the returns on senior high school and technical college education were 21.0% (53.2%–32.2%) and 48.8% (81.0%–32.2%) higher than those on junior high school education, respectively. The returns on college and university (bachelor's degree) education were 72.0% (125.2%–53.2%) and 150.1% (203.3%–53.2%) higher, respectively, than those on senior high school education. Meanwhile, the returns on a master's degree education were 136.5% (339.8%–203.3%) higher than those on a bachelor's degree education.

If years of education, namely three-year junior high school education, three-year senior high school education, three-year technical college education, three-year college education, four-year university education, and three-year graduate education, are taken into account, the data indicates the annual education returns of junior high school, senior high school, secondary-level technical college, technical college, bachelor's degree, and master's degree to be 10.7%, 7.0%, 16.3%, 24%, 37.5%, and 44.1%, respectively. All the previous analyses took primary school graduate and below as the control group. If we set a lower education level as the control group, the education returns of junior high school, senior high school, secondary-level technical college, technical college, bachelor's degree, and master's degree are about 32.2%, 15.9%, 18.2%, 24.4%, 34.7%, and 45.0%, respectively. Consecutively, the annual education returns of junior high school, senior high school, technical college, college, bachelor's degree, and master's degree stand at 10.7%, 5.3%, 6.1%, 8.1%, 8.7%, and 15.0%, respectively. We noted similar education return variation trends when treating the year data with regression methods or when adopting mixed data: the higher the education level, the higher the returns.

Judging from work experience and the estimated coefficient of its square, an individual earns the highest salary in his or her working life at around 30 years old, and this is represented by an inverted U-shaped curve. The annual virtual variables of the mixed cross-section data's estimated results are all well above zero, and they increased each year, which indicates that salaries are increasing as time goes by.

When an individual considers whether to pursue further education in the case that he or she was educated to some extent, the return to the next level of education may be an important factor affecting his or her education decisions. As shown in Table 2.2, our study calculated the returns on education at various levels according to the regression results in Table 2.1. From 2002 to 2009, the returns on education at various levels (excluding junior high school education) failed to keep the upward trend, differing from most previous studies, which hold that education returns were ever-increasing. The education returns of senior high school, secondary-level technical college, and technical college showed signs of decline from 2002 to 2009, while the education returns on bachelor's degrees and master's degrees tended to remain flat amid fluctuations.

Estimated results of extended Mincer equation

The estimated results of the ordinary Mincer equation should be considered as aggregate returns because the impact of other variables were uncontrolled. To obtain a more accurate education return, or the net return on education, other variables that might have a similar impact on education degrees and salaries should be controlled. Table 2.3 shows the estimated results when other variables were controlled. After a series of controlled variables were introduced, the education returns decreased dramatically compared to results generated by the ordinary Mincer equation (see Table 2.1). This effect indicates that a large part of an individual's education return is achieved through employment.

By the logarithmic transformation of the estimated coefficients, we found that, compared to primary school graduates and below, the salaries of junior high school graduates, senior high school graduates, technical college graduates, college graduates, bachelor's degree graduates, master's degree graduates are 21.3%, 37.4%, 55.5%, 83.8%, 127.3%, and 207.8% higher, respectively. Taking primary school graduates and below as the control group, we concluded that the returns on senior high school and technical college education are 16.1% (37.4% − 21.3% = 16.1%) and 34.2% (55.5% − 21.3% = 34.2%) higher than that of junior high school education. The returns on technical college and university bachelor's degrees are 46.4% (83.8% − 37.4% = 46.4%) and 89.9% (127.3% − 37.4% = 89.9%) higher than that of senior high school. Meanwhile,

Table 2.1 Estimated returns on education at various levels (using the ordinary Mincer equation)

	2002	2004	2006	2008	2009	Mixed Data
Junior high school	0.14796	0.19396	0.26706	0.34878	0.36722	0.27898
	(6.93)*	(8.37)*	(8.94)*	(11.85)*	(11.87)*	(21.63)*
Senior high school	0.32735	0.35603	0.43047	0.47454	0.49443	0.42641
	(15.47)*	(15.49)*	(14.50)*	(16.25)*	(16.08)*	(33.28)*
Secondary-level technical college	0.51756	0.54803	0.57927	0.6286	0.63876	0.59342
	(23.87)*	(23.22)*	(19.08)*	(20.64)*	(20.00)*	(44.93)*
Technical college	0.72026	0.77693	0.80243	0.85134	0.86082	0.81167
	(34.46)*	(34.01)*	(27.04)*	(28.98)*	(27.77)*	(63.09)*
Bachelor's degree	0.97439	1.084	1.09044	1.15944	1.1717	1.10966
	(44.11)*	(45.86)*	(36.32)*	(39.20)*	(37.55)*	(84.80)*
Master's degree	1.29881	1.59106	1.44368	1.52502	1.51727	1.48106
	(29.11)*	(42.03)*	(29.71)*	(42.33)*	(38.59)*	(80.09)*
Exp	0.04785	0.04678	0.04642	0.05219	0.04903	0.04885
	(33.24)*	(32.83)*	(35.06)*	(37.00)*	(36.00)*	(75.93)*
Exp^2	-0.00073	-0.00074	-0.00075	-0.00093	-0.00085	-0.00082
	(21.13)*	(22.15)*	(24.58)*	(28.93)*	(27.67)*	(55.26)*
2004						0.20358
						(45.43)*
2006						0.42447
						(95.55)*
2008						0.73387
						(161.94)*
2009						0.81384
						(184.39)*
Sample size	68,735	77,800	84,930	99,840	97,997	429,302
R-squared	0.13	0.13	0.12	0.12	0.12	0.20

Note: *p < 0.01

Table 2.2 Gross returns on education at various levels (%)

	2002	2004	2006	2008	2009
Junior high school	15.95	21.40	30.61	41.73	44.37
Senior high school	19.65	17.59	17.75	13.40	13.57
Secondary-level technical college	20.95	21.17	16.04	16.66	15.53
Technical college	22.47	25.72	25.00	24.95	24.86
Bachelor's degree	28.93	35.94	33.38	36.08	36.46
Master's degree	38.32	66.04	42.37	44.13	41.28

the return on obtaining a master's degree is 80.5% (207.8% − 127.3 % = 80.5%) higher than that of obtaining a bachelor's degree.

Taking education years into account, including three-year junior high school education, three-year senior high school education, three-year secondary-level technical college education, three-year technical college education, four-year bachelor's degree education, and three-year graduate education, we determined that the returns on each of these education levels is approximately 7.1%, 5.4%, 11.4%, 15.5%, 11.5%, and 30%, respectively. All the previous analyses took primary school graduates and below as the control group. If we set a lower education level as the control group, the returns on junior high school, senior high school, secondary-level technical college, technical college, bachelor's degree, and master's degree are about 21.3%, 13.2%, 13.2%, 18.2%, 23.7%, and 35.4%. Consequently, the annual returns on junior high school, senior high school, secondary-level technical college, technical college, bachelor's degree, and master's degree stand at 7. 1%, 4.4%, 4.4%, 6.1%, 5.9%, and 11.8%.

Analyzing the salary difference of varied groups using the estimated coefficients of other controlled variables and their significance, we found that the salary levels of females are lower than that of males. We identified that the average salaries of Category 2, 4, and 5 industries are lower than that of Category 1. Meanwhile, the average salary of Category 3 is higher than that of Category 1. The average salaries of employees from urban collective economic entities, urban self-employed or private enterprises, reemployed retirees, and other employees are lower than that of employees of state-owned organizations and employees from other economic entities; and urban self-employed or private enterprise employers have higher average salaries than that of state-owned economic unit employees. The average salary in the western region is higher than it is in the central region, but it is lower than it is in eastern region.

Table 2.4 lists the net returns on education at different levels. The net returns on junior high school education climbed between 2002 and 2008, and it declined in 2009. The net returns on education at other levels fluctuated or fell slightly during the period from 2002 to 2009.

Table 2.3 Estimated returns on education at various levels (using the extended Mincer equation)

	2002	2004	2006	2008	2009	Mixed Data
Junior high school	0.10416	0.13781	0.20263	0.22491	0.24692	0.19336
	(5.10)*	(6.23)*	(7.18)*	(8.60)*	(9.12)*	(16.52)*
Senior high school	0.23421	0.2686	0.3424	0.3383	0.36218	0.3145
	(11.47)*	(12.17)*	(12.20)*	(13.02)*	(13.37)*	(27.20)*
Secondary-level technical college	0.34586	0.40996	0.45914	0.45539	0.47172	0.44168
	(16.28)*	(17.99)*	(15.77)*	(16.63)*	(16.58)*	(36.32)*
Technical college	0.488	0.58349	0.62559	0.64002	0.65491	0.60866
	(23.21)*	(26.29)*	(21.74)*	(24.11)*	(23.48)*	(50.99)*
Bachelor's	0.65352	0.80621	0.8402	0.86634	0.88253	0.82107
	(29.72)*	(34.93)*	(28.63)*	(31.94)*	(30.88)*	(66.79)*
Master's	0.89932	1.21536	1.11054	1.1916	1.189	1.12412
	(20.81)*	(33.87)*	(23.44)*	(36.50)*	(34.10)*	(66.87)*
Exp	0.04434	0.04261	0.04196	0.04058	0.03619	0.04069
	(31.55)*	(30.57)*	(32.77)*	(33.30)*	(32.57)*	(70.90)*
Exp^2	−0.00074	−0.00073	−0.00074	−0.00076	−0.00064	−0.00072
	(22.03)*	(22.43)*	(25.06)*	(26.51)*	(25.05)*	(53.82)*
Female	−0.1894	−0.20897	−0.21489	−0.20985	−0.20239	−0.20798
	(29.34)*	(32.76)*	(34.49)*	(32.84)*	(33.62)*	(73.22)*
Industry 2	−0.08713	−0.02246	−0.00354	0.09349	0.00487	−0.00134
	(2.72)*	(0.72)	(0.12)	(2.42)*	(0.17)	(0.09)
Industry 3	0.14531	0.22334	0.18505	0.22576	0.13523	0.1856
	(4.42)*	(7.14)*	(6.46)*	(5.08)*	(4.56)*	(12.58)*
Industry 4	−0.07921	−0.02312	−0.0284	−0.00038	−0.07173	−0.03828
	(2.43)*	(0.73)	(0.99)	(2.53)*	(0.01)	(2.41)*
Industry 5	0.23664	0.20625	0.13253	0.17702	0.09035	0.16492
	(7.57)*	(6.70)*	(4.68)*	(4.59)*	(3.06)*	(11.15)*
Urban collective economic unit employee	−0.33562	−0.28553	−0.24403	−0.17758	−0.17908	−0.25402
	(20.36)*	(20.17)*	(17.22)*	(12.99)*	(11.99)*	(37.97)*

	2002	2004	2006	2008	2009	Mixed Data
Other economic unit employee	0.1388	0.05898	−0.03708	−0.00816	−0.02518	0.00774
	(9.89)*	(5.53)*	(3.98)*	(0.98)	(3.19)*	(1.83)*
Urban self-employed or private enterprise employers	0.04726	0.02632	0.10278	0.19778	0.16565	0.12548
	(2.88)*	(1.74)*	(7.74)*	(14.60)*	(14.11)*	(20.22)*
Urban self-employed or private enterprise employees	−0.26702	−0.32763	−0.36779	−0.22183	−0.19837	−0.2547
	(16.47)*	(23.24)*	(28.46)*	(22.73)*	(23.05)*	(50.17)*
Re-employed retirees	−0.49819	−0.49028	−0.4803	−0.55409	−0.53015	−0.50774
	(23.42)*	(25.36)*	(25.95)*	(25.23)*	(24.93)*	(55.19)*
Other employees	−0.48682	−0.60613	−0.66991	−0.41985	−0.43641	−0.51335
	(20.56)*	(26.74)*	(26.26)*	(25.43)*	(26.94)*	(56.16)*
Central region	−0.06559	−0.04162	0.02215	0.12654	0.06728	0.02899
	(8.29)*	(5.03)*	(2.62)*	(13.37)*	(7.85)*	(7.42)*
Eastern region	0.20312	0.25641	0.33297	0.40683	0.33597	0.31619
	(27.02)*	(33.29)*	(42.08)*	(46.79)*	(43.24)*	(87.05)*
2004						0.19937
						(46.42)*
2006						0.42194
						(99.17)*
2008						0.74281
						(169.82)*
2009						0.82916
						(193.68)*
Sample size	68,733	77,798	84,927	99,647	97,777	428,882
R-squared	0.22	0.22	0.21	0.19	0.2	0.28

Note: *p < 0.01

Table 2.4 Net returns on education at various levels (%)

	2002	2004	2006	2008	2009
Junior high school	14.78	22.46	25.22	28.01	21.33
Senior high school	13.89	15.04	12.01	12.22	13.21
Secondary-level technical college	15.27	12.34	12.41	11.58	13.23
Technical college	18.95	18.11	20.28	20.10	18.17
Bachelor's	24.95	23.94	25.40	25.56	23.67
Master's	50.55	31.04	36.73	34.50	35.40

Time trend analysis on the returns on education

The changes over time of the returns on education are particularly appealing to researchers. However, effective research results are challenging, due to the scarcity of existing data. Two factors often account for significant differences in the results obtained for returns on education, the first being inconsistent variables used by different researchers, and the second being a difference in control variables in the Mincer regression equation as discussed above. Thus, the results of different studies on returns on education are generally incomparable. In this section, we drew from data across many years and analyzed it using an integrated method, making it possible to look at the development trend of returns on education.

In order to study the longitudinal differences in returns on education at all levels at different times, this section draws from the research of Chen et al. (2003) for comparison, as it used the same data sources that we do in this study. Two points should be noted. The first point is that Chen et al. classified the sample of four-year education or above as a subsample. The number of the subsample is negligible, as samples with a master's or doctoral degree were a very small proportion of China's working population from 1991 to 2000. In contrast, during the period from which we drew samples for our research, there was explosive growth in the number of people with a graduate education. Thus, the sample of bachelor's degree holders provided by this study is more comparable with the sample of those with a four-year university education or above that Chen et al. used. The second point is that there are differences between the ways in which we and Chen et al. analyzed the data, which provides the possibility of looking at the changes over time of returns on education in different periods.

Figure 2.1 illustrates the changes over time of returns on education at all levels, with dotted lines showing calculation results by Chen et al. and solid lines depicting the results provided by our study. For the bachelor's degree level, the returns showed a clear upward trend from 1991 to 2000 with an average annual compound growth rate of 36.4%. However, according to our analyses, the compound growth rate of returns on obtaining a bachelor's degree was

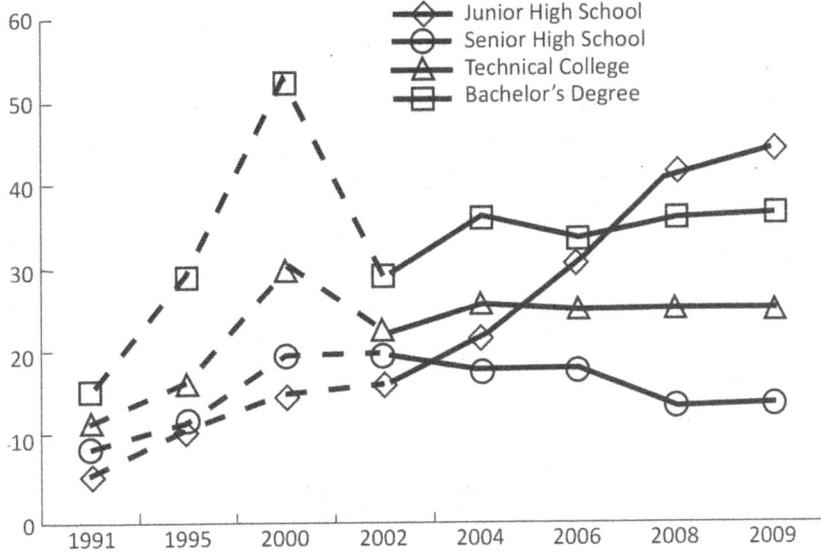

Figure 2.1 Time trend of returns on education at all levels (1991–2009) (%)

around 3.9% from 2002 and 2009, compared with 0.36% from 2004 to 2009, far less than the figures obtained by Chen et al.

Figure 2.1 shows that the returns from obtaining a four-year university education fluctuated moderately compared to the returns from obtaining a senior high school education; the returns from obtaining a three-year college education reached their highest level in 2004 and then fell afterward when compared to the returns from obtaining a senior high school education. The returns from obtaining a senior high school education peaked from 2000 to 2002 and then began to decline when compared to the returns from obtaining a junior high school education. The returns on education at the junior high school level remained on an upward trajectory compared to the primary school level or below. This could be because there was an increase in returns on junior high school education, or because there was a decrease in returns on primary school education or below. After nine-year compulsory education was implemented, workers with an educational background of primary school or less likely had difficulty finding employment, as a junior-high-school education or above is usually a minimum qualification for new employees.

Conclusions

The scale and structure of China's education system have undergone unprecedented changes since the start of the twenty-first century, with basic education covering more people and the number of higher education students rapidly rising. What are the implications for individual returns on education amid tremendous changes in supply and demand for employees with different educational backgrounds? How will these changes impact national economic development and income distribution? Does education expand or narrow the income gap? What influences does education have on the division of social class? How will these influences develop in the future? To answer these questions, we need a sound and comprehensive estimation analysis of the level of education obtained so as to monitor changes over time in the returns on education. Using the urban household survey data (2002 to 2009) from NBS, our study looked at the returns on education at all levels and the changes in such returns over the past decade. And it has led us to the following conclusions.

Regarding education levels, the longer one spends in school the higher their wages and returns on education will be. Variables such as industry and employer type play a significant role in returns on education. As for the changes over time, our findings showed that in recent years – except for junior high school education – returns on education failed to maintain rapid growth and instead gradually reached a plateau or even declined slightly in spite of existing literature that suggests significant upward movement in returns on education at all levels in the 1990s and early 2000s.

The findings of this study are worthy of attention, though they need to be further tested to determine whether they are robust enough to hold true for the future. The reasons for flat and even declining returns are complicated, and they have never been seen in empirical studies using data from earlier periods. The changes in returns on education may either reflect how Chinese society recognizes and values the production function and the signaling function of education; they may reflect the impact of government reforms that were imposed on income distribution; or they may even be closely related to the structure and efficiency of the allocation of social resources.

With a supply and demand analysis of China's education system over recent years, it is understandable that the growth of returns on education has slowed. First, growth is related to the number of people receiving education. Demand for employees with higher education has started to lag behind the rapid expansion of education across the country, which may push down returns on education. Second, growth is related to the competencies and skills of the people receiving education. If the competencies and skills of people with education opportunities follow a marginally decreasing assumption, the higher proportion of educated people will lead to a decrease in average competency skills, which may cause a decline in returns on education, especially when there is a mismatch between the competency skills provided by the education system and what the market demands. Third, growth is related to such factors as the economy, industrial restructuring, and technological progress. People with higher education experience are needed to develop advanced technologies, which in turn improve returns on education and initiatives for schooling. Returns on education tend to decline when talent training outpaces the development of technology.

Supply of education and returns on education influence each other. The slow-down in the growth of returns on education may cause people's pursuit of education to wane, resulting in notions of "useless degrees." However, slackening growth is also likely to make people adjust education choices and their allocation of educational resources, and encourage them to improve the quality of their education. In addition, technological progress can be boosted, as falling returns will cut development costs. The creation of new technology requires more talent, thus increasing returns on education and initiatives for schooling.

In conclusion, the reasons for, and the results of, changes in returns on education are complicated and diverse, requiring further theoretical explanation and empirical analysis.

References

Card, D. 1999. "The Causal Effect of Education on Earnings." In O. Ashenfelter and D. Card, eds, *Handbook of Labor Economics, 1801–1863*. Amsterdam: North Holland.

Chamberlain, G. & Z. Griliches. 1975. "Unobservables with a Variance-Components Structure: Ability, Schooling, and the Economic Success of Brothers." *International Economic Review* 16(2): 422–449.

Chen, X. Y., L. K. Chen & X. Chen. 2003. "Rates of Return to Schooling in Urban China: Changes in the 1990s." *Peking University Education Review* 2: 65–72.

Ding, X., Q. Yu & H. Yu. 2012. "Research on the Returns on Education at all Levels and the Changes thereof for Urban Residents in China during 2002–2009." *Research on Education Development* 11: 1–6.

Fan, J. B. 2011. "Tracking China's Returns on Education between 2003 and 2008." *Statistics and Information Forum* 8: 47–52.

Li, S. & S. Ding. 2003. "The Long-Term Trend of China's Urban Returns to Education." *Chinese Social Science* 6: 58–72.

Navarro-Lozano, S. 2002. *Matching, Selection and the Propensity Score: Evidence from Training in Mexico*. Working paper presented at the Seventh Annual Meeting of the Latin American and Caribbean Economic Association (LACEA) in Madrid, Spain.

Qian, Z. & Y. Yi. 2009. "The Estimation and Analysis of the Rate of Return on Education in China – A Comparison of Parametric and Semiparametric Estimation Methods." *Statistical Research* 7: 43–48, 50.

Wang, M. J. & L. K. Chen. 2008. "Comparison of Different Estimation Methods for Rates of Return on Education." *Application of Statistics and Management* 3: 404–408.

Zhong, F. & H. Liu. 2011. "Empirical Studies on the Returns on Education at all levels and the Variation for Urban Residents in China." *Chinese Social Science* 6: 58–72.

3 Analysis of factors affecting Chinese higher education graduates' employment satisfaction

Yue Changjun

Since the implementation of Reform and Opening-Up Policy in 1978, China's higher education institutions (HEIs) have not steadily expanded along with the country's rapid economic development. There were only two periods in which college and university enrollment experienced more than 10% growth. The first was in 1992 and 1993, when the annual growth rate reached 21.6% and 22.5%, respectively, but this rapid growth only lasted for two years (NBS 2012). The second period was from 1998 to 2005, when enrollment experienced more than 10% growth for seven consecutive years. In 2006, the growth rate of college and university enrollment decreased to less than 10%, where it has been ever since. China's college and university enrollment expansion plan, which was launched in 1999, had met citizens' increasing demands for more higher-education opportunities. And it was at this time that people began to focus on the qualitative aspects in addition to the quantitative aspects of higher education.

As college and university enrollment increased from 1998 to 2005, the number of higher education graduates between 2002 and 2008 also increased by more than 10% a year for seven consecutive years. Thus, the problem of finding employment became more pronounced for higher education graduates. From 2009 onward, however, the growth rate of higher education graduates dropped to less than 10% and the initial employment rate stabilized. Therefore, since 2009 employment pressure has decreased. People's primary concern, however, with regard to higher education graduates has shifted during this same period from the amount of graduates employed to the quality of their employment. It was no longer strictly a matter of whether or not graduates could find a job, but whether they could find a "good" job.

The way that higher education graduates feel about their employment status is an important measure when it comes to determining the quality of their employment. Employment satisfaction can be defined as a higher education graduate's subjective feeling about his or her job. Graduates also use this measure to evaluate their employment status. In terms of quality employment outcomes, job satisfaction is a good indicator of job quality. The first job a recent graduate holds after finishing his or her degree is very important, as a relatively high starting point in a person's career is conducive not only to career development, but also to job mobility. In the job search process, satisfaction can be used to examine the quality of university employment services and equity in the labor market. In the cultivation of human resources, job satisfaction can be used to examine the quality of career training offered to higher education students. Therefore, studying employment satisfaction of China's higher education graduates is theoretically and practically significant.

Concept and research overview

Employment satisfaction generally refers to how job seekers perceive the quality level of their employment. The level of employment satisfaction depends on the difference between job seekers' actual employment perceptions and their employment expectations. Higher education graduates' employment satisfaction can be summarized by the following formula:

Employment satisfaction = Actual employment perception − employment expectations

Many factors affect employment satisfaction, including salary, promotion opportunities, relationships with colleagues, and type of employment. As each person's psychological expectations are different, their evaluation of employment satisfaction will be different. Based on the above formula, factors affecting employment satisfaction can be placed into two categories. The first category involves job-related factors. When it comes to certain employment expectations, graduates' actual perceptions are different, that is, the same graduates may have significantly different experiences with different jobs. For instance, the job preferences of China's higher education graduates are generally quite similar: most of China's graduates want to work in eastern coastal cities, large and medium-sized cities, monopoly industries and emerging industries, the public sector, and professional technical and management positions. Graduates obtaining such jobs may have higher employment satisfaction than those who do not. High-paying jobs and jobs with good development prospects also tend to increase the level of graduates' employment satisfaction.

The second category involves non-job-related factors, such as demographic characteristics, human capital, social capital, higher education institution characteristics, and job search status. When it comes to actual employment perceptions, graduates' employment expectations can be different, that is, different graduates may have significantly different expectations of the same job. Higher education graduates who have high academic qualifications and who graduate from elite universities and those graduating with popular majors tend to have higher job expectations of and may show lower employment satisfaction with the same job in comparison with graduates from non-elite universities and from those graduating with degrees in lesser-known majors.

Employment satisfaction is a relative concept. Different people may have the same employment satisfaction with different jobs. Therefore, many complicated factors affect employment satisfaction. However, employment satisfaction is defined as a graduate's subjective feelings about his or her employment, and it refers to the overall view of the graduate after taking a variety of factors into consideration, so it can accurately reflect their experience of employment quality. Graduate groups with overall low employment satisfaction should be given more attention by scholars and officials alike, so as to determine whether there are specific common characteristics among the group that might be tied to lower employment satisfaction. Doing so will likely help the Chinese government formulate education and employment policies that will improve employment satisfaction.

There are many domestic and international research studies on employment satisfaction. Trow (1974) and Sanyal (1987) compared higher education and employment situations, and found that conditions for higher education students' employment are getting worse and that employment satisfaction is decreasing as higher education expands, especially after the transition from elite to mass higher education. Ball and Chik (2001) compared graduates' employment satisfaction in Malaysia to higher education graduates in the US and the UK, and found no significant differences in employment satisfaction between these groups. Using an econometric regression model, Florit and Vila Lladosa (2007) analyzed the influence of number of years of schooling and the degree of fit between major and job on employment satisfaction. Wharton et al. (2000) studied the link between social relations and employment satisfaction based on a multi-level linear model.

Many countries have conducted surveys and studies on higher education graduates' employment satisfaction. The US National Science Foundation (NSF) has conducted the National Survey of College Graduates since the 1970s to determine employment satisfaction among recent higher education graduates (NSF 2012). The survey includes the overall rating of employment satisfaction (divided into four options of very satisfied, somewhat satisfied, somewhat dissatisfied, and very dissatisfied), as well as employment satisfaction evaluation in nine different categories (salary, benefits, job security, job location, opportunities for promotion, intellectual challenge, level of responsibility, degree of independence, and contribution to society). The US National Association of Colleges and Employers conducts specialized surveys on the employment situation of higher education graduates each year, among which is a satisfaction survey (NACE 2012).

Funded by the European Union, from 1998 to 2000 the Career after Higher Education: A European Research Study (CHEERS) Project conducted extensive research on higher education graduates in eleven European countries and Japan who had completed school within the past four years. The studies involved respondents' social background, academic background, job-seeking process, early career, education and employment linkage, and evaluation of the education they had received. It focused particularly on employment satisfaction (Schomburg & Teichler, 2006).

In recent years, many Chinese scholars have also carried out empirical analyses on higher education graduates' employment satisfaction. Using the empirical research method and questionnaires, Tu (2007) analyzed the individual characteristics affecting higher education graduates' employment satisfaction. The study showed that it was more difficult for those higher education graduates who found jobs in a dependent manner, such as through school recommendations or family connections, to achieve a high level of job satisfaction. Higher education graduates' expectations in terms of their starting salaries and whether their jobs were aligned with their majors are also important factors that affect employment satisfaction. Liu (2007) studied how higher education graduates' career expectations affected employment satisfaction and found that graduates' overall employment satisfaction was not high. Graduates' employment satisfaction correlated significantly with their gender and major, but not with their family or cultural background.

Through questionnaires and interviews, Huang (2008) investigated higher education graduates' satisfaction toward career guidance services. The study revealed that the overall satisfaction toward university career guidance services was low, as the number of respondents who chose "dissatisfied" was similar to the number of respondents who chose "very satisfied." In an overall assessment of schools' career guidance services, more respondents chose "dissatisfied" than "very satisfied." Wang (2005) used the semi-parametric ordered Probit model to analyze female higher education students' employment satisfaction, studied major factors affecting their employment satisfaction, and made many recommendations for how to improve employment satisfaction and make it easier for female higher education graduates to find employment. Cao (2012) used data from the 2011 Sample Survey of Employment of National College Graduates from Peking University to analyze the influence of intrinsic and extrinsic factors on higher education graduates' employment satisfaction. The study found that both intrinsic and extrinsic factors significantly affected higher education graduates' employment satisfaction. Some of the factors that significantly affected employment satisfaction included higher education students' human capital and social capital characteristics, whether the jobs fit with students' degrees, and job characteristics.

The present study adopts data from a survey of Chinese higher education graduates in 2011, which was conducted by the Institute of Economics of Education at Peking University. It divides employment satisfaction factors into two categories – job-related factors and non-job-related factors – and uses the econometric regression method for significance testing of each affecting factor of employment satisfaction in order to provide an empirical basis for formulating policies to improve student employment quality.

Data description and empirical research methods

Sample description

Data used for this study came from the Sample Survey of Employment of National College Graduates in 2011 conducted by a research team at Peking University. The survey covers thirty higher education institutions in eight provinces in the eastern, central, and western regions, which include ten HEIs in Shandong and Zhejiang, nine HEIs in Jiangxi and Hubei, and eleven HEIs in Chongqing, Sichuan, Gansu, and Ningxia. Among them, there are three key Project 985 universities, four key Project 211 HEIs, nine common colleges, seven vocational colleges, four private HEIs, and three independent HEIs. Between 500 and 1,000 questionnaires were distributed to each college or university based on graduates' majors and academic levels. A total of 19,768 valid questionnaires were completed and collected.

Graduates from junior college and higher vocational colleges account for 38.9% of the valid samples; undergraduates accounted for 55% of the valid samples; postgraduates accounted for 5.5% of the valid samples; and doctoral graduates accounted for 0.3% of the valid samples. The ratio of male to female graduates was 49.1% to 50.9%. Graduates from key Project 985 universities accounted for 8.4% of the valid samples; graduates from key Project 211 HEIs accounted for 15.7% of the valid samples; ordinary colleges accounted for 28.4% of the valid samples; vocational colleges accounted for 25.5% of the valid samples; private colleges accounted for 12.8% of the valid samples; and independent colleges accounted for 9.2% of the valid samples.

Variable description

In this study, the dependent variable is employment satisfaction. The twenty-fifth question in the questionnaire is about higher education graduates' overall evaluation of their employment, which is divided into the following categories: "very satisfied," "satisfied," "ordinary," "dissatisfied," and "very dissatisfied." From a statistical description of the results, the evaluation of higher education graduates' employment satisfaction in 2011 was relatively high. The percentages of "very satisfied," "satisfied," "ordinary," "dissatisfied," and "very dissatisfied" are 11.1%, 43.6%, 40.0%, 4.7%, and 0.7%, respectively.

Explanatory variables are the various factors that affect higher education graduates' employment satisfaction. In this study, as mentioned above, these variables are divided into two categories – job-related factors and non-job-related factors. Specifically, job-related factors affecting higher education students' employment satisfaction comprise eight variables: monthly income, job location, geographic region of employment, organization type, industry category, job role, degree of fit between major and job, and employment status.

Non-job-related factors affecting employment satisfaction comprise demographic characteristics, human capital, social capital, HEI characteristics, and job search status. Demographic characteristics comprise the following variables: gender, nationality, and being the only child. Human capital comprises the following eight variables: education level, academic record, scholarship awards, Chinese Communist Party (CCP) membership, student leader experience, qualifications, minor or dual degree, and internship experience. Social capital comprises the following five variables: home city/town location, per capita annual family income, parents' average education level, parents' occupation, and family and social relations. HEI characteristics comprise HEI type and HEI location. Meanwhile, job search status comprises job search cost, job search frequency, job search network, and career guidance.

Econometric regression model

In order to investigate factors affecting higher education graduates' employment satisfaction, this study used the ordered logistic regression model. The regression equation is:

(1) The dependent variable is the higher education graduates' employment satisfaction. According to the questionnaire about the evaluation of employment, the twenty-fifth question used a Likert scale with the following responses: "very satisfied," "satisfied," "ordinary," "dissatisfied," and "very dissatisfied," with each response being numbered one to five, respectively. The explanatory variable X_j includes factors affecting employment satisfaction. Coefficient β_j stands for marginal impact of explanatory variables on employment satisfaction. A positive coefficient indicates that the explanatory variable has a positive effect on employment satisfaction. This study adopted dummy variables for the categorical explanatory variables involved in the model. The last column in Table 3.1 describes the control groups.

Analysis of factors affecting employment satisfaction

This study adopted the ordered logistic model of regression analysis on factors affecting graduates' employment satisfaction. First, a regression analysis was used to analyze all job-related factors pertaining to employment satisfaction, Second, non-job-related factors were then added and a regression analysis was conducted again. Statistical test results showed that, in the two regression models, chi-square statistic values are large with significance levels up to the 0.01 level, indicating that the each model as a whole is statistically significant. Due to the large number of explanatory variables, a multicollinearity test was conducted in the two regression analyses. The maximum variance inflation factors (VIFs) in the two regressions were only 2.31 and 4.04, showing that there was little multicollinearity. Statistical test results show that the result of the regression model is credible and explanatory. The numbers of observation samples in the two regressions were 6,649 and 3,314, respectively, with a difference of over 3,000.

According to different explanatory variable groups, the results of the two regressions are explained below (see Table 3.2).

Table 3.1 Explanatory variables description

Factor category	Specific variable	Variable description
Job-related factors	Monthly income	Continuous variable operating (unit: RMB)
	Job location	Large and medium-sized cities and non-large and non-medium-sized cities (control group)
	Geographic region of employment	Beijing, Tianjin, and Shanghai region; eastern region; central region (control group); and western region
	Organization type	State organizations, public institutions, state-owned enterprises, foreign-funded enterprises, private enterprises (control group), and others
	Industry category	Manufacturing (control group), electricity, gas, and water production and supply industry, finance and IT industry, science education, culture, health and sports industries, public administration, non-profit sector, and others
	Job role	Technician, manager, service position (control group), and other positions
	Degree of fit between major and job	Yes (control group) and no
	Employment status	With permanent local residence status and without permanent local residence status (control group)
Demographic characteristics	Gender	Female (control group) and male
	Nationality	Han (control group) and ethnic minorities
	Being the only child	Yes (control group) and no
Human capital	Education level	Junior college education, undergraduate education (control group), and postgraduate education
	Academic record	The top 25% in class, the middle 25%–50%, and the bottom 50% (control group)
	Scholarship awards	Yes (control group) and no
	CCP membership	Yes (control group) and no
	Student leader experience	Yes (control group) and no
	Qualifications	No (control group), English, computer-related, professional, and others

Factor category	Specific variable	Variable description
Minor or dual degree	No (control group) and yes	
Internship experience	No (control group) and yes	
Social capital	Home city/town location	Large and medium-sized cities and small cities (control group)
	Per capita annual family income	Low income (3,000 RMB and below); middle income (3,001 to 5,000 RMB; control group); and high income (more than 5,000 RMB)
	Parents' average education level	Continuous variable (unit: year), calculated according to parents' education level
	Parents' occupation	Non-managerial technical occupations (control group) and managerial technical occupations
	Family and social relations	Narrow (control group) and wide
HEI characteristics	HEI type	Project 211 HEIs, ordinary four-year HEIs (control group), vocational colleges, and other colleges
	HEI location	Eastern region, central region (control group), and western region
Job search status	Job search cost	Continuous variable (unit: 1,000 RMB)
	Job search frequency	Continuous variable (unit: times)
	Job search network	Employment information from school (control group), relatives and friends, networking, and other channels
	Career guidance	Courses and lectures for career guidance are helpful and not helpful (control group)

Note: Since the measurement model includes thirty explanatory variables and some categorical variables are too detailed, I merged sixteen variables in order to analyze the data and explain the results. These variables are job location, geographic region of employment, organization type, industry category, job role, degree of fit between major and job, academic record, home town/city location, per capita annual family income, parents' average education level, parents' occupation, family and social relations, HEI type, HEI location, job search network, and career guidance.

Table 3.2 Regression analysis results of factors affecting employment satisfaction

Explanatory variable	Coefficient	Standard error	Significance level	Coefficient	Standard error	Significance level
Logarithm of monthly income	0.613	0.054	0.000	0.908	0.094	0.000
Large and medium-sized cities	0.248	0.061	0.000	0.297	0.090	0.001
Beijing, Tianjin, and Shanghai	0.014	0.116	0.903	0.271	0.195	0.165
Eastern region	0.076	0.060	0.208	-0.014	0.109	0.897
Western region	-0.027	0.065	0.682	0.080	0.117	0.495
State organizations	0.280	0.132	0.034	0.339	0.206	0.100
State-owned enterprises	0.310	0.065	0.000	0.311	0.097	0.001
Public institutions	-0.128	0.096	0.185	-0.001	0.141	0.997
Foreign-funded enterprises	0.069	0.095	0.468	0.255	0.135	0.059
Other organizations	-0.075	0.102	0.459	0.049	0.145	0.737
Water, coal, and electricity industry	0.127	0.128	0.321	0.128	0.182	0.484
Finance and IT industry	0.268	0.079	0.001	0.187	0.116	0.109
Education, science, culture, health, and sports	0.221	0.099	0.027	0.037	0.147	0.800
CCP and government organizations	0.388	0.190	0.041	0.708	0.282	0.012
Other industries	0.261	0.073	0.000	0.201	0.110	0.067

Explanatory variable	Coefficient	Standard error	Significance level	Coefficient	Standard error	Significance level
Managerial positions	0.435	0.072	0.000	0.169	0.106	0.111
Technical positions	0.055	0.067	0.414	0.020	0.100	0.842
Other positions	0.075	0.080	0.352	0.070	0.121	0.564
Degree of fit between major and job	0.458	0.050	0.000	0.469	0.074	0.000
Permanent local residence status	0.425	0.053	0.000	0.501	0.082	0.000
Served as student leaders				0.129	0.075	0.083
Family and social relations				0.281	0.108	0.009
HEIs in western region				−0.253	0.133	0.058
Job search cost				−0.042	0.023	0.067
Job search frequency				−0.004	0.002	0.092
Job search network				0.282	0.101	0.006
Career guidance				0.521	0.070	0.000
N	6,649			3,314		
Pseudo r-squared	0.098			0.143		

42 Factors affecting employment satisfaction

1 Influence of job-related factors on employment satisfaction

(1) Monthly income has a significant impact on employment satisfaction. The higher the income, the higher employment satisfaction becomes. (2) Job location has a significant impact on employment satisfaction. Employment satisfaction is higher in large and medium-sized cities. (3) With the central region as the control group, the geographic region of employment does not produce a significant impact on employment satisfaction, indicating that there is no significant difference between the Beijing, Tianjin, and Shanghai region; the eastern region; the western region; and the central region in terms of employment satisfaction. (4) With private enterprises as the control group, organization type has a significant impact on employment satisfaction. In state organizations and state-owned enterprises, employment satisfaction is significantly higher than in private enterprises; employment satisfaction in public institutions and other organizations is almost the same as in private enterprises; and employment satisfaction in foreign-funded enterprises is higher than in private enterprises, but only the coefficients in regression two are significant. (5) With the manufacturing industry as the control group, industry category has a significant impact on employment satisfaction. Employment satisfaction in CCP and state organizations, finance and information technology (IT), and other industries is significantly higher than in the manufacturing industry. Employment satisfaction in the education, science, culture, health, and sports industries is higher than in the manufacturing industry, but only the coefficients in regression one are significant. There is no significant difference in employment satisfaction between the water, coal, and electricity industries and the manufacturing industry. (6) With the service position as the control group, job roles have a significant impact on employment satisfaction. Employment satisfaction in managerial positions is significantly higher than in service positions, but only the coefficients in regression one are significant; there is no significant difference in employment satisfaction between other positions and service positions. (7) Major matching has a significant impact on employment satisfaction. The higher the major matching is, the higher the employment satisfaction becomes. (8) Forms of employment have a significant effect on employment satisfaction. Offering employees permanent local residence status can significantly improve their employment satisfaction.

In summary, employment satisfaction can be significantly improved depending on job-related various factors. It is higher when graduates have high-paying jobs, when they work in large and medium-sized cities, when they work in state organizations, CCP and government organizations, the finance and IT industry, when they work in managerial positions, when there is a strong fit between their majors and their jobs, and when they have permanent local residence status.

2 Influence of demographic characteristics on employment satisfaction

Regression coefficients of gender, nationality, and being the only child in one's family are not significant, showing that the demographic characteristic variables have no significant impact on employment satisfaction.

3 Influence of human capital on employment satisfaction

Among the eight variables of education level, academic record, scholarship awards, CCP membership, student leader experience, qualifications, minor or dual degree, and internship experience, only the regression coefficients of the student leader experience variable are significant. The regression coefficients suggest that higher education graduates serving as student leaders will likely have higher employment satisfaction.

4 Influence of social capital on employment satisfaction

Among the five variables of location of graduates' home town/city, per capita annual family income, parents' occupations, parents' average education level, and family and social relations, only the regression coefficients of family and social relations are significant. Regression results show that, the wider family and social relations are, the more satisfied graduates become with their employment.

5 Influence of HEI characteristics on employment satisfaction

The regression coefficient of HEI type is not significant, indicating that there is no significant difference in evaluating employment satisfaction for graduates in Project 211 HEIs, vocational colleges and universities, other colleges, and ordinary colleges. The regression coefficient of western HEIs is significantly negative. The results indicate that graduates' employment satisfaction in western HEIs is lower than in central HEIs, and that there is no significant difference between eastern and central HEIs.

6 Influence of job search status on employment satisfaction

The regression coefficients of the variables of job search cost, job search frequency, job search network, and career guidance are significant. The results indicate that job search status has a significant impact on employment satisfaction. Among the four variables, the regression coefficients of job search cost and job search frequency are significantly negative, indicating that the more money and time an individual invests in his or her job searches, the lower his or her employment satisfaction will be. The regression coefficients of career guidance (i.e. courses and lectures) are significantly positive, implying that career guidance is likely to increase employment satisfaction. Compared with higher education employment information, the regression coefficients of online job searching are significantly positive, while the regression coefficients of relatives and friends and other channels are not significant. Using the Internet is a more equitable, competitive, and independent channel for job searching. Graduates are more satisfied when they obtain jobs via such a channel.

In summary, higher education graduates influenced by non-job-related factors, which include higher education graduates who had student leadership experience, graduates with wide family and social relations, graduates in eastern and central HEIs, graduates who think that career guidance is helpful, and graduates who get jobs via the Internet, are more satisfied with their employment.

Factors affecting job choice

The coefficients of the variables in the results of the two regressions are different. In addition, the significance of the regression coefficients of foreign-funded enterprises; education, science, culture, health, and sports; and managerial positions is inconsistent. There are two main reasons for this. First, the sample sizes for the two regressions are very different. Second, there are up to thirty kinds of explanatory variables in regression two. Although statistical tests show that there is little multicollinearity, some variables are somewhat relevant. Non-job-related factors and especially job-related factors are not completely independent. Demographic characteristics, human capital, social capital, HEI characteristics, job search status, and other factors influence the types of jobs that graduates can obtain.

Next, the seven job-related factors, namely, monthly income, job location, organization type, employment category, job role, degree of fit between major and job, and employment status, significantly affect employment satisfaction were used as the dependent variables, and twenty-two non-job-related factors were used as explanatory variables for regression. The monthly income variable is a continuous variable (introduced in logarithmic form). Based on the multiple linear regression model, this study used ordinary least squares (OLS) to conduct regression, and other dependent variables are dichotomous variables. The variables have to do with whether graduates work in large and medium-sized cities, whether they work for state organizations, the CCP and government organizations, the finance and IT industry, whether they occupy managerial positions, whether there is a strong fit between their major and their job, and whether they obtain permanent local residence status. This study used the ordered logistic model as applied to dichotomous dependent variables to conduct the regression. The seven results of the regression are shown in Table 3.3 and are explained below.

1 Influence of demographic characteristics on employment

Male graduates of Han nationality are more likely to find "more satisfactory jobs." The four regression coefficients of males in monthly income, large and medium-sized cities, state organizations, and permanent local residence status are significantly positive. The regression coefficients of minorities in CCP and government organizations, and finance and IT industry are significantly negative.

2 Influence of human capital on employment

Among the eight variables, only the regression coefficients of the internship experience variable are not significant. Graduates with a postgraduate education background, who are in the top 25% of their class, who have won scholarship awards, who have CCP membership and student leadership experience, who are English-certified, and those who graduated with a minor or dual degree are more likely to find "more satisfactory jobs."

3 Influence of social capital on employment

Graduates from families with high incomes, with highly educated parents, and wide family and social relations are more likely to find "more satisfactory jobs." The regression coefficients of family location and parents' occupations are both positive and negative.

4 Influence of HEI characteristics on employment

Compared to graduates from ordinary colleges, graduates from Project 211 HEIs are more likely to find "more satisfactory jobs," while vocational college graduates are less likely to find "more satisfactory jobs." Compared with central HEIs, graduates from western HEIs are more likely to find "more satisfactory jobs," while the regression coefficients of eastern HEIs are both positive and negative.

5 Influence of job search status on employment

Some of the regression coefficients of job search costs, job search frequency, job search network, and career guidance are significant. Each variable has either a positive or a negative coefficient, which has an uncertain impact on finding "more satisfactory jobs."

Table 3.3 Regression results of factors affecting employment

	Monthly income	Large and medium-sized cities	State org.	State org., finance and IT industry	Major matching	Manag. positions	Perm. local residence status
Male	0.092***	0.361***	0.497***	−0.054	−0.240***	−0.091	0.156*
Minorities	−0.040	−0.126	0.025	−0.573***	0.159	−0.058	−0.228
Being the only child	0.014	−0.186*	0.056	0.098	0.125	0.031	0.353***
Junior college education	−0.217***	0.064	−0.637***	−0.193	−0.438***	−0.451***	−0.615***
Postgraduate education	0.310***	0.335	0.318**	−0.217	−0.169	0.737***	0.580***
Top 25% in academic record	0.052***	0.336***	0.116	0.052	−0.192*	0.295***	0.049
Bottom 25% in academic record	0.03*	−0.007	−0.005	0.131	−0.223	−0.169*	0.109
Scholarships	0.029*	−0.046	0.274***	0.278***	0.020	0.014	0.138
CCP member	0.005	0.007	0.173*	0.289***	0.098	−0.021	0.209
Student leader	0.053***	0.142	0.075	−0.220***	0.118	−0.035	0.200*
English certificate	0.042***	0.200*	−0.120	0.128	0.082	−0.011	0.201*
Computer certificate	0.015	−0.261***	−0.055	−0.245***	−0.161*	0.008	0.220***
Other certificates	−0.039*	0.005	0.082	0.045	0.119	0.040	−0.263***
Minor or double degree	0.006	0.134	0.069	0.139	0.420***	−0.114	−0.037
Internship experience	−0.027	−0.178	−0.080	0.008	0.105	0.170	−0.067
Families in large and medium-sized cities	0.021	1.117***	0.004	0.027	−0.157*	−0.019	0.251***
Low-income families	−0.006	−0.033	0.321***	0.188	−0.331***	0.211*	0.020
High-income families	0.064***	0.131	0.190*	0.361***	−0.033	−0.068	0.017
Years of parents' education	0.009***	0.081***	0.053***	0.034*	0.025	−0.005	0.011

	Monthly income	Large and medium-sized cities	State org.	State org., finance and IT industry	Major matching	Manag. positions	Perm. local residence status
Parents' managerial and technical occupations	−0.027	−0.274*	0.263*	0.136	−0.013	0.093	0.236*
Wide family and social relationships	0.038*	−0.182	0.483***	0.309***	0.396***	0.015	0.270*
Project 211 universities	0.125***	0.120	0.408***	−0.150	0.081	0.398***	0.657***
Higher vocational colleges	−0.152***	0.123	0.458*	−0.333*	0.252	−0.025	−0.707***
Other colleges	−0.076***	0.082	−0.225	−0.163	0.384***	−0.119	−0.538***
Eastern colleges	0.031	−0.349***	0.004	0.014	−0.010	0.205*	0.676***
Western colleges	−0.028	0.012	0.203	0.034	0.073	0.216**	0.260**
Job search cost	0.014***	−0.054*	0.124***	0.071***	0.075***	−0.022	0.139***
Times of job search	0.001***	0.008*	−0.005**	0.008***	0.000	−0.006***	−0.013***
Channels of relatives and friends	−0.093***	−0.416***	−0.314***	−0.027	0.186	−0.340***	−0.512***
Network information channels	−0.054***	−0.022	−0.103	0.614***	0.174	−0.175***	−0.606***
Other job-search channels	−0.060***	−0.194	−0.176*	0.270***	0.241*	−0.166*	−0.110
Job-search guidance courses	−0.024*	−0.109	0.072	−0.031	0.122	0.153*	0.161**
Constant	7.551***	0.442	−2.286***	−1.950***	−1.695***	0.305	−0.349
N	3,473	3,568	3,685	3,685	3,593	3,615	3,520

Notes: ***, **, * represent statistical significance levels of 0.01, 0.05, and 0.10, respectively.

Conclusion and policy suggestions

This study conducted an empirical analysis of higher education graduates' employment satisfaction based on the data from the 2011 Sample Survey of Employment of National College Graduates, which was conducted by the Institute of Economics of Education at Peking University. The main conclusions of the empirical research are summarized in this section.

First, job-related factors have a significant impact on employment satisfaction. In this study, the regression coefficients of seven of the eight variables (monthly income, job location, organization type, industry category, job role, degree of fit between major and job, and employment status) are statistically significant.

Second, regression results show that employment satisfaction can be improved significantly by having a high-paying job; working in large and medium-sized cities; working for state organizations, the CCP and government organizations, and in the finance and IT industry; working in managerial positions; having a better fit between one's major and one's job; and being able to obtain permanent local residence status.

Third, some non-job-related factors also have a significant impact on employment satisfaction. In this study, from among twenty-two non-job-related factors in five categories, eighteen non-job-related factors and in four categories (human capital, social capital, HEI characteristics, and job search status) have significant regression coefficients, and only the coefficients for the three non-job-related factors in the demographic characteristics category are not significant. Regression results show that among graduates who are more satisfied with employment are those who served as student leaders, those with wide family and social relations, those from eastern and central HEIs, those who find career guidance helpful, and those who find jobs through networking.

Fourth, although some non-job-related factors have no significantly direct impact on employment satisfaction, they can affect higher education graduates' job choice and indirectly have an impact on employment satisfaction. Regression results show that graduates who are male, of Han nationality, among the top 25% in their HEI's academic record, scholarship awardees, CCP members, former student leaders, English certificate holders, possessors of a minor or double degree, members of families with high incomes, offspring of highly educated parents, possessors of wide family and social relations, and graduates of Project 211 HEIs are more likely to find "more satisfactory jobs."

It is clear that higher education graduates' employment satisfaction depends mainly on "good" or "bad" work. Everyone seems to have the same opinion about so-called "good" work, which reflects that there is extreme imbalance in China's labor market and serious market segmentation. Graduates with higher human capital and social capital as well as graduates from eastern and central HEIs are generally more satisfied with their jobs partly because they have obvious advantages in competition for "good" jobs.

The above-mentioned results of empirical research have significance because they can improve employment quality for graduates. First, the main factors affecting employment satisfaction are primarily job-related. There is obvious labor market segmentation in China, specifically with respect to job location (city versus countryside), region, organization type, industrial category, and position. These differences result in significant income disparity. Graduates who enter the main labor market are generally more satisfied with their jobs, while graduates who only enter the secondary labor market are less satisfied with their jobs. Establishing an equitable, just, and competitive labor market and narrowing the income gap by reforming irrational institutional factors can help improve graduates' employment satisfaction.

Permanent local residence status also has a significant impact on graduates' employment satisfaction, so the government should further liberalize constraints on higher education graduates' residence status, and thereby increase their mobility. Meanwhile, an archives management system that is more conducive to graduates should be set up so that the system no longer charges fees for archiving.

Second, the employment service system for higher education graduates should be strengthened. Empirical results show that career guidance courses and lectures significantly affect employment satisfaction. Thus, strengthening career guidance and career planning education processes will help improve quality of employment.

Obtaining job information from the Internet is a more equitable and competitive employment channel. Graduates who get their jobs via the Internet are likely to be more satisfied with their employment. Therefore, employment networking via the Internet should be further improved and strengthened.

Third, employment of disadvantaged groups should be given special attention so as to help improve their employability. The research results of this study show that graduates in the following categories are less likely to find "more satisfactory jobs": females, minorities, students attending junior college or less prestigious colleges, students with poor academic performance, students with no scholarships, non-CCP members, students with no student leadership experience, students without English-language certification, students from low-income families, students from households where parents had a low average level of education, and students whose families lack significant social relationships and connections.

References

Ball, R. & R. Chik. 2001. "Early Employment Outcomes of Home and Foreign Educated Graduates – the Malaysian Experience." *Higher Education* 42(2): 171–189.

Cao, X. 2012. *Analysis of Factors Affecting Employment Satisfaction of College Graduates.* Unpublished master's thesis. Beijing: Peking University.

Florit, E. F. & L. E. Vila Lladosa. 2007. "Evaluation of the Effects of Education on Employment Satisfaction: Independent Single-Equation vs. Structural Equation Models." *International Advances in Economic Research* 13(2): 157–170.

Huang, P. 2008. *University Graduates Career Guidance Satisfaction Study.* Unpublished master's thesis. Chongqing, China: Southwest University.

Liu, X. 2007. *Impact of College Graduates' Career Expectations on Employment Satisfaction*. Unpublished master's thesis. Chengdu, China: Sichuan University.

National Association of Colleges and Employers (NACE). 2012. *Student Survey*. Bethlehem, PA: NACE. Available online at http://www.naceweb.org/home.aspx. Accessed October 12, 2012.

NationalBureau of Statistics (NBS). 2012. *China Statistical Yearbook*. Beijing: China Statistics Press.

National Science Foundation (NSF). 2012. *National Survey of College Graduates*. Washington, DC: NSF. Available online at http://www.nsf.Gov/statistics/srvygrads/. Accessed October 12, 2012.

Research into Employment and Professional Flexibility(REFLEX). 2012. *European Graduate Survey*. Available online at http://www.fdewb.unimaas.nl. Accessed October 12, 2012.

Sanyal, B. 1987. *Higher Education and Employment: An International Comparative Analysis*. London: The Falmer Press.

Schomburg, H. & U. Teichler, 2006. *Higher Education and Graduate Employment in Europe: Results from Graduate Surveys from Twelve Countries*. Dordrecht: Springer.

Trow, M. 1974. *Problems in the Transition from Elite to Mass Higher Education*. Paris: Organisation for Economic Co-operation and Development (OECD).

Tu, X. 2007. "Empirical Study on Influence Factors of the Degree of Graduates' Employment Satisfaction." *Higher Education Exploration* 2: 117–119.

Wang, Y. 2005. "Semi-Parametric Analysis of Employment Satisfaction of Female College Students." *Statistics and Decision* 22: 71–74.

Wharton, A. S., T. Rotolo & T. Bird. 2000. "Social Context at Work: A Multilevel Analysis of Employment Satisfaction."*Sociological Forum* 15(1): 65–90.

4 Studying abroad or internationalizing on campus

University students' global competence training

Wen Dongmao, Lu Jiao and Wang Youhang

Problem statement

The internationalization of higher education has a long history. Teaching and studying abroad was common as early as the Ancient Greek period (Chen 2007). With the unceasing advancement of economic globalization and world integration, internationalization has become an important trend in current higher education development. Some modern scholars even believe international cooperation or international cultural exchange to be the fourth function of the university (Chen 1998; Ji 2007).

There are still different opinions in academia surrounding the basic question: "What is internationalization of higher education?" For example, in *The Dictionary of Education*, internationalization of higher education is defined as

> a development trend of higher education in each country with global concentration on the basis of domestic concentration. Major performance: one is strengthening foreign language teaching by adding a large number of courses, majors, and departments about international issues to train professional personnel engaging in the study on international affairs and international issues; another one is carrying out extensive international personnel exchange; the third one is carrying out multinational cooperation on education and scholarism.
>
> Gu (1991)

Arum and Van de Water (1992) define internationalization of higher education as various activities, projects, and services of educational institutions performed in the process of international research, international education, and technical cooperation. Knight, a Canadian scholar, states that internationalization of higher education refers to the "process of integrating an international intercultural dimension into the teaching, research and service functions of the institutions" (Knight 1994: 7). In a later volume co-authored with de Wit, Knight once again defines internationalization of higher education as a process "of integrating an international/intercultural dimension into the teaching, research and service function of the institution" (Knight & de Wit 1997: 8). However, through careful reading, it is determined that "trend theory," "activity theory," and "process theory" all deal with the change of relevant activities to include teaching and scientific research in higher educational institutions as the basic approach or major content of higher education internationalization. Theories aside, in reality it seems that national governments, colleges, and universities currently promote the international mobility of teachers and students.

Student mobility was institutionalized in Europe through the Erasmus Programme (1987) and the Socrates Programme (1994), while the intensity of recruiting international students also increased in the United States, Canada, Australia, Japan, and other countries. The Chinese government has expanded state-funded study abroad initiatives through its State-Sponsored Postgraduate Study Abroad Programs and has adopted various measures to attract foreign students to study in China. *U.S. News & World Report* regards the percentage of students studying abroad and the percentage of international students on campus as important factors to take into consideration when evaluating universities.

In these times of globalization, it is incontrovertible that institutions of higher learning should train students to possess global vision, the master the ability to communicate and engage internationally, and to develop multicultural understanding. There are two basic approaches to cultivating students' global competence: one is self-supporting or state-funded studying abroad, and the other is internationalizing at home (Knight 1994) by "internationalizing on campus," which depends on the availability of college or university resources. Although studying abroad allows students to directly experience life in other countries, the cost of transportation, board and lodging, and tuition is high, a cost which only a few students can afford to pay. Although "internationalizing on campus" saves both time and labor with relatively low cost, it may sometimes seem ineffective as an alternative.

This chapter addresses the following questions: (a) In terms of international resource utilization, what is the difference between students who study abroad and those who do not? (b) What influence does studying abroad have on the development of students' global competence? and (c) How do students choose between studying abroad and internationalizing on campus?

Study design and sample description

This study assumes that the cultivating of university students' relevant global competence is based on certain resources, including personnel, funds, materials, and information. These resources can be divided into those provided by national organizations ("national resources") and those provided by international organizations ("international resources"). International resources can be divided into resources that involve studying abroad and campus resources that can be utilized on domestic university campuses. Campus resources include personnel resources such as international students, foreign specialists, and exchange scholars; information resources such as Internet access, foreign-language electronic databases, and foreign-language literature provided on campus; and an internationalized environment consisting of international student apartments, international conferences, and international activities. On this basis, this study assumes a difference between the influence on students of studying abroad and the influence on students of internationalizing on campus (i.e. utilizing internationalized resources like those just mentioned). Consequently, this difference is also found in how studying abroad and internationalizing at home influence the development of students' relevant global competence.

In order to research how international resources are being utilized and how international resources affect students' relevant global competence, this study divided students into two groups: those who have experience studying abroad (including short-term and long-term exchanges) and those who do not. It then compared the utilization condition of international resources and campus resources by these two student groups through a questionnaire survey. Finally, it analyzed the relationship between how international resources are being utilized and how students' relevant global competence is being developed.

Peking University was chosen as the subject for our case research, as it is a prominent university in China and pays a great deal of attention to international cooperation and students' global competence. Peking University's overall talent cultivation objective as of 2006 is to train "leading talents who own international view and spirit of innovation, and play the guiding role in all industries for the country and nation" (Lin 2006: 2). Because of its analysis of the internationalization condition at Peking University and its practice, methods, and results, this study will serve as a highly valuable reference for researchers and policymakers seeking to learn about the status of international resource utilization in China's colleges and universities and wanting to potentially bring about education reform.

For this study, we administered a survey to students with Chinese nationality from Peking University in May 2007. This survey adopted a stratified sampling method, by which we selected the School of Mathematical Sciences, the School of Physics, the Law School, and the Department of Chinese Language and Literature as our surveyed units. The survey was then administered to 200 participants from each school or department using random selection criteria. The total sum of questionnaires administered was 800, and the total number of completed questionnaires was 665, indicating an 83.1% response rate. Of this 83.1%, the sample percentages of the above four schools or departments was 28.6%, 27.1%, 22.9%, and 21.5%, respectively, and the percentages of undergraduate, postgraduate, and doctoral students who responded were 78.2%, 11.9%, and 9.9%, respectively.

In order to know how international students at Peking University are using relevant resources, as well as the contact and interaction effect between international students and Chinese students, we conducted a survey-based study for international students at Peking University in April 2009. This study used a simple random sampling method. The total sum of questionnaires administered was 600, and 402 completed surveys were returned. Of the 402 completed surveys, 400 were effective, indicating a 66.7% response rate. Participants were from 35 countries on five continents, with 58.6% of participants being South Korean students. The second and third highest groups were Thai students (7.0%) and Singaporean students (6.7%). The percentage of undergraduates, master's degree candidates, doctoral candidates, and students without a degree was 59.2%, 5.8%, 2.0%, and 33.0%, respectively. The international students came from 18 schools or departments, with those students from the Department of Chinese Language and Literature making up 18.7% of the total number of students surveyed. The second and third highest number of participants came from the School of Chinese as a Second Language (14.4%) and the School of International Studies (13.9%), respectively. The analysis in the present study is mainly based on this survey (from April 2009) and the one discussed above (from May 2007).

Status of studying abroad and international resource utilization

Studying abroad places students in a unique environment, in which they are immersed in foreign language, culture, life, and learning. This firsthand experience of politics, economics, scholarship, and technology is referred to as "total immersion learning." After investigating and analyzing the experiences of Peking University Chinese students who studied abroad and those of international students who came to China to study, we have come to the following conclusions.

The opportunity for students to study abroad is limited

At Peking University, opportunities for students from different schools or departments to study abroad are not readily available. Undergraduates from the Guanghua School of Management and the School of International Studies have many opportunities to study abroad for short periods of time, while those from science departments prefer to study abroad after graduation. However, the 2007 survey results show that, of the participating students from four schools at Peking University, only 28 students, or 4.2% of all participants, have studied abroad. Meanwhile, the percentages of undergraduates, master's degree candidates, and doctoral candidates who have studied abroad are 2.9%, 5.1%, and 13.6%, respectively, which shows that for undergraduates there is little opportunity to study abroad.

The percentage of opportunities for studying abroad is also unbalanced in different schools, being 2.7% in the School of Mathematical Sciences, 6.7% in the School of Physics, 4.6% in the Law School, and 2.8% in the Department of Chinese Language and Literature. The length of time of study abroad programs is generally short, with 53.6% of programs being one month or less, 39.3% being for one to six months, and 7.1% being for six months to one year in duration.

Since 2008, the Chinese government and Peking University administrators have promoted student opportunities to travel to foreign countries. According to statistics from the end of 2009, approximately 22% of Peking University undergraduates had experienced studying abroad in the past four years (Jin 2009). However, at present, the percentage of college students with study abroad experience is still rather limited throughout the country.

The depth of international communication during study abroad programs needs to improve

Among students who have studied abroad, in terms of purpose and task, 33.3% went to attend an international conference, 18.5% participated in scientific research cooperation projects, 22.2% went to gain course credit, 25.9% went for other reasons, and none of the participants went as part of their degree program. In terms of accommodation abroad, 40.7% of students lived with Chinese students or ethnic Chinese, 40.7% of students lived independently, 11.1% of students lived with other international students, and 7.4% of students lived with local students. When participants were asked about difficulties they experienced abroad, 57.7% students answered the "language barrier." Students were given a multiple choice questionnaire to determine where the language barrier was most difficult aspect of their experience, and 46.2% indicated that "attending a lecture or during communications in class" was most difficult, while 34.6% indicated "daily life" as being the most difficult obstacle and 23.1% indicated that "making friends" was the hardest part of their experience.

From the data presented above, it is clear that the extent of studying abroad for students from Peking University is still mainly limited to short-term academic programs or visits, while the percentage of those students who go for the opportunity to receive instruction at foreign colleges and universities is very low. Although these students live in foreign countries, most of them do not live in internationalized environments. Even though they are students from Peking University, most of them experience language barriers to some degree. This obstacle will inevitably influence the depth and breadth of students' international communication.

There is a lack of communication between international students and Chinese teachers and students

The frequency with which Chinese students are utilizing international resources after studying abroad is influenced by factors such as visit duration, foreign language speaking level, and cultural psychology. How are international students utilizing Chinese resources (i.e. international resources) after coming to China? Through the survey of international students at Peking University, we can conclude that the communication between international students and Chinese teachers and students is relatively limited both during and after school, as well as in daily life.

In terms of academic communication, the percentage of students "participating in frequent classroom discussions" is 38.2%, while 33.6% is the percentage of international students "frequently discussing learning problems with Chinese students after class"; 36.7% is the percentage of international students "mainly reading Chinese literature after class"; and 18.1% is the percentage of international students "communicating with teachers alone at least once every week."

In terms of participating in extracurricular activities, 12% of international students frequently participate in "club activities organized by Chinese students"; 11.5% undertake "collective travel with Chinese students"; 15.3% are "learning language in pairs with Chinese students"; and 40% or more students have "no participation" to speak of in these three activities.

In terms of accommodations at Peking University, 51.5% of international students live in international students' apartments on campus, and 48.5% of international students live off campus, among which only 5.5% live with Chinese students. It is thus clear that the majority of international students do not live with local residents during their time abroad, which will also influence the opportunity, depth, and breadth of the communication between Chinese students and foreign students.

Status of international communication on campus and campus resource use

Peking University is a major site for international academic communication in China, with more than 2,500 international students and more than 500 foreign specialists and foreign language teachers on campus in any given year. The university has established school-level cooperative relationships with more than 200 foreign colleges and universities, introducing a large number of excellent curricula to campus. Hundreds of international academic conferences are held at Peking University every year. The following survey results indicate that, despite how abundant international campus resources are, students may not be taking full advantage of them. The frequency and universality of student participation in international communication on campus are low.

Table 4.1 shows that from among Peking University students, 38.2% "frequently" use foreign language network resources and foreign language teaching materials; 40.1% "repeatedly" use these resources and materials; 14.2% "frequently" or "repeatedly" take foreign language courses as electives, take courses taught by foreign language teachers, or participate in international conferences; and only 12.6% "frequently" or "repeatedly" communicate with international students. However, it should be mentioned that over 40% of

Table 4.1 Participation of Chinese students at Peking University in international communication on campus (%)

Activity	Frequently	Repeatedly	Occasionally	Never
Participating in international conferences	3.8	10.4	38.1	47.8
Communicating with international students	3.2	9.4	42.7	44.7
Taking classes that are taught by foreign language teachers or foreign language classes as elective courses	3.1	11.1	48.5	37.3
Using foreign language network resources	17.0	21.2	40.0	21.8
Using foreign language teaching materials	15.6	24.5	42.3	17.7
Reading foreign language academic theses	18.5	15.8	32.6	33.1

students never participate in international conferences, or communicate with international students, while more than 30% of the students never read foreign language academic theses.

There is significant variation in how campus resources are utilized across different schools and departments

This survey has shown that there is a pattern to how students from different schools utilize international campus resources. Students from science departments use information resources more frequently than do students from social science and humanities departments. For example, the percentage of students who "frequently" or "repeatedly" read foreign language academic theses and use foreign language teaching materials is 27% and 39.6% in the School of Mathematical Sciences, 71.6% and 60.9% in the School of Physics, 22.0% and 31.2% in the Law School, and only 9.9% and 23.8% in the Department of Chinese Language and Literature.

Relatively speaking, the availability of personnel resources by student from the Department of Liberal Arts is higher. For example, 22.5% students from the Law School and 11.2% students from the Department of Chinese Language and Literature "frequently" or "repeatedly" communicate with international students. However, this percentage in the School of Mathematical Sciences and the School of Physics is only 9.6% and 8.4%, respectively. Among the six listed activities in Table 4.1, the School of Physics has four activities with the highest percentage, while the Department of Chinese Language and Literature has only four activities with the lowest percentage. This also shows that the number of students utilizing international resources is influenced by subject characteristic and the status of available resources. It may also be connected to school requirements and specific activities.

The different education levels of students will significantly influence the use of campus resources

This study indicates that, the higher the education level is, the higher the utilization degree of international campus resources will be. The utilization of information resources by doctoral students and postgraduates is much higher than that of undergraduates. For example, the percentage of those who "frequently" or "repeatedly" read foreign language academic theses is 93.9%, 75.9%, and 20.4% for doctoral, postgraduate, and undergraduate students, respectively. The percentage of those who "frequently" and "repeatedly" use foreign language teaching materials is 80%, 59.5%, and 32.1% for doctoral, postgraduate, and undergraduate students, respectively. The percentage of those who "frequently" and "repeatedly" use foreign language network resources is 90.7%, 69.9%, and 17.3% for doctoral, postgraduate, and undergraduate students, respectively. In terms of participating in an internationalized environment, the percentage of those who "frequently" or "repeatedly" participate in international conferences is 38.4%, 26.9%, and 9.1% for doctoral, postgraduate, and undergraduate students, respectively.

Relatively speaking, in terms of the utilization personnel resources, the difference among students with different education levels is minimal. For example, the percentage of those who "frequently" and "repeatedly" take courses that are taught by foreign language teachers or who take foreign language courses as electives 20.9%, 21.5%, and 12.2% for doctoral, postgraduate, and undergraduate students, respectively. Meanwhile, the percentage of those who "frequently" and "repeatedly" communicate with international students is 17.2%, 11.4%, and 12.2% for doctoral, postgraduate, and undergraduate students, respectively.

Utilization of international resources and students' global competence development

The main purpose of higher education internationalization is to improve students' academic level, international understanding, and other relevant comprehensive competencies through international communication and cooperation. This study shows that the utilization of international resources significantly promotes the development of students' global competence.

Studying abroad and students' global competence development

Studying abroad can help students tap into campus international resources more directly and conveniently and has thus been identified as an effective way for students to broaden their international views and develop their international understanding, and as tool to improve internationalization. This study has adopted a five-point Likert scale to carry out a survey on what students gain by utilizing international resources and campus resources, with 5, 4, 3, 2, and 1 meaning "agreeing completely," "agreeing," "agreeing generally," "disagreeing," and "disagreeing completely," respectively.

Through comparative analysis, we can identify the effectiveness of the influence of studying abroad on students' relevant global competence. Among those who have studied abroad, the most frequently attested benefit is "understanding international conditions, customs, and lifestyles." The percentage of "agreeing completely" or "agreeing" is 93.3%. As displayed in Table 4.2, the percentage of "agreeing completely" or "agreeing" for four other benefits listed on the survey – (1) "improving foreign language ability"; (2) "deepening understanding of foreign conditions;" (3) "deepening awareness of and respect for different cultures"; and (4) "strengthening national consciousness, paying more attention to words and deeds, and maintaining the image of the home country – is above 80%. As for the evaluation of the other eight benefits, the percentage of "agreeing completely" or "agreeing" is above 70%. The independent-sample T test of scores on each benefit from the two categories of "using campus resources" and "studying abroad" shows that there is a significant difference between them.

Table 4.2 Comparison between the benefits of using campus resources and studying abroad

	Average score		Significance of difference
	Using campus resources	Studying abroad	sig.
Deepening knowledge of major	3.53	4.04	0.015
Improving practical skills and abilities related to major	3.29	4.04	0.000
Improving foreign language ability	3.77	4.15	0.031
Improving working ability	3.47	4.00	0.004
Enhancing self-confidence	3.51	3.96	0.015
Strengthening interpersonal communication skills	3.63	4.00	0.039
Developing friendships abroad	3.10	4.00	0.000
Understanding foreign conditions, customs, and lifestyles	3.49	4.31	0.000
Deepening awareness of and respect for different cultures	3.68	4.15	0.009
Deepening understanding of foreign conditions	3.72	4.19	0.002
Understanding foreigners' view of China and the Chinese	3.56	4.12	0.001
Strengthening national consciousness, paying more attention to words and deeds, and maintaining image of home country	3.68	4.15	0.003
Changing attitude toward life to one that is more positive and open	3.31	4.04	0.000

Notes: $p < 0.05$ is significant; $p < 0.01$ is highly significant

Utilization of campus resources and students' global competence development

The relationship between the degree to which campus resources are utilized and students' relevant global competence can be illustrated through Spearman's analysis. Table 4.3 illustrates the impacts of utilizing different types of campus resources on the development of students' specific global competence. There is a significant correlation between "participating in international conferences" and the development of each ability and competency. The influence of communicating with international students on the development of specialized knowledge and skills is not obvious, but the correlation with other benefits is significant ($p < 0.01$). The correlation is significant ($p < 0.01$) between using foreign language network resources" and foreign language teaching materials," "reading foreign language academic theses," and the improvement of specialized knowledge and skills, and foreign language ability. However, the correlation between using foreign language network resources and foreign language teaching materials and reading foreign language academic theses, and making foreign friends, "deepening understanding of foreign conditions," and promoting international understanding is not obvious.

It is worth noting that there is no significant correlation between "taking those that are taught by foreign language teachers or in foreign language as elective courses" and the development of students' specialized knowledge and relevant skills, and understanding foreigners' views of China. Except "enhancing international understanding," the other benefits also are not significantly correlated with "taking those that are taught by foreign language teachers or in foreign language as elective courses."

In addition, the analysis also finds out that if we calculate the average scores of each student utilizing six kinds of internationalized resources and the development of ability and competencies in 13 aspects, the correlation between these two average scores is significant (Pearson's $r = 0.263$, $p < 0.01$). The correlation rate shows that the more internationalized campus resources are utilized, the more global competence develops.

Conclusion and recommendations

Internationalization is an important trend in higher education development and an important way to improve the comprehensive strength of colleges and universities. It is also an important way in which to promote the development of students' global competence. Through the analysis of the data from the Peking University surveys, this study has shown that both studying abroad and utilizing campus resources can effectively promote the development of students' relevant global competence. Relatively speaking, the effect of studying abroad is more obvious, but the cost is high and the benefit group is small.

In general, the utilization of internationalized resources is currently insufficient for both Chinese and international students on campus and abroad. We therefore believe, based on our findings, that the government and colleges and

Table 4.3 Correlation between the use of campus resources and the development of students' global competence

	Participating in international conferences	Communicating with international students	Taking foreign language courses as electives	Using foreign language network resources	Using foreign language teaching materials	Reading foreign language academic theses
Deepening knowledge of major	**	N	N	**	**	**
Improving skills related to major	**	N	N	**	**	**
Improving foreign language ability	**	**	*	**	**	**
Creating friendships abroad	**	**	*	N	N	N
Deepening understanding of different cultures	**	**	**	N	N	N
Deepening understanding of foreign conditions	**	**	*	N	N	N
Understanding foreigners' view of China and the Chinese	**	**	N	N	N	N
Strengthening national consciousness, paying more attention to personal words and deeds, and maintaining image of home country	**	**	*	**	**	**

Notes: * $p < 0.05$, ** $p < 0.01$, N = non-significant

universities should not only expand opportunities for students to study abroad, but encourage students to take full advantage of campus resources and promote the development of students' abilities and competencies through internationalization efforts on campus.

Expand opportunities for study abroad programs and improve the quality of communication abroad

In developed countries such as those in Europe and North America, many colleges and universities require all students to have completed a study abroad program before graduation. In China, as the cost of studying abroad is relatively high and the quota of students eligible to study abroad is limited, it will not be easy to require a high percentage of students to study abroad any time soon. However, expanding the opportunity for students studying abroad is possible and even necessary. Through the establishment of the Students Studying Abroad Project, Peking University has responded to the State-Sponsored Postgraduate Study Abroad Programs of the China Scholarship Council (CSC) by cooperating more actively with the CSC, committing funds to study abroad programs, and promoting opportunities for students to study abroad. For example, the Guanghua School of Management at Peking University recently signed an agreement regarding student communication with many foreign colleges and universities. Consequently, the percentage of undergraduates who study abroad increased from 20% during the 2006–2007 school year to approximately 85% during the 2008–2009 school year, essentially providing each student who is willing to go on exchange with the opportunity to do so.

In addition to providing students with opportunities for studying abroad, we should also make an effort to improve the quality of study abroad experiences students have. As for students of inter-school exchanges, colleges and universities should carry out preliminary exchange training sessions before the students study abroad to prepare them academically (including language study), emotionally, and psychologically for the experience. Colleges and universities should pay attention to the details of study abroad experiences – both with regard to their form and content – and place and emphasis on academic communication and social interaction requirements. Higher education institutions (HEIs) must put forward clear requirements for students to complete summary assessments after they return home to China from their study abroad experiences and encourage students to make good use of internationalized resources on campus in an effort to improve the quality and benefits of study abroad programs.

Expand opportunities for international communication on campus through hiring foreign visiting scholars and foreign language teachers, and attracting international students

With economic development, improvements in transportation technology, and increased international cooperation, the number of international specialists and scholars coming to domestic colleges and universities to visit, communicate, and teach every year continues to rise. These foreign specialists and scholars are an incredibly valuable workforce resource for internationalization and HEIs should take full advantage it. For example, Peking University is one of the most important windows for Chinese international communication, and the number of foreign visitors yearly is more than 20,000, more than 500 of whom are specialists and scholars, and 60–70 of whom are university presidents. The number of foreign professors (i.e. specialists and scholars) employed on a short- and long-term basis is around 100 and 200 per year, respectively.

Based on these precious educational resources, the form of international cooperation fostered by Peking University is gradually moving from international reception to international exchange and talent-training. This transition is slowly enabling more teachers and students to participate in all kinds of international exchange activities and to receive the benefits of international communication.

In the process of internationalizing colleges and universities, the most important factor – and the most ignored aspect – is the international student. International students are frequently regarded as "beneficial owners" of internationalization, "receivers," and "learners" of international exchange. In fact, not only is there a large number of international students with wide sources and connections to local teachers and students, but international students are also young and speak more common languages, have varied interests and hobbies, and are less prejudiced and biased when it comes to their peers. In addition, they are full of energy and are absolutely willing to play a more positive and active role in international exchange and cooperation.

According to the results of our surveys of international students at Peking University, the percentage of students who "take advantage of their mother tongue to carry out language teaching," "take advantage of their mother tongue to do translation work," and "introduce domestic culture" is 42.6%, 45.9%, and 39.0%, respectively. The percentage of those who are willing to do extra work, if it is available, is 87.8%, 81.2%, and 82.8%, respectively. The percentage of international students from Peking University who have worked as teaching assistants, research assistants, administrative assistants, and/or logistics owners is only 18.1%, 13.9%, and 13.5%, respectively, while the percentage of those who are willing to do work over and above what they are asked to do is 74.0%, 61.7%, and 58.4%, respectively. It is thus clear that there is an opportunity for HEIs to increase their utilization and employment of international students as a means to increase internationalization.

Emphasize the importance of fostering an internationalized campus culture to create opportunities for internationalization on campus

The mere fact that students attend the same HEI will not naturally bring about campus internationalization. Instead, campus internationalization comes through convenient, natural, and sufficient communication among multicultural teachers and students from different countries as practiced in the classroom, cafeteria, dormitory, and library. Historically, under the influence of communism, colleges and universities in China have adopted a "different management and treatment" policy for international students. These HEIs established specialized apartments and cafeterias for international students, taught them independently, and managed their affairs in a unique way, setting up artificial barriers to their communication with domestic students.

With the improvement of Chinese students' accommodations and lifestyles, and with the gradual changing of teachers' and students' worldviews, the communication between Chinese and international students has started to gradually improve. For example, in the Peking University–Yale University Joint Undergraduate Program, with Peking University as the teaching site, students from both institutions live in the same dormitory, study in the same classroom, and participate in the same extracurricular activities. The Peking University International Culture Festival organized by the Peking University Office of International Relations has been held annually for six years and has grown to be a significant event with the participation of students from more than 50 countries around the world. The festival helps Chinese and international students develop a mutual understanding, and its helps foster among Chinese students a deeper respect for foreign cultures.

Strengthen internationalization development strategies and systems to make internationalizing on campus beneficial to all teachers and students

There are many objectives when it comes to internationalizing China's colleges and universities. Such a process does not only foster academic development in HEIs, but it also promotes the awareness of foreign cultures across the country. Colleges and universities aim to help teachers and students widen their worldviews, increase their intellectual abilities, deepen their cultural understanding, and enhance their knowledge of the internationalization process. Therefore, the internationalization of colleges and universities should not be restricted to Western countries. Recruiting international students and dispatching Chinese students abroad should have a truly global reach and should not be restricted to economically advanced countries. The internationalization of colleges and universities should not be limited to a set of departments or a specific set of majors, and it should be solely based institutions' administrative needs. Rather, it should also consider the real requirements of teachers and students from each school who will participate in international exchange activities.

Each department should formulate its own unique internationalization development strategy and training program in accordance with the features and resource conditions of its subject. All teachers should take full advantage of teaching in class, carrying out research in their fields of expertise, and attending international conferences to train students' global competence. Campus resources can be utilized more fully to promote the internationalization of HEIs and their students. This increase in utilization can be achieved only through a corresponding institutional arrangement that transfers the focus of internationalization at colleges and universities at the department level to individual teachers and students.

References

Arum, S. & J. Van de Water. 1992. "The Need for a Definition of International Education in U.S. Universities." In C. Klasek, ed., *Bridges to the Future: Strategies for Internationalizing Higher Education*, 191–203. Carbondale, IL: Association of International Education Administrators.

Chen, C. 1998. "International Cooperation: The Fourth Function of Institutions of Higher Learning – Discussing the Internationalization of Chinese Higher Education." *Studies on Higher Education* 5: 11–15.

Chen, X. 2007. "Several Basic Issues on Internationalization of Higher Education." In China Association of Higher Education (CAHE), ed., *University Internationalization: Theory and Practice*, 15. Beijing: Peking University Press.

Gu, M. 1991. "Higher Education." In M. Gu, ed., *The Dictionary of Education*, 12. Shanghai: Shanghai Education Press.

Ji, B. 2007. "International Culture Exchange is the Fourth Basic Function of University." In CAHE, ed., *University Internationalization: Theory and Practice*, 55. Beijing: Peking University Press.

Jin, D. 2009. *Report on Teaching Management*. Paper presented at the Peking University Teaching Work Meeting in Beijing, China.

Lin, J. 2006. *Meeting Undergraduate Teaching Work Assessment and Promoting Peking University Undergraduate Education Development*. Beijing: Peking University Press.

Knight, J. 1994. *Internationalization: Elements and Checkpoints*. Ottawa: Canadian Bureau for International Education Research.

Knight, J. & H. de Wit (eds). 1997. *Internationalization of Higher Education in Asia Pacific Countries*. Amsterdam: European Association for International Education.

5 The influence of higher education on student development

Li Wenli

Different explanations of the development of personal abilities

Economist Theodore Schultz discussed the important concept of human capital in the early 1960s. He claimed that education is the largest investment a society can make in human capital. One corollary of this argument is that most economic abilities people possess are not innate, but are acquired while attending school. These acquired abilities can take any form, but they have tremendous implications because they can fundamentally change the quantities of people's savings and capital (Schultz 1963). Schultz's human capital theory gives unprecedented prominence to the economic function of education.

The core element of human capital theory is that education, by imparting knowledge and skills, enables people to acquire cognitive and non-cognitive abilities, which in turn results in greater abilities for social production and services. In this way, better-educated people will make greater contributions to the labor market and will thus receive higher income.

However, in the 1970s other theories, which present different explanations for the connection between education and labor market, challenged human capital theory. Such explanations mainly fell into two categories. The first category is represented by the selection hypothesis, which claims that personal abilities are developed early in life. Education simply legalizes these abilities and provides a convenient means to distinguish people with different abilities. There is no other way to determine this besides education. People's differences in productivity are largely attributable to the differences in their early abilities, which are not acquired in school or through training (Groot & Hartog 1995). The second category is represented by labor market segmentation theory and internal labor market theory. These two theories argue that differences in people's productivity are largely attributable to what they do for a living. The nature of a person's job determines his or her productivity and income. Furthermore, the kind of jobs people can get is a variable that is dependent on education, cognitive abilities, non-cognitive abilities, and innate characteristics (including gender, race, and family background) (DeFreitas 1995; Doeringer 1995).

Labor market segmentation theory presents vastly different explanations for how people's abilities are developed. As a matter of fact, human capital theory and the selection hypothesis give completely opposite explanations. Human capital theory contends that the productivity that brings economic gain is based on the cognitive and non-cognitive abilities that people develop in school. The value of these capabilities is then verified by the labor market. On the other hand, the selection hypothesis argues that personal abilities are acquired in familial and socioeconomic contexts rather than an educational context and that people do not develop these abilities equally. It is easier for children from families of higher socioeconomic status (with higher education levels, greater wealth, and higher political status) to develop the cognitive and non-cognitive abilities that could lead to high economic gain.

Although job characteristics theory, represented by labor market segmentation theory and internal labor market theory, does not make an argument that is runs directly counter to that of human capital theory, it does not underline the input–output relationship between education and an individual's cognitive and non-cognitive abilities. However, it does argue that personal abilities and education both equally determine what people do for a living. Figure 5.1 shows a simplified model of human capital theory, which argues that differences in income are basically attributed to differences in abilities that are acquired through education.

Figure 5.2 shows a simplified theoretical model of the selection hypothesis, which argues that education does not change one's abilities or income. The function of education is simply to select people with high abilities from the crowd.

Figure 5.3 shows a simplified model of job characteristics theory.

The differences among the various economic theories regarding the relationship between education, abilities, productivity, and income – especially the contention between human capital theory and the selection hypothesis – prompt us to ask the following questions. Should higher education aim to improve students' cognitive and non-cognitive abilities or merely serve as a means to pass on socioeconomic status and help people with higher abilities stand out from the crowd? How do education, personal abilities, and job

Figure 5.1 Explanation of the function of education according to human capital theory

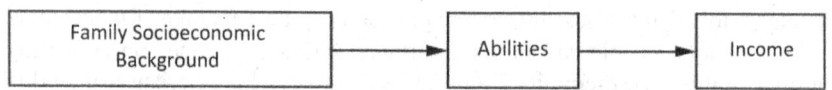

Figure 5.2 Explanation of personal abilities and income according to the selection hypothesis

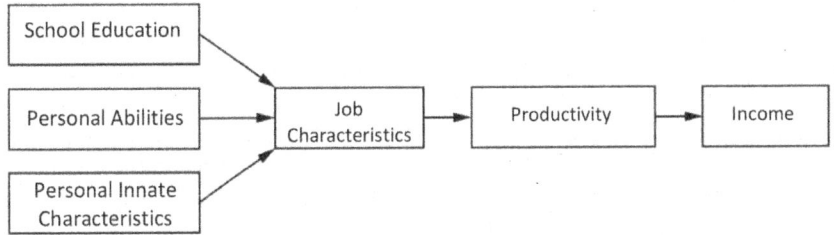

Figure 5.3 Explanation of the relationship between education, abilities, and income according to job characteristics theory

characteristics influence college students' career development? Does the influence better reflect the views of human capital theory or job characteristics theory? This study introduces a relevant theoretical model and uses quantitative analysis techniques to conduct an empirical study of the relationship between higher education and college students' ability and career development.

The educational input–output process in psychological theories

Both human capital theory and the selection hypothesis argue that education can increase economic benefits for an individual, but they disagree on the working mechanism of education. The controversy centers on whether the function of education is production or signaling. Human capital theory emphasizes the production function of education, while the selection hypothesis highlights the signal function. There have been an immense number of studies concerning both human capital theory and the selection hypothesis, but none has come up with a unified conclusion. Both theoretical paradigms prove valid under certain conditions. This study, however, will not spend much time on this topic, as it beyond its scope.

Human capital theory and other theories of educational economics consider education as an input and economic benefit as an output in human development. However, these theories fail to explore to any great extent the process between input and output, which remains a "grey area." Psychological research is concerned about personal development and focuses on people's cognitive abilities and social development. Some of the research uses college students as the subject of study. One example is the study carried out by Pascarella and Terenzini in 2005. After a review of the research done in this field since 1991, they came to an important conclusion: college education exerts a significant long-term impact on an individual's overall cognitive development and thinking (Pascarella & Terenzini 2005). Moreover, college experience lays a solid foundation in respect of cognitive skills for enhancing an individual's lifelong learning abilities and sustained intellectual development. Some other studies concluded that parents' educational background does not have cross-generation effects on their children's overall cognitive abilities, even though it does have an impact on their children's abilities in math, science, and reading (Terenzini et al. 1995). In addition, according to research done by Pascarella and Terenzini (2005), college education has a net positive effect on students' cognitive abilities and intellectual development, net effect here referring to the effect of college education alone (with the effects of other factors excluded). These studies mainly focused on students' critical thinking and reasoning abilities. The results showed that the improvement in students' critical thinking and reasoning abilities in college is completely attributable to the higher education they receive rather than to any other factor.

After a review of multiple empirical studies on the impact of college education on students' cognitive abilities and intellectual development, Pascarella and Terenzini (2005) concluded that students' self-reports on their cognitive abilities and intellectual development are consistent with the results of objective standardized tests, which validates the method of using students' self-reports to assess their individual capacity development. Two representative studies that obtained data about students' ability development from self-reports were those by Whitmire and Lawrence (1996) and Grayson (1996).

A series of empirical studies conducted on student development emphasizes the significant influence of higher education on students' capacity development and divided the factor of higher education into more specific categories. For example, the development theory regarding college students put forward by psychologists Pascarella and Terenzini posits that college students' development of learning and cognitive abilities is directly or indirectly influenced by factors in the following five areas: (a) students' family background and characteristics before admission to college, (b) structural or organizational characteristics of the institution of higher education, (c) the environment of the institution of higher education, (d) students' efforts, and (e) the teacher–student and peer-to-peer relationship. Based on the reality of Chinese universities, and in accordance with Pascarella and Terenzini's (2005) theoretical model, the research team from the Graduate School of Education at Peking University that conducted research on college students' development re-examined the factors in these five areas in a Chinese context. Figure 5.4 shows the interactions between factors of higher education and personal characteristics and their effects on students' academic achievements and cognitive development.

Dynamic model of college students' skill and career development

In order to examine the factors that influence the formation and development of college students' abilities, this study builds a theoretical scheme by combining the economic concepts of human capital theory, the selection hypothesis, and job characteristics theory with the psychological theoretical model of student development. The scheme is called the "dynamic model of college students' ability and career development" (see Figure 5.5). Its main purpose is to verify the role of higher education in promoting college students' capacity

Influence of higher ed. on student development 71

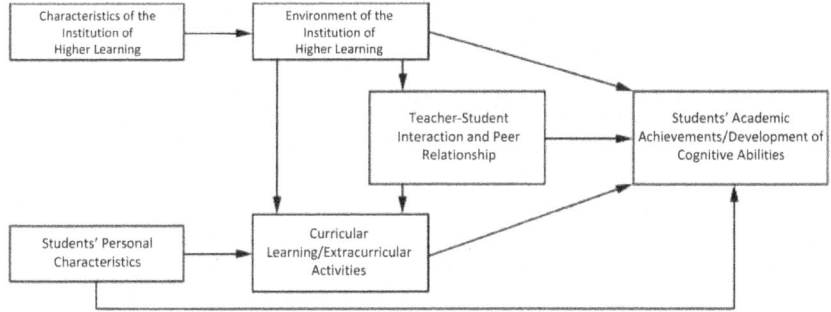

Figure 5.4 College students' academic achievements, cognitive ability development, and influencing factors

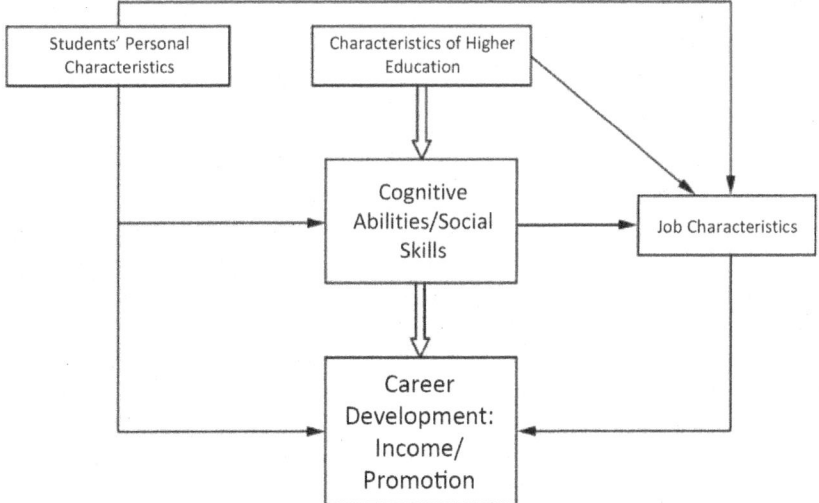

Figure 5.5 Dynamic model of college students' capacity and career development

development and to compare the three economic theories' explanations of the college graduate labor market. This study includes five major variables:

1. Knowledge and abilities

In this study, 27 questions were designed to assess college graduates' knowledge and abilities. Each factor is measured on a 1–5 scale. Using factor analysis, the 27 questions were divided into two categories: cognitive abilities and social skills. Cognitive abilities were further divided into two subcategories: basic cognitive abilities and expanded cognitive abilities. Basic cognitive abilities consist of breadth of knowledge, depth of knowledge, foreign language skills, computer skills, knowledge of economics, native language skills, writing skills, and attention span. Expanded cognitive abilities consist of planning and organizational skills, problem solving abilities, analytical abilities, learning abilities, innovation, hands-on skills, and ability to work independently. Social skills consist of understanding of the society, ability to work under pressure, accuracy in judgment, time management skills, negotiation skills, adaptability at work, teamwork coordination, good faith and credibility, insights, leadership and organizational skills, tolerance, and sense of responsibility.

2. Career development

In this study, current income and average annual promotions since graduation from college are used as variables to measure the career development of college graduates. Current income is the annual income from work, including wages, year-end bonuses, incentive bonuses, thirteenth-month pay, and other benefits. Average annual number of promotions is the total number of promotions since the first job divided by the number of working years.

3. Personal characteristics

Students' personal characteristics consist of gender, marital status, age, hometown, and parents' educational background (used to represent family background). Gender and marital status are dummy variables: 1 for male and 0 for female; and 1 for unmarried and 0 for otherwise. Hometown is a fivefold variable, including municipalities and provincial capitals, prefecture-level cities, county-level cities, towns, and residence in the countryside. The fivefold classification is hierarchical, reflecting the differences between China's urban and rural areas. It can more or less be viewed as an equal-interval variable for this analysis, the values being measured on a 1–5 scale from municipalities and provincial capitals to the countryside.

Parents' educational background is an eightfold variable, consisting of primary school and below, below junior high school, junior high school, senior high school (secondary vocational school and technical school), vocational college (junior college), bachelor's degree, master's degree, and PhD, reflecting the hierarchy of educational background. It can more or less be viewed as an equal-interval variable for this analysis, the values being measured on a 1–8 scale.

4. Characteristics of higher education

The higher education category can be divided into three levels, namely, junior college, college, and graduate school (including master's degree and PhD). The first two characteristics are expressed as two dummy variables in the model, namely, junior college and college, and the last is used as a reference. The next three characteristics of high education are the three types of assistantship, namely, the positions of research assistant, teaching assistant, and management assistant, which represent participation in teaching, research, and management during college; scholarships, which represents academic merit; and intern days, which indicate participation in social practice during college.

5. Job characteristics

Type of employer is set as a dummy variable. State-owned employers are given the value of 1, including state organizations, enterprises, schools, and research institutions; other types of employers are given the value of 0, including three types of foreign-funded enterprises, collectively owned enterprises, township enterprises, private enterprises, and others. Number of departments served in indicates flexibility for transfer to different positions. The questionnaire covers eight departments, consisting of research and development, production, marketing and sales, finance, human resources, administration and logistics, customer service, and other. A permanent labor contract can be defined as job stability in the legal sense. It is set as a dummy variable, with a value of 1 if a permanent contract is signed; otherwise it is assigned a value of 0.

Teamwork indicates interaction with the organization or the team in the workplace. It is a fivefold equal-interval measurement. Total dependence on individuals' skills and hard work has a value of 1; greater dependence on individuals' skills and hard work has a value of 2; equal dependence has a value of 3; greater dependence on teamwork has a value of 4; and prevailing dependence on teamwork carries a value of 5.

Participation in decision-making with regard to departmental affairs indicates the importance of an individual's position. It is an equal-interval variable on a 1–5 scale. No participation is given a value of 1; little participation has a value of 2; some participation carries a value of 3; quite a lot of participation merits a value of 4; and full participation earns a value of 5. As for the subjects who have worked for more than one employer, this study adds up their participation in the decision-making process, resulting in a total value over 5. Job consistency with major in college is set up as a twofold dummy variable. Consistency with major, minor, double major, or extracurricular learning is given a value of 1, while consistency with none is given a value of 0.

Based on the questions this study intends to resolve, we propose two hypotheses:

Hypothesis 1: Students' development of basic cognitive abilities, expanded cognitive abilities, and social skills is the joint result of the higher education they receive and their own personal characteristics. Of the two factors, higher education exerts a more significant influence on college students' development of basic cognitive abilities, expanded cognitive abilities, and social skills.

74 Influence of higher ed. on student development

Hypothesis 2: College graduates' career development (current income and promotion) is under the joint influence of personal characteristics, educational characteristics, job characteristics, and abilities, with the last two factors exerting the most significant influence.

Impact of higher education on college students' development of basic and expanded cognitive abilities and social skills

Sponsored by the Beijing Municipal Government and assisted by the Beijing Municipal Bureau of Statistics, the team in charge of the research "Development Trends of Higher Education and the Beijing Municipal Government's Coping Strategies" at the Graduate School of Education at Peking University carried out a survey in August 2006 on 501 employers in Dongcheng, Xicheng, and Haidian districts about their needs and expectations for college graduates. The survey covered 150 employers in Dongcheng District, 150 employers in Xicheng District, and 201 employers in Haidian District. Three employees with college backgrounds were randomly chosen from each employer. Altogether, 1,503 copies of the questionnaire were distributed, with 1,403 or 93.3% valid questionnaires returned. Table 5.1 shows the basic statistics of such variables as personal characteristics, higher education characteristics, and job characteristics for the effective sample, namely, employees from whom the questionnaire was validly retrieved.

In this study, college students' capacity development was placed into two categories: cognitive abilities and social skills. Cognitive abilities were further divided into two subcategories: basic cognitive and expanded cognitive abilities. Table 5.2 shows the basic statistics of the three types of abilities.

In order to determine the influence of higher education factors on college students' capacity development, and how significant a role students' personal characteristics and family background play in the formation and development of their abilities, this study established a multivariate regression equation that takes basic cognitive abilities, expanded cognitive abilities, and social skills as dependent variables, and personal characteristics and characteristics of higher education as independent variables. The result of the regression analysis is shown in Tables 5.3, 5.4, and 5.5. Furthermore, a multicollinearity test was performed on the relationship between the variables. The result is displayed under tolerance and variance inflation factor (VIF) in the last two columns of each table. VIF for all the variables is far below 10, indicating no multicollinearity. Therefore, a multivariate linear regression test can be used for parameter estimation.

Table 5.3 shows that the personal characteristics gender and hometown are significant factors that influence basic cognitive abilities. Men's basic cognitive abilities are significantly superior to women's, with a coefficient of 0.05. The influence of the student's hometown on the formation and development of basic cognitive abilities has a significance level of 0.01. The table also indicates that students who live in urban areas with socioeconomic and cultural prosperity

Table 5.1 Statistics of basic characteristics for effective samples of the survey

Variable	Number of participants	Min.	Max.	Mean	Standard deviation
Personal characteristics and family background					
Gender (dummy variable)	1,403	0	1	0.451	0.498
Age	1,403	20	44	28.795	5.008
Marital status (dummy variable)	1,403	0	1	0.553	0.497
Hometown	1,403	1	5	2.159	1.351
Father's educational background	1,402	1	8	4.208	1.459
Mother's educational background	1,402	1	8	3.761	1.497
Higher education characteristics					
Level of higher education (dummy variable, with postgraduate as reference)					
Junior college	1,391	0	1	0.215	0.411
College	1,391	0	1	0.575	0.495
Three types of assistantship (RMB)	1,403	0	640,000*	22125.070	1335.100
Scholarships (RMB)	1,403	0	63,000	1129.900	3667.777
Cumulative number of intern days	1,403	0	1,100	70.191	97.139
Job characteristics					
Type of employer					
State-owned employers (dummy variable)	1,403	0	1	0.555	0.497
Number of departments served in	1,397	1	8	1.884	1.066
Permanent labor contract (dummy variable)	1,403	0	1	0.121	0.326
Cooperation in the form of teamwork	1,403	1	5	3.078	0.899
Participation in decision-making	1,403	1	10	3.996	2.037
Job consistency with major in college (dummy variable)	1,403	0	1	0.92	0.406

Note: * The sample contains graduates of US and Hong Kong universities.

Table 5.2 Basic statistics of college students' cognitive abilities and social skills

Variable	Number of participants	Min.	Max	Mean	Standard deviation
Basic cognitive abilities	1,403	8	40	28.464	3.914
Expanded cognitive abilities	1,403	7	35	26.170	3.883
Social skills	1,402	12	60	45.685	6.116
General abilities	1,403	22	110	80.803	10.875

Note: Due to the different number of questions, the values for the three types of abilities are incomparable.

Table 5.3 Results of multivariate regression analysis of factors influencing basic cognitive abilities

Variable	Coefficient	Standardized coefficient	T-value	Significance	Tolerance	VIF
Constant	28.668		25.674	0.000		
Gender	0.525	0.067	2.454	0.014	0.932	1.073
Marital status	−0.136	−0.017	−0.495	0.621	0.569	1.756
Age	0.038	0.049	1.377	0.169	0.554	1.806
Hometown	−0.259	−0.089	−2.821	0.005	0.684	1.463
Father's educational background	−0.002	−0.001	−0.024	0.981	0.507	1.972
Mother's educational background	0.028	0.011	0.287	0.774	0.485	2.064
Junior college	−2.076	−0.218	−6.088	0.000	0.538	1.857
College	−1.198	−0.151	−4.223	0.000	0.537	1.861
Three types of assistantship	−3.6E-07	−0.002	−0.073	0.942	0.912	1.096
Scholarships	3.92E-05	0.037	1.287	0.198	0.856	1.168
Cumulative number of intern days	0.0013	0.032	1.170	0.242	0.908	1.101
R-squared	0.051					
F-value	6.169			0.000		
Observation	1,389					

before the age of 18 display significantly better development of basic cognitive abilities than those who live in areas with poor socioeconomic and cultural conditions.

As for characteristic variables of higher education, the level of higher education influences college students' development of basic cognitive abilities with a significance level of 0.001. The higher the level of higher education they

Table 5.4 Results of multivariate regression analysis of factors influencing expanded cognitive abilities

Variable	Coefficient	Standardized Coefficient	T-value	Significance	Tolerance	VIF
Constant	27.126		24.436	0.000		
Gender	0.731	0.093	3.436	0.001	0.932	1.073
Marital status	−0.190	−0.024	−0.699	0.485	0.569	1.756
Age	0.015	0.019	0.536	0.592	0.554	1.806
Hometown	−0.190	−0.066	−2.081	0.038	0.684	1.463
Father's educational background	−0.036	−0.014	−0.368	0.713	0.507	1.972
Mother's educational background	−0.057	−0.022	−0.579	0.562	0.485	2.064
Junior college	−2.024	−0.214	−5.971	0.000	0.538	1.857
College	−0.947	−0.120	−3.358	0.001	0.537	1.861
Three types of assistantship	−2.4E-06	−0.014	−0.499	0.618	0.912	1.096
Scholarships	5.12E-05	0.048	1.690	0.091	0.856	1.168
Cumulative number of intern days	0.0012	0.031	1.109	0.268	0.908	1.101
R-squared	0.050					
F-value	6.120			0.000		
Observation	1,389					

receive, the more developed their basic cognitive abilities are likely to become. A comparison of standardized coefficients indicates that, of the three factors that influence basic cognitive abilities, the level of higher education completed has the most significant influence on college students' development of basic cognitive abilities, followed by hometown (before 18 years of age) and by gender.

Table 5.4 shows that, among personal characteristics, gender and hometown (before 18 years of age) are significant factors that influence expanded cognitive abilities. Men's expanded cognitive abilities are significantly superior to women's. Students who live in urban areas with socioeconomic and cultural prosperity (before 18 years of age) display significantly better development of expanded cognitive abilities than those who live in areas with poor socioeconomic and cultural conditions.

As for characteristic variables of higher education, level of higher education influences college students' development of expanded cognitive abilities with a significance level of 0.001. Those with master's and PhD degrees display significantly better development of expanded cognitive abilities than with college and junior college degrees. A comparison of standardized coefficients indicates that the level of higher education exerts the greatest influence on college students' development of expanded cognitive abilities, followed by gender and hometown (before 18 years of age).

The findings demonstrate that higher education plays a positive role in promoting college students' development of cognitive abilities. Local socio-cultural capital represented by the students' hometowns exerts influence on their capacity development before college, but this influence might also be attributable to primary and secondary education. Furthermore, family cultural capital represented by parents' educational background has no significant influence on college students' basic cognitive abilities or expanded cognitive abilities.

Table 5.5 shows several differences between the influence of personal characteristics and higher education on students' development of social skills and students' development of cognitive abilities. The first difference is that the influence of gender weakens and is below the significance level of 0.05, while the student's hometown (before 18 years of age) significantly influences the development of social skills at the 0.05 significance level. The second difference is that the level of higher education still has significant influence on the development of social skills, but the influence is weaker than that on the development of cognitive abilities. Compared to individuals with master's and

Table 5.5 Results of multivariate regression analysis of factors influencing social skills

Variable	Coefficient	Standardized coefficient	T-value	Significance	Tolerance	VIF
Constant	46.774		26.397	0.000		
Gender	0.656	0.053	1.932	0.054	0.932	1.073
Marital status	−0.642	−0.052	−1.478	0.140	0.570	1.755
Age	0.025	0.020	0.563	0.574	0.553	1.807
Hometown	−0.327	−0.072	−2.242	0.025	0.683	1.464
Father's educational background	−0.025	−0.006	−0.159	0.873	0.507	1.972
Mother's educational background	−0.132	−0.032	−0.843	0.399	0.484	2.064
Junior college	−1.680	−0.113	−3.103	0.002	0.537	1.862
College	−0.677	−0.055	−1.502	0.133	0.536	1.866
Three types of assistantship	−1E-05	−0.037	−1.343	0.180	0.912	1.096
Scholarships	5.79E-05	0.034	1.198	0.231	0.856	1.168
Cumulative number of intern days	0.0034	0.053	1.904	0.057	0.908	1.101
R-squared	0.027					
F-value	3.126			0.000		
Observation	1,388					

PhD degrees, college graduates' development of social skills is not significantly different, while junior college graduates display significantly lower development of social skills than those with master's and PhD degrees at the 0.01 significance level. The third difference is that while the number of intern days influences the development of social skills at the significance level of 0.1, its influence on cognitive development is not significant. One possible reason for this, as suggested by the study's results, is that internships give students a more realistic view of the job market, strengthen their ties and communication with society, and foster their abilities to adapt to new surroundings and coordinate with people in a practical setting.

A comparison of the standardized coefficients shows that the factors that influence the social skills of college graduates in descending order of their influence are whether they receive college or higher-level education, the student's hometown (before 18 years of age), and participation in social practice during college years.

As shown in Tables 5.3, 5.4, and 5.5, higher education has significant influence on students' capacity development; in other words, higher education significantly improves their abilities. Therefore, Hypothesis 1 (listed above) is validated. This conclusion largely supports human capital theory.

Analysis of factors that influence college students' career development

Higher education has significant positive effects on college students' cognitive abilities and social skills. To determine whether the effects described in human capital theory are reflected in the economic abilities of college graduates, and in their economic contributions in the labor market, and whether the job characteristics of their work influence their economic abilities, we have further analyzed two representative variables of college graduates' career development, current annual income and average annual number of promotions since graduation, to validate Hypothesis 2 of our theoretical model (Table 5.6).

Based on the test results in Table 5.7, we find that the main factors that affect graduates' current income are age, level of higher education, abilities, job stability, and participation in decision-making. Among them, age indicates work experience. The more work experience they have, the higher income they are likely to receive. As for the education variable, the income of junior

Table 5.6 Basic statistics of graduates' career development indicators

Variable	Number of participants	Min.	Max.	Mean	Standard deviation
Current annual income	1,401	3000.00	450000.00	41316.181	28648.631
Average annual number of promotions	1,403	0.00	3.00	0.082	0.182

Table 5.7 Results of regression analysis of factors that influence income (logarithm used for income)

Variable	Coefficient	Standardized coefficient	T-value	Significance	Tolerance	VIF
Constant	5.500		10.396	0.000		
Gender	0.032	0.028	1.222	0.222	0.955	1.048
Marital status	−0.025	−0.022	−0.728	0.467	0.553	1.808
Age	0.291	2.599	8.844	0.000	0.006	171.154
Age squared	−0.004	−2.308	−8.016	0.000	0.006	164.318
Junior college	−0.420	−0.308	−10.086	0.000	0.543	1.843
College	−0.212	−0.186	−6.239	0.000	0.566	1.767
Abilities	0.002	0.048	2.027	0.043	0.917	1.090
State-owned employers	0.032	0.028	1.195	0.232	0.892	1.122
Number of departments served in	−0.013	−0.025	−0.945	0.345	0.715	1.399
Permanent labor contract	0.083	0.048	1.994	0.046	0.888	1.126
Cooperation in the form of teamwork	0.010	0.016	0.704	0.482	0.980	1.021
Participation in decision-making	0.043	0.155	5.717	0.000	0.689	1.451
Job consistency with major in college	0.013	0.010	0.417	0.677	0.970	1.031
R-squared	0.309					
F-value	47.153			0.000		
Observation	1,382					

college graduates and college graduates is significantly lower than that of postgraduates, and the income of junior college graduates is lower than that of college graduates. Clearly, the findings indicate that the higher level of education completed the higher the income one will receive. However, due to the limited size of the number of participants who hold a PhD, this study does not compare them with participants who have master's degrees.

The abilities variable has a significant influence on graduates' income. In this study, cognitive abilities and social skills are combined into the participants' overall abilities. The results suggest that cognitive abilities and social skills of graduates can translate into economic output, which is in line with human capital theory.

In addition, among the variables of job characteristics, job stability represented by permanent labor contract and participation in decision-making, also affects the level of income of the graduates, indicating that job characteristics to a certain extent influence an individual's economic contribution in the labor market.

Table 5.8 shows that age, abilities, flexibility for transfer to different positions, cooperation in the form of teamwork, and participation in decision-making significantly influence college graduates' promotion in the workplace. Here, age is inversely proportional to the average annual number of promotions, indicating that younger graduates receive more opportunities for advancement than their older counterparts. With the gradual improvement of the socialist market economy, there are more job opportunities available in the labor market and therefore more career development opportunities for youth.

It is worth noting that abilities have an extremely significant influence on opportunities for promotion. The greater abilities the graduate possesses, the more opportunities will be available for his or her promotion. The level of education completed does not have significant influence on promotion, which

Table 5.8 Results of regression analysis of factors that influence the average annual number of promotions

Variable	Coefficient	Standardized coefficient	t-value	Significance	Tolerance	VIF
Constant	−0.107		−1.750	0.080		
Gender	−0.005	−0.013	−0.491	0.623	0.961	1.041
Marital status	0.013	0.036	1.047	0.295	0.569	1.757
Age	−0.003	−0.073	−1.965	0.050	0.492	2.032
Junior college	0.026	0.059	1.711	0.087	0.562	1.778
College	0.0002	0.001	0.016	0.987	0.582	1.718
Abilities	0.002	0.092	3.426	0.000	0.923	1.083
State-owned employers	−0.001	−0.003	−0.124	0.901	0.891	1.122
Number of departments served in	0.039	0.228	7.466	0.000	0.719	1.391
Permanent labor contract	0.025	0.044	1.595	0.111	0.888	1.126
Cooperation in the form of teamwork	0.011	0.055	2.112	0.035	0.981	1.019
Participation in decision-making	0.005	0.060	1.929	0.054	0.694	1.440
Job consistency with major in college	−0.004	−0.008	−0.310	0.757	0.969	1.032
R-squared	0.078					
F-value	9.670			0.000		
Observation	1,384					

indicates that, in the maturing labor market, abilities are more valued for important positions than level of education completed. The findings more clearly verify the role of abilities in career development. The level of higher education shows no signal characteristics.

Among the variables of job characteristics, number of departments served in, which represents flexibility, cooperation in the form of teamwork, which represents cooperation ion the workplace, and participation in decision-making, which represents flexibility of organizational management, all display significant influence on opportunities for promotion. This indicates that graduates with greater flexibility for transfer to different positions are likely to be promoted; that graduates who work at a place with a high degree of teamwork or who possess abilities for cooperation are more likely to be promoted; and that graduates have more opportunities for advancement if their workplace offers greater opportunity for participation in decision-making or if graduates have more opportunities to participate in decision-making in the workplace.

Based on the test results in Tables 5.7 and 5.8, this study concludes that level of higher education, abilities, and job characteristics affect graduates' income, and personal abilities and job characteristics are key factors that influence their promotion at work. College graduates who display greater personal abilities, higher adaptability and flexibility at work, better cooperation in the form of teamwork, and participate more in decision-making have more advantages in career development. This conclusion corroborates both human capital theory and job characteristics theory.

Further study of factors affecting college students' career development

In order to gather further data on the factors that influence college students' career development, we included a self-assessment question in the questionnaire, which required graduates to rate the factors that might influence their career development on a 1–5 scale (1 and 2 = negative influence, 3 = no influence, 4 = positive influence, and 5 = very positive influence). We listed a total of 21 factors, including personal factors, schools that they attended, majors that they chose, their knowledge, and their abilities. We put these factors in the order of their ratings, as shown in Figure 5.6.

Figure 5.6 shows that giving out treats, gifts, and other favors is rated below 3 points. It indicates that giving out treats and gifts does not help career development, and that in fact it has negative effects. Besides giving out treats and gifts, alumni relations, family background, and other social capital factors are the four factors that receive the lowest rating. The five factors rated above 4 (indicating positive influence) are, in ascending order of rating, nice personality, high collaborative abilities, relevant work experience, good basic knowledge, and good technical knowledge. Obviously, the survey participants tend to believe in the positive effects of human capital factors like knowledge and abilities on career development. This conclusion also supports the claims of human capital theory.

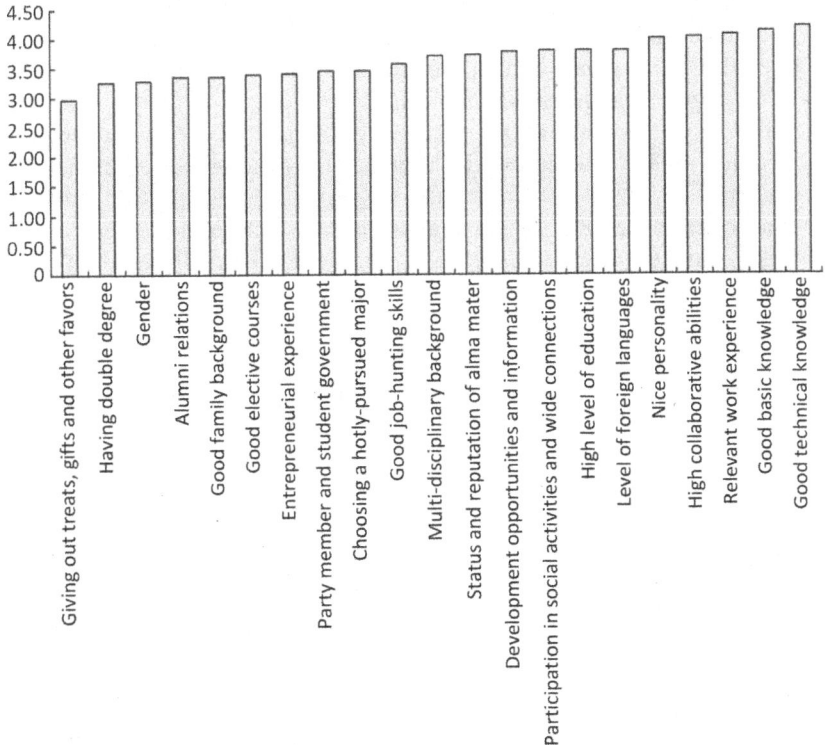

Figure 5.6 Factors that influence graduates' career development in the order of their importance

Conclusion

This study started with the economic concepts of human capital theory and the selection hypothesis, combined them with the psychological theoretical model of student development, and built a dynamic model of college students' ability and career development. It carried out an empirical analysis on the influence of personal and family factors and the level of higher education on college students' capacity development, as well as the influence of job characteristics on their career development. Based on the findings of this study, I have reached following major conclusions:

1. Of the factors that influence the development of basic cognitive abilities, the level of higher education has the greatest influence on college students' development of basic cognitive abilities: postgraduates display better basic cognitive abilities than college graduates, and college graduates display better basic cognitive abilities than junior college graduates. The second greatest influence comes from the student's hometown (before

18 years of age): students who grow up in areas with better socioeconomic and cultural development display better basic cognitive abilities. The third greatest influence comes from gender: men display better basic cognitive abilities than women.
2. Of the factors that influence the development of expanded cognitive abilities, the level of higher education has the greatest influence on college students' development of expanded cognitive abilities: postgraduates display better expanded cognitive abilities than college graduates, and college graduates display better expanded cognitive abilities than junior college graduates. The second greatest influence comes from gender: men display better expanded cognitive abilities than women. The third greatest influence comes from the student's hometown (before 18 years of age): students who grow up in areas with better socioeconomic and cultural development display expanded cognitive abilities.
3. The level of higher education has the greatest influence on college students' development of social skills: postgraduates and college graduates display significantly better social skills than junior college graduates do, but there is no significant difference between college graduates and postgraduates. The second greatest influence comes from the student's hometown (before 18 years of age): students who grow up in areas with socioeconomic and cultural prosperity display better social skills. The third greatest influence comes from participation in social activity during college: the more opportunities there are for social activity and contact, the more advantages individuals are likely to have in their development of social skills. Therefore, higher education plays a positive role in promoting college students' development of cognitive abilities and social skills.
4. As for the factors that affect income, individuals will earn higher income with more work experience, more education, more abilities, a more stable employment situation, and more opportunities to participate in decision-making.
5. As for the factors that affect promotion, the better abilities they possess, the more opportunities they have for promotion. The level of education completed does not have a significant influence on promotion, which indicates that in the job market abilities are more valued for important positions than education. In addition, greater adaptability and flexibility, better teamwork capability, and more participation in decision-making lead to more opportunities for promotion.
6. The survey participants place more faith in the positive influence of human capital factors such as knowledge and abilities on career development than that of social capital factors.

In the final analysis, compared with the selection hypothesis, human capital theory better explains the influence of higher education on college students' capacity development. In other words, higher education significantly improves college students' abilities. Family cultural capital, represented by parents' educational background, does not have significant influence on college students' capacity development. This conclusion largely supports human capital theory. Both human capital theory and job characteristics theory soundly explain China's labor market of college graduates. The significant influence of work experience and education on income is consistent with human capital theory. The significant positive effects of abilities on income further corroborate human capital theory. In addition, personal abilities, job stability, adaptability and flexibility at work, teamwork, and participation in decision-making play a positive role in promoting college graduates' career development. This conclusion not only validates human capital theory, but also indicates that job characteristics theory does, to a certain degree, explain China's college student labor market.

These findings have important policy implications. On the one hand, higher education could bring higher income and better career prospects for individuals. The national development of higher education could also boost economic prosperity and social development. On the other hand, improvement of the market economy and encouraging economic organizations (employers) to make innovations in technology could provide individuals with greater space for career development and thus facilitate overall socioeconomic development.

References

DeFreitas, G. 1995. "Segmented Labor Markets and Education." In M. Carnoy, ed., *International Encyclopedia of Economics of Education*, 39–44. Oxford: Elsevier.

Doeringer, P. B. 1995. "Internal Labor Markets and Education." In M. Carnoy, ed., *International Encyclopedia of Economics of Education*, 28–33. Oxford: Elsevier.

Grayson, J. 1996. *Value Added in Generic Skills between First and Final year: A Pilot Project*. Working paper. Toronto: Institute for Social Research, York University.

Groot, W. & J. Hartog. 1995. "Screening Models and Education." In M. Carnoy, ed., *International Encyclopedia of Economics of Education*, 34–39. Oxford: Elsevier.

Pascarella, E. T. & P. T. Terenzini. 2005. *How College Affects Students, Volume 2: A Third Decade of Research*. San Francisco, CA: Jossey-Bass.

Schultz, T. W. 1963. *The Economic Value of Education*. New York: Columbia University Press.

Terenzini, P. T., L. Springer, E. T. Pascarella & A. Nora. 1995. "Influences Affecting the Development of Students' Critical Thinking Skills." *Research in Higher Education* 36(1): 23–29.

Whitmire, E. & J. Lawrence. 1996. *Undergraduate Students, Development of Critical Thinking Skills: An Institutional and Disciplinary Analysis and Comparison with Academic Library Use and Other Measures*. Paper presented at the Annual Meeting of the Association for the Study of Higher Education in Memphis, Tennessee.

6 Decontextualization and recontextualization

Understanding reform practice through teacher discourse

Yang Fan and Chen Xiangming

Background and problems: investigating the change in meaning of "reform" from a discourse perspective

More than a decade ago, a new curriculum reform substantially changed the outlook of China's basic education. Yang (2007) stated that curriculum reform shattered the tedium of the classroom at elementary and middle schools, demonstrating to the vast teaching force another method of classroom teaching that has inspired innovation, change, and the pursuit of the autonomous, cooperative, and inquiring classroom. However, at the same time, many education scholars have noticed that despite the belief held by instructors that they are implementing teaching models and methods such as "inquiry teaching," "task-based teaching," and "cooperative teaching," that are in line with new curriculum concepts, few classroom activities conform to reform expectations, and many scholars are constantly corroding and distorting the meaning of the reform (Yang 2007). For instance, inquiry teaching, as interpreted and championed by some schools, simply turns the cramming or "spoon-feeding" method of teaching into a learning experience characterized by "a class barraged with questions" (Zhong 2006). Conversely, task-based teaching and cooperative teaching only exist in activities such as playing games for the sake of playing games and dividing children into groups for the sake of dividing children into groups. In short, the initial meaning of the term "reform" in the Chinese context has shifted during the transition from theory to practice.

Education experts and experienced teachers have very different views on whether the meaning of reform has been distorted in practice. Colen's probe into the relationship between instructional policy and teaching practice is a famous research case study. Colen chose Mrs. Oublier, a teacher who thought she was successfully compliant with the new instructional policy, as the study subject. Colen observed her classroom and compared her teaching practices to the traditional class teaching approach. The findings suggest a paradox, revealing that the innovations in her teaching had been filtered through a very traditional approach to instruction. Oublier eagerly embraces change and believes that she has made significant efforts to change her teaching and that she has in fact done so. However, experts note that her classroom has no history of progressive pedagogy (Colen 1990). Colen's study illustrates the existence of the problem, but fails to explain the process and mechanism that contribute to the degeneration of the meaning of change.

The present study adopts the approach of tracking the analysis of Chinese school teachers' instruction following the reform and investigates the process of change in the meaning of the term "reform." Based on existing research, discourse analysis offers one of the most desirable perspectives from which to examine the relationship between school environment and reform. It can also reveal the tension between the "local, practical, and mundane" school culture and "general, authoritative, and professional" reform ideals, that is, the relationship between micro and macro discursive phenomena. However, as will be seen, some researchers disagree on the various findings of this study, particularly with regard to the role of the local and individual discourse of schools in the reform.

Freeman conducted a study on the relationship between "spoken language" and the "professional discourse" practiced by teachers in a teaching development program. The study observed that the development of a professional discourse enabled the teachers to articulate and reflect on these tensions defined as "competing demands within their teaching," and to reconceptualize their understandings of their practice in the process. Hence, Freeman (1993) concluded that, in the course of reform, there was a certain degree of justification for the mandatory replacement of native discourse with appropriate technical terminology, that is, professional discourse.

Meanwhile, Elbaz-Luwisch (2005), using Bakhtin's theory of polyphony as a foundation, argued that the "internally persuasive discourse" and the "authoritative discourses" that teachers experience are entangled and constantly shifting. She was more concerned about individuals then about professions per se, as her study raised the alarm on professional discourse as a powerful ideology. The same stance was taken by Wu (2005) in his examination of China's curriculum reform process, in which he defined two different discourse structures as "top-down enforcement" and "bottom-up innovation." He also perceived the reform as a conflict-evolving process that oscillated between ideology control and individual struggle and resistance.

Existing research has begun to move from discourse to investigating education reform, but it still strongly emphasizes the "internal-external" and "top-down" binary relations as key aspects of the reform. However, this research overlooks the integration process of the individual in the curriculum reform and the relationship between native discourse and professional discourse. As a result of this oversight, the present study views reform as a unified process that combines professional development and social interaction and has as its goal the building of an analytical framework that will permit these concepts to be more fully understood.

The present study investigates how the meanings of the current national curriculum reform in China changed over time, meanings that were created in the context of an external authoritative mandate but which were transformed in the context of local school teaching practices. One focus of this study is to analyze how teachers understand the meaning of reform practice. "Reform practice" generally refers to a series of new instructional methods that teachers in the reform era have to adopt, and here the term specifically refers to new teaching methods advocated in the national curriculum reform of basic education.[1] This study investigates teachers' understanding of the meaning of the reform through an analysis of the methods they use to interpret reform practice.

Since "discourse" contains complex meanings in the social sciences, its definition in this study is the following: "a system of meaning, or the expression, of systematically organized and expressed meanings and values of an organization" (Kress 1985: 6). A series of premises lies behind this particular definition. First, discourse refers to the collection of meanings, which limits the capacity and boundaries of subject cognition and action. Second, society makes up all knowledge; in the present context, the so-called "corrosion and distortion" of reform practice by teachers are the result of discursive communication, negotiation, competition, and compromise with regard to the meaning of the curriculum reform. Third, the tactical observation of discourse is conducive to reflecting on the way that power is created, altered, and transformed in the act of oral communication, a process that is often opaque.

The present study borrows the concepts of "decontextualization" and "recontextualization" from Little (2003), who uses these concepts to observe and generalize the process that teachers use to understand and share the meaning of their practice. Decontextualization refers to teachers omitting details about their teaching situations that they feel are less important, so as to make it easier for the students to understand certain ideas or concepts. Recontextualization refers to when teachers use their individual experience to enrich the understanding of the subject matter, so as to avoid distracting students and keeping them focused on the intended material (Little 2003).

The present study modifies these two borrowed concepts in important ways. Little's study was carried out against the backdrop of teaching and research, whereas this study focuses on the observation of the reform process. Decontextualization in Little's study refers to the teacher intentionally overlooking details, whereas in this study it refers to the cognition and expression mechanism faced by individual teachers when reform practice is introduced from outside. Recontextualization in Little's study refers to the concrete contribution that teachers make to a given concept, whereas the present study identifies the process, carried out by teachers, of reconstructing and re-enacting the reform by resorting to their native discourse.

The decontextualization and recontextualization mechanisms reflect the representation capacity of school discourse over reform practice. "Representation" refers to the process that discourse brings to the subject matter. For teachers, representation defines the meaning of reform in understandable and acceptable terms.

Study method and process

This study employs a qualitative method to collect and analyze information, as this method is best suited to our objective of clearly explaining the ways in which elementary school teachers internalized and then changed the meaning of reform. To fully understand the problem, we looked at a case study to capture an entire sequence of events, and we employed discourse analysis to reveal how the meaning of curriculum reform changed. Discourse here has a dual nature in that it is both the object of research and the tool with we explain and understand the object of research.

In our case study, we followed all the steps in the lesson study cycle taken by all the Chinese language teachers at a Beijing primary school in line with a reform concept known as "thematic teaching." In essence, this change in classroom teaching is a constantly evolving process. However, for pragmatic reasons, we often decided, throughout the course of our qualitative research, to record and analyze typical events in the reform process in an effort to represent various opinions, conflicts, and relationships embodied therein. Now, with this theatrical basis, we are able to shine a light on the discursive structures of day-to-day interactions which have long remained opaque.[2]

Lesson study itself is not an innovative activity, its early form having emerged at the beginning of the twentieth century in China. Lesson study is a school-based teaching research method that has evolved from the traditional listening, talking, and commenting on lessons. Lesson study involves repetitive preparation, planning, teaching, and reviewing (Chen 2011), and it is a common way for teachers to enhance their instructional skills. In the case study that we examine in this study, the term "reform practice" refers to the thematic teaching approach to the Chinese language discussed by teachers who practice the lesson study method.

The thematic teaching method has rapidly advanced into both primary and middle schools in China in recent years. According to Chen et al. (2005), in the wake of the curriculum reform, primary and middle schools widely adopted thematic-unit-based textbooks. Dou Guimei, one of the most influential advocates of thematic teaching in China, defined thematic teaching as a dynamic form of instruction that seeks to connect with students' lived experiences. To put it simply, thematic teaching focuses on specific themes, emphasizes individual experience, and ultimately aims to create an open teaching environment by integrating multiple textbooks and other learning materials and by stressing the shared understanding that results from the learning experience (Dou 2004). In Dou's words, thematic teaching can be understood as follows: "learn textbooks well, transcend textbooks; have a foothold in the classroom, transcend the classroom; respect teachers, transcend teachers" (Dou 2010). Although these definitions and explanations appear vague, they reflect to some extent the opinions of those who have spearheaded thematic teaching on how their method differs from traditional Chinese language instruction. In other words, the traditional Chinese language teaching method, in their eyes, focuses primarily on the indoctrination of knowledge and places too much emphasis on instrumental tasks such as memorizing vocabulary and summarizing a paragraph. It ignores the humanistic aspect of the Chinese language and the ways students' lives can be enriched. Thematic teaching, however, is aimed at disrupting teacher-centered and subject-centered teaching methods. It seeks to leverage teachers' literary training and, thereby, to harness and develop student interest in the material (in this case, Chinese literature). According to this method, courses should be designed with flexibility in mind, and teachers should encourage student inquiry. Courses should also seek to expand students' reading abilities. With all this in mind, teachers can provide their students with an experience that fosters comprehensive Chinese language literacy.

For over two months, we closely followed a lesson study on "thematic teaching." As a teacher-initiated seminar on class-teaching reform, it started with an observation exercise. We sat in on a thematic-teaching demonstration class taught by the Dean of Students of "S" Primary School, Li Jin,[3] who is also a Chinese language teacher there, Tian Tian, a Chinese language teacher at "S" Primary School, and Wang Jun, a Chinese language teacher at another primary school. The text to be taught was a chapter from Xiao Hong's autobiographical novel, *The Story of Hulan River*, entitled "Garden of Grandfather." This chapter was from a unit in the second volume of "Chinese Textbooks for Primary Students" (for fifth graders) published by People's Education Press. The two young teachers were very excited after taking some time to observe the class. Tian Tian expressed a wish to prepare for the class by simulating the class with her colleagues beforehand, whereas Li Jin suggested inviting other experienced Chinese language teachers to form a lesson preparation group, thus making the session into a one-class, multiple-round lesson study.

In the process of observing reform practice spreading throughout the school, we noticed the formation of two different but interconnected levels between classroom and school. First, the cognition of thematic teaching by the Chinese language teachers originated from an open class. Second, particular teachers acquired an individualized understanding of this method from experience. However, the class-teaching reform was not strictly aimed at the behavior of individual teachers, as much as it was aimed at having teachers collectively participate in, discuss, and reflect on the school community. The significance of thematic teaching lies in its emphasis on group sharing and consensus. So it is not only about individual teachers graining a new way in which to conceive of the physical classroom, but about the teachers as a group having a collective understanding of the new pedagogy before they implement it in the classroom. The present study uses transition of different states of meaning as the thread to investigate the process of changes to the reform meaning.

It should be noted that in addition to spending more than two months gathering the data for the present study, we had also gone to "S" Primary

School to conduct fieldwork three years ago. Since then, our relationship with school's administration and its teachers has strengthened. We have gotten to know each other, and as a result we have developed a deep sense of trust. All of us are committed to improving the practice of classroom teaching at the school. For more than three years, then, we, as researchers, have been gradually accepted as associate members of "S" Primary School in light of its effort to bring about the changes of the reform. Without such a status, it would have been difficult for us to observe the entire reform practice process in our case study.

Findings: reconstructing the meanings of reform in native discourse

Based on the discourse fragments that we have recorded, we focus below on the dialogues of Chinese language teachers of "S" Primary School in the lesson study process and keep track of teachers' understanding of thematic teaching and reform practice. At the same time, we pay particular attention to how the meaning of "reform practice" changed in teachers' perception and understanding, and we seek to reveal the mechanism or mechanisms by which this change in meaning occurred.

Decontextualization: individualized understanding of the meaning of reform

When a teacher attempted to borrow an effective teaching practice and apply it to their own class, their understanding of the meaning of the reform practice differed from that of their colleague. Tian Tian can only introduce to other teachers some of her most profound impressions: "He (Teacher Wang Jun) only made 'Grandfather's Garden' a prelude, and then spent the bulk of the time expanding on *The Story of Hulan River*. He learned from that experience that many students would read the novel after the class. I had been hoping for this, and wanted to try it. The students had a lot to read, while the teacher lectured very little. He selected a great chapter, and his choice of the resounding words of the last paragraph of the novel was clever."

Tian Tian, for the first time, is able to isolate an important aspect of thematic teaching, which is the streamlining of course content and using personal experience to deliver it. She directly associates Wang Jung's technique with reform practice, but what she understands is only one of its components (another component being the self-selection of course content). While she has understood the form of thematic teaching, she has essentially overlooked the qualities (or "content") of thematic teaching, which include inculcating a respect for humanity, instilling a sense of inquiry, transcending the classroom, and fostering students' overall literacy.

In this case, it is clear why Tian Tian was only able to obtain a simplified understanding of reform practice. First, a teacher cannot comprehensively understand reform practices implemented by an instructor just by observing a class. Fullan (1999) demonstrates in his tri-level model that the fundamental driving force for system-wide reform consists of invisible sub-level results, which is why reform is difficult to spread and proliferate. Tian Tian noticed the effect that Teacher Wang Jun created in his classroom. Apparently, when the substance of reform mixes with a teacher's personal style, the definition of reform may become less clear. Second, when a teacher observes a class they gain personal experience, but they often have difficulty transmitting what they learn from this experience to others. Therefore, Tian Tian and Li Jin were only able to summarize what they learned from the demonstration class. From our own observations, Tian Tian's introduction identifies a few key characteristics of thematic teaching, most notable of which is the self-selection of the course content. She also noticed that Teacher Wang Jun centered his class discussion not on the text of "Grandfather's Garden" but on the content of *The Story of Hulan River*. However, she was not able to inspire sympathy when describing the class to her colleagues. On the contrary, her colleagues were confused about the exact condition of the class, thinking that the class had lost its focus and that appropriate time management was not used. This misunderstanding was mainly due to Tian Tian's simplified introduction, which was detached from the original context. Although it is a commonplace for key information to be omitted and/or lost in its relay from one person to another – which leads to the same event being understood differently by different people – what we stress here is that, in their dialogues with one another, teachers often failed to completely convey to their colleagues the substance of they have learned.

We refer to this process in this study as "decontextualization." Regardless of how competent the teacher is who taught the demonstration class, or how well the observing teacher relays their opinions to other teachers, the "visible" contents of their opinions are actually supported by "invisible" discourse as what we like to call "meaningful resources." These meaningful resources comprise either practical knowledge of individual teachers or the collective culture at the school developed in the wake of the introduction of the reform. When a reform practice is introduced by a teacher from another school, the original discourse that gives meaning to the reform practice is somewhat diluted due to its elusive nature.

Meanwhile, decontextualization of the meaning of reform practice(s) also reflects the actual need for teachers to introduce reform on their own. Thematic teaching contains within it a variety of complex ideas as well as a knowledge network that operates at a deep level.[4] What has sparked Tian Tian and others to take the initiative to learn and practice thematic teaching is that they felt that this method could make up for the shortcomings of their class teaching (e.g. by only explaining vocabulary and analyzing the main ideas of paragraphs of a given text). The pragmatic inclination commonly shown by many teachers in this regard, especially teachers in China, is quite evident. When facing reform, a teacher's focus is not on "absorbing new knowledge," but on seeking a solution based on their individual perspective.

Moreover, although teachers may take the same pragmatic approach, teachers in different stages of their career and at different levels of professional competence will differ in their understanding of thematic teaching, as the direction of their "focal awareness" and the scope and structure of their "subsidiary awareness" will diverge.[5] Therefore, decontextualization signifies that, in their dialogues, teachers place their attention on focal awareness integration, while intentionally or unintentionally reducing the disruption that their subsidiary awareness may cause in the discussion process.

This study considers decontextualization to be the first mechanism of school discourse representation in the reform process. As the "specified way of addressing issues by certain groups," discourse represents the selection and screening (shielding) process of the object of cognition. When teachers attempt to express their understanding of reform practice through thematic teaching, they may curtail and otherwise modify its meaning. This study does not attempt to judge this process of "curtailment," but does point out that it is not easy for the meaning of reform to be universally understood and represented. When a reform practice is required to be transmitted through the medium of teacher discourse, its meaning will become distorted as a consequence of the limited number of representation methods available.

Native discourse: the language of sharing the meaning of classroom practice

Reform is not an individual undertaking. Reform will not become a reality in the classroom as long as teachers are applying reform practice based on individually perceived understandings of what it entails. Reform will become relevant school-wide only when teachers convey the meaning of reform to other teachers and are proactive about its practice. Hence, sharing the meaning of reform is vital.

The essential path to effectively sharing this meaning is dialogue. At present, research that has been conducted on teacher dialogue centers on the discussion of the ideal systems, including Paulo Freire's dialogue theory, which stresses the fact that dialogue should not involve one person acting on another, but rather people working together, and Jürgen Habermas' communicative action theory, which identifies an "ideal speech situation" in which people are able to raise moral and political concerns and defend them by rationality alone (Fan 2008). This study does not pursue directly the ideal model of dialogue that allows people to seek liberation or reach consensus, but rather investigates the process by which the meaning of reform in a specific context change in reality. Therefore, we face the discourse system bearing the historical and cultural characteristics, which is also the cause for this study to choose discourse as the focus of the investigation.

This study determines the discourse system used by teachers by using an approach that captures native concepts. When Tian Tian and Li Jin gave their accounts of the highlights of the demonstration class to other teachers and expressed interest in conducting thematic teaching lesson studies, the other teachers were bewildered. When asked whether the teachers were familiar with this method, Li Jin responded that the most critical part of the program would be the research project for higher grades, and how to teach classes geared toward these students. Li Jin's suggestion was to instruct the students in *Ding Pian*.

The first native concept that emerged from the teachers' dialogues,[6] *Ding Pian* is the standard technique used in Chinese language and literature education. *Ding Pian* helps students gain a deeper understanding of texts and helps students appreciate fine art. It is highly dependent on the systematic use of textbooks (Wang 2007). Chinese language textbooks have included *Ding Pian* principles for a long time, and teachers and students have been analyzing them for several years. Most of the teachers learned *Ding Pian* texts as students, and they are more likely to teach these principles as teachers. Therefore, studying *Ding Pian* is likely to help aspiring teachers become more qualified. Over the past few decades, a vast number of lesson plans have been constructed using the *Ding Pian* method. Teachers feel quite comfortable emulating this lesson plans that employ this pedagogical technique. And for teachers who are experienced in *Ding Pian*, it is not difficult to construct a lesson plan around it. Consequently – and unsurprisingly – many teaching and research activities in the past (at "S" Primary School and across China) have employed *Ding Pian*.

Reform practice is currently encountering its first direct hurdle – traditional teaching and a school-wide research culture. When individual teachers attempt to change class teaching by introducing the thematic teaching method, the new teaching approach fails to integrate with the existing teaching and research discourse. Thematic teaching requires teacher flexibility in organizing course content, accentuating individual experience, transcending the textbook, and integrating themes with existing curricula. When one teacher attempted to introduce this innovative pedagogy, the first reaction from other teachers was to question his motives and wonder why he did not teach *Ding Pian*. *Ding Pian* discourse likes to emphasize hard work, traditional teaching skills, and fundamental knowledge points, and such notions in and of themselves, if left alone by the reform, would not raise an alarm. However, if these notions, mixed with teachers' customary practices, were interfered with or modified during the teaching process, then they would become causes for resisting the reform.

Besides *Ding Pian*, other native concepts all appear in the teachers' discussions about thematic teaching, with many teachers voicing their concerns about the new method:

> "We teach what is called **tradition and legacy foremost**" (doubtful of Tian Tian's practice of abandoning textbooks).
>
> "It's about **finding roots**. You can't abandon your **roots**, while replanting **a new branch**" (doubtful of Tian Tian's abandoning the teaching practice of inculcating basic knowledge points).

"Classic texts are a **feast, which should be eaten bite by bite**" (doubtful of Tian Tian's flexible selection of teaching materials, which is the teachers believe hinders students' ability to easily obtain important knowledge points, which is something *Ding Pian* would allow).

"The student cannot even grasp the organization of the text, failing to find the **eye-catching focal point**" (doubtful of the flexibility of Tian Tian's teaching method, which is considered a hindrance to students' understanding of texts' basic themes and arguments).

Some native concepts represent traditional teaching principles ("tradition and legacy foremost"); some are habitual similes that teachers hold for traditional teaching methods ("feast" and "root and branch"); and others are metaphors associated with subject characteristics ("eye-catching focal points"). As Chen (2011) has observed, they are all commonly found in teacher discourse describing and criticizing classroom teaching methods. Inasmuch as these principles and metaphors are applied on a daily basis, they have almost acquired the status of rules. They have what we like to call "the rationality of existence," and they uniquely represent teachers' practical knowledge and skills.

In this case, teacher's native concepts form a mutually supportive system of interpretation that affects different teachers' understanding of the meanings of reform. This interpretive system confines the scope of teaching activities accepted by teachers, and it deserves particular attention in terms of research and investigation. To these teachers, teaching should be based on current textbooks: using other texts or expanding into literary works beyond the textbooks would be premature. Article selection for textbooks is part of a massive curricular system that rationally and effectively organizes key principles and a corresponding study sequence. Textbooks are a fundamental element of education. The classic texts in the current textbook should be given top priority. The majority of the teachers' instructional hours should be spent working with the textbooks; otherwise, students will miss basic knowledge points, and the teaching would therefore be considered ineffective. Since the current textbooks are founded on complete, rigorous, and compact course arrangement, Chinese language teaching can only achieve its core instructional objectives by following several planned steps. When teachers apply such criteria to judging the thematic teaching points presented by Tian Tian, it is very difficult for them to understand the value of reform practice.

These theoretical concepts are tied to some prevalent teaching principles, which give them a strong sense of rationality. However, when employed in real life, these concepts inevitably become mixed with teachers' various idiosyncratic habits and inclinations – which are a result of native thinking – and come to be enmeshed in a native discourse, which gives them special meaning. As an example, the "tradition and legacy foremost" concept is rational at the theoretical level, meaning that in the perspective of systematic curriculum design, the textbook represents a more scientific and effective approach to content arrangement, making textbook-based teaching the most logical

96 *Reform practice and teacher discourse*

choice. The "tradition and legacy foremost" concept is so widely used, thanks to its sweeping rationality, that people do not challenge its theoretical basis, and they intuitively employ it when selecting textbook content. When teachers of "S" Primary School judged Tian Tian's behavior with the "tradition and legacy foremost" concept, instead of on the merits of what was being presented to them, the concept itself provided direct justification the teachers to insist that they use the current textbook and not "Grandfather's Garden" and/or the original literary work. What teachers may not be aware of is that the "tradition and legacy foremost" concept has strayed from its general meaning to become a parochial native discourse that points to certain teaching practices (Figure 6.1).

The open concepts of "tradition and legacy foremost," "root and branch", "feast," and "eye-catching focal points" have acquired native meanings due to the sheer frequency with which teachers use them, interconnecting their meanings and making them mutually supportive. As a consequence of this process, which results in a consensus about instructional technique, it is very difficult for teachers to break with tradition when faced with having to institute reform practice. It is very difficult for them to accept the image of the classroom presented by the new pedagogy.

Recontextualization: reform practice adapting to the native school discourse

A series of native concepts constitutes the basic elements of the teachers' discourse. Due to the fact that their practical knowledge often goes unvoiced, teachers tend to opt for and use familiar discourse to describe and assess practice. Thus, the native concepts that emerge in the teaching and research process (as mentioned above) form what we like to call the teachers' "professional" discourse, which is closely associated with specific instructional decisions and which therefore renders a degree of rationality (or perceived rationality) to teachers' intuitive resistance to reform practice.

Since the introduction of reform practice is affected by decontextualization, the new teaching method struggles to gain acceptance among teachers due its

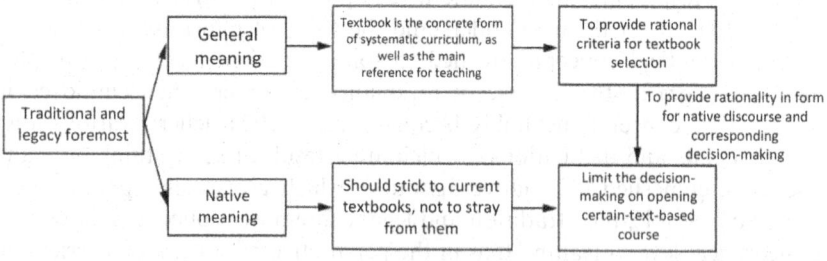

Figure 6.1 Divergence process of the local "tradition and legacy foremost" discourse

inability to achieve gain a foothold at the level of discourse, which would prove its rationality. In order for other teachers in "S" Primary School to accept the thematic teaching approach, leaders like Li Jin need to take the initiative in advancing the reform. On the other hand, the rationality of reform practice also needs to be shown through the lens of teachers' native discourse. It needs to be recontextualized through the process of representation.

In this case, when Tian Tian gave an account of the highlights that she witnessed in the demonstration class to her fellow teachers, she failed to fully communicate her message. Her colleagues, who were more familiar with the native concepts of *Ding Pian*, "tradition and legacy foremost," and "eye-catching focal points," argued with Tian Tian about the rationality of such a teaching design. In response to their inquiries, Tian Tian gradually shifted the focus of her explanation from "the thematic teaching highlights I have seen" to some details not directly associated with thematic teaching. And we note that Tian Tian's subsequent explanations correlate with the teacher group's native discourse. Table 6.1 includes parts of Tian Tian's discussions with her colleagues and parts of her written reflections on these discussions, both revealing the efforts she made in advancing reform and helping the "S" Primary School teacher group better understand reform practice. This information

Table 6.1 Corresponding relationships between Tian Tian's explanation and the teacher group's native discourse

Sequence number	Tian Tian's explanation	Native discourse
1	Though "Grandfather's Garden" is not in the Beijing textbook, it's still an important entry in the People's Education Press textbook.	"Tradition and legacy foremost" "*Ding Pian*"
2	Teacher Wang Jun did well in his whiteboard writing. "People," "object," "event" (written down) followed by all the teaching content, which was all written on the blackboard.	"Root and branch"
3	Actually that day, Teacher Wang Jun focused on the "freedom" paragraph, "everything is alive", along with the three laughs by grandfather. He only captured two points in the entire article, but he didn't read grandfather's laugh into it, and only mentioned it briefly.	"Eye-catching focal points"
4	If you want to know the flavor of pear, you must taste it yourself. We can't replicate the flair of an outstanding teacher, but we may replicate this class. Can we observe the class of "Grandfather's Garden" taught by the outstanding teacher? In the course of personal observation of the class, perhaps we can find answers to the long thinking, and we can find the teaching style suitable to us through deliberate replication and simulation.[7]	"Feast"

helped us understand the process by which the meaning of reform changed as it was transmitted from Tian Tian to her colleagues.

In order to link reform practice and native discourse, Tian Tian explained thematic teaching as she understood it based on native concepts, similes, and metaphors. From a positive perspective, this process breaks the habitual connection between native discourse and the traditional teaching process, pointing to some new pedagogical methods and behaviors. For instance, the "tradition and legacy foremost" turned from "currently used textbooks foremost" as the teachers supported earlier into "may use other textbooks;" the simile of "root and branch" transitioned from "teaching around basic knowledge points," which many teachers were concerned about earlier, to the idea that the content of the "class has a core while expanding." The "eye-catching focal points" metaphor function progressed from "to capture the core vocabulary and sentence" to "to capture the entry point of further reading." The implication of "feast" evolved from referring to the abundant study content for students to judging whether text has the identical meaning of learning and development for teachers. Tian Tian's efforts have undoubtedly expanded the possibility of decisions that teachers can make in their classrooms.

This study defined recontextualization as a process by which teachers are cognitively restricted by a "thinking map," which forces them to process pedagogical changes within the framework of their native discourse. The meaning of thematic teaching is understood and reprocessed in the local teaching context. It is clear that at the heart of the teachers' native discourse is a powerful interpretive system. It supports and reinforces teachers' daily instructional habits, and it helps them inspect, understand, and transform a reform practice with which they may be unfamiliar.

Figure 6.2 illustrates the process of thematic teaching being introduced into "S" Primary School. New definitions have been applied to the same native concepts undergoing recontextualization, which are used to identify changes in how thematic teaching was understood by teachers at the school.

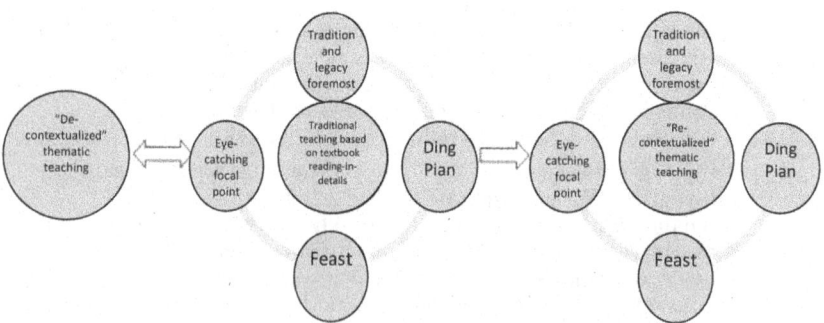

Figure 6.2 Reform practice goes through the process of recontextualization

The recontextualization mechanism represents the process by which outside reform practices are given new meanings in a new context. This process contains a few key points that can be beneficial to understanding the reform process.

First, the discursive context and the cultural context of the school in which reform is implemented are of paramount importance, and they are also areas that have not attracted much scholarly attention in previous studies. Understanding the classic teacher culture theory often begins with an analysis of teacher relations. As cited by Deng and Bao (2005), renowned education professor Andrew Hargreaves groups teacher culture into several categories: individual, collaborative (both natural and personal), divisive, and postmodern. It seems that they are categories based on external observation. From the "internal" perspective of the school, despite the fact that outside researchers make judgments about whether its culture of teaching is individualistic, collaborative, or divisive, such judgments often lack reliable standards of measurement. Teachers' acceptance or rejection of newly introduced reform practices often occurs inadvertently. Under many circumstances, teachers strongly identify with their own school's collaborative culture (as is the case with the teachers at "S." Primary School). However, their shared interpretive model of classroom practice often rejects the introduction of externally imposed reform.

Second, due to the presence of native discourse in local schools, and especially at "S" Primary School, the meanings of outside reform practices are obscure to teachers. The mechanism of recontextualization is necessary in order for teachers to better comprehend the essence of reform practice in terms they can easily understand. Although their meanings can be opaque, the new reform practices do not necessarily lack demonstration, explanation, or clarification. However, due to the marked differences between professional reform discourse and native discourse, the meanings of the reform tend to be unfamiliar to teachers. Therefore, recontextualization is a transformation mechanism that reconstructs the meaning of reform using terms and concepts that are prevalent in teachers' native discourse. This notion can explain the conflict phenomenon between related theory and practice.

Third, recontextualization is not only the process of reorganizing reform practice in a local context, but it is also the process by which school discourse (i.e. native discourse) can expand it horizons and encompass new meanings. In the case study, in order to get her colleagues to see and accept the rationality behind thematic teaching, Tian Tian explained the new concept using concepts and terminology from native discourse, something which had helped her understand thematic teaching in a new light. In her subsequent teaching experiments, instead of guiding students to read the content of *The Story of Hulan River* on their own alongside the textbook article "Grandfather's Garden," which is what Teacher Wang Jun had done, Tian Tian confined her teaching materials to the texts found in the People's Education Press textbook. The theme-based class taught by Tian Tian is closer to traditional teaching in its form and structure, and it is unable to achieve the goal of "transcending the textbook" championed by proponents of thematic teaching. On the other hand, many teachers have since changed some of their deep-rooted opinions through cooperative deliberation and discussion, expanding the limits of their native discourse to encompass a broader array of meanings. For instance, some teachers did not insist on interpreting the concept of "tradition and legacy foremost" as "currently used textbooks by school foremost," but instead began accepting textbook content from other textbook editions.

However, the degree to which school discourse has been adapted and changed by reform practice, as can be seen from Tian Tian's use of native discourse to reinterpret thematic teaching practices, pales in comparison to the degree to which native discourse has changed the meaning reform practice. This perhaps derives from the fact that the "S" Primary School teachers' daily discourse is their medium of reflection and that it is very difficult for most of them to use discourse to reflect on discourse. It is also unrealistic to effect significant change at the practical level (by changing and altering the scope and structure of native discourse) overnight.

Significance of the study and suggestions for future research: reconsidering the path of classroom reform

According to Zhong (2005), the ongoing education reform in China is in part founded on the process of reconceptualization (concept-rebuilding), which means that reform must confront one issue – how the meanings of reform practice transition from one discursive system to another. The sluggishness and lethargy exhibited by teachers in the reform process is not only the result of an increased workload and pressure to perform, but it is largely the result of feelings of aimlessness and meaninglessness, and the loss of a sense of identity that has been caused by problems of communication and understanding. These feelings often accompany the varied criticism and blame placed on practitioners by outside researchers and administrators. One value of the present study is that, through explaining how the meaning of reform is shared and reconstructed, it identifies how native discourse (as the teachers' main resource for understanding the reform) inevitably reconstructs the meaning of reform practice imposed from the outside. Starting from this understanding, researchers can now reflect on some of the existing education reform approaches being used in China's primary schools.

Top-down education reform approaches boast holographic and "forceful intervention." The so-called "holographic approach" is defined as "reformers transmitting the most critical and core part of reform practice in its entirety and original form to the teachers, depending on a series of educational technologies, coaching by outstanding mentors, video recording, and technology breakdown" (Lan & Fan 2012). The notion of high-leverage teaching practices, which has recently become popular in the United States, is representative of this approach. An individual-based educational philosophy lies at the heart of this approach, which is not so much concerned with the sharing of meanings within the teacher group, as it is with preventing the loss of meaning of reform by reducing middle layers. This approach is more beneficial for pre-service teachers and has less of an impact on teachers who are entrenched in a school's local discourse. For the latter, it is very difficult to accept reform, especially in its entirety and in its original form, because of their customary ways of thinking and speaking about classroom teaching.

The so-called "forceful intervention approach" has been defined as occurring when "reformers, through broad participation in schools' daily teaching management, introduce a set of education concepts with high theoretical value, in hopes of improving and enhancing teachers' understanding of self-practice and cultivation." This reform approach often forces teachers to adopt a set of terms employed by college researchers to express and reflect ideas, and the school's native discourse no longer remains the dominant way in which meaning is interpreted. To a certain extent, this approach reduces the amount of distortion that native discourse causes to the original meaning of reform, but it typically exposes outside researchers' "fatal vanity and conceit." The imposition of a foreign discourse at the expense of local school teachers by those in positions of power unavoidably affects the former's instructional practices, restricting their motivation and sense of initiative. Moreover, outside researchers' participation in primary and middle school practice is quite often not as profound and sustained as they claim it to be.

Of the bottom-up reform approaches, the construction process of the fashionable "learning community" concept also deserves reflection. The learning community, with school-based research at its core, integrates cooperation with universities and families, attempting to foster organic reform. Historically, numerous schools have achieved positive results in terms of benefitting from additional human resources and in terms of building an overall culture of cooperation, but the process of classroom reform has suffered repeated setbacks. Cooperative culture does not lead to reform. It is relatively easy to establish interpersonal cooperative relations, but it is a daunting challenge to break out of the confines of a discourse system that interprets teaching practice in a predisposed way and that exists at the collective and unconscious level. If reform cannot advance and be driven by a deeper level of thinking, its acceptance among teachers will often only be superficial. If the learning community can, at a certain level, attend to the understanding and amendment of school discourse, reform will be able to transcend the limit set by traditional cooperative culture theory: it will be able to integrate reform at the level of school culture as well as at the level of practice.

This study has determined that school-based research and training require enriched models of teacher exchange. Learning community construction and school-based research have been undertaken mostly in the form of dialogue. School discourse is often rooted in teachers' daily discussions, and the ingrained ways of thinking enabled by this discourse subtly limit teachers' behaviors. Therefore, it is necessary to enrich the ways in which reform concepts are represented in school-based research. Studies indicate that teachers can have diverse practical knowledge representation forms such as "image," "metaphor," "behavior formula," "embodiment," "narrative," and "case" (Chen 2011). If, in the collective discussion phase (brainstorming), teachers intentionally employ various approaches to represent the meanings of reform and get their colleagues to engage is serious reflection, then perhaps reform initiatives will be able to gain some real traction. While school discourse is not merely a way to describe and explain practice, practice reform is not merely a change in teacher behavior. The complexity of reform is rooted in school culture and even in broader collective culture, and relevant discourse should be recognized as a significant part of this culture. Of course, as stated earlier, reflecting on their own discourse is a daunting challenge for teachers, and that is why the successful implementation of school reform requires the continued presence in schools of what we like to call "cross-discourse-border practice researchers." These teachers have the passion for reform, while being familiar with a variety of discursive systems, which enables them to play the role of communicator as well as mediator, bridging the gaps between the policy, academic, practice, and native discourses of different schools. Such a role not only facilitates the transmission of the meanings of reform, but it also spurs the enrichment and innovation of these meanings.

Notes

1. As far as the term "reform practice" is concerned, it must be stressed that it also applies to teachers' behaviors in school beyond the immediate context of the classroom. For the purposes of space, the present study focuses on the concept only as it pertains to classroom teaching.
2. This is concept was often referred to as the "light of power" in the seminar given by Ying Xing entitled "Narrative Methods of Chinese Social Research," which was given at Peking University on July 8, 2012.
3. All teachers' names in this study are pseudonyms.
4. The Chinese language thematic teaching method, which possesses native characteristics and originates from frontline practice, may be more complex on the conceptual level than other reform practices. Besides the brief introduction of Dou Guimei's thinking (above), there is much for to be gleaned on this particular method from the teaching practice of frontline teachers with years of teaching experience, much of which is currently in semi-theoretical state.
5. Michael Polanyi described this interplay between subsidiary and focal awareness as "indwelling." People indwell their interpretive frameworks so that they order and select their impressions. See his *Personal Knowledge: Towards a Post-Critical Philosophy* (Guiyang: Guizhou People's Press, 2000).
6. "Ding Pian" referred by this study is a native concept, meaning that it did not come about as a result of academic research. Although some academic articles in recent years have referred to this concept, it was formed at the grassroots level.
7. Paragraph 4 of the text is from a shared teaching plan between Tian Tian and some of her fellow teachers.

References

Chen, X. 2011. *Bridging Praxis and Theory: A Study on Teachers' Practical Knowledge.* Beijing: Science and Education Press.
Chen, X., C. Liu & G. Zheng. 2005. "Thinking on Thematic Unit Teaching." *People's Education Press* 15–16: 19–22.
Colen, D. K. 1990. "A Revolution in One Classroom: The Case of Mrs. Oublier." *Educational Evaluation and Policy Analysis* 12(3): 311–329.
Deng, T. & C. Bao. 2005. "A Renewed Understanding and Construction of Teachers' Culture: Commentary on Andrew Hargreaves's Perspective on Teachers' Culture." *Studies in Foreign Education* 32(8): 6–10.
Dou, G. 2004. "Thinking on and Practice of Thematic Teaching." *People's Education Press* 12: 21–34.
Dou, G. 2010. "Face a Great Thing – New Thinking on Thematic Teaching. *People's Education Press* 5: 42–47.
Elbaz-Luwisch, F. 2005. *Teachers' Voices: Storytelling and Possibility.* Greenwich, CT: Information Age Publishing.
Fan, Y. 2008. "Teachers' Reflection Discourse State." *Peking University Education Review* 6(1): 79–91.
Freeman, D. 1993. "Renaming Experience/Reconstructing Practice: Developing New Understandings of Teaching." *Teaching and Teacher Education* 9(5–6): 485–497.
Fullan, M. 1999. *Change Forces: The Sequel.* Philadelphia, PA: Falmer Press.
Kress, G. 1985. *Linguistic Processes in Sociocultural Practice.* Geelong, Australia: Deakin University Press.
Lan, Y. & Y. Fan. 2012. "The High-Leverage Practices and Education Practice Curriculum Exploration." *Global Education* 41(6): 32–38.
Little, J. W. 2003. "Inside Teacher Community: Representations of Classroom Practice." *Teachers College Record* 105(6): 913–945.
Yang, X. 2007. "Standpoint of Practice and Representation of Theoretical Educators (Reflections on Problems in the Implementation of the New Curriculum)." *Educational Research and Experiment* 4: 20–23.
Wang, R. 2007. *Listen to Professor Wang Rongsheng Commenting on the Class.* Shanghai: East China Normal University Press.
Wu, Z. 2005. *Teachers' Knowing in Curriculum Change: A Critical Discourse Study of Language Teaching.* Beijing: Foreign Language Teaching and Research Press.
Zhong, Q. 2005. "Concept Rebuilding and China's Curriculum Innovation – A Discussion with the Author of "Seriously Confronting the Educational Trend of Not Treating Knowledge Seriously." *Peking University Education Review* 3(1): 48–75.
Zhong, Q. 2006. "Challenges Faced by Reform on Curriculum and Reflections." *Xiao Zhang Yue Kan* [*Principal's Reading*] 12: 21–25.

7 State and public education
A new analytical framework

Wang Rong

Over the past five decades, economic research on public education has been dominated by functionalist paradigms in general and by human capital theory in particular. According to the mainstream definition of the term, "human capital" is defined as knowledge, attitudes, and skills that are developed and valued primarily for their economically productive potential, and it refers to the productive capacities of human beings as income-producing agents in an economy (Hornbeck & Salamon 1991). "Human capital formation" is the name given to the process by which such capital is deliberately developed, and the expenditure of human capital (e.g. in time and in money) is called "human capital investment" (Becker 1987).

Under the functionalist paradigm, the analysis of the evolution and development of education is normally mixed with the analysis of its functions. The demand for skilled labor is used as an analytical framework with which to explain the evolution and development of education. However, the key issue when it comes to the evolution of education is how it responds to such demands. Currently, evidence shows that this response has been neither fast nor spontaneous in nature. As Randall Collins explained over thirty years ago, school education fails to provide specific skills (as is claimed by the functionalist framework): "Apart from industrial skills, that are gradually refined, other reasons account for the historical model of education development" (Collins 1971: 1002–1019). However, people always doubt and criticize the appropriateness of modern education. Education and economic development are frequently decoupled from one another in research, and this has been the case throughout the entire history of education development (Green 2004).

Some scholars correctly point out that individuals and society reap different rewards, as it were, from education. The economic return on education may be different among different individuals and groups within society. For example, Pritchett (1996) argued that the educational environment has been distorted in many countries and that, as a result, it has done a significant amount of human capital harm to economic growth. In other words, education can improve productivity and society therefore constantly demands more educated labor. However, such a demand may be a waste or even counterproductive for a society as a whole, even though individuals within that society may benefit from it. For example, in a large bureaucratic organization, or in a country with redundant employees in state-owned enterprises or government organizations, the overall economic output can stagnate – and even drop – even though individuals' salaries will increase as they obtain higher educational qualifications. This is due to the large number of non-economic factors exist in the education sector. In order to clearly demonstrate his point, Pritchett took an example from 1998, when more than 50% of university students in Saudi Arabia were studying humanities, religion, and theology. Pritchett (1996: 43) stated that "these fields of study that may not raise economic output per worker are obviously of no concern to those so engaged."

This study builds upon some of the other factors that contribute the historical model of education development presented by Collins (1971), and looks at different returns on education for individuals, groups and for society as a whole. It will then propose a holistic framework with which to examine public education, namely, a new human capital theory. This article consists of three parts. The first part analyzes several prototypical education systems from an historical perspective. The second looks at human capital, which can be classified into two dimensions: productive human capital and private objectified human capital. These conceptual frameworks lay the foundation for the new human capital theory. Finally, the third part will discuss the prominent issues that exist in the relationship between the state and public education.

The historical perspective

Before the modern education system was established, several educational system prototypes existed in China and in Western countries. They were (1) the church-based education system in Western societies; (2) the guild system in China and Western societies; and (3) the imperial examination system in China. These prototypes served as "genetic elements" for establishing modern Chinese and Western education systems.

Church-based education system

The establishment of the modern Western education system was closely tied to religion. Such a "genetic" explanation has been widely recognized by academics. In his book entitled *The Evolution of Educational Thought*, Emile Durkheim (2003) systematically explicated this relationship. Durkheim believed that the fact that schools originated in the Church in Western societies was due to the spread of Christianity. In particular, he pointed out that cathedral schools and cloister schools gave birth to the Western education system and to Western academic organizations. In his view, "this and this alone does and can explain certain essential features which our education has exhibited in the course of its history, or which it has retained right down to our own times" (Durkheim 2003: 30).

According to the historical explanation provided by Durkheim, the public education system sprouted up from the learning that occurred at churches thanks to the promotion of learning by imperial authority. At that time, King Charles tried to control the regions of Western Christendom under his sole power, and he employed the education system as a tool with which to do it. Education systems were not only used as a tool to unify people's culture and thoughts within a given political jurisdiction, but they were also a tool with which to popularize such culture and thoughts across the Frankish Empire.

As Durkheim (2003) proposed, church-based education systems have three main characteristics. First, the instructors showed initiative and tried to control their students' ideologies during the learning process. For this kind of education, to some extent, instructors influenced the minds and beliefs of learners. Preachers were obligated to preach. According to their religious requirements, Christians are obligated to preach the truth to people around them. What a Christian is charged to watch over is not only his own personal salvation but the salvation of humanity as a whole. Second, the contents of teaching and learning integrated. The purpose of religious education was to take charge of the whole person. Previously, in ancient times, students received tutoring from different teachers, and these teachers had no relationships whatsoever with one another. On the contrary, Christian schools gathered the public to learn under the same roof and followed the same moral standards, thus in this context education was unified. Third, education was popularized: with the development of a church-based education system, learners from different backgrounds all had an opportunity to receive an education.

The guild system

In the past, the guild system had been widely adopted by both Chinese society and Western societies. If seen through from a human resources perspective, the apprenticeship stage is an important part of the guild system. As pointed out by Epstein (1998), the first stage of human beings' acquisition of technical knowledge was through a formal or informal long-term mentoring relationship. According to Epstein, apprenticeship was the most widespread arrangement for transmitting technical knowledge outside the family devised by human societies. The benefit arrangement between masters and apprentices was a key issue in this arrangement. From this angle, Adam Smith (2002: 116) provided a definition on an apprentice as "a servant bound to work at a particular trade for the benefit of a master during a term of years, upon condition that the master shall teach him that trade." Interpreted through the lens of human capital, the apprenticeship was a kind of trading relationship, in which learners received the chance to acquire skills by working for the benefit of instructors.

Accordingly, apprenticeship exhibited the following characteristics. First, in contradistinction to the mass education that occurred in the church-based education system, the guild system strictly controlled the number of learners, and collective norms were established to control personal behaviors (Olson 2007). Second, in the church-based education system, religious knowledge was preserved. However, the knowledge and skills transmitted in the guild system were hardly codified and standardized. And third, such knowledge was difficult to spread through printouts and other media. Instead, it was taught by the master through verbal instruction. Technological knowledge that was spread across regions relied on the mobility of the masters/instructors.

It could be concluded that the church-based education system and the guild system differed in terms of the kind of knowledge transmitted and codification and standardization of this knowledge. Such differences were not only due to different kinds of knowledge and skills that were taught, but they were also due to the instructors' respective motivations. First, masters would be punished for accepting more apprentices than was customary. Under such regulations, people were less motivated to codify and standardize all self-owned or community-owned knowledge and skills and make that organization known to the public. Second, the guild system had higher economic and social requirements on admission. Such economic requirements as not receiving salary and a paying tuition fees during the apprenticeship period were the most important in the guild system. According to the research on the weaver guild in Germany in the 1500s-1600s conducted by Ogilvie (2004), young men, in order to be admitted to an apprenticeship, needed to pay the registration fee to the guild and admission fee to the masters, as well as material costs and community resident fees. Meanwhile, certain social groups were prohibited from entry, such as women, criminals, Jews, Catholics, and Calvinists. These were social entry thresholds.

The imperial examination system

In the past, the imperial examination system was the dominant education system in China. The system was differed significantly from the church-based education system and the guild system.

First, the emergence and development of the imperial examination system was dominated by the state, which aimed to ensure its own long-term operation and political governance. In early times, Chinese rulers and scholars had realized the political function exerted by education. After defeating the other six states, the Qin dynasty adopted a series of measures to unify China. Among these measures, the establishment of a unifying ideology was the most important one. Li Si, the Chancellor, submitted a memorial to the Qin Emperor:

> Of old, the world was scattered and in confusion ... Men valued what they had themselves privately studied, thus casting into disrepute what their superiors had established. At present, Your Majesty has united the

world ... Yet there are those who with their private teachings mutually abet each other, and discredit the institutions of laws and instructions ... If such conditions are not prohibited, the imperial power will decline within and partisanships will form at the grassroots level.

(Qian 2008: 1736)

Such political ideology was gradually cemented during the reign of Emperor Wu of the Han dynasty. In ancient Chinese society, government officials had to learn Confucianism with its six scriptures. Confucianism became the official political ideology for the official school system, laying a foundation for the shortlisting of government officials via the imperial examination system through Chinese history.

Second, the imperial examination system not only served as an education system, but it also served as a political recruitment system. Qualified students would be awarded government posts and increased salaries. Since then, "government officials selected from good scholars" had become a tradition in China.

Fang (1996: 6) has argued that the imperial examination system exhibited four characteristics: openness, universality, competitiveness, and limitation. Three important factors accounted for these four characteristics, namely, admission scope, examination method, and examination content.

First, due to the implementation of the imperial examination system, the Chinese civil service nomination system became open and universal for the first time. The imperial examination system broke the political power that traditionally been monopolized by hereditary nobles. In principle, people from the lower social classes had a chance to become government officials. The imperial examination system greatly strengthened the capability of the central government to unify Chinese society, and thereby significantly increased its legitimacy. Meanwhile, recruiting talented young men, mostly intellectuals, from all corners of society ensured the intellectual quality of government officials. Second, the imperial examination system was competitive: it had multiple layers and multiple subjects. In this way, a recruitment process that consisted of several rigorous levels was established. Third, the complex examination system, with its strict competitive ethos, had many limitations. In short, only a few intellectuals could enter a political career through the imperial examination system, although nearly all intellectuals participated in the examination system. It was also very expensive to study for the system and to enter into it. Thus, officials recruited from the imperial examination were normally from wealthy families even though the examination was open to all segments of society. And it was in this way that political stability was ensured through this recruitment system.

Apart from these characteristics summarized, it must be noted that the gist of the imperial examination system was to safeguard Confucianism as the official political ideology of the state so as to secure imperial authority. In order to participate in the imperial examination, the candidates had to read classical Confucian works many times over. This was how learners were ideologically brainwashed by such repeated reading and testing (Liping 1996).

New human capital theory: an analytical framework

Productive human capital and distributive human capital

Through examining several typical education systems under the genetic model, namely, the church-based education system, the guild system, and the imperial examination system, I will establish an analytical framework in order to classify human capital into two dimensions. The first dimension is the productive nature of human capital. Productive human capital is a concept that corresponds to distributive human capital. The second dimension is the private nature of human capital, which could be further classified into private objectified human capital and collective objectified human capital. In the past, traditional concepts of human capital were limited to productive and private objectified human capital. Nevertheless, I would like to argue that both in the past and in the present public education centered or centers on the transmission of distributive human capital and collective objectified human capital.

The term "productive human capital" here refers to knowledge, attitudes, and skills that are developed and valued primarily for their economically productive potential. It refers to the productive capacities of human beings as income-producing agents in an economy (Hornbeck & Salamon 1991). At the micro level, the increase of productive human capital improves personal productivity. At the macro level, it expands production and increases its economic aggregate. Productive human capital also refers to the capability of individuals, as those at the center of economic and production activities, to control the elements of production and ensure they are in balance.

Distributive human capital is an important component of non-productive human capital, as it is related to whether a group, organization, or government maintains/alters the current wealth distribution among individuals and groups within a state as well as among states.[1] Such necessary human capital is known as distributive human capital, which we have narrowly defined as knowledge, attitudes, and skills that are developed and valued primarily for their potential involvement in wealth distribution. It is no surprise that the state is the primary entity in need of distributive human capital.

In Weber's (2004) classical works on state, politics, and power, we can find a concept similar to distributive human capital. According to Weber's political theory, the state is a relationship of men dominating men, a relationship supported by the means of legitimacy. For a state, two elements are worthy of attention: the evidence of state legitimacy and the resources for domination. Regarding such resources, Weber (2004: 201) pointed out that "organized domination, which calls for continuous administration, requires that human conduct be conditioned to obedience towards those masters who claim to be the bearers of legitimate power. On the other hand, by virtue of this obedience, organized domination requires the control of those material goods which in a given case are necessary for the use of physical violence."

Weber's political theory mainly consists of three parts. First, Weber classified human resources needed by the state to dominate matters of finance, war, and law according to the concept of "expert officialdom," which is based on the division of labor. In this regard, he stated the following:

> The state purely plays technical functions. In Europe, expert officialdom, based on the division of labor, has emerged in a gradual development of 500 years. The Italian cities and seigniories were the beginning, among the monarchies, and the states of the Norman conquerors. But the decisive step was taken in connection with the administration of the finances of the prince ... The development of war technique called forth the expert and specialized officer; the differentiation of legal procedure called forth the trained jurist. In these three areas – finance, war, and law – expert officialdom in the more advanced states was definitely triumphant during the sixteenth century.
>
> (Weber 2004: 213)

Second, he clearly pointed out the self-investment process gone through by professional staff. Weber explained that:

> the administrative staff, which externally represents the organization of political domination, is, of course, like any other organization, bound by obedience to the power-holder and not alone by the concept of legitimacy, of which we have just spoken. There are two other means, both of which appeal to personal interests: material reward and social honor. The fiefs of vassals, the prebends of patrimonial officials, the salaries of modern civil servants, the honor of knights, the privileges of estates, and the honor of the civil servant comprise their respective wages. The fear of losing them is the final and decisive basis for solidarity between the executive staff and the power-holder. There is honor and booty for the followers in war.
>
> (Weber 2004: 201–202)

Third, Weber divided expert officialdom into five historical categories based on function: clergy, literati, imperial nobility, landed gentry, and professionals (i.e. lawyers). With regard to the church-based and the imperial examination systems mentioned above, Weber's discussion about clergy and literati is highly instructive. He explained it thus:

> Confronting the estates, the prince found support in politically exploitable strata outside of the order of the estates. Among the latter, there was, first, the clergy in Western and Eastern India, in Buddhist China and

Japan, and in Lamaist Mongolia, just as in the Christian territories of the Middle Ages. The clergy were technically useful because they were literate ... The humanistically educated literati comprised a second such stratum. There was a time when one learned to produce Latin speeches and Greek verses in order to become a political adviser to a prince and, above all things, to become a memorialist. This was the time of the first flowering of the humanist schools and of the princely foundations of professorships for "poetics." This was for us a transitory epoch, which has had a quite persistent influence upon our educational system, yet no deeper results politically. In East Asia, it has been different. The Chinese mandarin is, or rather originally was, what the humanist of our Renaissance period approximately was: a literator humanistically trained and tested in the language monuments of the remote past.

(Weber 2004: 222–223)

Based on Weber's theory, distributive human capital could be further divided into four categories. The first is military human capital. The army and the police force are tools for all countries to ensure their security and defend themselves against invasions. The army and the police force employ a large number of people. These personnel need to receive professional training. The special skills required by this social function are referred to collectively as "military human capital." From the historical perspective, education has a long-term relationship with military human capital. As explained by Peiqing (2002), in Chinese education history the title of teacher originated from the term *Shi*, which was the title for military officials. *Shi Shi* referred to senior military officials, while "master" referred to military officials who had a higher rank than *Shi Shi*. In the Western Zhou dynasty, the *Shi Shi* acted as the captain of the security force that protected the emperor. Aside from this duty, the *Shi Shi* was also responsible for educating children of the royal family and of the nobility. These children would become future rulers, and they therefore received military training. Since then, *Shi* became a title for educators. Later, administrative officials responsible for education were also called *Shi*.

The second category is ideology-related human capital. This refers to the knowledge and skills that it takes to produce, maintain, and preserve the beliefs and attitudes regarding how a group or a society distributes social benefits. Such beliefs and attitudes are collectively referred to as "ideology." In traditional society, apart from military force, deifying the legitimacy of their rule and status is another way for states, rulers, and social elites to maintain their political, financial, and legal dominance. The establishment of their legitimacy involves "spiritual labor," which includes rituals of sacrifice as well as the creation and spreading of other related ideological products. As stated in the *Chronicle of Zuo*, "the great affairs of a state were war and sacrifice." In other words, ideology is created and maintained; it doesn't emerge naturally. A state needs a great deal of resources to establish and promote its ideology, including human capital possessing professional skills and a great deal of knowledge. Such human capital is different from the human capital that is needed for state administration in general and in particular from the human capital for required for state finance as discussed by Weber. Thus, this type of distributive human capital is its own unique category.

In both Chinese and Western societies, the birth of the bureaucratic education system was closely related to the ruler's investment in ideology-related human capital. As described by Durkheim, the public education system sprouted up from the church-based education system thanks to the promotion of learning by imperial authority. For rulers such as King Charles, an education system was not only a tool to unify people's cultures and thoughts within a governing region, but also a tool to popularize such cultures and thoughts across his empire. Von Hayek (1997) has pointed out that, in modern society, mass education does not only serve the purpose of spreading knowledge: its most important function is to share certain kinds of knowledge and beliefs so as to effectively run and maintain democracy.

In higher education today, there are many subjects and research areas that focus on ideology-related human capital, and such study is normally not related to personal beliefs or ideologies. It is commonplace for the study of and research into ideology-related human capital to be objectified or commodified and seen as utilitarian, something which attracts a great deal of personal investment from students. Such courses have quickly become a widely circulated commodity, bringing with them monetary returns to both producers (teachers, researchers) and investors (students) alike.

With the development of political forms, "sacrifice" and "war" no longer meet the needs of state governance. Thus, the demand for administrative human capital emerged, that is, human capital in the form of officials who would be responsible for administering the daily affairs of the state. Such human capital is normally shortlisted from the qualified "brainworkers" who have received professional education and training. Administrative officialdom is a structure bound by law and which is mainly responsible for daily state administration. Official positions are arranged according to competencies and a bureaucratic hierarchical structure. Although this system of governance is operated by officials, it is separated from the ownership of the administrative tools. That is to say, the people who occupy these positions have no right to own technical resources that accompany them. Administrative officialdom is employed according to the qualifications of candidates. They must deal with public affairs according to regulations and laws (Weber 2004).

Weber (2004: 201–204) also noted that "the significance of the lawyer in Occidental politics since the rise of parties is not accidental. The management of politics through parties simply means management through interest groups … The craft of the trained lawyer is to plead effectively the cause of interested clients."

In addition, in modern society the state monopolizes judicial power, which is implemented by legal human resources. The skills and knowledge of legal human capital are mainly used for formulating and implementing laws and regulations. However, the extent of such special skills and knowledge in a given state is subject its political organization and its political system. The hierarchical officialdom interpreted by Weber refers to this as "technical resources and capabilities" in state governance. On the other hand, the technical resources and capabilities required for legislation, enforcement, and judicial matters in modern democratic societies are referred to as "legal human capital."

Historically, economists have often discussed the concept of non-productive human capital. Karl Marx and Adam Smith, for example, asserted that a national economy has philosophers, poets, pastors, and professors apart from farmers, manufacturers, and merchants – the latter corresponding to the three main industries: "A philosopher produces ideas, a poet poems, a clergyman sermons, a professor compendia, and so on" (Marx 1998: 349). In today's world, ideas, poems, sermons, and compendia no longer serve as the content of a spiritual noble's self-entertainment. Instead, they have become objectified as tradable commodities. A philosopher is educated and employed to produce and sell ideas. Without analyzing such a process, we cannot understand the context of today's education system.

It has also been observed that the state decides the investment return on distributive human capital as its main demander. In founding a new state, military human capital has higher investment returns. When a state is less exposed to military threats, the social status of military talent will be lowered. In the process of founding a state, ideology-related human capital plays an important political role. This viewpoint was shared by Chinese rulers and scholars in ancient times. The Qin dynasty adopted a series of measures to unify China. Among those measures, unifying ideology was the most important one. Such political ideology had been gradually cemented during the reign of Emperor Wu of the Han dynasty.

In ancient Chinese society, government officials had to learn Confucianism and its six scriptures. Confucianism became the official political ideology of the state and therefore of the state school system. Later, the imperial examination system was gradually formed, and it was this system which can be considered as an incentive system for ideology-related human capital (later known as "bureaucratic" or "administrative" human capital). As society – and the economy – continued to develop, administrative and legal human capital both became a lot more valuable. Those with legal and administrative skills came to occupy senior positions in government. Studies have shown that the elites who receive higher education in law and management science occupy a large portion of the leadership roles regardless of the political and economic system in which they find themselves (Zang 2001).

Given the analysis presented above, it is clear that education is closely related to distributive human capital. From the perspective of economists, most investments in education – the consumption element in a dualistic economic structure – are investments in distributive human capital, which are investments that deliberately sacrifice current benefit for future gain. As with the interpretation of clergy and literati made by Weber, higher education in human society was a process of investing in distributive human capital. The purpose of receiving a humanistic education was to become a political consultant for the King. The King's demands for men with such advisory skills brought humanistic training and the schools that provided it to the first peak of their development. As a basis for higher education, rather than for a liberal arts education (as some have suggested), humanistic education was utilitarian in nature. Meanwhile, those people with higher education backgrounds were owned and controlled by the power-holder. They not only accepted the legitimacy of the state, but also received financial rewards and social honor for their service. Thus, their learned knowledge and skills could be considered as a form of "self-investment."

For a state, higher education is not just for training future officials and political advisers, it is also for carrying out research that will support and sustain its legitimacy for years to come. First, as stated by Holcombe (1997), history, language, and the social sciences received state subsidies because those disciplines would bolster the ideas and theories of state legitimacy. Second, research in the natural sciences was seen as having many applications for military technology: the state therefore also subsidized the natural sciences.

Private objectified and collective objectified human capital

Inasmuch as human capital has been heavily commodified, it could be divided into two essential categories: private objectified human capital and collective objectified human capital. Here, we can use the concept of utility interdependence to distinguish between private commodities and collective commodities. Private objectified human capital has a low degree of utility interdependence, while collective objectified human capital has a high degree of utility interdependence. In the case of the latter, owners want people to obtain as much knowledge and skills as possible. The more people who hold such commodities, the more value will be added to these commodities.

Indivisible return is one of the main features of pure collective objectified human capital. For a group or an organization, all members will enjoy the same amount of utility when private human capital investment is increased. As opposed to increasing competitive human capital, bringing in a sizable amount of private human capital will increase owners' personal gain and will not damage their economic interests. Owners' interests are not in conflict or at odds with the wide dissemination of this kind of human capital.

Private objectified human capital

In society, if a given kind of human capital has low utility interdependence, then personal utility is not related to whether other people have or obtain such human capital. In such circumstances, the owners of such human capital are less motivated to help others obtain it because it is private and objectified.

The utility of productive human capital is negatively correlated to the number of people who have it. In short, owners' utility will be reduced when the number of owners is increased. This kind of human capital is often referred to as "competitive human capital." The concept of competitive human capital can be illustrated with an example given by Adam Smith. In the seventh chapter of his An Inquiry into the Nature and Causes of the Wealth of Nations ("Of the Natural and Market Price of Commodities"), he stated that "a dyer who has found the means of producing a particular color with materials which cost only half the price of those commonly made use of, may, with good management, enjoy the advantage of his discovery as long as he lives, and even leave it as a legacy to his posterity" (Smith 2002: 55).

The dyer previously relied on "proprietary" and monopolistic human capital to obtain extra profit, namely, techniques and knowledge proprietarily owned by laborers. The dyer's benefits would be compromised by sharing such proprietary human capital with others.

Whether the owners of pure competitive human capital are willing to transmit human capital depends on whether they can benefit from such an act. If they cannot, human capital transmission will not take place, even if there is a high demand from learners for education and/or training. As stated previously, in the guild system craftsmen did not want their skills to be widely circulated. Competitive human capital was only transmitted within a community, such as the family and the clan. Such communities consisted of instructors and learners who shared the same interests. Thus, in the guild system new craftsmen were trained from apprenticing with senior craftsmen.

There are two preconditions for the transmission of pure competitive human capital outside the family or the clan (i.e. the community) to other pre-established communities. The first precondition is when there is large demand in the market and when there are diminishing economies of scale. The guild system provides a good example of this. In the handicraft sector, for example, productivity was often constrained due to the fact that craftsmen had a limited amount of time in which to ply their trade and limited physical strength. Thus, producers would often need to expand production in order to meet increasing market demand, something which required the addition of more skilled workers. The second precondition is when the instructors can receive compensation for sharing their skills. Such compensation would offset the direct costs of training new workers, such as the opportunity cost and the direct costs which come as a result of lost production. More importantly, the compensation can offset individual loss caused by the reduction of the marginal rate of return on human capital because of the increasing aggregate human capital supply. This compensation system, as it were, typically has two main models.

The first model is when instructors form a close-knit interest community with learners. In such a structure, instructors and learners form long-term, and even life-long, cooperative relationships. During the training period, learners can pay tuition or receive lower salary as a way of compensating the instructors. At the end of training period, such compensation would continue. The instructors can continuously share the benefits of the learners' output, similar to the interests of material capitals. Actually, such compensation is, in essence, the "return on investment" for the instructors, who had shared their knowledge and skills with their apprentices. Thus, senior workers receive more compensation despite having a lower output. This income distribution scheme is based on and a result of the formation of an interest community.

The second model is the impersonalized contractual system supervised by a third party. In such circumstances, the instructor and the learners do not form an interest community. As a matter of fact, they have no contact at all. Instead, under a consistent and legally binding system, the instructors can obtain the value of their skills and knowledge from the products made by the learners as a result of their acquisition of human capital. Proprietary ownership of intellectual property is a typical example of such an arrangement.

Collective objectified human capital

In society, if a given kind of human capital has high utility interdependence, then the increase of personal utility is closely related to whether other people have or are capable of obtaining this kind of human capital. In such circumstances, people who possess human capital would like to help others obtain it.

Collective objectified human capital is always bound by economies of scale: the realization of personal utility is based on how many people share human capital. Language is a good example of this. Language is a communicative tool, and it cannot realize its utility when only one person commands it. Ideology-related human capital, religious belief, for example, is another example of human capital bound by economies of scale. (and there is no shortage of examples). When preaching a minority religion, the main proponents (officials, clergy, etc.) often try to expand the number of followers. However, when a religion is dominant in society, believers (on the whole) are not as enthusiastic to preach.

Collective objectified human capital is based on corresponding "collective" carriers serving the group. And this group can also be called an "interest group." The interest group can be classified into two types. One is a "productive interest group" consisting of a productive body (i.e. companies, craftsmen), which directly participates in the production process that leads to the creation of wealth. The other type is a "distributive interest group" consisting of a distributive body, which is not directly engaged in the production process. Instead, it obtains funds through rent-seeking. In reality, only a few interest groups are pure productive or distributive interest groups. Many productive interest groups, such as guilds, become distributive groups when formulating producer regulations and norms. Distributive groups, such as states, are normally not satisfied with rental benefits collected from producers, and they therefore become directly involved in some highly profitable sectors of the economy.

This classification can help us see why different interest groups have different attitudes towards access. The main task of productive interest group is to protect the interest of internal producers. Companies compete with one another in the marketplace. Thus, they do not wish newcomers to share the market. Preventing newcomers was one of a number of key tasks for guilds. The apprenticeship system is related to this objective (Olson 2007). Under these circumstances, productive interest groups aim to establish monopolistic status or protect it once established. Education and training are used as a means to determine who gets to join the group and who does not.

The situation is different for distributive interest groups. Generally, groups compete with one another to seek rent. The expansion of the group's economy of scale will increase group competitiveness so as to ensure rent-seeking benefits. In such circumstances, the interest group will aggressively expand its scale. In such a context, education develops fast as a means to build group recognition and attract new members, and this is exactly what happened in the church-based education system. Education in this context is a process of transmitting collective objectified human capital.

This study asserts that the transmission of collective distributive objectified human capital is closely related to the emergence and development of public education. The "original sin" of public education is the transmission of collective distributive objectified human capital. After the gradual improvement of the education system, the transmission of collective distributive objectified human capital becomes the main task for basic public education, while higher education is responsible for training high-end distributive human capital, which is needed by the state for governance. Certain conditions need to be satisfied in order to include the transmission of private productive objectified human capital in public education. Those conditions are related to ideology, values, and the transferability of such human capital, and they vary at different levels of economic development and in different economic and political systems.

For the transmission of collective distributive objectified human capital, it is assumed that there are two mutually competitive interest groups. Those two groups use education as a means to attract new members and find their self-identities. For Group A, there are two different means of gaining recognition. The first has to do with gaining legitimate recognition, as Group A strives to expand its legitimate group interests. The second means has to do with confrontation, and it is either initiated by the competitor of Group A or by Group B, which is held down by Group A.

Accordingly, society is composed of four types of people: (1) Group A elites, the instructors promoting the legitimacy of Group A; (2) the Group A public, the learners accepting the legitimacy of Group A; (3) Group B elites, the instructors promoting confrontation with Group A to question its legitimacy; and (4) the Group B public, the learners accepting the recognition of Group A as an entity to be confronted. In the process of Group A defeating Group B, the capability and power of Group B elites to confront Group A are diminished and Group A wins over the Group B public. As such, the collective objectified human capital owned by Group B is dispelled. For example, we consider Group A as a ruling state government and Group B as an opposition group, such as a civil group (internal) or an invading force (external). The emergence and development of public education is about gathering all the political tools of a ruling authority to a single point of focus as a means to diminish the ability of the elites from the confronting group to teach their ideology. Under such circumstances, everyone is required to accept the education system recognized by the state. Such education becomes compulsory. This is an important reason for the state to monopolize education and form a public education system that is compulsory for all. This is an important part of the concept of public education.

According to the analysis presented above, we find that what is considered to be "legitimate" content taught in public institutions is subject to past and current challengers of the state's legitimacy. The nature of the transmission of collective objectified human capital via public education varies in different states, depending upon its political circumstances: a newly independent state that has just succeeded overthrowing its colonial rulers will not have the same rules as state that seen ethnic disputes become commonplace or a state dominated by a party representing a certain class' social and political interests. The change in a state's disposition towards how collective objectified human capital is disseminated depends on how it sees the forces (internal and external) that challenge its legitimacy and how such forces act.

In this regard, whether or not the state permits non-government organizations to control schools – that is, whether it will allow the development of private education institutions – very much depends on how it assesses the forces that challenge its legitimacy. If a state permits the development of private education, it means that the state allows the transmission of collective objectified human capital and that it can control how future generations will challenge the state or its rulers. Such government-curtailed public education may be easily found in a state founded upon the fierce struggle between interest groups.

In addition, a common feature of public education is its inclusivity. For example, different religious or cultural content is often included in the curriculum. Schools run by different interest groups are included in the education system. Different countries, of course, have different policies in this regard. However, regardless of the political system, such differences lie in how the state or the dominant power group perceives threats to its legitimacy. If the aforementioned religious or cultural content are not considered as confrontation, they are likely to be included in public education. However, this does not mean that certain states don't refrain from ensuring that this content does not encourage confrontation.

The state and public education

The complex relationship between public education and the state is one of the key obstacles to public education reform. In some countries, education not only serves as a tool for political recruitment, but it also serves a basis for legitimate governance. In this regard, we can simply divide states into two types.

In Type A states, the government and the various political parties are similar to manufacturers and vendors in the market, while the general public consists of consumers. In politics, manufacturers compete with one another. Public services provided by vendors are considered as the commodity in the market. States and governments hold a social contract with their citizens. The government is a result of an election and is subject to public opinion. In addition, the general public directly takes part in public policy decision-making, which is one of the pillars of state legitimacy.

Type B states share three characteristics: (1) in politics, the state adopts an ever-lasting bureaucratic system consisting of elites; (2) the relationship between the government and different interest groups is contradictory; and (3) with regard to the economy, property ownership is re-arranged and defined through a bureaucratic administration. The state satisfies its own motives and maintains its political legitimacy through ongoing economic growth.

In Type B states, political legitimacy is based on the person or persons who form the government and the process of shortlisting elites. As a representative of the public, such elites are shortlisted in a transparent manner by following objective "moral" standards. The influence of stratum and class interests is maximally excluded or hidden in such a process. Such elites decide the legitimacy of re-arranging and defining property ownership in their society. Such legitimacy also comes from the process of shortlisting officials.

In such states, the relationship between education and political recruitment, and the relationship between education and political legitimacy are clearly institutionalized. Education is intermixed with the political recruitment process. Disadvantageous groups have a chance to enter the government bureaucracy through an open, universal, competitive, and restricted examination system. Through education, the political system strengthens its political governance and legitimacy: it recruits talent from all social strata, thereby increasing social mobility. The political legitimacy of the state will be affected by any problems that occurr in such open, universal, competitive, and restricted examinations. This is a fundamental reason why reforming an examination system, such as the imperial examination system in China, is so difficult.

For Type B states, the most important issue is to strike a balance between aggregate investment and aggregate returns, between productive human capital and distributive human capital. If the aggregate investment in distributive human capital or personal return is not sufficient, the state will cease to function or fail to recruit sufficient and reliable talent to administer its territory. This will jeopardize the interests of the people and the various interest groups. On the other hand, if aggregate distributive human capital is overabundant, then productive human capital will be reduced in aggregate as a social resource, and the state economy will lose rental income. If the return on distributive human capital is too high, economic activities will be less attractive for talented people and economic growth and innovation will stall. Therefore, the fundamental issue of talent deployment is to balance the investment and return on productive human capital and distributive human capital.

In Type B states, the return on distributive human capital is higher than the return on productive human capital. Distributive human capital is not deployed and supplied based on a market approach. Furthermore, its supply is monopolized by the state. In the process of the popularization of secondary and tertiary education, students and parents are keen on distributive human capital investments due to the higher returns they will receive. In such circumstances, various social groups compete for government positions that involve a degree of authority over social wealth distribution. This situation forces the education system to provide more educational opportunities related to distributive human capital. The supply and demand of distributive human capital are mismatched. On the one hand, the education system lowers the investment threshold to encourage supply, such as through lower admissions and credit requirements (the latter including student loans provided by the government). On the other hand, distributive human capital has a rigid level of demand in society. If such rigidity cannot be retained, insiders will see their returns reduced and the threshold of investment will be tightened. This will cause an oversupply of distributive human capital and the polarization of distributive human capital. The group with distributive human capital that will have the chance to realize their investment will have a higher return, while the group without equal opportunities in this regard will not be able to recover their investment.

In some circumstances, the government can predict the above result that is caused by education expansion. The government will restructure the education system and prevent education providers (i.e. schools) from expanding the distributive capital supply aiming to meet learners' demands. Namely, the government will promulgate policies in favor of vocational education. However, if the government does not solve the return gap between distributive human capital and productive human capital, there will be a perpetual problem with it comes to the government's system-wide adjustment, people's demand for distributive human capital investment, and schools' ability to meet such demand.

In Type B states, the government maintains its legitimacy through offering a higher return on distributive human capital. Apart from this, the return on productive human capital is low in the context of education. This is because the bureaucracy decides how property ownership will be re-arranged and defined, leaving personal or group properties without proper protections. When intellectual property is not adequately protected, innovative knowledge and skills – the most important output of productive human capital – will not become a tradable commodity separated from the creators and will not be widely transmitted through the formal education system. In such circumstances, the transmission of advanced productive human capital relies on individual human capital owners. Teaching productive skills and knowledge is a division of labor for education. However, the formal education system often fails to keep up with the latest industrial and commercial developments and teaches students outdated concepts and skills.

In 1996, Pritchett raised the question, "Where has all the education gone?", which led people to pay more attention to the relationship between education and economic growth and economic activities. Given the analysis presented above, we are able to answer this question from two perspectives. First, formal education tends to train through a distributive human capital approach, in which it is difficult for people to realize a return on investment. Second, formal education only provides superficial vocational education; it does not teach practical knowledge and skills needed in productive activities. Both kinds of education are non-cost-recovery human capital investments. To this extent, educational failure means a country's failure, and education reform shall begin with the state being able to recognize that there is a need for it.

Note

1 It's noted that distributive human capital does not only refer to non-productive human capital.

References

Becker, G. 1987. *Human Capital*. Translated by L. Xiaomin. Beijing: Peking University Press.
Collins, R. 1971. "Functional and Conflict Theories of Educational Stratification." *American Sociological Review* 36(6): 1002–1019.
Durkheim, E. 2003. *The Evolution of Educational Thought*. Translated by L. Kang. Shanghai: Shanghai People's Press.
Epstein, S. R. 1998. "Craft Guilds, Apprenticeship, and Technological Change in Pre-Industrial Europe." *Journal of Economic History* 58(3): 684–713.
Fang, N. 1996. "The Imperial Examination System and the Modern Civil Official System: An Interpretation of Modern Politics from the Perspective of the Imperial Examination System." *Strategy and Management* 6: 66–69.
Green, A. 2004. *Education and State Formation: Europe, East Asia, and the USA*. Translated by W. Chunhua. Beijing: Educational Science Publishing House.
Holcombe, R. G. 1997. "A Theory of the Theory of Public Goods." *Review of Austrian Economics* 10(1): 1–22.
Hornbeck, D. W. & L. M. Salamon (eds). 1991. *Human Capital and America's Future: An Economic Strategy for the Nineties*. Baltimore, MD: The Johns Hopkins University Press.
Liping, S. 1996. "The Imperial Examination System: A Mechanism to Shortlist Elites." *Strategy and Management* 5: 38–45.
Marx, K. 1998. *Economic Manuscript of 1861–1863*. Beijing: People's Publishing House.

Ogilvie, S. 2004. "Guilds, Efficiency, and Social Capital: Evidence from German Proto-Industry." *Economic History Review* 57(2): 286–333.

Olson, M. L. 2007. *The Rise and Decline of Nations: Economic Growth, Stagflation, and Social Rigidities*. Translated by L. Zenggang. Shanghai: Shanghai People's Press.

Peiqing, S. 2002. *The History of Chinese Education*. Shanghai: East China Normal University Press.

Pritchett, L. 1996. *Where Has all the Education Gone?* Policy Research Working Paper 1581. Washington, DC: The World Bank.

Qian, S. 2008. *Records of the Grand Historian*. Beijing: Zhonghua Book Company.

Smith, A. 2002. *An Inquiry into the Nature and Causes of the Wealth of Nations*. Translated by G. Dali & W. Ya'nan. Beijing: The Commercial Press.

Von Hayek, F. A. 1997. *The Constitution of Liberty*. Translated by D. Zhenglai. Beijing: Joint Publishing.

Weber, M. 2004. *Politics as a Vocation*. Translated by Q. Yongxiang. Guilin, China: Guangxi Normal University Press.

Zang, X. 2001. "Educational Credentials, Elite Dualism, and Elite Stratification in China." *Sociological Perspectives* 44(2): 189–205.

8 Technology in the development of education

Guo Wenge

Background

In the traditional narrative of the history of education, technology is not given much emphasis. The main reason for this lies in the slow development of educational technology as a whole. Remarkable changes in media technology (or communications technology) have occurred only a few times throughout the long stretch of recorded history. Within a certain historical time frame, its influence is often hardly able to be directly observed or specifically recognized. For example, from the fifteenth century to the twentieth century it was the printing press that served as the major media technology supporting educational development. Yet it played a more or less "silent role" in this process, supporting significant changes in educational theory, educational content, and educational approaches. And so this is how technology has come to occupy a minor role in the history of education.

The rapid development of electronic media in the twentieth century aroused the enthusiasm of academics researching human communication. The fields of communication studies and educational technology (among other related disciplines) had their origins in the middle of the twentieth century. In the 1960s, Marshall McLuhan form the University of Toronto, Eric Havelock from Harvard University, Jack Goody from the University of Cambridge, and the famous French structuralist Claude Lévi-Strauss from the University of Paris all published their research on media, oral traditions, and literacy. This new research triggered discussions about orality and literacy, and sparked a huge debate in the intellectual circles of the West, a debate that lasted throughout the second half of the twentieth century and involved professors from almost every discipline in the humanities (Havelock 2003). Works published in the late twentieth century on book history (Barbier 2005; Cang 2007), reading history (Manguel 2004), social history (Burke 2000), and intellectual history (Le Goff 1996) all involved a great deal of analysis on printing technology and paper-making technology. At the turn of the twenty-first century, Western views on education and technology influenced China's educational policies regarding online education, and both the former and the latter should be understood and interpreted in light of the aforementioned debate.

There are subtle differences in the objectives of the various strands of media technology research. In fact, this research is as diverse as the many definitions that have been given for the term "media" itself. For example, some research has focused on the development and evolution of the means of mass communication, such as newspapers, magazines, and television programs, while other research has focused on carriers of content, such as papers, printers, compact discs (CDs), digital video discs (DVDs), and computers. The history of media is often viewed from the perspectives of media technology and mass communication (Briggs & Burke 2009). Scholars in the mid-twentieth century who specialized in these two fields were particularly interested in the influence of media technology on social development and human expression. And it is this research that has led to the sub-fields of media analytics and oral communication.

The study of media technology was initiated by Canadian economist Harold Innis (Innis 2003; 2004). McLuhan considered himself a student of Innis and, based on Innis' research, resonantly asserted that "the medium is the message" (McLuhan & Zingrone 2000). Media analytics scholars have long been interested in a series of changes that occurred before and after major media technology transformations, such as the transition of ancient Greek civilization from oral tradition to literacy in the fourth and fifth centuries BC, and the change in the appearance of books and the way which their contents were organized before and after advent of printers in the middle of the fifteenth century. These scholars have linked these "discontinuous" changes to remarkable transformations in technology. Basing their analyses on a rather large historical timescale, they outline the entire process by which media technology influenced society and brought about social change. Such a macro-analysis based on a large time span boasts the ability to observe with a bird's-eye view the general trend of how media technology helped bring about social transformation. However, its disadvantage is that it lacks detailed observations on the transformation processes caused by specific new media technologies. Therefore, some academics have made the criticism that the analyses of media analytics scholars of social transformations are oversimplified and are tantamount to a sort of "technological determinism" (Briggs & Burke 2009). Since the emergence of the Internet, however, and as humans face one more tremendous change in media technology, the viewpoint of the "media analysis school", as it were, has gained a great deal of attention. Works produced by scholars from this school[1] have bene translated into numerous languages and have exerted a great deal of influence on research in such fields as communications, education, intelligence research, knowledge engineering, and artificial intelligence.

Scholars researching oral tradition include Eric Havelock (2003), Jack Goody (2005), and Walter Ong (2000). Their analyses of the transition (mentioned above) of ancient Greek civilization from oral tradition to literacy; the cognitive and expressive features of oral tradition (Ong 2000); and the processes experience storage, memorization, and duplication (Goody

2005; Havelock 2003) during oral expression provide us with rare insight into the role that "media" plays in human expression, knowledge storage and summarization, as well as knowledge processing, sharing, and use.

The achievements of the media analysis school and their research into oral tradition offer us a unique perspective (having examined an abundant amount of historical materials) on the educational transformation brought about by the Internet, allowing us to understand that "information technology exerts a revolutionary influence on education development" (Ministry of Education 2010). However, due to the overly extensive scope of communications technology that affects politics, economics, culture, and education, these works present a vast quantity of historical data and explanatory arguments, making it hard for readers to gain a clear picture of how media technology and educational development in particular are related.[2] It is a fundamental task for education technology researchers, then, to sort out and clarify the arguments that pertain to how media technology has affected educational development.

I first started to pay attention to media-related issues when the first Internet bubble burst in 2000, and I started to focus my research on the media when I decided to carry out a study on the topic "Research on the Policy Transition of and Future Reaction to Modern Remote Education Pilot Programs," which was listed Ministry of Education as a key subject in its tenth five-year plan for national education science. During my research on network education positioning and my analysis of network education policy transitions, I started to see a lack of analysis on the topic of how technology has related historically to education. Probing the interrelationship between media technology and education, and looking at the historical relationship between these two phenomena from the macro perspective of education development history will be of great importance for the "top-layer design" of IT-based education, positioning network education, and helping society form a consensus around developing "new media and new education."

In the following sections, I will first present and explore a select number of Western academic works on the topic of media analysis and oral tradition. Second, I will propose a definition for "media technology," which holds that a new media technology can be defined with the use of four dimensions, namely, symbols, carriers, copying methods, and dissemination characteristics. This fourfold definition will serve as a basic observation unit (variable) for my subsequent analysis of media technology and educational development. Third, based on my new definition of media technology, I will explore what I take to be the five historical stages of media technology development, arguing that each kind of "new media" brings with it something new; finally, on the basis of my analysis, I will propose a framework of the history of technology in the development education, so as to be able to interpret the interrelation between "media" and "education" from a historical perspective. In short, I will try to use the five stages of media technology development to determine the ways in which technology has influenced educational development.

Defining "technology"

The word "technology" has many connotations. Standard definitions range from describing pure hardware to describing specific ways to solve problems. John Kenneth Galbraith, an American economist, defines technology as a "systematic application of scientific or other organized knowledge to practical tasks." However, at the mention of the very word "technology," many people still think of computers, CD players, space shuttles, and various other sorts of technological products (Smaldino 2008). This shows that "technology" can refer to either a specific kind of product or to a specific process.

In the broadest sense, all technologies influence the development of human education, but with regard to what educational technology is concerned with, "technology" does not refer to all "technologies" in general. Briefly speaking, educational technology mainly focuses on a specific kind of "technology," that is, media (or communication) technology. Both printing technology and radio and television (TV) can be classified into the extensive category of communication technology. IT is, by its very nature, also a sort of communication or media technology.

In human history, the following media technologies have facilitated human expression, exchange, and communication: oral language; pictographs; the alphabet; the use of diagrams, bones, or tortoise shells for inscriptions; bamboo slips; papyrus; man-made paper; parchment; the movable-type printer; Morse code; the telegraph; the telephone; the analog electric signal; film; radio; TV; recording type; the video tape; the CD; binary digits; the computer; the DVD; and the Internet. Such technologies are what allow for the existence of "World 3" in the theory of three worlds proposed by Austrian philosopher Karl Popper. One can see that human scientific exploration, education/teaching, and social organization are all generated and developed with the support of such technologies.

It was less than 100 years ago that researchers saw such technologies (some of them, at any rate) as remarkable influencing factors on education. The emergence of educational technology as a field shows just how much had changed in this period: within the last 100 years, remote electronic communication technology has developed by leaps and bounds. Therefore, in educational technology research the concept of "technology" has been constantly varying along with development of electronic communications technology and, as a result, has not come to be regarded as a steady analysis variable and observation unit.

The basis of academic research lies in the development of a core concept. What sort of "unit" serves as a core variable for observing and analyzing relationships between phenomena plays a crucial role in formulating sound arguments. A poorly defined core concept is likely to result in "useless" disputes in academic research. For example, are the categories "multimedia" and "interaction" two variables that are independent from each other, or are they two different properties of a "media technology"? This question has generated much debate in educational technology research. In this field, the debate on the relationship between "media theory" and "study theory", the discussion on "materialized technology" and "intelligent technology," and the change of research focus from "media" to "interaction" all originated from a failure to clarify the relationship among three key core concepts: technology, multimedia, and interaction.

Therefore, providing a clear definition of "technology" is the first step in analyzing the historical relationship between "media technology" and "education." Due to a lack of space, I will not run through an exhaustive list of definitions of "technology"; rather, I will focus directly on the term I introduced above, namely, "media technology."

Media technology

It is worth noting that when people mention "media technology," they generally refer to the combination of several technologies rather than to a certain singular technology. For example, when we speak of "printing technology," we usually refer to words as symbols of expression, paper as a writing carrier, what is written being copied by printers, and books being shipped by train or by plane. When we mention "IT," we refer to "ideographic symbols" (words, sounds, and video); "storage and communication symbols" (binary digital signals); and "carriers" (computers). IT content is transmitted by way of copying, pasting, and sending; and information is communicated by the flow of electric charge. Likewise, when we talk about vocal music, literacy, and TV, we refer, respectively, to a group of symbols, carriers, copying methods, and a series of dissemination characteristics that arise therefrom. Therefore, in defining media technology, such properties as symbols, carriers, copying means and dissemination characteristics should be taken into consideration.

Additionally, since "media technology," as I have just defined it, will be examined in the context of its historical link the development of education, it is necessary to effectively explain the main educational developments of the past. Presently, the most prominent theories offering explanations for educational transformation are the "four intellectual revolutions" proposed by Ashby (1983), the "three crises" of Western education triggered by media transformation proposed by Postman (2004a), and the four stages of the evolution of education communication technology proposed by Nan (2005). Upon further analysis, one can see that the later three revolutions in Ashby's theory were triggered by media technology and that these three media technology revolutions (as it were) are more or less identical to the "three crises" proposed by Postman, which refer to the transitions from oral tradition to literacy, from literacy to printing, and from printing to electronic communication media. Due to technological limitations of the times in which they wrote, Ashby and Postman did not differentiate between the Internet (digital media) and TV (electronic media). Nan explores the relationship between the Internet and TV, but he ignores the transformation that came about as a result of printers. He combines the stages before and after the creation of printers into a single stage which he calls "literacy," a methodological move which obviously fails to explain the enormous transformations brought about by printers. Based on overall analysis presented in this study, the history of media technology is divided into five major stages: tradition, literacy, printing, electronic media (TV as a typical example), and digital media. This categorization has the advantage of being compliant with major views on the history of communications.

The definition of media proposed herein also borrows from definition of media technology proposed by Kozma and research on media carried out by the so-called "media ecology school."[3] According to Kozma, media "can be defined by their technology, their symbol systems, and their processing capabilities" Kozma (1991).[4] He argued that the most distinctive feature of media is technology; however, the influence it has on teaching mainly comes from the other two features – what symbol system it supports and what processing capability it presents. The media ecology school holds that the emergence of new media technology will gradually cause changes in symbol expression, human-machine interaction, and social communication structure, and that it will subsequently change – in a systematic way – the communication ecology and social environment of society.

To summarize the foregoing analysis, media technology can explain several major transformations in the history of education. Media technology is a sort of technology that supports human expression, exchange, and communication. It has four dimensions or sub-properties: expression symbols, carrier types, copying methods, and dissemination characteristics. Expression symbols refer to such symbol systems as oral language, alphabetic writing, images, visual and aural language, electronic impulse signals, and binary system signals. Symbols are the basic units of human expression. They determine what kinds of expression a given media technology supports. Carriers refer to the materials used for the writing, storage, communication, and display of content. Papyrus, parchment, man-made paper, recording tapes, CDs, TVs, computers, CDs, hard disks, flash drives, and the Internet all fall into this category. Copying methods refer to the ways in which content is duplicated and include oral tradition, literacy, machine printing, TV broadcasting, and uploading and downloading. Content copying methods exert a decisive influence on the accuracy and speed of communications. Finally, dissemination characteristics refer to the difference between human-machine interaction and interpersonal interaction caused by differences in the expression symbols, carrier types, and copying methods involved. Dissemination characteristics determine the communication ecology of a society and exert a profound influence on a given society's political, economic, and education systems. "Unilateral," "bilateral," "synchronous," "asynchronous," and "interactive" are all adjectives used to describe the dissemination characteristics of media communication.

This fourfold definition of media technology serves as the basis for the present study. Below, it will be taken as the core variable for analyzing the influence of media technology on human scientific exploration and educational communication.

History of media technology development

Starting from the definition of media technology (discussed above) and based on what I have borrowed from theory of media ecology, I will now use the four dimensions of symbol, carrier, copying, and dissemination as a basis for reorganizing the historical development of media technology into the following scheme.

Table 8.1 shows the analytical framework for the five stages of media technology development.

When, in the past, oral tradition gave way to literacy, and electronic communication gave way to digital communication (to name two transformations), one or more of the above-mentioned media technology dimensions were present. Each such transformation resulted in a brand new social communication ecology and a significant change in society's political, economic, and education systems.

Oral tradition age

The main features of media technology with regard to oral tradition are as follows: expression symbols comprise oral language that is made up of various syllables produced from the throat. People are both creators and carriers of content. The recording of human experience and wisdom has to rely solely on human memory, as it cannot rely on an external recording carrier.

To facilitate memorization, oral rhetoric mainly relies on rhythmic poems, proverbs, and other means to present human observations on external natural phenomena and historical events, and to record what has occurred. In the age of oral tradition, those engaged in "recording" and "copying" were minstrels. Homer was an excellent example of a minstrel.

In spite of this, the contents of oral tradition are often forgotten or revised by minstrels (intentionally or unintentionally) during the process of recitation or singing. As time goes by, the "recording" of facts gradually turns into the recitation of a story, which then turns into a legend and a fable. Therefore, few people took Homer's epic poems as serious historic works (in the modern sense of the term "history"). It was only in the nineteenth century when Heinrich Schliemann, a German archeologist who discovered ancient Troy (in modern-day Turkey) based on clues provided in Homer's *Iliad*, that people realized that the *Iliad* is a "traditional history" and that it was the defects of tradition that turned these once true "recordings" into fables and legends.

In the oral tradition age, human communication mainly relied on "shouting." People could basically only interact and trade with those within shouting distance. This also determined the scale of organized human cooperation. In that age, humans mainly lived in tribes and were for the most part quite self-sufficient when it came to meeting their basic everyday needs.

Table 8.1 History of media technology development

Age	Symbol	Carrier	Copying	Dissemination
Oral tradition: before the fourth century BC	Oral language	People	Those performing traditions/memory holders going around	People: Synchronous and bilateral communication Social communication agent: minstrels
Literacy: from the mid-fourth century BC to around 1450	Alphabetic writing	Papyrus, parchment and man-made paper	Literacy, people going around/traveling by horse	Paper: Asynchronous and unilateral communication, Social communication agent: scribe
Printing: from 1450 to the present	Alphabetic writing	Man-made paper	Printer, means of transportation	Paper: Asynchronous and bilateral communication, Social communication agent: Book publication, newspaper, periodicals, magazine, printing, and paper-making
Electronic communication: from 1830 to the present	Ideograph: Storage and transmission symbol	Recording tape/video tape, CD, platter, TV	Radio and TV station, video transcription	Radio/TV: Unilateral communication; Social communication agent: TV Collection/compilation/broadcasting/compilation/direction/performance
Digital communication: from 1990 to the present	Ideograph: Storage and transmission symbol	Hard disk, CD, monitor, speaker	Copy, paste, upload, download	Network: Synchronous, asynchronous, and bilateral communication Social communication agent: you

Literacy age

Compared with oral tradition, literacy presented two innovations. First, the ancient Greeks created a new set of expression symbols – alphabetic writing. Second, carriers for recording content changed from people to external material, namely, papyrus and parchment.

The introduction of this new carrier for writing saw the start of a new chapter for human civilization: "Symbols for one thing do not equal that thing itself; symbols may be used when the very thing is not present" (Goffman 2009: 213). The separation of content from its source brought with it a revolutionary transformation in the size and scale of social organization. Papyrus, for example, made possible organized human coordination beyond the level of "shouting." The scale of social organization expanded rapidly, and a series of innovations were made in politics and academic research. Official documents written on papyrus became essential tools and came to be the basis for the political operation and administration of the city-states of ancient Greece. Thanks to the use of papyrus, Aristotle developed the very first organized academic research facility in human history. The Library of Alexandria accumulated 500,000 books as papyrus rolls, establishing itself as the one of the world's earliest large-scale knowledge repositories.

In this age, content "copying" solely relied on manual writing by "scribes." Manual writing was slow and error-prone. Moreover, papyrus and parchment were rare and expensive. In the Middle Ages, parchments were mainly in the hands of the Church. This hindered the spread of knowledge about the ancient world: the achievements of Greek civilization had limited influence on local politics and culture. Though hand-copied books of various qualities could be bought at a reasonable price on the bookstalls of Athens and Alexandria, papyrus shortages would have occurred even in Egypt had education been even slightly more widespread (Wells 2001). In the literacy age, reading and writing were activities that only a small number of elites engaged in. Common people still relied on oral language for obtaining and exchanging information. As far as common people were concerned, reading and writing were not indispensable skills.

Printing age

Compared with literacy, printing technology brought about new changes in the two dimensions of "carrier" and "copying": first, man-made paper took the place of parchment; and second, printers took the place of scribes. The transformation of the two technologies thoroughly changed the depressive atmosphere of the Middle Ages in the West; Western societies were now on their way to modernization.

Man-made paper came in sufficient quantities, while printers were accurate and highly efficient in copying. The results caused by these two technological transformations were that anyone could get enough to read so long as they wanted to read, and that anyone could get enough man-made paper so long as they wanted to write. Printing technology shaped a sort of brand-new social media ecology. This ecology, reliant on "letter symbols," based on paper, and supporting bilateral expression and exchange, provided fertile soil for the Renaissance, the Age of Discovery, the Scientific Revolution, and the Industrial Revolution. The historical point in time where the East (especially China) was eclipsed by the rise of Europe can be traced back to the invention of the Gutenberg printing press.

One hundred years after the creation of printers, reading and writing became indispensable skills, while book, newspaper, and journal publication started to take off. A major innovation in human education, namely, the modern education system itself, gradually came into existence and spread across the globe.

Electronic communication age

As opposed to the carrier and copying dimensions, the greatest innovation in the field electronic communication arose in the expression symbol dimension in the form of the electronic impulse signal. A complete electronic communication process requires two kinds of symbols: ideographs and storage/transmission symbols. The former includes text, sound, and dynamic video images. During storage and transmission, ideographs are converted into electronic impulse signals; after arriving at the receiving end, electronic impulse signals are converted back into ideographs.

The separation of the ideographic and storage/transmission symbols produces two results: first, information is transmitted at the speed of an electronic impulse, so a piece of information can make several trips around the world instantaneously. With the scope of human communication now much larger than it has ever been, the world now rapidly turns into a "global village." Second, the interconversion between ideographs and electronic signals, and the mixed expression of multi-variety symbols – including text, audio, and video – brings human writing from an age dominated by the letter to an age dominated by the image. Once this transformation occurred, people started to record events with cameras. Oral tradition, at this stage, is already ancient history, as it were, with much of the richness and detail of oral tales having already been lost when they were put to paper. Image-based recording has the advantage of being able to be "read" by people with various educational backgrounds and of retaining a lot more information (e.g. scene, apparel, posture) than text. It is clear, then, that human communication (in terms of the recording and expressing of information) had entered into a new historical age.

Before the emergence of the Internet, electronic communication was in fact a closed information transmission network. Similar to what happened when literacy came to replace oral tradition, radio and TV came about in small stages: radio transmission channels were rare, and writing based on "film"

Technology in the development of education 133

was expensive and complicated. With all these obstacles, the right for "image-based writing" belonged to a group of professional craftsmen. Video programs that common people "watched" were generally completed by professionals engaged in collection, compilation, broadcasting, and direction. As soon as someone expressed interest in presenting their viewpoints on a carrier like TV, for example, they were immediately met with restrictions. Therefore, although TV was (and still is) an effective means of publicity for political and commercial propaganda, its role in education was severely limited because it was a form of "unilateral communication."

Digital communication age

Just as with electronic communication media, digital communication media, as represented by the Internet, also brought about two innovations. In this case, they were based on the "expression symbol" and "carrier" dimensions. First, the digital signal took the place of the analog signal; and second, the open communication of the Internet took the place of the closed TV network.

The Internet affected and influenced TV in the way the printer affected and influenced literacy. First of all, the Internet is a carrier for writing. It is like a "huge paper" covering the earth's surface. Each person who can access the Internet can write articles, post photos, play video clips, and publish songs on this "paper." Second, the Internet is an open publication platform, whereas the TV was a closed communication network. It simplified "publication," reducing it to a matter of "copying and pasting" and "uploading and downloading" and providing unprecedented opportunities for individualized expression and publication.

On the Internet, which was, at the time of its introduction, a new writing and reading platform, is where a series of new expression symbols started to appear and gain a great deal of popularity. The most typical of these was the network game. The newly arrived network games, in addition to presenting static content, let "readers" experience history in person through role substitution. And based on scenario and rule design, they also had "readers" going to different virtual locations so the latter could connect with each other online. This also helped them hone their strategic awareness and teach them tactical skills so as to be able to complete various complex tasks. Compared to traditional reading, network games provided an unprecedented kind of "immersed reading" for users (the "readers"). An education game in Hong Kong, for example, takes economic statistical data (for a certain number of years) and displays in which in such a way that students can visually experience the influence of periodic economic fluctuation on government policy decisions. Thanks to the way in which the game allows users to experience information, one no longer needs to thumb through endless pages of tedious annual reports.

The Internet seems to have come to dominate the media technology landscape. Printing technology, which dominated the educational communication

Media technology and social development: solving the Needham Puzzle

In the middle of the fifteenth century, both the Chinese and Europeans had grasped man-made paper-making and movable-type printer technologies. But why did modern science (ushered in through the Scientific Revolution) only emerge in Europe? Why was China surpassed by the Europe in spite of the fact that it was more technologically advanced than Europe in the Middle Ages? How did such a change happen? The process by which scientific and technological advances took hold in Europe, allowing it to surpass other areas of the world, is known as the "Great Divergence."

This puzzle can be partially solved starting with the fourfold definition of "media technology" explained above. In the middle of the fifteenth century, as I just mentioned, both the Europeans and Chinese had grasped man-made paper making and movable-type printing technologies, but the number of literacy symbols, that is, the quantity of movable types, gave rise to the following two issues. The first one had to do the nature of the work itself: European typesetters only needed to differentiate 26 letters, while Chinese workers had to identify 10,000 Chinese characters. The second issue had to do with typesetting efficiency: in Europe, to set a character, you had to choose one letter from 26 letters, while in China you had to choose 1 from among 10,000 characters. The combined effect of these two issues was a sharp increase in printed materials and literate populations in Western states in from 1400 to 1900. On the other hand, although China invented movable-type printing technology before Europe, its publication methods still relied on block printing, so its social reading culture and literate population remained on par with Europe in the Middle Ages. When the People's Republic of China was founded in 1949, half of China's population was still illiterate.

Taking this as the background for analyzing the reversal of development process of oriental and Western societies in the fifteenth century may probably help us understand and experience the influence of media technology on social advance and scientific development.

Technology in the development of education

Based on definition of "media technology" proposed in the paper, the mark for emergence of "new media" was made on the key time point of education history, and the analysis framework of five-stage education "technology" development history is obtained, as shown in Table 8.2.

From the perspective of the history of media technology as well as from the history of its connection with education, an innovative form of media technology generally initiated an educational transformation in two stages. In the

Table 8.2 Technology in the development of education

Media technology	Education goal	Education resource	Education method	Education organization pattern
Oral tradition	Development of minstrels	Oral education materials: kept in mind	Oral dialogue	Face to face
Literacy	Development of scribes	Manually copied education materials: Inconsistent content, formats and page numbers	Lecturing, memorization, debate	Benedictine education rules, mundane, common old-style private schools
Printed text	Popularized mandatory education	Standard teaching materials library	Experiment-based teaching, exploration-based teaching, case study	Class-based teaching mechanism, modern school mechanism
Electronic communication	Higher education, popularized distance education	Video teaching materials and education programs	Remote teaching: separation between teaching and learning in terms of time and space	Distance education through radio and TV
Digital communication	Life-long education: Education can be received by everyone everywhere and any time	Online materials based on multiple media	Individualized teaching	Mixed-style learning: Mixing of teaching materials and mixing of classrooms

136 *Technology in the development of education*

first stage, new media forms took the place of old ones, while the content they communicated generally remained the same. Using papyrus for recording traditional poems and using printers for copying manually written drafts were both typical examples of using new media for "carrying" old content. In the second stage, new content was carried by the new media. In the context of a new "expression" environment, new compositional approaches and knowledge communication methods emerged. "Abstract classification, formal logic inference and definition" came about in written form thanks to the emergence of papyrus, which later evolved into printed materials, Ramus teaching materials, and eventually the differentiation of academic disciplines (Ong 2008: 104).

Furthermore, from the perspective of the industrial chain, the influence of new media technology on education goes beyond the processes of teaching and learning to include research and development (R&D), communication, training, and business analytics. Under the influence of IT, not are industrial chain processes changed but, more importantly, the entire industrial chain itself is transformed, which means that certain processes and certain occupations come into existence, while others disappear completely.[5]

Now, I will turn to the five-stage stages of media technology innovation referred to above, so as to paint a more detailed picture of the history of human scientific advancement and its relationship with education and the passing down of knowledge from one generation to the next.

Oral tradition age

In Greece, in the middle of the fourth century BC, writing on papyrus with alphabetic language started to cut into the dominance of oral tradition in a major way (Innis 2003). Before this development, the Greeks mainly relied on oral language to "memorize" lived experience and ancient wisdom. This was the period of the transition from oral tradition to literacy. As Socrates did not write and in fact objected to writing, his thoughts were passed on until today by his student Plato (i.e. the dialogues). So it is safe to say that the boundary between oral tradition and literacy probably lay between Socrates and Plato.

Expression in tradition age

As it was, at one point, impossible to store human lived experience by means of written documents, human expression had to facilitate memory storage and memory activation. And this was able to be achieved, for example, at various kinds of celebratory activities (e.g. festivals, commemorations) that were often held in traditional societies. Individual memory was activated and engaged with the use of performance, sound, movement, and image.

Basic structures of expression in the oral tradition age were cliché and parlance. At that time, "the whole oral tradition knowledge circle or thinkers all relied on ... parlance to construct thoughts ... already obtained knowledge had to be repeatedly stated, otherwise it would be forgotten; fixed and set thinking patterns were a must for wisdom and valid management" (Ong 2008: 42).

Traditional expression relied on aural perception and lacked such abstract means of expression as classification and inference: "Tradition culture could not tackle with geometric figures, abstract classification, formal logic inference and defining at all" and the "use of analysis-based questions to train students and others seemed to emerge as late as in the late stage of text-based learning" (Ong 2008: 17, 42).

Education in oral tradition age

Obviously, the oral tradition age had not seen a transition akin to a move from, in the words of Ashby, "family to Christian church or synagogue" (Ashby 1983: 37). Family-based tribes used fables and stories, usually in gatherings, to ensure that their children would learn about ancient traditions and learn certain social responsibilities.

In the oral tradition age, there existed a group of men who were like minstrels and who were responsible for "storing" cultural traditions of their own tribes. During local gatherings, they would sing by heart what they had memorized in their minds. The duty of these minstrels to record their culture and move it forward made them akin to "oral books," as it were, or a set of "oral education materials." The education of these minstrels mainly relied on a teacher-pupil relationship: it was individualized. The collective experiences and wisdom of a culture were "copied" and "inherited" by way of repeated recitation and practice.

Literacy age

In the literacy age, the basic symbol system of communication changed from oral language to alphabetic writing. Interestingly, the texts that first appeared on papyrus were oral tales like Homer's epic poems. Immediately, new communication media technology gave rise to new means of expression, and formulation styles like classification and analysis started to emerge.

With papyrus as an external recording carrier, it was now possible for people to collect observations of natural phenomena scattered all over the world and gather them in the form of letter symbols. And with these symbols, they were able to express comparison, differentiation, classification in a symbolic system of knowledge representation. Such "knowledge" differs from discrete individual observations and thinking. Rather, it is built upon the basis of the observation and communication of social communities; it is a form of social construction. Such "social construction" can serve as a point of entry for thinking about and researching the relationship between media technology and in-depth knowledge.

Papyrus and the academic research of Aristotle

Thanks to the help of papyrus, Aristotle developed the first organized research center in human history. Over an extended period of time in the fourth century, Aristotle hired over one thousand people to carry papyrus and visit sites in Greece and in other places in the ancient world so as to collect and record natural and historical information on his behalf. These people had not received any specific academic research training. Their main task was to collect oral legends from around the ancient world, record them on papyrus, and take them back to Athens.

How did Aristotle process the huge amount of information collected by these "researchers"? Unfortunately, there is no answer to this question because (somewhat ironically) no record of detailing his proves survives. Obviously, Aristotle needed sufficient space to unroll these papyrus records for reading, and he likely established a classification/indexing system based on location and chronological period. Aristotle needed to establish some kind of scientific baseline in order to make logical sense of the many contradictory legends. Basic data analysis techniques such as classification and inference started at this time.

As an epitomizer of the philosophy of ancient Greece, Aristotle stressed the concepts of differentiation and comparison, and he set the stage for future researchers seeking to gather and analyze vast quantities of information. Behind his great undertaking, of course, were the "new" media technologies of papyrus and alphabetic writing.

THE LIBRARY OF ALEXANDRIA

According to historical records, over the course of the third and second centuries BC, the Ptolemaic Dynasty in Egypt established Library of Alexandria. The cost of this undertaking was steep, to say the least, for the monarchs had to engage people for copying, writing, editing, and merging documents in addition to those they hired for the construction of the structure. During its heyday, the library boasted the largest number of volumes, the largest variety of document types, and most complete set of records in the world.

At that time, all commercial ships entering Alexandria's port were subject to rummage; all papyri and manuscripts were copied by Egyptian scribes. All original copies were kept in the Library of Alexandria while duplicated copies were given to their owners. Additionally, the Ptolemaic Dynasty also collected and purchased, at great cost, volumes from all over the world. At its pinnacle, the Library of Alexandria accommodated 500,000 volumes, including translated manuscripts for the very first Greek version of The Old Testament (i.e. The Septuagint or LXX); all verse manuscripts of the works of Homer, the ancient Greek epic poet; and the authentic manuscripts of Euclid's *Elements of Geometry*, and authentic manuscripts three major Greek tragedians, Aeschylus, Sophocles, and Euripides.

The process of gathering of vast quantities of scrolls in Alexandria also attracted elites from all over the world to travel there where so as to undertake their own teaching and research activities. The ancient Greek astronomer Eratosthenes and the philologist Aristarchus were once curators of Library of Alexandria, and the philosopher Aenesidemus and the mathematician and physical scientist Archimedes once lectured or sought education there. Alexandria was also provided with a great many lecture halls. Many students traveled there from afar to receive advanced education in the city.

In addition to the library, museums, astronomical observatories, laboratories, dissecting rooms, botanical gardens, and zoos were also founded in Alexandria, serving as the very first research institutes and educational organizations set up by a state in the history of human civilization.

THE DEVELOPMENT OF EDUCATION IN ANCIENT GREECE AND ROME

Schools in Roman times roughly fell into three categories: elementary schools, which were private-pay schools; grammar schools, where grammar and the works of the great poets of old were learned; and elocution schools, which were schools for advanced study. The teaching objective of elocution schools was to form elite Roman citizens and politicians. The curriculum at such schools included such fields as astronomy, mathematics, music, philosophy, ethics, logic, and law. Additionally, students were instructed in the art of rhetoric, receiving training in how to control their tone, rhyme, cadence, facial expression, posture, manner, and bearing while speaking. Instructors usually had students memorize and recite famous speeches of the past (i.e. from Greek and Roman history) and eventually write their own set speeches (i.e. commemorative speeches, deliberative political speeches) and debate one another in class (Quintilian 1989).

The essential educational strength of the elocution school was the rigorous training it provided in logic and rhetoric (oral expression) with the aid of written materials. This meant, however, that the school and social affairs at Rome still very much relied on oral communication.

In fact, due to the limited number of papyri, the slow speed of manual manuscript copying, and the poor supply of reading materials, literacy education still was restricted to a small number of people. In common social activities, major communication still relied on the use of oral language: it was based on "hearing" and "saying." Therefore, although we trace our modern education system back to ancient Greece and ancient Rome, it may be premature to hold that education system in the classical world had been the result of substantial development.

THE STAGNATION OF EDUCATION IN THE MIDDLE AGES

Western scholars have provided varied explanations for the decline of reading and writing and the decrease in the literate population in the Middle Ages.

One of them holds that the churches' control of parchment texts negatively affected the popularization of education. The transition from papyrus to parchment resulted in the monopoly of churches over knowledge. Therefore, heretical works were ignored while Christian works were valued: "Regarding all knowledge other than the Bible, if it is harmful, sentence it to death; if it is useful, record it ... Mundane knowledge was forbidden while theological research was given priority" (Innis 2003: 35).

Another view holds that in order to achieve a superficial degree of splendor, manuscript fonts were exceptionally bright and ornate in the Middle Ages. Books in that age were extremely luxurious, but they were not for reading at all: "People wrote in neat fonts just to kill the time ... The demand for books in this period was so negligible that contents were not cared for; people decorated books in a sumptuous way just for the court or for some mundane or religious VIPs. All these showed book distribution was very slow ... Besides, books were not for reading by people at all. They were only additions to the wealth of church treasuries and to gains of some of the rich. They were economic wealth rather than treasures of thoughts ... extricate manuscript books became luxury" (Le Goff 1996: 6).

Due to the limited number of writings and the low level of publication efficiency, most of the population in the Middle Ages were illiterate and did not read at all. Education in the Middle Ages for the most part did not involve writing: it was delivered through oral instruction. Students completed their education with apprenticeships and "on-the-job training." The salient feature of schools in the Middle Ages was a "lack of grading mechanisms to arrange programs based on subject difficulty, synchronous teaching of various subjects, mixing of students at varied ages and free course selection by students" (Postman 2004a: 20).

In the Middle Ages, school teaching materials mainly consisted of texts that had been manually copied by the teachers themselves or by others whom the teachers had do the work for them. As a result, the same subjects in different schools tended to be taught in a different sequence, and the content of similarly themed lessons was often inconsistent. And since it was only the instructors who had access to the pedagogical materials, teaching merely relied on the latter delivering information through lecturing and students memorizing as much information as they could: memorization by rote was inevitable.

Printing age

In the fifteenth century, it was in fact two technologies that ushered the West into printing age: from the twelfth to the fourteenth centuries, paper-making technology invented by a Chinese man named Cai Lun gradually spread over the whole of Europe. In the middle of the fifteenth century, Johannes Gutenberg invented the movable type printer. The sufficient supply of man-made paper broke the monopoly of the churches on parchment. Improvement in the accuracy and copying efficiency of printers made it possible for everyone in need to get a copy of any book they wanted. The accuracy of written expression fueled the development of scientific exploration, education, and teaching in an unprecedented way. It allowed Western society to embark on a fast track to modernization. Over time, reading and writing became the requisite elements for scientific advancement and development all across the world.

Written expression

What first appeared on printed books in the literacy age was the Bible. New media forms took the place of old ones while their contents remained virtually unchanged. Next, along with these new media technologies came written expression symbols and an entirely new expression structure.

First, vernaculars like Italian, French, and German replaced Latin and became the main written languages of several Western European countries. Second, innovations in the format or style of written communication kept on evolving during this period. Martin Luther, for example, used a large number of brochures in his religious reform movement as a way to publicize his theological claims. In 1701, the very first English-language daily was born. Edison created the "editorial" for newspapers to replace brochures and short articles. Defoe further reformed the brochure, making news narration a part of the newspaper. In 1779, James Harrison founded *The Novelist* and by doing created to the first ever numbered serialized magazine (Innis 2003).

The content and structure of written expression grew increasingly complex and diversified as time went on. Michel de Montaigne published his personal essays; John Bunyan, a British writer, introduced dialog between two persons in his novel *The Pilgrim's Progress*; and Daniel Defoe introduced story plots into his novels. In 1742, Samuel Richardson integrated plots, figures, depictions and dialogs into his work, making it a novel in the full sense of the term (Innis 2003).

Writing played an increasingly important role in daily life as well. Richardson, for example, compiled a "collection of daily letters covering practical subjects drawing common attention," that is, the Pamela series, to serve as an example of the epistolary style and to have the purpose of "letting country readers learn to write letters" (Innis 2003: 39).

Limited by memories, the quantity of words had been finite and their meanings kept changing. Black text on white paper fixed the meanings of words while the quantity of words then started to keep increasing. Dictionaries and lexicons soon became reference books that were indispensable to intellectuals, while lexicons also established books as symbols of authority.

Written expression enabled humans to, in the world of letters, process complicated temporal-spatial relationships, describe complicated aspects of human nature such as external representation and psychological conflict, explain observable phenomena, and explicate scientific theories. This new ability undoubtedly provided humans with a new means of expression, enabling them to recognize and communicate the natural world and the social environment in which they lived. As mentioned above, printing technology was responsible for the innovation of the existential space and organizational structure of "World 3" in Karl Popper's theory of three worlds. The trivial observation and comprehension of "World 1" by the human brain ("World 2") had a "space" in which to exist, and the "innovation" in expression that letters made possible provided human knowledge with a technological organization and structure.

Thanks to printing media technology, humans managed to gather records on, among other things, various stories and legends, geological surveys, species, political regimes, and economic systems from the ancient world until modern times, and as a result have formed a subject-specific knowledge system. As a result, "what we know about the world in 600 BC is virtually more detailed than whatever living person lived in that age" (Wells 2004: 144). Such an all-around, multi-perspective and multi-tier knowledge system established based on printing technology pooled together human observations and experiences from all over the world.

Printing media technology produced two important concepts that would have a great deal of influence over the fields of modern academic research and modern education and teaching, respectively. First, in the field of academic research, we have the emergence of the scientific research criteria stating that experiments must be "repeatable and verifiable." Second, in the field of education and teaching, there emerged a new way to organize and structure knowledge which is often referred to as the "Ramus method."

Modern academic research criteria: repeatable and verifiable

In the Middle Ages, churches gradually obtained the power to judge what constituted "knowledge" by using their control over the parchment supply. Printing technology broke the monopoly of churches over writing materials and the power of churches to say what was and what was not considered to be knowledge. Amidst the battles between Copernicus and Galileo and Roman Curia, the scientific research criteria of "repeatable and verifiable" began to took shape.

In the sixteenth century, Copernicus proposed the theory of Heliocentrism. To avoid direct conflict with the Roman Curia, he did not formally publish his *De Revolutionibus Orbium Coelestium* (*Revolution of the Heavenly Spheres*) before the end of his life. As soon as the book was published, it was immediately deemed as a treasonous and heinous heresy by the Roman Curia. Giordano Bruno, an Italian scholar, was burned to death on the Campo dei Fior in Rome just because he spread Copernicus' theory. Galileo was sentenced to life imprisonment by Roman Curia as he developed the very theory.

However, once thoughts are expressed and once they are communicated, they obtain an objective existence independent of their maker. So long as churches failed to destroy *De Revolutionibus Orbium Coelestium* the way they had destroyed the parchment it was written on, the spread and growth of the thoughts and ideas contained therein could not be checked. After the death of Copernicus, printing technology passed the baton, as it were, of proving and developing Heliocentrism to later astronomers and scientists. And indeed, many European scholars were influenced by Copernicus' theory and its associated ideas. Based on Copernicus' research, astronomers all over Europe made tremendous observations and accumulated further data in support of Heliocentrism. Eventually, Copernicus' research came across the desk of another brilliant scientist, the German Johannes Kepler. Based on a large volume of data, Kepler made various calculations and carried out a great deal of analysis that would finally validate Copernicus' theory. He later proposed what came to be known as Kepler's laws of planetary motion.

Due to the fact that they had a limited number of versions and copies, respectively, traditional oral stories (oral tradition) and handwritten manuscripts (literacy) experienced a more or less linear transmission, while printed texts (printing technology) underwent a dispersive style of transmission. For example, Copernicus' astronomical observations and research were not only taken up Kepler but by Galileo Galilei as well. In the early seventeenth century, Galileo further improved upon Copernicus' Heliocentric theory with the use of various technological tools (most notable of which was the telescope) and the use of scientific thought experiments. In 1632, Galileo published *Dialogo Sopra I Due Massimi Systemi Del Mondo (Dialog Concerning the Two Chief World Systems)*, which specifically described the surface of the moon as seen with a telescope; used relativity theory to answer people's questions about the revolution of the Earth, and used the revolution of the Earth around the sun to explain why we experienced four seasons during the year.

During the century that followed the original introduction of Copernicus'[6] Heliocentrism, printing technology had a threefold role to play in its further expansion and development: (1) it created direct and indirect opportunities for scientists of all ages and places to share their observations and research; (2) it allowed astronomers of all ages and places store and gather their observations; and (3) it facilitated opportunities for the dissemination of new thoughts and ideas throughout the scientific community. In this period, printing technology effectively fueled the rapid scientific and technological development of Western society because of the open and dispersive ways in which information was able to be communicated over large distances.

This is the first time in human history that scientific exploration was able to shape and mold a new view of the universe based on scientific argumentation based on large-scale observation and experimentation. It silently paved the way for the Scientific Revolution. "Repeatable and verifiable" was the new mantra for scientists in the West. Their experiments from now on had to repeatable and verifiable by their colleagues across the world. By then, organized academic research, initiated by Aristotle (based on papyrus technology) had become commonplace feature of human activity. An enormous scientific community started to emerge. Scientific exploration became an essential way in which to understand the nature of the physical world and ensure the further development of human society.

Change in textbooks

The invention of printers directly influenced the publication format and the content structure of textbooks.

In the literacy age, font sizes, map sizes, and image proportions varied from book to book, and this can especially be seen in representations of humans and the human anatomy. In addition, manually copied books did not have page numbers, indices, or tables of contents. In the middle of the sixteenth century, standard formats for book publication gradually took shape. In 1516, Johann Froben used page numbers for the first time in the first edition of The New Testament by the Dutch scholar Desiderius Erasmus. From then on, tables of contents, indices, notes, as well as punctuation, paragraphs, paragraph headers, title pages, and page headers started to emerge one after another. By the end of the 16th century, books printed by machines were already similar to today's books in terms of external appearance.

When people revised textbooks for the sake of printing, subject-specific contents and organizational methods were also revised. For example, in the Middle Ages few law teachers had run through the whole of Irnerius' *Summa Codicis* (the first medieval system of Roman jurisprudence), so those teaching the work could not describe to either themselves or their students just how each law was related to the complete juridical system presented therein. However, starting from 1553 a new generation of legal scholars began to edit and organize legal manuscripts. Their tasks included reorganizing each part of a given text so as to relocate them to in specific paragraphs based on their content and making indexes for quotations. In the case of the *Summa Codicis*, they made this classic work entirely legible to readers: its style was easy to understand and the internal logic was clear and coherent. They thoroughly reformed this landmark work of law and the field of law itself (Postman 2004b).

The same changes happened to other fields. In the literacy age, the same subject was often treated by several textbooks, which presented the relevant information in various formats and sequences that were often inconsistent with one another. According to Neil Postman, "The mere preparation of different graded textbooks for teaching varied disciplines encouraged a re-assessment of inherited procedures and a rearrangement of approaches to diverse fields" (Postman 2004b: 46). Determining what should come first and what should come later had become a process where the textbook author reformed a subject or discipline by determining how it would be taught and subsequently understood.

An example of Ramus teaching material

The linear content organization which is characteristic of printed books (often known as the "ABC pattern,") is different from the style of content organization that is characteristic of handwritten manuscripts (which can sometimes show the organizational influence of oral tradition). Manuscripts are full of dialogues, admonitions, and aphorisms, while statements in textbooks seem by comparison to be plain and straight to the point, covering a wide array of topics. The closed expression structure brought into being by printing technology is not only present in literary works, but also exists in works of analytical philosophy and the natural sciences. The most typical example of such an expression structure is the Ramus teaching example.

Petrus Ramus created a standardized form for teaching materials for all subjects, including dialectic, logic, rhetoric, grammar, and arithmetic: first comes the cold subject definition and classification, from which further definitions and classifications are introduced, until each and every detail of the subject has been elaborated and processed. Ramus-style teaching material did not contain within it any interaction with any ideas or concepts external to it. The Ramus-style textbook won't cover disputations: the term "rival" never appears in them (Innis 2003).

According to Ramus' standardized form for teaching materials, so long as you define and classify concepts appropriately, everything in the textbook will be self-evident, and the teaching materials themselves will be perfect and self-sufficient. Ramus allocated difficult issues and debate with rival philosophers to his various lectures, introducing them under the rubrics of dialectic, rhetoric, grammar, and arithmetic (Innis 2003).

Currently, most teaching materials are compiled according to Ramus' standardized form. After the advent of printing technology and the subsequent printing, publication and revision of numerous textbooks, the contents of said textbooks came to be more varied and subject-specific. Nowadays, we can hardly find scholars with an encyclopedic knowledge like those of the Renaissance. Today, most experts are highly specialized and focus on ever-narrowing fields of expertise. And this is probably a part of the heritage left to us by the printing age.

MODERN EDUCATION MECHANISM

The existence of standardized textbooks and a sufficient quantity of writing materials laid a foundation for the creation and development of the what I like to call the "modern education mechanism." Briefly speaking, the main features of the modern education mechanism are as follows: (1) Teaching is specific to subjects; teaching activities are developed based on varied levels of difficulty and on various grades; (2) Students are put into grades according to their ages; and (3) Routine teaching activities are organized by subject according to a classroom structure. In the modern education mechanism, students in the same class are in the same age group and follow courses of instruction with a level learning difficulty that is roughly suitable to them (i.e. their level of development). Writing is the means by which teachers can check students' learning outcomes and obtain specific feedback on their learning.

After a period of over 100 years since the creation of printers, the modern education mechanism that centered on "class-based lecturing" was formally established. In the roughly 400 years that followed, is mechanism spread from Europe to North America and other locations around the world. It was spread from Japan to China around the turn of the twentieth century.

Afterwards, the educational system, based on exams as evaluation mechanisms, and the entire academic degree-granting mechanism kept on improving and evolving to form today's modern education system. It can be said that the entire mechanism of education that we have been accustomed to was solely founded on the basis of that very new media technology invented over 500 years ago, that is, printing technology.

Electronic communication age

Electronic communication media, represented by TV, mainly exerts influence on social communication ecology in two ways: first, information is spread at electronic speed and the world is subsequently turned into a small "global village;" and second, with the transition from literacy to image-based writing, human expression went from pure letter-based expression into an audio and video age where expression is made with language, music, and image.

"Audio and video" education

The rich audio and visual effects brought about by film and TV immediately attracted the attention of education researchers. There were many optimistic predictions about the influence that video media would have on education. In 1913, Thomas Edison once predicted that "before long books will soon be obsolete in the schools ... it is possible to teach every branch of human knowledge with the motion picture. Our school system will be completely changed in the next ten years" (Gagné 1992: 14).

Starting from "audio and video education," the field of educational technology formally entered onto the historical scene. However, too much attention to electronic media and multimedia programs caused many in educational technology to confuse the "subject history" of educational technology with the "practice history" of the field, wherein media technology drove the development of human learning. They rejected the "old technologies" that supported human education development before the advent of the modern era. Some would even argue that the blackboard, the letter, paper, the printed book, and conventional media alike were not actually educational technologies.

From the perspective of content presentation, the "audio and video education" movement which endeavored to turn the "single medium" into "multimedia" did not substantially reform the school system apart from adding some multimedia teaching materials to the class curriculum. Edison's dreams were soon was dashed. The enormous human education system still relied at this stage on the communication ecology created by printing technology.

Limitations of electronic communication media

TV only plays a limited role in the education realm because the TV communication network is a closed system. It is a unilateral communication channel and does not support bilateral mutual communication. TV "writes" with images that are broadcast by TV stations. Image-based "writing" is both complicated and expensive. There are only a small number of TV stations and radio stations that are also relatively closed to the public. Common people cannot use TV to express their feelings and their thoughts. In a communicative process that is akin to the teacher's lecture (as it is one source communicating to many), TV boasts the advantage of scale, but on the other hand the teacher can use dialogue, examination, and homework to determine what their students had learned. For such an education feedback loop to occur electronically, one would have to rely on printing, telephone and other media technology. This is the way in which universities and other HEIs develop distance education programs.

Only media technologies supporting bilateral mutual communication, however, can bring about a revolution in traditional school education. Judged from this perspective, the influence of electronic communication media on education is similar to that of literacy. Its main mission was to explore "image-based writing" skills and accumulate "image-based writing" resources, and thus pave the way for what became known as the "Internet Revolution."

Significance of TV in the world of "rapid" publication and serious "reading"

Among all the changes brought about by TV, three of them are worth noting here. They are likely to exert a greater influence on academic research and classroom teaching in the present and future Internet-dominated communication ecology.

First, TV "records" what happens around the world every day. Owing to efforts of those engaged in the TV sector in all corners of the world, TV cameras record "facts" as they happen. These enormous volumes of "fractioned facts" influence the way in which people receive and perceive information. However, it is worth noting that "fractions" are not equivalent to knowledge. In the words of Postman, "what is obtained from TV is often some specific sections without education, while what is obtained from reading is often related to the knowledge we have in mind and features stronger education" (Postman 2004a: 198).

Second, TV programs are also a sort of "fast track" means of publishing vast quantities of information. For example, China Central Television's (CCTV) "Covering the Wall Street Storm," and Beijing TV's "5 Hits in a Row about Finance and the Economy" produced a number of discussions on the dispute between Gome and Chen Xiao, and thus published a great deal of information in short order. These programs helped viewers ("readers") learn about the events that took place and learn a great deal of financial and economic knowledge. In particular, executives at the China Business Network (CBN) (a TV channel in Shanghai) launched a series interview programs with Ma Yun, Ma Huateng, Li Yanhong, and Guan Guoguang, and these programs likely constitute a better source of information on the Internet than any textbook.

Third, TV also provides a large volume of serious or formal "reading materials." Presently, it is not accurate to simply position TV as an entertainment medium. TV "writing" falls into various categories, including "fiction," "documentary," "news," "reality," and so on. The US news magazine "60 Minutes" and the TV documentaries produced by the US National Geographic Magazine are all significant reading materials in China airing on CCTV. When watching these programs, readers not only play them back, but the often take notes. In future academic papers, it will not be uncommon to see citations from such TV programs.

Digital age

The Internet is the epitomizer of all communication media technologies. It features fast communication speed, an extensive communication scope, rich expression symbols, accurate recording technology, and support for bilateral communication. Integrating all these advantages, the Internet comes with unprecedented features in terms of recording, expression, and communication structure, thoroughly transforming the original electronic social communication ecology. The digital age will definitely initiate a revolutionary transformation in academic research and classroom teaching. Judged from the point of view of the history of technology and its relationship to educational development, the educational transformation triggered by the Internet will follow a certain historical logic and spark the following changes.

Changes in the goals of education

Since the emergence of the Internet, a series of transformations have occurred in, among other areas, political fundraising, manufacturing, commerce (i.e. e-commerce), and financial payment (i.e. FinTech). Such transformations will eventually change the traditional ways in which society is organized and therefore finally cause change in the goals of education. Here, I will take the fundraising methods employed for a US presidential candidate as example with which to analyze the influence of the Internet on the political realm. I will also further analyze how such an influence may translate more broadly into changes to the goals of modern education.

US presidential candidates prior to George W. Bush mainly raised funds for their campaigns through face-to-face communication, an example of which is the classic fundraising dinner. The fundraising process inevitably involved intermediate costs for such things as activity venues, meals, accommodations (of donors), round-trip flights, and clothes. If every guest donated merely US$200, that amount could hardly cover such costs. Obama used the Internet for his donation strategy. He changed the donation means and the donation process, thus saving large volumes of "intermediate costs." Therefore, although 80% of donations to Obama were below US$200, he still became the presidential candidate who raised the most election funds ever in US history, establishing him as the very first "Internet president" in the world.

The influence of the Internet on politics goes well beyond the process of fundraising; what's more important in this regard is the expression of public opinion and the communication of political ideas so as to influence public opinion. In our present environment characterized by various kinds of media technologies, the expression of public opinion and the gathering of data on public opinion can be costly. There are also more ways than ever to communicate ideas around the world, and this will affect how politicians choose to gather data and relay their messages. Therefore, the internal governance of modern nations and even global communication and data-gathering processes (e.g. for political and economic purposes) are subject to the influence of the Internet.

The numerous changes that have been and will be brought about by the Internet in such fields as political fundraising, manufacturing, commerce (i.e. e-commerce), and financial payment (i.e. FinTech) will greatly change the way in which humans work, negotiate, and coordinate in the future and will pose a series of new requirements on how society educates its youth and what objectives they will set. The current worldwide emphasis on education reform is primarily due to nations' realizing that they need to find ways to prepare their youth for a world that is more interconnected than it has ever been in human history.

Innovation in media technology will spark transformations the field of education in two stages: in the first stage, new media will take the place of old ones, while the content they relay will essentially remain the same; and in the second stage, new content will be developed for and carried by the new media.

The very nature of IT-based education lies in the transition of "writing" from the "paper" to the "network." Therefore, the first step in this transition is the changing of the format of instructional content from the old media to the new media. Currently multiple IT-based education programs carried out in China, including fine course construction, multimedia teaching, and whiteboard teaching, are all at this stage in the transition.

The revolutionary influence of IT on education, however, is exhibited mainly in the second stage – new content carried by new media. The further development of educational informatization lies in the innovation represented by this change. The development of IT-based education in the second stage should, on the one hand, focus on new forms of "writing" and the brand-new knowledge structure that cannot be contained within paper books; on the other hand, attention should be paid to the reconstruction of the education process itself in multiple spaces. Influenced by the Internet, today's classrooms are equipped with multiple communication subsystems. The presence of the "body" of a student can no longer ensure that teaching and learning will actually take place. Teachers should think about how to effectively arrange various teaching activities and tasks in multiple spaces like the classroom, factory workshop, hospital, and virtual classroom such that their instruction can promote their students' growth in a truly effective way.

The influence of the Internet and IT on education goes beyond the processes of teaching and learning. Instead, it affects the whole industrial chain of education from academic research and publication to communication and teaching. Under the influence of IT, the processes of the industrial chain of education undergo a transformation and, more importantly, the chain as a whole undergoes a significant change.

Here, special attention should be paid to the challenge posed by the Internet to traditional academic research process which had long been based on printing media. Survey research supported by printing media, for example, often relies on collecting information after an event has happened, where sampling is done to get a picture of the occurrence of the event. Moreover, the process of carrying out survey research supported by paper media is bound to take a great deal of time. As a result of this time lag and the inherent limitations of sampling, the survey research process runs the risk of being distorted. For example, sometimes written or spoken words do not accurately convey the ideas they are supposed to represent; those being surveyed by intentionally or even unintentionally (i.e. out of ignorance about a topic) sabotage their responses. Such distortions can affect the accuracy of statistical results. In the past two years, housing price and residence expenditure data published by China's National Bureau of Statistics (NBS) have been heavily criticized. This shows just how problematic traditional sampling-based statistical approaches can be.

In an Internet- or IT-based environment, large volumes of human data can be recorded in real time and uploaded to network databases by way of bank cards, e-commerce platforms and the future Internet of Things. Statistical and analytical results based on calculations from this new type of data have started to influence major decisions taken by the Chinese government. For example, China's foreign trade import and export situation is monitored using Alibaba's e-commerce platform; and the pattern of urban consumption is formed based on analysis of data obtained from bank cards. This new trend in data acquisition and analysis has started to attract the attention of finance departments all over China. The recent dispute about the withdrawal of foreign stock-holding rights from Alipay (the erstwhile subsidiary of Alibaba) also involved issues having to do with data acquisition and analysis. New knowledge organization based on the Internet also comes into existence. For example, "Follow the Money" (Guo 2009), dubbed "best science video in 2009" by US scientists, was an academic paper written with "images." The "paper" presents multi-dimensional research results with dynamic video; it is hard to constrain such work within the limits of traditional paper-based publication.

Summary

Summarizing the history of how technology has influenced education will often lead one to reflect on the revolutionary transformation in education brought about by IT and Internet technology. And such a transformation has three components.

First, from oral tales, to papyrus and parchment to printers, the different ways in which humans have produced knowledge over the years have varied tremendously. At present, the dispersive social community environment shaped by the Internet has created an unprecedented connection between "research" and "practice," even giving rise to the "economies of scope" phenomenon to a certain degree. As a result, humans have entered the age of the knowledge economy and knowledge production has evolved from Mode 1 to Mode 2. The dispersion of information and the production of knowledge according to "economies of scope" will have a structural influence on future academic research and on higher education as an institution.

Second, the evolution of media technology has led to a corresponding evolution and change in the ways humans store and communicate knowledge. When new media replaced the old media, the knowledge systems from the oral tradition age, the literacy age and the printing age were loaded onto a new expression system that was the Internet. In the future, interactive means of expression, such as online games, and interactive organizational structures such as hypermedia, databases, and search engines will start to incubate new means of communicating and organizing knowledge within the Internet environment. This will thoroughly change the publishing sector as we know it and will fundamentally change the way people use knowledge and the way they read and write.

Third, IT brings human education closer to the educational goal of "individualized teaching," while the increase in instructional options[7] also largely adds to complexity of decision-making in education. Along with the development of IT-based education, "cramming education," which had been introduced at the behest of industrialization, is likely to be deconstructed into several segmented education markets with their own features. Education organizations and learners alike will, based on the criteria of selection and combination, form feature-specific teaching schemes to meet the demand for differentiated study regimes. This will serve as the starting point for the top-tier design of IT-based education in China in the years to come.

152 Technology in the development of education

In conclusion, the research presented in this paper has mainly used information from Western media history, while it has not used data from Chinese media history. And there are two reasons for this. First, to the present day, analytical information on the history of media technology in China has not yet be made available. Second, China's history of media technology development is very special. Its history of literacy and block printing lingered until the nineteenth century, while such media technologies as printers, radios, films, TVs, computers, and the Internet emerged in the twentieth century (mainly in the latter half of the twentieth century). Therefore, the influence of printing technology, electronic media, and digital media was felt at the same time, making it hard to observe the distinct influences of each medium. So although the framework of the development of media technology and its historical influence on education proposed herein has been established on the basis of Western media history, it can still serve as a reference point for thinking about the past and the future influence of technology on education in China.

Notes

1 Starting from 2000, a series of works published by scholars from the media analysis school have also been translated into Chinese. They mainly include the following: *Empire and Communication* and *The Bias of Communication* by Harold Innis, *Understanding Media: The Extension of Man* and *The Mechanical Bride: Folklore of Industrial Man* by Marshall McLuhan; *The Disappearance of Childhood, Amusing Ourselves to Death*, and *Technopoly: The Surrender of Culture to Technology* by Neil Postman; *No Sense of Place: The Impact of Electronic Media on Social Behavior* by Joshua Meyrowitz; *The Soft Edge: A Natural History and Future of the Information Revolution, Mind at Large: Knowing in the Technological Age*, and *Cellphone: The Story of the World's Most Mobile Medium* by Paul Levinson; *Orality and Literacy: The Technologizing of the Word* by Walter Ong; *The Media Ecology* by Casey Man Kong Lum; and *The Printing Press as an Agent of Change: Communications and Cultural Transformations in Early Modern Europe* by Elizabeth Eisenstein.
2 Works by the media analysis school are references for "The Basis of Education Technology," a mandatory course for postgraduates at the Peking University Graduate School of Education. They are also optional books for their reading lists. When reading these books, students tend to have difficulty gleaning the main points because there seem to be too many penetrating insights: it is hard to organize these insights into systemic explanations. The definition of media technology proposed in this study, along with the proposed framework for understanding how technology has effected educational development, have been communicated to students taking classes at Peking University. Based on their feedback, the definition and framework proposed here can, in a relatively clear and systematic way, explain the changes brought about by media technology over time.
3 The media ecology school arose out of the media analysis school. After Marshall McLuhan passed away, the basis of media analysis research shifted from Toronto to New York. Neil Postman, a professor at New York University, and his students Joshua Meyrowitz, Paul Levinson, and Casey Man Kong Lum are leading academic figures in this school. In 2000, *Media Ecology*, compiled by Casey Man Kong Lum and published by Peking University Press, described the development and main academic views of this academic school.

4 To avoid confusion with academic disputes in the field of media education, in this study the view of the media ecology school is adopted and the word "media" is used.
5 Scribes, typesetters, and the entire sector transcription industry have all disappeared. Along with the invention of TV came the emergence of the film and advertising sectors. Likewise, the Internet will cause the disappearance of certain occupations and bring about the emergence of some new ones.
6 "Copernicus" is added to differentiate his theory of Heliocentrism from the one presented in Alexandria many centuries earlier.
7 For example, regarding specific teaching objects and teaching goals: what sort of teaching resources should be chosen? Where should teaching be done? and How does one reasonably arrange and organize various teaching activities among multiple physical and network spaces such as classrooms, laboratories, workshops, video conference rooms and network classrooms? These choices, which have been enabled by the advent of IT, add to the complexity of curriculum design.

References

Ashby, E. 1983. *Adapting Universities to a Technological Society*. Translated by Teng, Dachun and Teng, Dasheng. Beijing: People's Education Press.
Barbier, F. 2005. *History of the Book*. Translated by Liu Yang et al. Guilin, China: Guangxi Normal University Press.
Briggs, A. & P. Burke. 2009. *A Social History of the Media*. (3rd edition). Cambridge: Policy Press.
Burke, P. 2000. *A Social History of Knowledge: From Gutenberg to Diderot*. Translated by Jia Shiheng. Taipei: Rye Field Publishing Co.
Cang, L. 2007. *Research on the Cultural Sociology of Book Communication and the Social Development of the Publishing Sector*. Beijing: Capital Normal University Press.
[EB/OL]. 2011. "Entries on Homer's Epic." June 10. Available from: http://baike.baidu.com/view/15908.htm.
[EB/OL]. 2011. "Follow the Money." June 15. Available from: http://video.sina.com.cn/p/tech/d/v/2010-02-21/193060486584.html.
[EB/OL]. 2011. "Library of Alexandria." June 10. Available from: http://baike.baidu.com/view/25310.htm.
Gagné, M. E. 1992. *Instructional Technology: Foundations*. Translated by Zhang Jiefu; Edited by Wang, Jiqing and Qian, Qingyuan. Beijing: Science and Education Press.
Goffman, E. 2009. *The Presentation of Self in Everyday Life*. Translated by Feng Gang. Beijing: Peking University Press.
Goody, J. 2005. "Memory in Oral Tradition." Translated by Hu Xiaohui. *Studies of Ethnic Literature* 1: 133–140.
Guo, W. 2009. "'Invasion' of Online Learning into the Classroom." *Distance Education in China* 6: 36–37.
Havelock, E. 2003. "The Orality-Literate Equation: A Formula for the Modern Mind." Translated by Bamo Qubumo. *Folklore Studies* 4: 14–34.
Innis, H. A. 2003. *The Bias of Communication*. Translated by He Daokuan. Beijing: China Renmin University Press.
Innis, H. A. 2004. *Empire and Communication*. Translated by He Daokuan. Beijing: China Renmin University Press.
Kozma, R. 1991. "Learn with Media." *Review of Educational Research* 61(2): 179–212.

Le Goff, J. 1996. *Intellectuals in the Middle Ages*. Translated by Zhang, Hong; Edited by Wei, Maoping. Beijing: The Commercial Press.

Manguel, A. 2004. *History of Reading*. Translated by Wu Changjie. Beijing: The Commercial Press.

McLuhan, M. & F. Zingrone. 2000. *Essential McLuhan*. Translated by He Daokuan. Nanjing, China: Nanjing University Press.

Ministry of Education. 2010. *Outline of the National Medium- and Long-Term Program for Education Reform and Development (2010–2020)*. Beijing: Xinhua News Agency. Available from: http://news.xinhuanet.com/edu/2010-07/29/c_12389320_15.htm.

Nan, G. 2005. *Educational Communication*. Beijing: Higher Education Press.

Ong, W. 2000. "Oral-Tradition-Based Thinking and Expression Features." Translated by Zhang Haiyang. *Folklore Literature Studies*: 18–31.

Ong, W. 2008. *Orality and Literacy: The Technologizing of the Word*. Translated by He Daokuan. Beijing: Peking University Press.

Postman, N. 2004a. *Amusing Ourselves to Death*. Guilin, China: Guangxi Normal University Press.

Postman, N. 2004b. *The Disappearance of Childhood*. Guilin, China: Guangxi Normal University Press.

Quintilianus, M. F. 1989. *Selections from the Education Works of Quintilianus*. Translated and Edited by Ren, Zhongyin. Beijing: People's Education Press.

Smaldino, S. E. 2008. *Instructional Technology and Media for Learning* (8th edition). Translated by Guo, Wenge. Beijing: Higher Education Press.

Wells, H. G. 2001. *The Outline of History*. Translated by Wu, Wenzao et al. Guilin, China: Guangxi Normal University Press.

Wells, H. G. 2004. *The Outline of History*. Translated by Man, Yeping and Li, Min. Beijing: Yanshan Press.

9 Education's role in economic growth patterns

Min Weifang

After thirty years of rapid economic growth, China has become the world's second largest economy, with a per-capita gross domestic product (GDP) that reaches the level of middle-income countries. In the next ten years, the most significant and urgent task for China to complete in terms of economic and social development is to transform its pattern of economic growth so that its national economy can progress in a harmonious and sustainable manner. If it were to fail to complete this task – and it is no small task – China would fall into the "middle-income trap." This fate would be caused by, among several factors, the overuse of limited natural resources and energy (to the detriment of its current ecological environment), weak domestic demand, a weak investment climate, and prominent social contradictions – all of which would contribute to economic recession. Although a variety of factors deeply influence patterns of economic growth, education plays a fundamental role in the process of economic transformation. Chinese universities must better understand the mission of education and promote the accumulation and improvement of human capital (therefore paying attention to matters of quantity and quality, respectively) by strengthening education reform, speeding up educational development, and improving education quality. In the meantime, these institutions should establish an effective mechanism with which to join economic growth to education reform and scientific innovation so as to lay the groundwork for the successful transformation of the latter (i.e. into a new, more productive and beneficial pattern).

Education transforms economic growth from a resource- and investment-driven pattern to an innovation-driven pattern

Since implementing market-oriented reforms in the late 1970s, China has maintained rapid growth for over thirty years, with an average annual growth rate of over 9%. However, natural resources and investment have primarily driven China's economic development in the past. Such growth strategies have caused severe problems because they are often imbalanced, uncoordinated, and unsustainable. Problems of unreasonable economic and industrial structures remain, and further efforts should be made to improve the quality and efficiency of economic growth. China faces multiple challenges when it comes to economic progress, which include its enormous population, its limited natural resources, and the potential damage that rapid economic growth has done to the environment. China's possession of energy resources per capita is less than half of the world average, while its energy consumption per unit of GDP is three to four times greater than that of developed countries. China is one of the world's most resource-poor countries when it comes to water resources, and its per capita water resource utilization is only 28% of the world average. However, China consumes 1,340 tons of water for every US$10,000 in GDP, while Japan consumes 189 tons and the US consumes 491 tons. Thus, the failure to accelerate the transformation of its economic growth pattern to one of sustainable economic development has produced many negative environmental and ecological consequences for China.

The ideal economic transformation would see a high-investment, high-consumption, high-pollution, low-output, low-quality, and low-efficiency growth pattern changed into one that focuses on low investment, low consumption, low pollution, high output, high quality, and high efficiency. For a state, economic growth requires transforming the way in which it approaches productivity, and it requires it to be willing to adjust its overall economic structure, improve its industrial structure, contribute to the success of its high-tech and strategic emerging industries, foster scientific and technological progress, strive to achieve management innovation, seek out ways to improve labor quality, develop green technologies, and adopt an overall positive attitude toward sustainable development. In sum, one key factor for transforming economic growth is (as mentioned above) to shift from an investment-driven pattern to an innovation-driven pattern. China is currently far behind advanced countries in terms of innovation in the fields of science, technology, and management. There are relatively few original ideas or concepts in the fields of science, technology, and management in China today. There are, however, many "copies" or borrowed ideas. Currently, only 10% to 15% of independent, high-tech innovation-related achievements in China have generated significant economic scalability, with the rate of contribution to economic growth at only about 20%, while the rate in developed countries is above 60%.

Many high-tech products manufactured in China are sold across the world, with the production values included in the calculation of China's GDP growth. In fact, the majority of these products are manufactured with imported high-end equipment and core parts. Thus, in proportion to sales volume, most of the profits from these high-tech products go to foreign intellectual property owners, high-end device makers, and core parts suppliers, with a small portion of the profits going to domestic manufacturers who depend on the consumption of natural resources and energy to make a living. For example, globally influential technological innovations, such as the Internet, were invented in developed countries, most notably the US. China lags behind such nations in terms of the production of sophisticated hydraulic components, high-end bearings, seal components, and high-end numerical control systems. China can produce high-speed trains, but all the bearings used for these trains are imported from abroad. China has to import the majority of its bearings it uses for the gearboxes that go into domestically produced wind turbines. China lags far behind European and American countries in the fields of aviation and aerospace.

As the "world's factory," China has a large but not sufficiently independent industrial sector, with foreign countries controlling most of the core technologies used therein. In terms of agriculture, there are over one million technicians in China, which happens to have the world's largest agricultural research system. However, China has to import at least 90% of the fine seeds it needs to produce high-end fruits, vegetables, and flowers. Thus, it is up to Chinese universities to take the lead in helping to change this situation as soon as possible. They need to help improve the capacity of local innovation and help facilitate an innovation-driven national movement. Along with the rapid progress of scientific technologies and the rise of the global knowledge economy, education has become increasingly important to promoting innovation-driven economic growth. The key lies in the innovation of science, technology, and management, since the basis of transforming economic growth is the shift from an investment-driven growth pattern, which inevitably consumes a large amount of natural resources and energy, to one that is innovation-driven, which depends largely on progress in science and technology. Technological transformation evolves internally and it depends on labor quality and the quality of management personnel. Thus, technological innovation ultimately depends on the institutions that possess the spirit of innovation and the ability to carry out the activities required to see it realized, the latter including the ability to attract high-quality talent. China should develop these innovative institutions and help ensure that they have the personnel needed to transform its national economic growth pattern. And it should do so by vigorously developing education to improve the quality and quantity of human capital and by deepening education reform to improve the quality of instruction being delivered at all levels. Acemoglu (2003), a scholar at the Massachusetts Institute of Technology, discovered in his studies that stock of human capital, represented by average years of schooling, is positively proportional to economic growth (see Figure 9.1).

Human capital stock is both a quantitative concept and, more importantly, a qualitative one. China lags far behind developed countries in higher education, which plays a vital role in the development of high-quality human capital. According to the experiences of developed countries, colleges and universities are an important part of the national innovation system, playing a vital role in achieving innovation-driven growth. Colleges and universities hold a dominant position when it comes to conducting research and are some of the most important sources of technical innovation. Gerhard Casper, former President of Stanford University, has pointed out, in his lecture "The Advantage of the Research-Intensive University," that "high-tech companies

158 *Education's role in economic growth patterns*

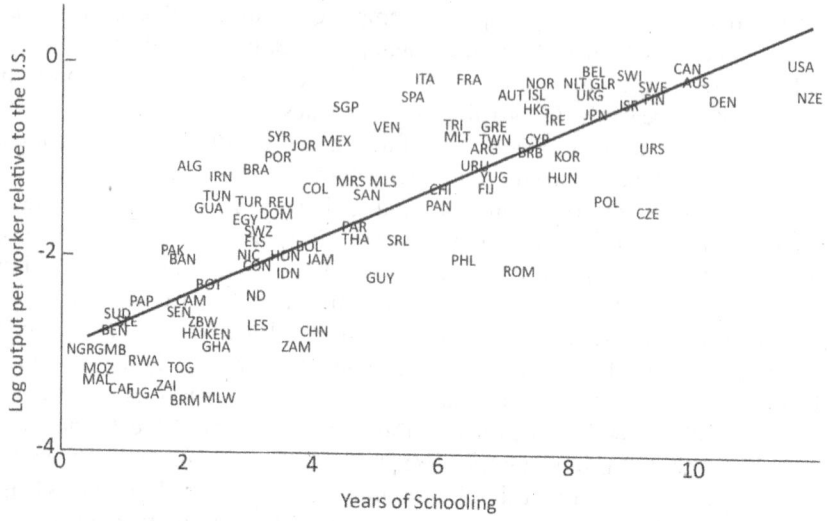

Figure 9.1 Significant positive correlation between human capital stock and per capita GDP
Source: Adapted from Acemoglu (2003).

in Silicon Valley alone recorded earnings of 85 billion dollars in 1995, and according to one estimate, 62% of those earnings can be tracked back to companies whose founders had connections to Stanford" (Casper 1999: 110). China has developed the world's largest higher education system. However, if Chinese colleges and universities do not improve their innovation capacity, they will not cultivate top graduates and attract top faculty members in international academic fields. If these institutions are only interested in the quantity of papers published in science journals, it would, in the end, be pointless to develop the country through science and education and to build a powerful country based on the talents of its human resources: China would never be able to fundamentally transform its economic growth pattern.

Six million college students and over 400,000 postgraduate students graduate every year in China, and over 50,000 are doctoral graduates. Although China ranks first in the world in terms of the quantity of graduates, Chinese graduates are much weaker than their foreign counterparts in terms of critical thinking skills, ability to innovate, and adaptability to economic, scientific, and technological change. Thus, in order to give pride of place to education in the transformation of its national economic growth pattern and in order to achieve sustainable economic growth, China must promote education reform and emphasize the need for innovation when it comes to administration and operation of its higher education institutions (HEIs) and the cultivating of its college and university students. Chinese HEIs must build an institutional environment that promotes the spirit of innovation and the capacity for innovation. This means that those charged with governance in the higher education system in China must not only pay attention to curriculum development and pedagogical techniques, but also identify ways to improve the system itself, which should include strengthening innovative education, promoting systematic innovation, and cultivating a large number of top graduates and faculty members so the economy can ultimately experience innovation-driven growth.

Education provides human resources for the improvement of industrial structure

One key measure China can take to transform its economic growth pattern to one that is driven by innovation is to constantly promote the improvement of its industrial structure. The improvement of a nation's industrial structure refers to the transformation of its economy from a low-level (unbalanced) state to a high-level (balanced) state. On the one hand, it involves the change from raw-materials-based, low-value-added, and labor-intensive industries to high-value-added and high-technology-intensive industries. On the other hand, from the perspective of the national economy, the improvement of industrial structure also refers to a shift from a focus (by the state) on primary industries to a focus on secondary and tertiary industries. The balance of a nation's industrial structure is inextricably linked to the speed and efficiency of its economic growth and the sustainability of its economic and social development. There are several serious problems with China's industrial structure. First, China's primary industries are weak, with peasants' annual income seeing slow growth in recent years. Agriculture is the basis of China's national economy, as it is the guarantee of (and the industry that fuels) rapid economic growth and it is the primary condition for economic security. The low income of Chinese farmers has to do with low consumer demand in the rural market, and it therefore affects the driving force behind the country's economic development. Second, China's secondary industries are large and in the process of growing, but they are generally not strong, with weak equipment manufacturing and independent innovation capacity. Multinational organizations own most of China's core technologies. Many regions rely to a great extent on heavy industry and the chemical industry, both of which generate huge economic output but also generate a great deal of pollution. These industries consume tremendous amounts of energy and water, and they put an immense strain on the environment. Third, China's tertiary industries remain relatively undeveloped and are currently experiencing slow growth. And this leaves the state having to rely rather heavily on its secondary industries for its economic growth.

China's service sector is relatively small, with low-grade supporting facilities, and the comprehensive service function is not well developed. Therefore, the environment for opening-up to the outside world needs to be further improved. The output of the comprehensive service sector in China accounts for only 43.1% of GDP, less than the world average of 51% and less than the average for developed countries, which is between 60% and 70%: the figure for developed countries is over 40%, while the US has reached 78.4%. The proportion of tertiary industry activity in China is much lower than it is in the US. The population employed in China's service sector accounts for only 34.6% of the total employed population, much lower than 70% figure recorded for developed countries. In the modern world economy, the service industry has expanded faster than any other industry, and it has become the driving force behind economic growth. The modern service industry has emerged along with the innovations brought about information technology (IT) and the knowledge economy that have generated demand, encouraged consumption, and provided high-value-added, knowledge-intensive production and day-to-day services for society. The vigorous expansion of the modern service industry has played a significant role in expanding employment, improving people's standard of living, expanding the diversity of countries' industrial structure, and transforming patterns of economic growth. In 2009, the World Bank conducted studies on the relationship between human capital and the improvement of nations' industrial structures. The results showed that the more high-quality human resources a country possesses, the easier it is able to improve its industrial structure and raise its aggregate productivity (see Figure 9.2).

In Figure 9.2, the horizontal axis represents the percentage of population that has received higher education, while the vertical axis represents the output value of the tertiary sector as a percentage of GDP. This figure illustrates the significant role that education plays in the improvement of industrial structure. The world is on the verge of a new revolution in science and technology and it is on the verge of a new industrial revolution. More

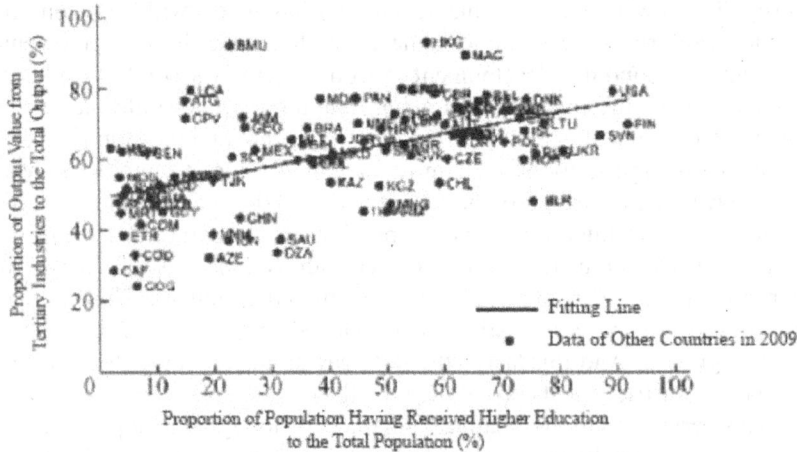

Figure 9.2 Relations between human capital and industrial structure improvement in different countries
Source: Adapted from The World Bank (2009).

importantly, in order to improve its industrial structure, China must learn from global development trends in the fields of science and technology. By doing so, China will able to seize an historical opportunity to vigorously develop strategically emerging industries that are knowledge- and technology-intensive, that are characterized by a low resource consumption, and that have high growth potential and a good comprehensive benefit. They will serve as role models for the long-term sustainable growth of the economy and of society as a whole. There are many strategically emerging industries, such as next-generation IT, intelligent high-end equipment manufacturing, biological manufacturing, advanced materials manufacturing, and green technology or "GreenTech" (including recycling and renewable energy). Each of these industries relies heavily on high-quality human resources that include highly trained individuals and future-oriented organizations that are focused on innovation and creativity. The Organisation for Economic Co-operation and Development (OECD) has explained the major challenges that the world economy will be facing by 2060 and has pointed out that the accumulation of human capital is becoming increasingly important for economic growth. Many examples in China and in the rest of the world show that the level human resource development is highly connected with – and in fact determines – industry structure quality. In 1995, Bill Gates, the founder of Microsoft, said the following during a visit to Peking University: "If Microsoft Corp. lost its 50 best people, Microsoft Corp. would be 'nothing.'" The progress of the US' Silicon Valley in California has revealed that highly educated employees are the dynamic resource driving the improvement and optimization of the US' industrial structure. The formerly desolate valley was finally developed into a world-famous incubator of high-tech industries thanks to the plethora of learned and resilient personnel who graduated from renowned US universities such as Stanford and the University of California, Berkeley. It is not an exaggeration to say that without these high-level universities Silicon Valley would not exist. The prosperity of high-tech zones such as Silicon Valley helps to promote deeper integration between the processes of industrialization and informatization in the US, which boosts the improvement and optimization of country's traditional industries. In recent years, many similar examples could be witnessed in China. One is *Zhongguangcun*, a high-tech economic zone in Beijing.

The significant and indispensable role of education in the expansion of domestic demand

Another key factor for the successful transformation of China's economic growth pattern and for the achievement of sustainable development is to expand domestic demand, shifting from a foreign-demand and investment-driven pattern to a domestic-demand-driven growth pattern. Over the past decade, China's dependence on foreign trade has increased, and foreign trade now accounts for 50% of the nation's total balance. The ratio of imported crude oil to total consumption exceeded 56% in 2011, and the import volume of iron ore accounted for over 60% of the total world's iron ore trading volume. That same year, the final consumption rate of Chinese residents was only 35%, much lower than 70% for developed countries. It will become increasingly difficult for China to promote economic growth while still depending on foreign demand, since many developed countries suffered an economic downturn during the global financial crisis. This is in addition to other export-negative factors, such as frequent trading friction (caused by trade protectionism) and the appreciation of the Renminbi (RMB) against various foreign currencies. As far as China is concerned, it is no longer possible to achieve long-term, sustainable economic growth by depending heavily on foreign investment. It can no longer be "business as usual." Thus, in order to maintain rapid economic growth, China must expand domestic demand and, in particular, enlarge consumer demand, which shall be seen as a significant and strategic basis for both economic and social progress.

The expansion of domestic demand, especially consumer demand, of course, can be affected by a variety of factors. The most significant factor is the improvement of residents' income and the health of the social insurance system. Expanding domestic demand needs to be able to narrow the income distribution gap and change the economic unfairness caused by the education system and intergenerational mobility. Only through a more equitable income distribution structure can citizens' incomes be improved. If this were to be achieved, domestic consumer demand may expand. Educational equality is the basis of social and economic equality. The core step to narrowing the urban-rural income gap and expanding consumer demand is to vigorously develop the education system, increase investment in human capital, and promote the equitable distribution of educational resources to urban and rural areas. As an important factor of intergenerational mobility, education helps improve the economic status of children from low-income families in an equitable system. However, in the absence of support for policies demanding such reforms, education may continue to fuel the unequal social economic structure now present in China. Studies show that in Project 985 national key universities, the number of students from low-income families is much lower than the number of students from high-income families. Instead, in ordinary universities and colleges, the number of students from low-income families is higher than the number of students from high-income families (Li & Min 2006). The imbalance in the regional economy only exacerbates the regional educational development gap. For example, at the national level, the average expenditure for public higher education is 8,956 Yuan per student. This figure is 23,275 Yuan in some more affluent provinces, while it is only 4,292 Yuan in some relatively low-income provinces. The higher figure is five times that of the lower one (DOF & NBS, 2011). Studies on intergenerational mobility showed that there is a significant correlation between children's education level and their parents' occupation and income. Consequently, children's education level affects their future vocation and income. That is to say, high-income parents transfer high incomes to their children through education (Guo & Min 2007). This situation must be changed so that economic income distribution can become more balanced. The Chinese government needs to promote social equality in education regulations and provide an active education-funding framework which involves increased state funding of education, more funding for children from low-income families, and a shift financial policy that more fiscal support goes to economically underdeveloped regions. Under such a framework, Chinese universities will be able to offer education and training to more people, especially those from low-income families. And such a framework would also help positively adjust the current income distribution pattern (see Figures 9.3 and 9.4).

Figures 9.3 and 9.4 show that under the active income distribution structure and a sound labor market system, along with an increase in education investment and the gradual equalization of high-quality education resource allocation, the well-educated population number increases greatly, their competitive strength drops gradually in the labor market, and their relative income decreases. Conversely, the low-income-educated population drops to a remarkably low level, and their relative income rises due to the decrease in labor supply in the market. Thus, supported by positive policies, education helps move economically vulnerable groups upwards and drives economic income distribution in a better direction, thus facilitating the expansion of domestic consumer demand, lowering dependence on foreign markets, promoting economic growth, and driving sustainable economic growth.

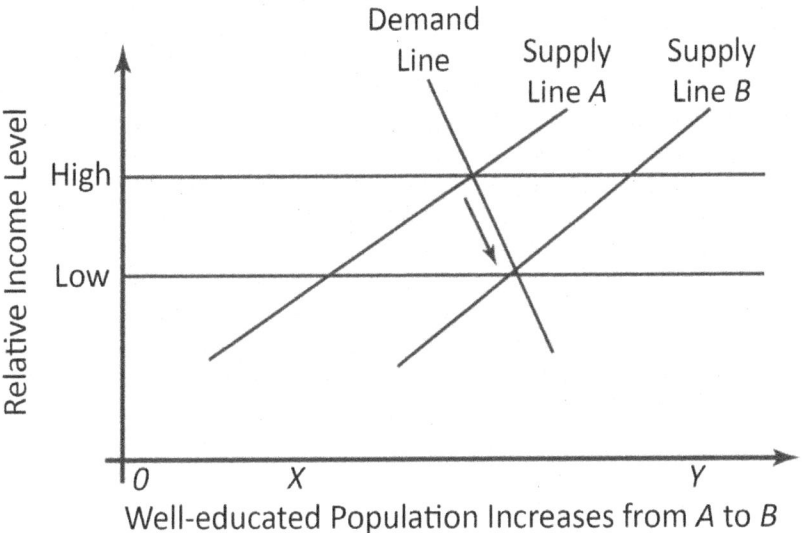

Figure 9.3 Changes in income and quantity of a well-educated population

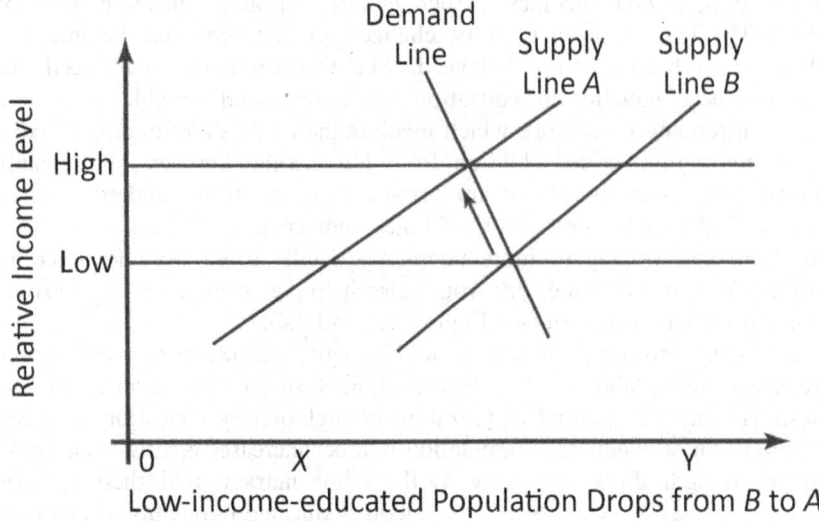

Figure 9.4 Change in income and quantity of a low-income-educated population

Improving the quality of education is the basis of education's role in the transformation of China's economic growth pattern

Education plays a significant role in economic growth in three important ways: (1) it transforming an investment-driven growth pattern to an innovation-driven growth pattern; (2) it promotes and leads to the improvement of a state's industrial structure; and (c) it expands domestic demand. The best way for the government to effect a positive change in China's economic growth pattern through education is to focus on the quality of education that students receive, especially at China's colleges and universities. In 2010, there were approximately 120 million postsecondary students in China, which is equal to the total population of Britain and France combined. Moreover, the number of college graduates increases by over six million every year. China ranks number one in terms of college graduates. In general, however, China lags behind developed countries in terms of the quality of higher education. Generally, China's undergraduate students behave well during examinations, review the material after class, pay attention in class, and are able to master specialized knowledge on a narrow topic. Far from being generally unintelligent or lazy, Chinese students typically study very hard, from primary school and middle school all the way to college and university. These students pass numerous examinations, such as entrance exams for universities, final exams for junior middle school courses, entrance exams for graduate courses, and entrance exams for doctoral programs and other postgraduate courses. According to one professional working in a university, "students have formed conditioned responses to examination questions." Indeed, at this level of study students have been trained, with regard to both their train of thought and their behavior, to generally look for similarities instead of differences. Thus, one can say that their sense of individuality has, for the most part, not been developed comprehensively. Students' unique abilities and their own individual potentials are not nourished. Rather, students are developed into "studying machines" that perform well in examinations, but fall short when it comes to critical thinking skills and independent thought.

Thus, students lack the spirit of innovation and the capacity for innovation. They often lack an ability to adapt and be flexible, and they are unable to respond quickly to changing economic and social change. Chinese students lack these skills, compared to students at foreign world-class universities. As colleges and universities expand enrollment and the number of students increases sharply, they pay little attention to the development of each student's individuality and fail to "teach students according to their aptitudes" and develop students' innovative abilities. Despite the fact that the quality of China's undergraduate education lags behind that of other developed countries, the situation is far worse when it comes to the quality of its graduate education. This is why many of China's excellent university students go abroad for graduate study. The famous scientist Qian Xuesen, known as "the father" of China's aerospace industry, has pointed out several times that:

> China is far from being well developed. An important reason is that no universities are operated in the mode in favor of the development of creators, scientists, and inventors. They have no unique innovative characteristics. They fail to "develop" outstanding graduates. It is a big problem.

The quality of postgraduate education is closely correlated with the level of scientific research in universities. Over the past few decades, China has accomplished several impressive scientific and technological feats thanks to the research programs of several of its main universities. These programs have contributed, for example, to the detonation two nuclear devices and the launching of a satellite to space. There can be no doubt that Chinese universities have made great progress when it comes to scientific research, and this is reflected in the fact that China is ranked second in the world in terms of the total number papers published in international foreign academic journals. However, Chinese universities must keep in mind that quantity and quality are two distinct things. Statistics released in 2005 showed that among the world's researchers whose papers were most frequently cited, 3,410 were from the US, 380 were from Britain, 207 were from Germany, 193 were from Japan, and only three were from China. So although, as we have just seen, Chinese universities have made progress in scientific research in recent years, they still lag far behind foreign world-class universities in terms of scientific research quality. And the situation remains unchanged today. Since the founding of the People's Republic of China (PRC) close to 70 years ago, China has developed into the world's second largest economy. However,

Chinese universities have yet to make any key breakthroughs considered to be worthy of a prestigious Nobel Prize in a scientific field.

The ability of Chinese universities to recruit and develop quality talent and conduct scientific research has a direct bearing on the role they will play in transforming China's economic growth pattern and in achieving an innovative development strategy. Thus, China must develop higher education in accordance with the thirty measures released by the Ministry of Education and give priority to education quality (DOF & NBS 2011). The gap in talent development is mainly a result of China's failure to develop students' critical thinking skills and of its failure to train students to value their own unique potential for creativity. This has led to a plethora of students without the spirit of or capacity for innovation, which is a hindrance to China when it comes to transforming its economic development pattern. Going forward, Chinese universities must therefore pay special attention to relaxing the teaching environment in their HEIs (especially within the classrooms itself), respecting students' individual development, and advocating for academic freedom and the idea that both teachers and students alike can make progress by learning from one another. No modern "research universities," in the truest sense of the term, will be created without academic freedom. Former Prime Minister Wen Jiabao said the following at the 2012 Academicians Conference of the Chinese Academy of Sciences and Chinese Academy of Engineering:

> We must advocate an academic freedom atmosphere in which scholars are energetic, free from restraint, brave in invention and creation. We encourage debate over academic research. Only debate may inspire the thinking of criticism, which is indispensable in modern society. It's a type of independent thinking. We must respect individuality. A society without individuality has no vitality or creativity. When considering whether a nation, or a state, can prosper or not, the key lies in whether the mass's huge creation potential and independent thinking are developed. We must make talent discovery and training a priority to have the youth exert their ability. Many important scientific phenomena were discovered by youth. We must create conditions for the youth.

The content of undergraduate teaching should be aligned with the trends of integration and general knowledge in order to improve student adaptability and flexibility with regard to the rapidly changing demands of society and the economy. Thus, Chinese universities should grant more freedom to students when it comes to selecting their course of study, update teaching content on a regular basis, add technical disciplines, and teach more basic theories that have wide application and universal significance. Chinese universities should not only try to continuously expand their course offerings and build a flexible curriculum, they should also promote integrating arts, science, and engineering in an effort to provide teachers with greater flexibility. Moreover, teaching content should be enriched and diversified: Chinese universities should pay special attention to the development of students' overall character, innovative spirit, and innovative ability, and they should teach students according to their aptitude, thus fully developing the potential of every student. This requires Chinese universities to focus teaching activities on inspiring students' independent thinking in; to give prominence to training and nourishing critical thinking skills; and to enhance student independence and creativity when it comes to their studies. The higher education system in China needs to get students to forecast, predict, and imagine what the future will bring and in which direction the country will go in terms of the economy. Meanwhile, Chinese universities should place a lot of emphasis on the connection between campus and society, and between theory and practice. They should encourage students to participate in social practice while studying on campus, so as to gain experience and to get inspired about their future.

The quality of teaching and the quality of scientific research are complementary and closely related concerns. International experience has shown that when teachers bring high-level scientific research into the classroom and get students to experience knowledge innovation, they produce high-level creative graduates. To fundamentally improve their scientific research programs, Chinese universities should keep an appropriate balance between basic and applied research. On the one hand, these HEIs should enhance demand-oriented applied research with regard to the development of the economy and society. On the other hand, they should pay special attention to the enhancement of students understanding of basic research. Globally, scientific and technological progress tends to benefit from achievements in basic research. Thus, most winners of the Nobel Prize have worked in areas of basic research. Without a series of major achievements in basic research in the twentieth century, there would be no remarkable leap in a series of scientific technologies and no rapid development in the knowledge economy today. Six years ago, researchers at a US university put forward what they termed "compressed sensing theory," which applied research scientists used to make key breakthroughs in computed tomography (CT) imaging. There are many such cases in scientific history. Thus, it is worth repeating here that Chinese universities should not only emphasize applied research, but they should also pay attention to basic research. In recent years, total expenditure on basic research accounted for 12% to 26% of the total cost of scientific research in developed countries such as the US, France, Italy, Japan, and South Korea. This figure is less than 5% in China. China's basic research covers a wide array of topics, but its development is at a relatively low level. It takes a long time for progress to be made. Recently, a journalist asked Cambridge University's president why his school has generated so many Nobel Prize winners. The president gave the following reply: "The latest winner is engaged in a field about which no one is optimistic. I have waited for him for fourteen years. Quality needs patience and time." Koichi Tanaka, a Japanese winner of the Nobel Prize for Chemistry, had published a few papers before winning the prize. These few papers were published in smaller journals. When he was awarded the Nobel Prize, the local Shimadzu government and the Japanese federal government offered him scientific research funding that was one hundred times greater than the total amount that he had received in the past twenty years, expecting him to make further scientific advances.

A country with a low level of basic research can never become a leader in science and technology. In order for a state to nurture its basic research infrastructure, its universities should be granted adequate funding to carry about scientific experiments; they should forge ahead with a pioneering spirit in an environment that fosters academic freedom; and they should avoid contributing to an environment that focuses solely on the quantity rather than the quality of their academic publications. If the state, and China in particular, is able to do the above, HEIs will fundamentally improve the quality of their scientific research and will assume a national role in economic change, a role that they very much ought to have. Only when teaching quality and scientific research are improved can Chinese universities contribute to the development of an innovative development strategy to achieve sustained economic growth.

References

Acemoglu, K. D. 2003. "Human Capital and The Nature of Technological Progress." The AstraZeneca and StoraEnso Lecture. December 11. Stockholm.

Casper, G. 1999. "The Advantage of the Research-Intensive University." In X. Wei, W. H. Ma & X. M. Chen, eds, *The University of the 21th Century*, 151–160. Beijing: Peking University Press.

Department of Finance of the Ministry of Education & National Bureau of Statistics (DOF & NBS). 2011. *China Educational Finance Statistical Yearbook 2011*. Beijing: China Statistics Press.

Guo, C. B. & W. F. Min. 2007. "Research on the Relationship between Education and the Intergenerational Income Mobility of Chinese Urban Households." *Educational Research* 5: 3–14.

Li, W. L. & W. F. Min. 2006. "Higher Education Access in China." *IAU Horizon* 12(2): 12–13.

The World Bank. 2009. *World Development Report 2009*. Washington, DC: The World Bank.

10 The political logic of non-government/private education (NGPE) in rural China

Evidence from a northern county

Yan Fengqiao

In 2006, the Standing Committee of the National People's Congress amended and adopted the *Compulsory Education Law of the People's Republic of China* (*Compulsory Education Law*). Since the law went into effect, China has implemented a free education policy (i.e. tuition and miscellaneous fees) toward school-age children at the (compulsory) elementary level. As a result of the passing and execution of this policy and other financially beneficial educational policies, household expenditure on school-age children's education has moderately declined. Meanwhile, the working conditions in Chinese schools have gradually improved and teachers' actual income in the wake of the adoption by schools of a performance-based salary system has increased by a significant margin. Of course, such changes have recently occurred in the public education system. In this context, what is the attitude of local government toward private education? How has Article 49 of the *Law of the People's Republic of China on the Promotion of Privately Run Schools* – which states: "Where a people's government entrusts a privately run school with the task of compulsory education, it shall, in accordance with the agreement of entrustment, appropriate the necessary amount of funds for education" – been implemented? How does local government handle the relationship between financial assistance and profitability when it comes to private schools? Will students still opt for fee-paying private schools now that all tuition and miscellaneous fees for public schools have been waived? Will the development of public education impact private education? How does the private education system manage the balance between examination-oriented education and quality-oriented education? With these questions in mind, I, along with a visiting doctoral student from Harvard University, Zachary Barter, went to a northern county (hereinafter referred to as "County J") from October 8 to October 9, 2011, to conduct a field study on the development of local private education. We held discussions with investors, administrators, teachers, students from three private schools, as well as with administrative officials from the local education department; observed classroom teaching; visited campuses and their associated living facilities, and viewed local government work reports, local leaders' speeches, and related media reports. Having had valuable firsthand experience watching the private education system in Country J in operation, we subsequently came to the following conclusions about the nature of private education development in rural China.

The findings of our investigation showed that the amended *Compulsory Education Law* and other financial assistance policies favorable to public education have indeed affected some private schools, as some private schools in County J and neighboring counties have closed down due to a lack of enrollment. The number of private schools in County J shrank from 24 in 2007 to 13 in 2011, as enrollment fell from 22,000 to 17,000. In 2009, County J built several rural public boarding schools, which provided transportation for students and which provided them with food and accommodation subsidies. This lured away a number of private school students, and hence some small-scale private schools experienced lower enrollment and were subsequently forced to suspend their operations. However, while some private schools had to suspend their operations or even face closure, others have managed to hold their ground with a steady increase in enrollment owing to their ability to improve the quality of education and reduce costs. The viability of private education in China had proven itself after the private system had undergone various trials and tribulations and survived the challenges posed by market forces and public policy changes.

This paper aims to study the actual operation status of private education in County J from the perspective of political logic. The so-called "political logic" analytical approach refers to how government, public schools, and private schools interact with each other under the current school administration system, and the impact of this interaction on the development of private education. In this study, private education was the subject, while government and public school behavior were the influencing factors. The abstract concepts and the logical relationships that will dealt with can only be sufficiently and vividly exhibited through specific storylines. This paper therefore attempts to apply anthropological analytical methods to the observation of specific issues impacted by state policies while we try to illustrate the nature of our personal experiences with County J's private school system. We will try to situate our observations and experiences with those found in previous research on the Chinese education system. We aim to demonstrate the presence of a particular pattern taking place in rural China with regard to the interaction between the government, the public education system, and the private education system. As our conclusions are based on a rather limited investigation, they should not be seen as anything other than tentative arguments in need of further study and elaboration.

Basic facts of social and private education development in County J

County J, located in northern China, has jurisdiction over eight townships covering an area of 593 km^2. Rural residents constitute 88% (280,000) of the county's total population of 320,000. In 2005, County J's GDP came in at more than RMB 2.1 billion, with per capita GDP at RMB 6,700. Primary, secondary, and tertiary sector outputs of RMB 360 million, RMB 1.04 billion, and RMB 740 million make up 16.7%, 48.5%, and 34.8% of overall output, respectively.[1] The data above shows that although County J is a rural administrative unit, its agricultural production constitutes a relatively small proportion of its overall economic activities. In 2005, County J's budgetary expenditure stood at RMB 200 million, an amount over five times its budgetary revenue of just over RMB 36 million: the county was apparently dependent on fiscal subsidies from higher levels of government to maintain its operations. Like other rural areas in China, pronounced social changes have happened in County J. The share of agricultural production in the overall economic activities has gradually declined, alongside the dwindling ratio of rural residents who specialize in agricultural production, as more and more people have migrated to towns or even to major cities inside or outside the area. County J is currently undergoing the related processes of industrialization and urbanization.

Rural private education was established as a result of a movement for educational reform, and it developed under the market supply-demand mechanism. The advancement of rural economic reform from the perspective of supply and demand created the conditions for the establishment of a private education system. From a demand perspective, due to the development of the rural economy and the promotion of increased standards of living, parents in rural households have attached greater importance to the next generation's education. They now have a better ways of taking the initiative to improve their children's education experience, such as opting for fee-paying education, which includes having their children attend public schools that require students to pay a non-permanent residence fee, or by having their children attend private schools (Zen & Ding 2010).

From a supply perspective, the achievement of rural reform also brings with it a drive for expanding individual freedom, as behavioral freedom has gradually spread from the production sphere to the non-production sphere. For example, individuals are now permitted to open private schools. In 1995, the Provincial People's Congress passed regulations having to do with the running and administering of schools by social (i.e. non-governmental) entities. In 1997, the State Council released *Regulations on the Running of Educational Institutions with Social Resources*, the first administrative regulation on private education in China, which spearheaded the development of private education on the policy front (Sun 2003). The earliest private school in County J started operating in 1998. The sponsor of the school, who was motivated by a desire to raise his annual income and improve his standard of living, left his previous job in the public sector work and started raising funds to open a private school before finally receiving the appropriate official government approval. He founded a private school that could accommodate over one hundred students by first leasing various buildings and then obtaining the official government permit to run the school a year later. That same year, namely 1998, two additional private schools were open with the approval of local government. One of them, founded by an entrepreneur running a hardware business, has grown into the biggest and most reputable private school in County J (hereinafter referred to as School Q). So far, student enrollment at the county's first private school has reached 1,300, as school assets have ballooned from RMB 5,000 at the beginning of its existence to RMB 20 million. This case testifies to the fact that although the Chinese Constitution as amended in 1982 granted legitimate status to social entities running schools, and the first private school in County J appeared sixteen years later. The time lapse is the result of the gradual formation of an education market. At the outset, the desire to establish and or run private schools was a result of a desire of many to find a way out of poverty and become prosperous. So the drive to establish private schools was intimately connected with the concept of profitability.

After more than a decade, private education in County J has grown considerably. In 2011, the whole county had 13 private schools occupying 683 mu (0.4567 km^2) of land and 272,000 m^2 in floor area. The total worth of their total fixed assets was RMB 280 million; the total number of students was over 17,000, and the total number of full-time teachers was over 1,300. Private education has taken on quite a significant role in County J's overall education system. In terms of quantity, private schools teach about one-third of the total student population. In terms of quality, the number of admissions to university and college, and the number of outstanding students taking senior high school entrance exams at private schools include almost half of the total student population. These two ratios reflect the developmental momentum of local private education to some extent. Over the past ten years, no single public high-school graduate has been admitted into Tsinghua University or Peking University. However, from 2005 to 2011, thirty-seven graduates from School Q (our private school) attended Tsinghua University, Peking University, and highly selective universities in Hong Kong. Personnel at the County J Education Bureau disclosed that even local government civil servants and public school teachers are willing to send their children to School Q.

In terms of enrollment, School Q, which has only been in existence for a dozen years, has surpassed the top middle school in County J, which has just recently celebrated the centenary of its founding. In addition, private schools are not bound – as public schools are – by the legal requirement to recruit students from the local neighbourhood. They are not limited by geographical restrictions. As a result, private schools have recruited many students from other counties. Out of the 17,000 private school students currently enrolled, more than 5,600 – or approximately one-third of the total student body – come from other counties. With regard to private school faculty members, more than 60% of just over 1,300 full-time teachers come from other counties. Hence, the private education system in County J exhibits two main features: cross-regional competition for students and cross-regional teacher mobility.

Public school behavior and private education development under government restrictions

In an open society, the value of private schools is on full display due to recognition they gain from competing with public schools. To study the logic of private school development in China, it is necessary to discuss the behavioral characteristics of the dominant public schools, as well as their limitations, the latter having made it possible for the development of private education in the first place.

Government, as a super-organization, is much larger than both the public and private school systems combined. Both the political system itself and government-formulated policies have conspicuous impacts on the behaviors of these two types of educational institutions. The public school system operates within the larger governmental system, while the private school system can grow beyond the confines of the governmental system. Investigative research and numerous educational documents have shown, however, that the latter exerts a decisive influence over the administration of both types of schools. From the perspective of administration, a non-economic tie exists between the government and public schools. While they receive funds and other forms of governmental support, public schools are required to vigorously adhere to the policies and regulations formulated by governmental departments. In the course of achieving government-set compulsory education objectives, county public schools are in the position of being selected by many students and must unconditionally accept the majority of school-age students, as inclusive public policies that target all students can be easily implemented in public schools. In recent years, under the political climate of overcoming the drawbacks of examination-oriented education and undertaking quality-oriented education advocated by the government, county public schools have also conducted a variety of experimental reforms on quality-oriented education, such as reducing student course-load and the volume of student homework; guaranteeing students' self-study and rest time; changing traditional teaching methods; and increasing extra-curricular activities. Therefore, county public schools are prohibited from assigning homework that would take up students' time during the evening and/or weekend.

By contrast, private schools are not restricted by such government policies to the same degree as their public counterparts. Private schools usually adopt a boarding system, a closed campus administrative style, and a timetable that includes weekend breaks every two weeks. They also have shorter public holidays than public schools, which are regulated by the government. During our fieldwork, public organizations had just reopened after long National Day holiday (formally the "National Day of the People's Republic of China"), which is set by the government. Meanwhile, private schools in County J had returned to their normal schedule a few days earlier. As a result, private school students will spend more time in class and doing their homework than their public school peers. According to initial estimates, if private schools take thirty less weekends off per year than public schools – and each weekend is calculated as a total of sixteen hours over two days – then private schools would dedicate more than 480 hours to classroom teaching per year. With taking the university entrance exam as their top priority, private school students will most likely outperform their public school peers on test scores due to the greater number of study hours per year in private schools. In rural areas, it is easier and more efficient for examination-oriented education to deliver results that influence schools than long-term, quality-oriented education.

As mentioned above, for various legal and administrative reasons the accountability relationship between public schools and the government is more forceful than that between private schools and the government. For the same reason, the accountability relationship between public schools and public school students and their parents is weaker than that between private schools and private school students and their parents. According to one office worker in the County J Education Bureau, private school administration is more efficient than public school administration. In fact, the information gathered during our investigation helped us understand the salient features of private school administration. In 2003, the General Office of the State Council issued the *Notice on Successfully Managing the Employment of Rural Workers in the Cities and their Access to Public Services*, removing the policy obstacles for rural migrants to seek employment in China's cities and spurring the migration of surplus rural laborers to urban areas. Left-behind children, that is, children who were left to live with relatives when their parents headed to the city to find work, have recently emerged as a common phenomenon in County J. While parents seek employment elsewhere, childcare and schooling will become a realistic challenge for the country administration. Public schools, due to their inability to find effective solutions for a lack of student housing, have failed to cope effectively with growing social pressures.

Private schools, however, have discovered development opportunities in the "social gap" left open by the public schools. They have started providing lodging to students, adopting a closed-off management system on campus, and implementing such measures as having a 24/7 teacher presence on campus, a move which ensures that students will be well looked after, secure, and secure. And this measure has gone a long way to reassure parents who work away from their hometown. The principal of a local private school indicated that left-behind children made up over one-third of the school's overall student population. During spring and autumn, two peak influenza (i.e. flu) seasons, in order to prevent the spread of the illness, the school supplemented students' drinking water with Chinese herbal medicine. Safety is paramount in the private school system: without assurance that their children will be safe, parents will not leave them in the care of private schools and private schools will not be able to survive. Internally, private school administrators can stay true to the social accountability relationship they have with students and parents through various organizational means. They devolve and delegate responsibilities for looking after students' personal well-being to each lecturing teacher and each childcare-providing teacher. To some extent, this has protected students from various social malaises such as Internet addiction and truancy.

As for public school administrators and teachers, they can sometimes adopt strategies of inaction out of self-interest so as to avoid or evade certain responsibilities. Examples of such strategies are shunning responsibility for students' after-school safety and shifting some instructing responsibilities to parents. High-level government organizations formulate policies and labor protection measures such as the eight-hour workday and public holidays to safeguard public school teachers' rights and interests. However, public school teachers, when pursuing individual development objectives such as meeting requirements for professional title assessment, may do so at the expenses of their teaching work and/or their students' personal development. The effectiveness of teacher evaluations and the corresponding incentives and punitive measures at public schools pales in comparison to those at private schools. Private school sponsors or administrators can dismiss a teacher for misconduct and/or negligence, while this is much more difficult to do at public schools. During discussions that we had at two local public schools, a few teachers indicated that they felt greater responsibility and more pressure when working at private schools even though their possibilities for career advancement were better.

Survival and development of private schools

During our investigation, we wanted to know how it was that some private schools continued to operate and even have more appeal than public schools when it was the public schools that have received extensive support from the government. The following analysis was taken from our case study of School Q.

From its founding in 1998 until 2011, School Q's enrollment has increased from 400 to over 7,000 students, making it the biggest and most renowned local private school. Because County J boasted ir's larger educational capacity, the local government mad a special allocation over 1,000 mu (0.6667 km^2) of land to set up a school park for the purpose of teaching and learning. Hence, the School Q campus is located inside the school park, occupying 260 mu (0.1733 km^2) of land, and it pays a rental fee to the government each year for its use. School Q has a total floor area of 8,700 m^2 and had received an initial investment of RMB 140 million. School Q includes all grades from the elementary level to the senior high school level. Its various performance indicators at college entrance examinations for the past seven years have steadily improved. In 2011, School Q's rate of admissions into Tier 2 universities exceeded 75%. It is noteworthy that a total of thirty-seven School Q graduates have been admitted into prestigious universities, such as Tsinghua University and Peking University, for the past four years.

The driving force behind School Q's achievements is the fact that it strives to meet parents' keen expectations for their children to receive a high-quality pre-college education, a fact that has debunked the myth that rural students cannot get into Tsinghua University or Peking University. School Q's founder and the chairman of its Board of Directors said: "What parents are most concerned about is whether their children's academic performance can steadily improve and whether they can get into competitive universities; all of our school administration activities are focused on meeting this core task, that is, meeting the parents' demands. Since we have delivered results, parents are willing to send their kids to our school." School Q's curriculum is based on meeting parents' demands for their children to get into reputable universities, and it has utilized the supply and demand relationship of the educational market to satisfy parents' demands and become a well-known private school in County J. From a theoretical standpoint, the most difficult part of school administration is the lack of objective standards and measurements with which to evaluate the school's performance, whereas the easiest part is to highlight students' test scores and admission rates, although these indicators are not without their flaws and may sometimes give a misleading picture of a school's administration.

School Q has made students' achievement of academic excellence its ultimate objective and therefore the cornerstone of its most critical administrative rules. Therefore, it is fair to say that School Q is the most faithful follower and the most effective executor of examination-oriented education. The reason that School Q has adopted a school administration model is the powerful social foundation for examination-oriented education in the rural areas of China, as test scores are the effective currency for receiving higher education and social mobility. The leading middle school in County J, not far from School Q, has undertaken educational reform, virtually cutting students' daytime class hours in half and eliminating homework altogether. However, we have not discovered in School Q and other private schools in County J any evidence that they have done anything similar to the educational reform conducted at County J's top-ranked middle school.

From the perspective of its sponsors, the key to helping School Q students improve their academic performance and test scores is very simple. School Q recruits the best students and best teachers and it implements a vigorous management style, thus advancing its university admissions goals.

When we spoke with him, the founder of School Q cautioned that some private schools, during the early stages of their development, were overwhelmed with applications and faced the risk of taking on more students than they could handle. This problem was a result these schools having a single-minded desire to expand their student recruitment without the use of proper screening procedures. School Q has learned many lessons from these schools' experiences. Instead of implementing a zero-threshold acceptance policy, it adopts a selective approach and recruits students with solid academic records at any cost. For students who perform well on the senior high school entrance exam, School Q not only waives their tuition fees, but also provides them with financial aid. For students whose test scores reach the threshold mark for its senior high school, School Q determines their tuition based on their scores on the senior high school entrance exam and adopt a ten-point tuition bracket. Among the senior high school students that we interviewed, some with a solid academic record pay a little over RMB 2,000 per semester in tuition fees, while some with an average academic record pay over RMB 7,000 per semester in tuition fees.

School Q has a particular interest in recruiting returning students who had high scores on previous year college entrance examinations but have decided to take the exam again in the hopes of getting an even higher score and gaining entry in to a higher-ranked university. School Q spares no effort in attracting students with the potential to get into Tsinghua University or Peking University. Among the twelve 2011 graduates who were admitted to Tsinghua University or Peking University, eleven were returning students. In addition, School Q always seeks to expand the areas from which it recruits its students: three-quarters of the thirty-seven students accepted by Tsinghua University or Peking University are from other counties, with only a little over a quarter are from County J. School Q will award RMB 200,000 to each student who is admitted to top universities such as Tsinghua University and Peking University in addition to a handsome award to their lecturing teachers. On the school's 2011 College Entrance Examination Honor List, we noticed that each of the twelve students admitted by Tsinghua University or Peking University received an award of RMB 200,000. Five teaching teams each received a financial award of between RMB 50,000 and RMB 190,000, with the top-performing teacher receiving RMB 64,400.

This practice of financially enticing outstanding students and rewarding those who perform well on university entrance examinations while common in the private system is not permitted in the public system. This is the slight edge that private schools have in competing with public schools for students. School Q has put into place a salary scale that ties pay to performance. In senior high school, teachers' average monthly salary is RMB 4,000, with the lowest being RMB 3,500 and the highest being RMB 6,000, and the bonuses range between RMB 4,000 and RMB 6,000. The award amount tends to increase the closer a teacher gets to teaching twelfth grade, as teachers' incomes are closely tied to their students' scores at college entrance examinations. From an external point of view, School Q teachers' actual income is higher than that of local public school teachers and other private school teachers. From an internal point of view, there is a real income gap among teachers and it is starting to expand. The founder and president of School Q's Board of Directors asserts that the Board aims to stimulate teachers' motivation to work hard and take the initiative with higher salaries. With enviable income and award packages, School Q is able to recruit outstanding teachers. However, School Q has also implemented a vigorous teacher employment policy. Teachers can only start in-class lecturing after scoring over 80% on subject tests and passing a lecture rehearsal. A teacher can only be employed on a permanent basis when 60% of their students achieve "excellent" marks or more than 90% of the students achieve "OK" marks.

All management decisions at School Q are centered on improving students' test scores. To this end, School Q has adopted a contract-responsibility system and a lowest-place elimination system. The contract-responsibility system refers to the arrangement in which several students are contracted out to one teacher by the school. The teacher takes responsibility for the students' academic performance and the teacher's salary and overall standing in the school is tied to these students' performance. The lowest-place elimination system refers to the transfer to lower grades of teachers whose class test scores are lowest. It may also involve their outright dismissal from the school. School Q is a boarding school, as students from grades one to twelve all live in school dorms and are allowed to visit their families once every two weeks. At school, students must obey a set of rules referred to as the "Ten Noes." School Q sets up ten untouchable signs, each of which has its own admonitions. One, for example, forbids students from using electronic products (e.g. cell phones, MP3 players, computers) or reading books unrelated to the curriculum in school. In addition to regular classes and physical exercise periods, students have morning and evening self-study time and almost no leisure time. When we asked students about their school life, some of them said that studying almost makes up the entirety of their life and that they hardly have any time for extracurricular activities. What they feel most stressful about is the monthly test and the subsequent ranking of their test score.

The headmaster of the school gave us a copy of the forty-three-page administration policy document (amended in 2011), which covered a wide array of rules and regulations. In short, those who commit minor infractions will be fined by the school, while severe offenders will face possible dismissal.[2] Such rules and regulations would be almost impossible to implement at public schools, where state law protects teachers' and students' rights and interests.

Profit is a topic often discussed in the process of formulating private education policies. Among the thirteen private schools in County J, only two have not applied for reasonable return on investment (ROI), as the other eleven have already done so, seeking permission to earn a profit from tuition fees.

The sponsor of School Q has been open about his intention to profit from running the school, stating that "parents are most willing to spend on children, and hence it is easiest to make money from students." He only attended school for six years and knows little about education, but he is an expert at making money. Before founding School Q, he operated a highly profitable enterprise specializing in hardware, electrical products, and chemical products. From a management perspective, School Q's assumes a patriarchal management model, as the members of the Board of Directors are all from the founder's family, with the son of the president of the Board being the principal. School Q adopts a shareholding system, as shares are divided into eight portions and shareholders receive dividends according to the number of shares they hold. In the words of the founder, School Q has "broken even on revenue and expenditure after a few years in operation," and has enjoyed surpluses in some years. When asked about the surplus of administration funding at School Q, the staff at the County J Education Bureau responded that the local government did not understand School Q's financial situation and was unable to estimate its revenue, income, and possible surplus because School Q applies differential tuition standards to students with different academic performance records and offers financial incentives to teachers. In addition, there is a wide teacher income gap because School Q does not observe uniform teacher salary standards.

Above we have discussed the administrative characteristics of School Q, that is, taking a selective approach to recruiting students and teachers, aiming to meet parents' demands for their children on excelling on tests, getting into competitive colleges or universities, and implementing a performance-based compensation policy to improve students' test results.

The behavior characteristics of any private school are to some extent the result of government policies or management practices. At the grassroots level, the local government has reinterpreted national private education policies and made some adjustments to adapt them to local conditions. The fact that private schools are outside national system restrictions have made it possible for School Q to adopt a school administration model that does not quite fit with the essence of the quality-oriented education policy championed by the Chinese government. School Q can formulate various management policies unimpeded by the state. The leader of the County J government pointed out unequivocally that schools providing basic education should be dedicated to sending more students to college.

Government's attitude and approach to private education

It is now time to turn to examining the behavioral logic of the local government. Public schools are more closely tied to the local government than private schools, and it is natural for the government to favor public schools while maintaining a laissez-faire attitude toward private schools. However, County J's government has presented a different case, as it has adopted policies that are more supportive of local private schools. They not only offered them financial incentives, but they also allocated a number of government-affiliated institutions' staffing quotas to private schools. Therefore, one has to ask the following question: under what circumstances does government support the development of private education? We have noticed that when the administration at private schools help local government improve its performance, local government provides them with more support. On the contrary, if private schools cause trouble for the local government, the latter will not support the former and may even object to the development of private education. In other words, the administration of private schools (i.e. their policies) precede government policies and measures, which squares well with Daniel Levy's conclusion that government policies on private higher education lag behind the real development of private higher education. Levy (1999) further emphasized that private higher education is not the result of government design but of natural evolution.

Under the current bureaucratic system, performance evaluation is the key element affecting government behavior. It is important here to stress that local government officials' performance evaluations will affect their chances for promotion. Performance is also the way in which the government can show that it brings value to the public, and thus the government's performance affects the reputation of local officials (and vice versa). The performance of county governments (and that of Country J in particular) is evaluated under the scope of the entire area, and it is easier to show visible evidence of performance. When it comes to the performance category of education, college entrance examination scores have the best comparability and visibility, and they have a great deal of what I like to call "socially persuasive power," just like GDP, which is a hard indicator of economic growth. Therefore, County J officials have put forth a specific "One Thousand People Target" (i.e. over 1,000 students will achieve the "admissions mark" on their college entrance examination), treating "college entrance examination score" as the biggest "popularity-winning project" that will show that it is performing well with regard to the "Steadfastly Improve Performance on College Entrance Examination" category. And this category is stressed by the County J Education Bureau, the highest level of government in County J, as being vital to their performance evaluation.[3] While the county tries to advance quality education even as it has institutions in its jurisdiction providing examination-oriented education in a no-nonsense fashion, passing the college entrance examination is considered to be the essential objective of its education policy. As Zhao wrote in his book *Farmers' Politics*, "the grassroots people each take what they need from the documents of higher level government for both understanding and implementation, and each acts according to the interests of their own department" (Zhao 2011: 144). The detachment of quality-oriented education from examination-oriented education may be explained by the fact that politicians' efforts to implement the national government's policy on quality-oriented education are thwarted by executive bureaucrats who want to well on their performance evaluations. To do so, they need to score well on the college admissions rate category (Zhao 2011).

The local government's support of private education is a result of both the stellar performance of local private schools with respect to the provision of senior high school education and the scores of their students on college entrance examinations, and a host of economic considerations. Private education has stimulated the county's economic development with regard to both consumption and employment. Among the more than 17,000 students enrolled in private schools, over 5,600 of them do not live in County J. If the annual tuition and consumption expenditure per student were calculated at RMB 5,000, the total annual expenditure would be RMB 28 million, making up 4% of County J's tertiary sector output of RMB 700 million. Hence, a county leader once remarked in a speech that education is not only about cultivating talent, but about increasing the employment rate and contributing to the public's well-being. Education cannot be undertaken as an industry, but its stimulating effects on industries should not be overlooked.

County J's government has a specific objective – and has formulated detailed measures – to facilitate the development of private schools. In 2003, County J's Party Committee released the document *Opinion on Encouraging the County Education System to Accelerate the Cultivation of High-Quality Talent*. Article Six of the subsequent County J government document No. 19, 2007, *Preferential Policies of Encouraging and Supporting the Development of Private Education*, states that the government awards RMB 50,000 to each student who is admitted to Tsinghua University or Peking University. County J's government set aside RMB 350,000 in 2007, RMB 820,000 in 2008, and RMB 640,000 in 2009 to honor this financial commitment to private schools and private school teachers.

The number of full-time teachers on staff in private schools is the key element affecting teaching force stability and private schools' ability to recruit outstanding teachers. Hindered by the fact that the power of resolving this problem lies not with the education department, but with the national government and the local government, social pressure notwithstanding, there is no unified strategy to acquire public institution employee status for private school teachers. Perhaps due to its enviable planning capacity and its foresight, County J formulated specific approaches to this problem in its official document No. 47, 2008, *Notice of Individual Amendments and Improvements on Preferential Policies of Supporting the Development of Private Education*. These approaches can be summarized as follows:

1 Candidates with a bachelor's or a master's degree are eligible for recruitment. Candidates who have been working at County J's private schools for over three years with outstanding teaching performance and who have met any of the following requirements are qualified to be recruited to County J public schools: junior high school teachers under age 35; senior high school teachers under age 40; junior high school teachers who graduated from junior college; and senior high school teachers with a bachelor's degree.
2 School size: schools with over 1,000 students can resolve the status issue for three teachers; and public teacher status is granted in increments of 500 students. Senior high school size: for every 420 students, one status is given. College entrance examination contribution: for every 100 liberal arts and science and engineering students admitted to Tier 2 universities or above, one status is granted.
3 Children of private school teachers originally from other counties are entitled to the same treatment as local students; private schools should tackle issues such as housing, social insurance, and subsidies based on years of teaching and employment for teachers from other counties.

This policy has been considered the most compelling measure taken to date to support private education. To implement this policy, County J allocated thirteen teacher status licenses to private schools in 2009 and thirty such licenses in 2010. Private schools pay the salary of these private school teachers who enjoy public teacher status.

In 2008, the County J Party Committee held a College Entrance Examination Award Ceremony at a private school and commended two students from the school who were admitted to high-level institutions, the first to Tsinghua University and the second to Peking University. The local government awarded this school RMB 100,000 along with RMB 20,000 from the County J Education Bureau. During the ceremony, the county leader made the following remarks: "The president of the private school is a businessman noted for his great social responsibilities, and parents sending their children to this private school have both vision and foresight, and teachers at this private school deserve our heartfelt respect." Undoubtedly, his speech was a most palpable gesture of governmental support for private education. Compared with urban areas, rural areas can be characterized by a less complex political environment and can therefore support, make, and implement policies favorable to private education with little conflict and controversy. It is plain to see that local government can move faster than the national government, as supportive policy for private education from the latter is still in its infancy, while the former has turned such a concept into a reality.

On the other hand, competition is brewing among governments at the same level, and some people have called this recent phenomenon a "political tournament" or a political "bidding war."[4] To highlight performance, local governments have unveiled County J's policies. In 2007, County J released official document No. 19, *Preferential Policies of Supporting the Development of Private Education*, which offered incentives to schools which attract senior and intermediate teachers from other counties, such as awarding one school RMB 2,000 for recruiting one intermediate teacher, and RMB 3,000 for recruiting one senior teacher. The County J government has fulfilled its commitment by disbursing over RMB 200,000 from 2007 to 2010 to award the schools that had successfully recruited outstanding teachers from other counties.

Investigation: questions and answers

Through this investigation, we have begun to answer the questions raised at the beginning of this paper. First, what is the local government's attitude toward private education? In 1998, County J's first private school made its debut. In 1999, the County Education Bureau officially approved the educational qualification for three of its first private schools. In 2007, two graduates from a County J private school were admitted into Tsinghua University and Peking University. In 2007, County J's government unveiled incentive measures and subsequent policies supporting the development of private education. We can infer from this fact that the government's supportive policies for private education were sparked by private school students' impressive performance on college entrance examinations. After 2007, eleven private schools left the competition due to a shortage of students, while the local government did not take special rescue measures but instead opted to "let them go." Hence, the government's attitude toward private education can be encapsulated by the decision to "support the strong and leave the weak alone" (Wu 2007: 366). In the *Twelfth Five-Year Education Development Plan*, County J identified the centerpiece of private education as "putting stress on the scale of education, supporting big and prestigious schools, and creating schools with brand recognition."

For public education, which exists within the federal system, local government can either take the "support the strong and leave the weak alone" policy based on efficiency, or take the "support the weak and leave the strong alone" policy driven by fairness. For private education, which exists outside the system, local government is inclined to support it insofar as it succeeds in market-oriented competition, "supporting the strong and leaving the weak alone." Based on the development of private postsecondary education in the US, Zumeta (2011) emphasized three types of public policy postures of different states: (1) laissez-faire, in which state government takes no action on private higher education; (2) central planning, in which state government gives the same treatment to private higher education as it does to public higher education, adopting an integrated planning management approach; and (3) market competition, in which state government adheres to the law of market development, resorting to an indirect regulation and control management method with regard to private higher education instead of direct intervention. County J's private education policy seems to be transitioning from a laissez-faire approach to a market competition approach.[5]

Second, how have the provisions of Article 49 of the *Law of the People's Republic of China on the Promotion of Privately Run Schools* been implemented? This article states the following: "Where a people's government entrusts a privately run school with the task of compulsory education, it shall, in accordance with the agreement of entrustment, appropriate the necessary amount of funds for education." In the case of County J, though many private schools are providing compulsory education, they are doing so voluntarily and not as a result of being entrusted to do so by the government, and they have therefore not received any regular government funding. Hence, the government funding mentioned in the *Promotion Law* has not materialized. It can only be said that the defining statement in this provision gives a legitimate excuse for government inaction. In fact, close to one-third of school-age students in County J have received compulsory education at private schools that charge fees and have not received any public funding subsidies, a sign that China as a whole is drifting away from the national inclusive policy of free compulsory education. In this regard, the private education situation in County J is not an exception and is similar to that of other counties and regions. In addition, the tendency of private schools to follow the market competition model (just discussed above) and a shortage of government education funding have also contributed to the inability of private schools to receive public funds.

Third, how does local government handle the relationship between financial assistance and the profitability of private schools? We need to first look at private schools' profit-making activities. Although private schools provide services, they have received administrative resources from the state and have accumulated a certain amount of assets while steadily expanding. For instance, the assets of the first private school in County J have increased by a factor of four thousand since its founding. Facing the issues of a budgetary deficit and asset depreciation, eleven out of thirteen private schools have asked for reasonable return on investment (ROI), leaving only two schools that have not made this request. Next, we must look at government financial support. As mentioned above, government does not provide regular budgetary funding to private schools, but offers awards to private schools for achieving various objectives, such as having many students perform well on college entrance examinations and successfully recruiting high-calibre teachers from other counties. In addition, government incentive policy doesn't distinguish between schools that take a non-profit approach and those that take a market competition approach, whether they have made a request for reasonable ROI or not, and whether they provide compulsory education services or post-compulsory-education services. Two points deserve our particular attention in this instance: (1) clear classification has been set at the grassroots level for both private schools that request reasonable ROI and those that do not; and (2) the ratio of private schools that request reasonable ROI is very high.

Fourth, will students still opt for private schools that charge tuition when public schools waive all tuition fees and miscellaneous fees? Though public schools boast many advantages, they are also restricted by the federal system, which leaves room for private schools to operate. One study conducted by Si (2009) shows that the lack of flexibility and adjustability in the system has forced village elementary schools into a disadvantageous situation. That conclusion also applies to our discussion of private education in Country J. Through competition in the gap left by the dominant public education system, private schools that have survived achieved a space in which they can thrive. On the one hand, private schools have met the unique educational demands of migrant laborers (for their children's education), and on the other hand private schools satisfy students' need to get into elite universities and improve their social status by excelling on college entrance examinations.

Fifth, will the development of public education affect private education? Owing to the relatively recent compulsory education law of 2006, which lays out benefits to public schools, and the 2008 financial crisis, private education has suffered significant setbacks in the last decade. The number of private schools in County J has declined from its peak of 24 in 2007 to 13 in 2011, as the enrolled student population plunged to 17,000 from 22,000. However, many private schools have survived the competition for resources and have even gained more social popularity and acceptance in some fields than public schools. County J did not encounter thorny problems when dealing with 11 closed-down private schools: as students were transferred to other schools, administration assets worth anywhere from a few hundred thousand RMB to a few million RMB were traded on the market, with the new owners using the assets for their own purposes.

Sixth, how does the private education system manage the relationship between examination-oriented education and quality-oriented education? The senior high school and college entrance examinations have significant influence on private schools' administrative activities. From the perspective of local farmers, college entrance examinations are unquestionably an important way in which their children can move to urban areas and improve their economic situation. It is also natural for parents to pay special attention to children's academic performance and for local schools to stress examination-oriented education. It is a rational choice for rural populations to migrate to the city to seek high-quality higher education, and neither governments nor other stakeholders have the right to make decisions for them. If the social foundation in the rural areas for examination-oriented education does not change and university admissions policies remain unchanged, private schools will continue to offer examination-oriented education as always. On the other hand, if any link in the supply-and-demand chain were to break or to rupture, the whole operating mechanism of private schools would fail. It is a long process, but to improve private education requires macroeconomic controls to be implemented from the national government and meaningful discussions to be held between society and schools. And of course, significant change will not happen overnight.

Finally, we would like to briefly place China's private education system in a global context. Education has always been considered one of the public functions of the government. National governments in some countries began providing education to their citizens in the middle of nineteenth century, as national education systems gradually started to take shape. At the turn of the twentieth century, major industrial countries had already achieved universal primary education, and in 1960 nationally subsidized secondary education was almost fully realized in all OECD countries (Tanzi & Schuknecht 2005). Developing countries are following the path taken by developed countries, as the penetration and coverage of education have steadily increased over the past decades. Hence, the basic outlook of global education development today is that compulsory education has been widely established, while public education remains the fundamental form of basic education. There are some differences between countries with regard to this overall pattern. For instance, in the US the private sector has been influential by providing various types of education and funding, as government and the private sector have formed a cooperative, rather than a confrontational, relationship (Salamon 2008). To overcome the limitations of public education and to enhance education quality and efficiency, other countries have been learning from the US experience and have undergone privatization reforms, which include the issuing of education bonds, the expanding of student choice when it comes to schools, the development of private schools, and the establishment of public-private partnerships. China's private education system has been developing in the context of a lack of public resources and a transformation in the country's social structure. As a result, the education quality of private schools and the latter's contribution to the public has been receiving more attention in recent years.

A new perspective on rural education development

The investigation that we conducted within a relatively short period of time cannot allow us to formulate general conclusions about the nature of private education in rural China, but the information and insight that we obtained does allow us to put forward a new perspective on the matter.

In the past, when studying issues of education development in rural areas, researchers have paid more attention to analyzing the result then they have to the process. Process analysis is a field of research that can provide us with a valuable perspective and which can lead interest groups and stakeholders alike to better understand the complexity of the Chinese education system and especially the institutional changes that take place therein. There are two main reasons to introduce local government into the research process. The first is the assessment of education development in rural China. Although rural education in China is still beset by many challenges such as a lack of funding, poor administration, old-fashioned educational concepts, deficient teaching quality, and relatively poor education quality, from the global perspective China has gained some experience and learned beneficial lessons from enforcing compulsory education in its rural regions. The national government has quite effectively galvanized the initiative of multiple parties in running schools; it has achieved the goal of universal compulsory education within a relatively short period of time; and it has resolved many problems of "developing great education under poor circumstances" while overcoming financial constraints. The hierarchical and "county-centered" basic educational administration system affirms the critical role of county governments in rural education development. Hence, issues or experiences cannot be addressed without the presence of county government.

The second reason has to do with a theoretical explanation offered by some economists to demystify the Chinese economic miracle known as "local governance theory." These interesting perspectives view political economics in terms of a rivalry between local governments – the Chinese government, with the mind-set of a developmental state, is dedicated to economic growth and views the GDP growth rate as a key governance objective. In addition, a highly decentralized financial system combined with a centralized official promotion model can also partially explain economic development in China

(Zhang & Zhou 2008). Though educational development differs from economic development, it is more problematic to evaluate and understand. The decentralized financial system and official governance characteristics (i.e. the official evaluation and promotion mechanism) most definitely have an effect on education development. In addition, as official evaluation contents change, the "political tournament" founded on economic growth has begun to incorporate social development indicators into its domain: "Local government becomes more focused on how to provide public services that satisfy public demand" (Zhou 2008: 321), as education is part of the public service. Hence, fieldwork on rural education development can be conducted under the framework of local governance theory.

The biggest difference between the education system in the 1980s and its predecessors lies in the introduction of decentralization and competition. Before the 1980s, China was dominated by a national-government-led three-level public finance management system, and a three-level (central, greater administrative area, and provincial) education funding budgetary system came into effect. Fiscal decentralization reform began after the 1980s. In 1980, "contract responsibility for revenue and expenditure by the central and local governments" was effective; in 1994, tax-sharing reform was launched, further specifying the financial responsibilities of the central and provincial governments (Ministry of Education 1999). The educational administration system adjusted to adapt to the changes to the national fiscal management system. In 1985, *The Decision of the CCP Central Committee on the Reform of the Education System* clearly mandated the need "to transfer the obligation to develop basic education to the local government; different levels holding different responsibilities," as county and township governments are mainly responsible for the administration of rural compulsory education. The *Compulsory Education Law* amended in 2006 states that "in compulsory education, the system shall be practiced under which the State Council shall provide guidance, the people's governments of provinces, autonomous regions, and municipalities directly under the Central Government shall make overall plans for its provision and the people's governments at the county level shall play the main role in administration." This clause elevates the main responsibilities for compulsory education from the township to the county level.

The traditional Chinese authoritarian system has evolved into a "fragmented authoritarian political system" (Qi 2011: 7) in the wake of rising regional autonomy; in other words, relations between the national government and local government has morphed into that of "local corporatism" and "economic federalism" (Tang 2010). Decentralization and the official promotion mechanism have stimulated competition among local governments, as well as competition between departments within local governments. When education has close ties with economy and society, that is, when it has the human resources needed for economic development, it becomes a scarce commodity, which results in the formation of a competition mechanism centered on the supply and demand of education resources. Its force has certainly been felt. In the case of education development in County J, competition is ubiquitous between public schools and private schools, private schools and other private schools, and even between county governments. Therefore, competition is undoubtedly a new lens through which to view rural education development in China. Research on competition in the education system has been conducted abroad, broadening the horizon of educational research and raising some policy recommendations for enhancing education quality and efficiency. For instance, studies show that intra-public school competition and public-private school competition are all conducive to improving education quality (Chen 2011).

The objects and forms of competition are can be seen in the following situations. First, there exists competition between schools. Public and private schools, administered by the government and operated under market conditions, respectively, exhibit distinctive behavior patterns. Students as consumers can "cast their vote with their feet" by choosing the type of school they want to attend based on a rational analysis of the educational services provided and the related costs, an analysis which determines the market distribution pattern of public and private schools. The theory that involves private education meeting students' excess and differentiated educational demands is the specific demonstration of such a supply and demand relationship.

Second, there is competition between local governments. When people have the freedom to move and choose their employment location, they tend to opt for areas with low taxes and high-quality public services; hence, local governments must enhance the quality of services they offer and the efficiency with which they offer them in order to attract students. This is the driving force of the competition among local governments. As a public service provided by the government, education naturally becomes a draw for talented individuals, but in doing so has become the cause for inter-governmental competition. For this purpose, local governments have formulated their own education development plans and talent policies, sparking both local education development and economic development. "Local protectionism" is the negative practice of restraining competition designed to allow "free competition," that is, restricting schools from other regions to recruit local teaching and student resources, and this is a distinct phenomenon in the private education field.

Third, competition is manifested by higher- and lower-level government relations. The superior-inferior government relationship is not an equal and competitive one; rather, it is a relationship between a "client" and an "agent." In such a relationship, local government faces less ideological pressure than the national government, but it controls more individual and local information (Zhou 2008). The regional impact of national government policy varies from region to region because of the discretionary power of local governments and different policy interpretations among local governments. Under the system of separating responsibilities, local government can even formulate more liberal and enlightened local education policies than the national government, spurring the latter to react and bring about "bottom-up" reforms. For instance, in 2008 the Hunan provincial government issued the *Hunan Provincial Government Decision on Advancing Private Education* and specified the private school as a "non-government public institution," breaking the definitional limit set by the national government as a "non-government, non-enterprise legal person," and generating considerable reaction nationwide. Certainly, higher-level government can exert influence over the behavior of lower-level government through the means of official evaluations, promotions, and funding. For example, County J was awarded with "outstanding county of non-government education" by the higher-lever government to strengthen its decision to open higher-quality schools and this better educational opportunities for its students. In the face of incentives from the higher-level government, lower-level government could exhibit some opportunistic behaviors. For example, it could overstate its performance to earn a better evaluation from higher-level government or it could underreport performance to gain funding for the purposes of fighting poverty.

Fourth, competition is manifested by the relationship between government and schools. Government may adopt "support the strong" or "support the weak" policies when it comes to its stance towards public schools in order to enforce the principle of efficiency or fairness, respectively. The *Promotion Law* stipulates that the governments at various levels shall incorporate private education initiatives into national economic and social development plans; hence, the development of private education becomes part of government performance evaluation. Government tends to adopt a "support the strong" policy, that is, it awards the administrative activities of private schools that help improve government performance through material and moral encouragement. As for the weaker private schools, they are left to live by the law of "survival of the fittest."

Notes

1 Data is from the 2006 Statistical Yearbook of a certain province. Out of the need for anonymity, this study does not indicate the province and does not use the exact numbers presented in the original source.
2 The following are some paragraphs from School Q's administration policy document: "During morning exercises, physical education, or computer class, if a student is caught not participating in the classroom or on campus, the teacher in charge of the class will be fined RMB 20 per student, the contracted teacher will be fined RMB 20 per student, and the teacher who is giving a lecture when the incident occurs will be fined RMB 40 per student" (13); "During the noon break, students are not permitted to stay in classrooms or to participate in activities on campus (they must return to their dormitory during this time period). If a violation occurs, the teacher in charge of the class will be fined RMB 20 per student, the contracted teacher will be fined RMB 20 per student, and the teacher in charge of moral education will be fined RMB 50 per student" (13); "The academic performance of the subject guided by the teacher in charge of the entire grade must be

ranked in the top 30%; otherwise, he or she will be replaced" (12); "At school-organized tests, a teacher who is caught for plagiarism will be dismissed immediately, and students who are caught for plagiarism will be persuaded to leave the school" (27); and "The school implements a lowest-place elimination policy. Grade ten and grade eleven teachers who place last two consecutive times at four unified examinations and grade twelve teachers whose classes place last at college entrance examinations will be eliminated or transferred to teach grade ten or grade eleven" (39).
3 This data comes from our investigation materials. The County J Education Bureau announced on its website its focused tasks for 2012, which include "striving to enhance education quality" and "steadfastly improving performance on college entrance examinations." According to the 2012 education "top ten project" list published on the County J Education Bureau website, its Bureau's project of getting 1,000 students above the admissions threshold on their college entrance examinations was ranked first in the nation. County J had fulfilled the objective of 1,000 students crossing the college admissions threshold in 2008, and had thereafter increased their target.
4 Zhou (2008: 89) in *Local Governments in Transformation* defined what he called a "promotion tournament" as local government officials of the same administrative rank being in competition for promotion. The criteria used to decide the winner could be GDP growth rate or other indicators such as fiscal revenue or the employment rate.
5 A few years ago, the author conducted a field study on the development of private higher education in Shaanxi Province and Huang Teng, President of Xi'an International University, and pointed out that people think that the rapid development of private higher education in Shaanxi is the result of wise local policies. However, the Shaanxi department of education did not formulate any specific policy at the outset of private higher education development in the province. Private higher education in Shaanxi has developed in the context of non-governmental interference, and only when it has grown to achieve a certain scale and acquired domestic influence did the government begin formulating supportive policies. Hence, private higher education in Shaanxi gave the public the impression that it is local policy that has empowered the development of private higher education.

References

Chen, Z. Y. 2011. *Study on Competition among Chinese Local Governments*. Jinan, China: Shandong University Press.
Levy, D. 1999. "When Private Higher Education Does Not Bring Organizational Diversity: Case Material from Argentina, China, and Hungary." In Philip G. Altbach, ed., *Private Prometheus: Private Higher Education and Development in the 21st Century*, 17–50. Westport, CT: Greenwood Press.
Ministry of Education. 1999. *50 Years of Education Development in the People's Republic of China*. Beijing: Beijing Normal University Press.
Qi, X. F. 2011. *A Study on Local Government Behavior Patterns in the Period of Transformation*. Beijing: China Economic Publishing House.
Salamon, L. M. 2008. *Partners in Public Service: Government–Nonprofit Relations in the Modern Welfare State*. Beijing: The Commercial Press.
Si, H. C. 2009. *A School on the Edge of a Village*. Beijing: Science Publishing House.
Sun, X. B. 2003. *A Study on China's Non-Government/Private Education (NGPE) Organization and System*. Beijing: China Youth Publishing House.
Tang, L. P. 2010. *A Study on Local Governance amid Competition among Chinese Local Governments*. Shanghai: Shanghai People's Press.

Tanzi, V. & L. Schuknecht. 2005. *Public Spending in the 20th Century: A Global Perspective*. Beijing: The Commercial Press.

Wu, Y. 2007. *A Small Town's Hustle and Bustle: A Township Political-Operation Play and Interpretation*. Beijing: Joint Publishing.

Zen, M. C. & X. H. Ding. 2010. *Efficiency, Equity and Adequacy: The Financial Reform of China's Compulsory Education System*. Beijing: Peking University Press.

Zhang, J. & L. A. Zhou. 2008. *Growth from Below: The Political Economy of China's Economic Growth*. Shanghai: Truth & Wisdom Press.

Zhao, S. K. 2011. *Farmers' Politics*. Beijing: The Commercial Press.

Zhou, L. A. 2008. *Local Governments in Transformation*. Shanghai: Truth & Wisdom Press.

Zumeta, W. 2011. "State Policies and Private Higher Education in the USA: Understanding the Variation in Comparative Perspective." *Journal of Comparative Policy Analysis: Research and Practice* 13(4): 425–442.

11 Shaking off adaptation theory, a historical misconception in higher education

Zhan Lixin and Chen Xuefei

Rationality is a thinking style that pursues truth and logically explains human activities. It consists of two parts: cognitive rationality and practical rationality. Cognitive rationality is rationality in pursuit of truth. Cognitive rationality is a thinking style that rationalizes cognitive activities, while practical rationality is rationality in pursuit of the *use* of truth, in that it involves rationalizing political, economic, and social activities. While practical rationality may be seen as the application of cognitive rationality, practical rationality is restricted by certain values and may sometimes be inconsistent with or even contradictory to cognitive rationality. Higher education is committed to improving people's cognitive abilities, but it is also responsible for satisfying social needs by delivering knowledge products. Therefore, from a rational perspective, the basic contradiction in higher education is the fact that cognitive rationality and practical rationality are at cross-purposes, where the former is the principal aspect of the contradiction and the latter is the secondary aspect of the contradiction. Such a contradiction can appear in various forms and be solved using different measures. This leads to a diverse array of alternative outlooks on higher education development.

Since the founding of the People's Republic of China (PRC), higher education has chronologically served as a means of industrialization, superstructure change, economic reform, and infrastructure development (primarily through the building of the world's top universities). The adaptation theory of higher education (hereinafter "adaptation theory"), illustrates this idea: the external contradiction of higher education (namely, the contradiction between higher education and social needs), which is believed by scholars to be its primary contradiction, is that the development of higher education must meet the basic needs of social development, or it will otherwise lose the basis for its reasonable and legitimate existence. As higher education has multiple functions, it is natural that the development of higher education must adapt in order to meet society's economic and social development goals. If the logic of adaptation theory is to be followed, the core value of cognitive rationality will be lost; academic autonomy will not be adequately protected; and the role of universities as knowledge producers will be marginalized. If adaptation theory remains an indisputable theory or law, then this idea will fetter the mind and discourage alternative approaches to higher education development.

The formation of an adaptation-theory-based outlook on higher education development was the result of a changing social needs and a misunderstanding of the nature of higher education activities. As a result, traditional theories of political economy sometimes restrict higher education development. Therefore, the study of multiple disciplines is necessary to re-examine adaptation theory and its prescriptions. This study takes a rational perspective primarily because rationality can interweave sociology, economics, education, and other disciplines. From a rational perspective, the relationships among internal and external higher education goals and measures can be explored with a view to re-examination and the ultimate formulation of a new theoretical foundation for the current and future development of higher education.

This study argues that the ultimate way to "shake off" the historical conception of adaptation theory and ensure the long-term and stable development of China's higher education system is to establish a sound domestic academic market.

This study will address the following five issues:

1 The predicament of instrumental rationality: outstanding problems faced by higher education in the pursuit of industrialization.
2 Political-rationality-based misjudgment: analyzing the causes of chaos in higher education institutions (HEIs) during the Cultural Revolution.
3 The dilemma of economic rationality: should higher education guide social development or adapt to economic reality?
4 The limits of practical rationality: the conflict between goals and measures in building the world's top universities.
5 Getting back to cognitive rationality: promoting knowledge innovation and fostering outstanding graduates through a sound academic market.

The predicament of instrumental rationality: outstanding problems faced by higher education in the pursuit of industrialization

In a broad sense, instrumental rationality includes any thinking style in which the communicative object is treated as a tool to achieve a realistic goal. Instrumental rationality is the opposite of communicative rationality in that it completely ignores independent human values and in that it utilizes communicative activities insofar as it only recognizes the use or practical value of a communicative object.

In a narrow sense, instrumental rationality is a thinking style that rationalizes HEIs' exclusive need to pursue industrialization, particularly in instances where they promote the development of heavy industry. Instrumental rationality falls under the category of economic rationality. However, because instrumental rationality places the state's industrialization over all other economic activities, in a strict sense it is a variation of economic rationality and it is able to exist as an independent category. The less industrially developed a country is, the more easily instrumental rationality can influence its people. Instrumental rationality consists of two basic characteristics. First, it prioritizes the historical role of national industrialization, giving it significant value, and second it is scientific in nature because of its strong logical and experimental nature and its emphasis on practicality. Instrumental rationality and cognitive rationality differ in that the latter pursues the idea that any knowledge innovation is independently valuable, while the former pursues the practical use of knowledge, meaning that knowledge that does not contribute to industrial development is more or less considered to be useless knowledge.

The higher education model of the former Soviet Union provides one example where the concept of instrumental rationality governed higher education policy. This model stemmed from Tsarist Russia, when there were many more polytechnic schools than other comprehensive universities and multidisciplinary higher industrial schools. After the October Revolution, the Soviet Union's higher education system became even more unique as it continued to separate more independent institutions from comprehensive universities and multidisciplinary higher industrial schools. In the meantime, it put higher industrial colleges and universities under the management of the People's Economic Committee and other economic authorities. Academic traditions such as academic autonomy were restricted to specialized activities. The integration of a highly centralized and planned economy system with a highly specialized industrial higher education model constituted the main feature of the Soviet higher education system. The great success of the Soviet industrialization program in the 1930s and 1940s made its higher education model particularly attractive and imitable to some economically and industrially underdeveloped regions and countries.

As early as March 1931, Zhu Jiahua, former Minister of Education of the Republic of China (ROC), suggested that China should imitate the Soviet higher education model. In May 1932, State Councilor Chen Guofu proposed a more radical plan of education reform, suggesting that:

> in a decade, specialized schools shall foster the number of graduates in agriculture, industry, and medical science required by the state's construction plan, and colleges and universities shall stop recruiting arts students so that the spending can be otherwise used for education in those science fields. State-financed students studying abroad shall also be limited to students in those science fields.
>
> (Su 2000: 78)

Many intellectuals disfavored and disputed this scheme when it was issued, and it was eventually relinquished. This demonstrates that even in the old China, the instrumental rationality-based thinking style in which higher education is deemed as a measure to achieve industrialization has been influential in government.

The PRC began to imitate the Soviet higher education model in the early 1950s, as colleges and departments were adjusted not merely in a quantitative way, but in terms of how they produced and disseminated knowledge. The latter adjustment introduced two HEI prototypes: Renmin University of China and the Harbin Institute of Technology. With regard to the first one, Zhou observed that "at Renmin University, an interesting thing was that no matter how many ministries and commissions there were at the central government, it literally had a corresponding specialty and therefore corresponding managerial personnel for each of them, except for military science" (Zhou 2004: 220).

Though a technological university, the Harbin Institute of Technology followed exactly the same practice with regard to the provision of specialties as did Renmin University of China. Knowledge production was classified as the meeting of academic or social needs. At that time, social needs prevailed, thereby excluding knowledge production as a means of meeting academic needs. Understandably, this reversed the mission of fostering profound scholarship through higher education during the era of the ROC. Although Chinese universities during the ROC period gave birth to "master" scholars, these experts did not effectively promote the state's industrialization. Since the founding of the PRC in 1949, the higher education system attached more importance to knowledge application and therefore accelerated the process of industrialization for a rather long period of time. However, such a system tended to suppress academic communication and politicize academic issues, which resulted in catastrophic consequences such as the Anti-Rightist Movement and the Cultural Revolution.

Later on, the leaders of the PRC quickly changed their views about the Soviet models of industrialization and higher education. In March 1958, during the Chengdu Meeting, Mao Zedong said that "in the early days of our new nation, we had no choice but to imitate the Soviet Union. Some practices were based on truth and some were not. We could not say copying is the only choice and we have no other choices" and stressed that "the sectors of industry and education were the most typical copiers" (PLRC 1996: 365). He then went on to say that the "Soviet Union's experience is one side, and China's practice is another. This is the unity of opposites. We can only follow the good points and abandon the bad points in the Soviet Union's experience. It is not to follow the good points if we look at the Soviet Union's experience in isolation without looking at China's reality" (PLRC 1996: 366). In September 1958, *Instructions of the Central Committee of the CCP and the State Council on Education* pointed out that "education was for a period divorced from production and labor and reality, and to some extent from politics and the Party's leadership" (Shanghai Higher Education Bureau 1979: 263).

Two risks were hidden when the Soviet model was introduced. First, as a country with a much less developed agricultural system, China could not necessarily adapt to the Soviet Union's models of higher education and industrial development. Second, with the advent of economic fluctuations, the higher education model of the Soviet Union, which integrated majors based on its own national strategic plan, would inevitably cause problems for China, including internal and external disproportion of higher education. Even if it were possible for China to suppress and/or ignore the contradictions and problems arising from copying a model tailored to the needs of another country as its national economy grew at a rapid pace, this would undoubtedly not be a viable option when it encountered an economic downturn in the aftermath of the Great Leap Forward of 1958.

In terms of the outlook on higher education development during this period, some contradictions between instrumental rationality and political rationality – and within instrumental rationality itself – appeared, as can be illustrated by the following three problems. The first problem is the conflict between instrumental rationality and political rationality. In the educational theories of the Soviet Union, because instrumental rationality was viewed as universal rationality in a seemingly scientific way, the role of political rationality was relatively downgraded and instrumental rationality and political rationality were mechanically integrated. At this point, Mao Zedong pointed out that "some educationists in fraternal countries such as the Soviet Union, like those idealistic theorists, are wrong in their pedagogy, especially Kaiipob's. However, Chinese people blindly worship him and treat him as a myth, and therefore he is perniciously influential" (PLRC 1992: 342). During the Cultural Revolution, government leaders remarked that education was for a period divorced from production and labor and reality, and to some extent from politics. The Chinese Communist Party's (CCP) leadership was in fact critical of the fact that in higher education, industrial-technology-related education was given unduly more time than political and ideological education.

Max Weber once classified the patterns of action of mankind into two basic types: value-rational action and means-end rational action. Value-rational action is culturally differentiated and individually selective and therefore cannot be proved by means-end rational action. In general, the more value-rational the action, the less means-end rational the action may be, and vice versa. Weber stressed in particular that value judgment cannot be demonstrated through empirical science, and "it does not belong in the university – but rather in political programs and in parliament" (Weber 2005: 145). Although instrumental rationality typically acts in accordance with an individual's values, as opposed to political values, it is actually more a matter of factual judgment. Instrumental rationality may therefore merge with opposing political values and cover up the so-called "problem of ideological differences."

During the industrialization of the PRC, leaders of the CCP and the state began to quickly realize that, along with the progress of the state's industrialization, intellectuals in every discipline would soon become political leaders even though their professional status did not necessarily mean that they would adopt or adapt their thinking the Party's ideology. Therefore, the ideological education of new and old intellectuals gained particular political significance for the state at this time. However, there remains the unanswered question about whether political rationality can be used to dominate and remold instrumental rationality and even cognitive rationality.

The second problem has to do with the dogmatism, extravagance, and waste caused by the Soviet industrial higher education model. Soviet industrial higher education primarily consisted of engineering education, which was divided into two stages – the basic stage and the advanced, applied stage. In the former stage, specialized courses are numerous and systematic, making student learning excessively burdensome and prolonged. In the latter stage, almost all actual production problems must be solved according to documented technical specifications, so that college students' learning is divorced from its application. Many engineering college students found after graduation that most of the basic knowledge they had acquired was useless in the workplace.

In his *People's Daily* article, renowned physicist Qian Weichang pointed out that:

> after we learned from the Soviet Union, the college curriculum became redundant, encompassing basic and specialized courses ending up with over 30 class hours each week. West German universities have only 17 class hours each week, and U.S. universities have only 20 class hours including experiments, but they have as well fostered high caliber graduates. It is not proper to make specialties too specific, because it is impossible to accurately forecast the demand for graduates.
>
> (Qian 1957)

With such problematic features as heavy workloads and excessively specialized majors, which were justified with the slogan of "integrating theory with practice," teachers and students were more likely to be viewed as dogmatic. After all, the teaching methods espoused by the Soviet model were stringent and highly regulated.

Another striking characteristic of engineering education is that it both embraces specialized knowledge and serves the social needs of individuals, families, communities, and the general public. The technical specifications that Soviet engineers developed took into account such factors as the culture, race, natural environment, living habits, and social development level of Russian society, which were far different from those of Chinese society. And this is why China suffered enormous economic losses during those periods when it had copied the Soviet industrialization and education models. Despite this unfortunate development, such problems gradually improved and were corrected in practice. Social needs were to have no substantial connection with whether or not certain educational strategies were adopted, adapted, or rejected.

The third problem is the compulsory expansion and contraction of the higher education system caused by China's planned economy. In an economic system where new majors are required to support their corresponding industries and technologies, the higher education system ends up undergoing constant expansion. In a report by a military engineering institute, it was pointed out that "in the early days of establishing the institute, we had only several departments for conventional weapons ... Later, as requested, our enrollment kept increasing to today's 7,000, still falling short of the demand" (Teng 2003: 834–835). Liu Bing, Deputy Secretary of the CCP of Tsinghua University, recalled that "in 1965, at a meeting of heads of China's HEIs, a member of the central leadership critically remarked that Tsinghua had grown too big and should be split into four. Because this criticism concerned Tsinghua's future, I felt gloomy" (Liu 2008: 400). Looking at it from another angle, we might say that without a fundamental understanding of university majors, simply providing majors that correspond with their respective industries and technologies will not lead to success in the long run.

From 1958 to 1960, under the influence of the Great Leap Forward movement, China's universities grew remarkably, far exceeding the capacity of the national economy. After the rectification and adjustment of national development policies in the early 1960s, the number of and enrollment in HEIs, though controlled, continued to grow until the Cultural Revolution began. The reason for this growth is that the planned economy required that higher education be developed ahead of time to prepare students with the necessary talent and technological skills to meet future demand for expanding the scale and sophistication of China's industrial production. When the national economy grows smoothly, the scale of higher education tends to expand; however, when the growth of the national economy slows down or even stagnates as a result of a lack of market regulation, the state will usually take administrative measures to force HEIs to adjust and rectify themselves accordingly. Though this can sometimes adapt the scale of higher education to economic growth, it deprives higher education of its autonomy along with its ability to develop on its own terms.

Many used to say that the Soviet planned economy system was a rigid national economic system, but we somehow neglected the other side of the equation: the industrialization-oriented higher education system is not only a major component but also a victim of the national planned economy.

The dominance of instrumental rationality over higher education practices requires certain social and historical conditions, as well as certain cultural traditions and a certain amount of cognitive understanding. Otherwise, fierce conflicts will arise between instrumental rationality and cognitive rationality and between instrumental rationality and political rationality. In China, adaptation theory, which was oriented toward industrialization and which governed the state's outlook on higher education development, actually problematized the development of higher education in two important ways.

First, higher education by its very nature is an enterprise that seeks to develop cognitive rationality, while instrumental rationality is only one of its many applications. Cognitive rationality is a dialectical thinking style that stresses critical reflection in academics and encourages people to challenge authoritative ideas. Furthermore, cognitive rationality opposes the treatment of knowledge production as a predictable or planned mechanical process. Instrumental rationality, however, is a mechanical thinking style, and despite the value of academic autonomy, instrumental rationality typically stresses absolute obedience to academic authority for the sake of efficiency, denying any substantial difference between knowledge production and material production. When instrumental rationality governs cognitive rationality, the vitality of the former will be stifled, and the latter will lack the momentum required for development.

Second, political rationality may strongly resist being under the control of instrumental rationality, which will likely further enhance the obedience of cognitive rationality to the latter. Although instrumental rationality and political rationality are contradictory, together they are the opposite of cognitive rationality. When instrumental rationality forces cognitive rationality to obey it, political rationality is then allowed to govern cognitive rationality. This is why almost all extreme practices in the Cultural Revolution, such as big-character posters, great debates, open-door schooling, and work-study programs, were put into practice prior to political turmoil. Influenced by the extreme left, political rationality could shake off the restriction of cognitive rationality more easily than instrumental rationality could, and it might ultimately evolve into absolute political irrationality, thus leading to the same unprecedented devastation that China's higher education suffered in the past decade.

Political-rationality-based misjudgment: analyzing the causes of chaos in HEIs during the Cultural Revolution

A thinking style that rationalizes political activities, political rationality is a specific application of cognitive rationality used in politics. Political values substantially integrate political rationality with cognitive rationality. The existence of political values is what makes political rationality and cognitive rationality mutually supportive of one another. Political rationality can prove its own rationality in ideas and actions only with the help of cognitive rationality. Under the guidance of political values, political rationality has the power to utilize and interfere with cognitive rationality in such a way so as to present political practices that differ quite markedly from cognitive activities. By its very nature, higher education is involved with the development of cognitive activities and not involved with political practice or political debate. Though influential, political values should never interfere with academic autonomy. Without such awareness, one may easily be distracted by political rationality and wrongly allow political values to interfere with and harm teaching and scientific research activities.

On the eve of the Cultural Revolution, the showdown between cognitive rationality and political rationality almost reached a fever pitch, as both academic and political activities became militant. In February 1966, a group led by Peng Zhen issued *An Outline of the Report of the Group of Five in Charge of the Cultural Revolution on Current Academic Discussion*. In the publication, the group stated that "(academic discussion) shall be based on the principle of seeking truth from facts, making sure that everyone is equal before truth and convincing people by reasoning rather than by acting like an arbitrary and bullying scholar-tyrant. We shall uphold truth and be always ready to correct our mistakes" (Liu 2008: 400). However, in May 1966, in the *Circular of the Central Committee of the CCP* issued by the Central Committee of the CCP, the slogan of "everyone is equal before truth" was severely negated. Instead, one found in the document the argument that "this slogan is a bourgeois one. They use this slogan to protect the bourgeoisie, stand against the proletariat, Marxism-Leninism and against Mao Zedong Thought, and positively negate the class nature of truth" (Liu 2008: 400). With such "evidence," Peng Zhen and some others were deemed to be "representatives of the bourgeoisie" and "counterrevolutionary revisionists." Thereafter, similar trumped-up charges were made, even against Liu Shaoqi, then state president.

Political values are at the core of political rationality, although political rationality does include the application of cognitive rationality, albeit cognitive rationality guided by political values. Political values can choose good cognitive activities while abandoning bad ones. Whether political rationality can supersede cognitive rationality is directly determined by the extent to which people recognize political values inherent in political rationality. If the power of cognitive rationality lies in logic and experiment, then the power of political rationality lies in belief and obedience: the "rules of the game," as it were, are completely different. In terms of political power, besides the slow massaging of public opinion and the use of propaganda, what was most essential to the official inception of the Cultural Revolution was whether support by the armed forces, the strongest political force, could be obtained. This is why *The May 7 Instruction of 1966*, a document outlining on the work of the army, was the political declaration of the Cultural Revolution.

During the three years of economic hardship that followed the Great Leap Forward, the People's Liberation Army (PLA) was a successful producer and was therefore able to support the national economy. In early 1966, *The Report of Further Improving the Army's Agricultural Work* by the General Logistics Department of the PLA was submitted to Lin Biao and then forwarded to Mao Zedong, who wrote a reply to Lin Biao on May 7 known as *The May 7 Instruction of 1966*. Three months later, the *People's Daily* included this reply in an editorial. *The May 7 Instruction* requested that each sector set up large schools like the one in the PLA, in which students "learn politics, military science, economics, culture, engage themselves in agricultural and sideline production, and set up some medium and small-sized factories to manufacture some products to meet their own needs" (NCNU/SNU 1982: 177). *The May 7 Instruction* also requested that in the education sector "the length of schooling shall be shortened, education needs a revolution, and the rule of schools by bourgeois intellectuals shall come to an end" (NCNU/SNU 1982: 177). On

August 8, in the *Decision on the Proletariat Cultural Revolution* passed by the Central Committee of the CCP, it was pointed out that "it is an extremely important task to reform the old education system, the old teaching principles and methods in this proletariat Cultural Revolution, in which the rule of schools by the bourgeoisie shall be totally changed" (NCNU/SNU: 1982: 179).

Early on in the Cultural Revolution, Chen Boda, the head of the Central Cultural Revolution Group, publicly argued that "our education system evolved from the one in late Qing Dynasty and later accepted a package from the revisionist Soviet Union. Our education system and teaching methods are largely capitalist ... We need overall eradication and overall construction" (NCNU/SNU 1982: 183). He also said that "the liberal arts need a complete reform, and science and engineering needs a teaching system to be designed" (NCNU/SNU 1982: 183). These statements actually reveal the political logic of the Cultural Revolution: whatever the people adhered to and developed during the seventeen years between the founding of the PRC and the start of the Cultural Revolution must be reversed. Otherwise, higher education development will not adapt to this political movement's basic goals. Therefore, the Cultural Revolution simply distorted and subverted the normal relationship between politics and academics, and between formal and informal education, as well as teaching relationships (i.e. teacher-student relationships and the relationship between teaching and production) in higher education. During the Cultural Revolution, differing political values frequently disrupted the normal operations of HEIs, as the following three issues clearly illustrate.

The first issue involves the mixing of politics and academics. Politics and academics are different types of activities: politics aims to redistribute political power and involves the separation and integration of political forces as well as the struggle between them. Academics aim to pursue truth, with its basic mode of action being dialogue and mutual criticism in the academic community. Politics and academics can partly overlap, but any academic issue should be solved through academic exchange. Political intervention is coercive and cannot help reach academic consensus. Academic freedom and academic autonomy primarily protect academics from being interfered with. However, during the Cultural Revolution, when academic autonomy was criticized and tagged as a value of the bourgeois right, academics were reduced to servants of the extreme left and for a long time fared quite poorly.

Supporters of the extreme left during the Cultural Revolution borrowed the so-called "theory of the two estimates": (1) before the Cultural Revolution, education was dictated by the bourgeoisie to rule over the proletariat; and (2) during this time most intellectuals had a bourgeois worldview (Hao & Long 2000: 384). With such "estimates," academic issues could be deemed political and political coercion could be used to handle academic disputes. Therefore, academics were ruled by a political movement, could not pursue truth independently, and worked in the service of political ideology. However, the "two estimates" were in essence value judgments imposed on intellectuals rather than facts obtained through investigation. Critics of the extreme left, however, had their own value judgment about the nature of education before the Cultural Revolution. Their view can be seen in the statement by Zhou Enlai regarding the state of education during the seventeen years prior to the Cultural Revolution. He said that "Chairman Mao's red line also shined upon the education front" (Hao & Long 2000: 401). Based on this view, therefore, the mixing of academics and politics was not a sound practice. They critics wanted to rectify the situation in Chinese academia and counterbalance the influence of the left. Efforts to do so by Zhou Enlai and Deng Xiaoping were inevitable and welcomed by many critics of the left.

The political trends during the Cultural Revolution were always unpredictable. To justify the reasonableness of the changing "revolutionary situation," some universities could not help but advocate an extreme left political position, and foremost among these universities were Peking University and Tsinghua University, which had writing groups that went by the pseudonym "Liang Xiao" (homophonous with "two schools"). Such political disturbances as the Criticize Lin (Biao), Criticize Confucius Campaign and the Repulse Right-Deviationist-Verdict Reversal Movement violated the principles of academic objectivity and justice, exerted a negative influence on the people's struggle against the Gang of Four, and left a shameful mark on the history of academic development in China.

The second issue is the relationship between formal and informal higher education. Formal higher education refers to teaching and scientific research activities targeted toward full-time, "off-the-job" college students, while informal higher education refers to teaching and scientific research activities targeted toward part-time, "on-the-job" college students. In general, formal higher education is the principal part and the model of higher education, while informal higher education is a supplementary part and makeshift form of formal higher education. During the period surrounding the Revolutionary Civil War, informal higher education was the main form of higher education in various revolutionary bases due to their limited material resources, but it still gained traction in terms of management and development experience. After the founding of the PRC, formal higher education became dominant once more, but because of the traditional ideas practiced and taught at HEIs, formal higher education was sometimes challenged by informal higher education.

After the Great Leap Forward, Liu Shaoqi promoted two education and labor systems, the first being the full-time school system and the eight-hour factory labor and governmental organization system and the second being the work-study school education system and the factory labor system, with the secondary technical and university system at the core. After Liu was deposed as the Chairman of the CCP, these two education and labor systems were tagged as another version of the double-track system of capitalist "talent education" and "laborer education" reflecting the bourgeois philosophy of education. However, during the Cultural Revolution, the two higher education institutional models, the July 21 universities and Zhaoyang Agricultural College, were still work-study schools. The coexistence of such part-time colleges and formal universities showed the continuance of the two education and labor systems. However, from the standpoint of extreme left politics, some people touted July 21 universities as "revolutionary institutions" and implausibly summed up the schooling experience as "open-door schooling," "brainwashing intellectuals," and "fostering successors to the revolutionary cause of the proletariat." On the contrary, Deng Xiaoping claimed that the July 21 university was just one of many forms of HEI and could not altogether replace the formal university. He also made it clear that HEIs would maintain their normal teaching and scientific research practices (NCNU/SNU 1982: 217).

The relationship between formal higher education and informal higher education is asymmetrical in that the former operates independently of the latter, but not vice versa. Informal higher education exists only by coexisting with and imitating formal higher education. The practice during the Cultural Revolution of using informal higher education to challenge or even replace formal higher education not only rapidly downgraded China's overall higher education system, but it also caused an increasingly serious shortage of human resources and several technological gaps, both of which impeded scientific and technological progress.

The third issue is the distorted relationship between teachers and students. First, the teacher-student relationship was misinterpreted as a hostile one. From the perspective of the extreme left, teachers who took responsibility for maintaining order were called members of a "bourgeois dictatorship," and they were arbitrarily labeled as "bourgeois intellectuals" and "reactionary academic authoritarians." Equal dialogue in teaching was misinterpreted as a cause for political struggle akin to big-character posters and the great debates. Teachers were accused of criticizing and denouncing students, failing in the supervision of students, and were completely deprived of the right to appeal and protest, often becoming victims of false accusations. Worker-peasant-soldier students born in the 1970s, though praised as "fresh activists in the Cultural Revolution movement," were actually victims who were unable to differentiate educational activities from production activities. Additionally, the relationship between production and teaching was totally reversed. Production practice is the intermediary step in the conversion of knowledge production into material production. Therefore, the higher education curriculum should account for production practice. As the knowledge production cycle is quite different from the material production cycle, higher education must maintain its independence and autonomy, and it cannot willfully change the process and order of teaching and scientific research for the sake of material production. However, in the "open-door schooling" campaign, such a typical phenomenon was seen at Peking University, as many science programs found it impossible to recruit students because "theories were often perceived as divorced from reality," and some arts programs were cancelled because they were "in opposition to workers, peasants, and actual production." The remaining degree programs were now required to allot less time to traditional classroom teaching and more time to workshops and production activities so that students could "learn what needs to be done and used at the moment" (Du & Sui 2000: 92). However, Jiang Nanxiang, former CCP Secretary and President of Tsinghua University, said: "If the principle of focusing on teaching is abandoned, the key work of the university will be off-track, causing losses and degrading the role of Tsinghua University" (Jiang 1998: 896). The reversal of the relationship between teaching and production undoubtedly downgraded the knowledge production function of higher education and place most of the emphasis on its material production function.

Many complex historical lessons can be drawn from the Cultural Revolution. The relationship between political rationality and cognitive rationality proved that the forcible domination of political rationality over cognitive rationality would have disastrous consequences for both political and cognitive rationality. In handling the relationship between cognitive and political rationality, the following three factors must be considered.

First, a natural tension exists between political rationality and cognitive rationality. Cognitive rationality can serve as an approach to political rationality; some other social factors such as beliefs, emotions, and customs can all be used in political propaganda and debate, and although they may also have a place in academia, they cannot be directly applied to activities related to the pursuit of cognitive rationality.

Second, political rationality and cognitive rationality have different modes of action. Political-rationality-based political practice is by default the competition between different political forces; it is partisan, organizational, and strategic. Cognitive-rationality-based knowledge production is by default an academic activity, which is nonpartisan, critically reflective, and academically normative. In academics, academic autonomy must not be affected by political movements. Third, in academics power and majority rules generally do not apply. Finally, political rationality must respect the independence of cognitive rationality. Cognitive rationality can exist and develop independently of political rationality, but it does not work in reverse. Political rationality cannot act without cognitive rationality in place. No matter how great the political forces of political rationality, it is impossible to force cognitive rationality to bend in favor of political rationality.

The dilemma of economic rationality: should higher education guide social development or adapt to an economic base?

Economic rationality is the way of thinking that rationalizes economic activities. Economic rationality is the specific application of cognitive rationality in material production and exchange activities. Economic rationality may often include instrumental rationality, and its scope of application extends from industrial production to the operation of the entire national economic system. The values of economic rationality are primarily oriented toward the growth of the national economy and the claim that higher education must adapt to economic growth and comply with and serve a fluctuating economy. When considering issues surrounding higher education, individuals who attach less importance to political rationality in favor of economic rationality tend to more readily accept an adaptation theory that requires higher education to adapt to economic activities. During the course of the reform and opening up, and in the context of the changing nature of economic activities, the economic adaptation theory was presented in three different variations corresponding to the following central components: the planned economy, the commodity economy, and the market economy. These three types of adjustment theories share one common characteristic: each of them understands an economic base according to specific basic economic activities so that the theory of economic base and superstructure can be used to strengthen their validity.

Shortly after the Cultural Revolution, the CCP and the government, led by Deng Xiaoping, rapidly shifted their focus from political instruction to economic construction. Deng believed that education and the economy were of equal importance, pointing out that "if a region or department only developed economy and neglected education, then they have not properly or fully shifted its key work. A leader who neglects education is short-sighted and immature and cannot lead modernization" (Liu 1990: 465). On the eve of National Day in 1983, he wrote that for Beijing Jingshan School, "education should be geared toward modernization, toward the world and toward the future" (RGHAED 2008: 41). Later termed the "Three Orientations of Education," this message has served as an important policy guideline for China's higher education reforms.

The three economic adjustment theories are very similar to Deng's Three Orientations. Requiring higher education to adapt to economic rules does not prevent higher education development from being geared toward the needs of modernization, the world, and the future. In fact, those originally behind the economic adjustment theories may not have seen any inconsistencies between adaptation theory and the Three Orientations. However, the Three Orientations theory is theoretically consistent with the idea of science and technology as a primary productive force and does not limit higher education to the realm of superstructure. Instead, the economic adaptation theory holds that higher education is an important constituent of superstructure, and it somewhat defines or restricts higher education based on a changing economy. Whether being used as instructions for leaders in education, or summed up by an authoritative higher education expert, the above-mentioned three adjustment theories are quite influential and should be critically considered. An analysis of these economic-rationality-oriented adjustment theories, including their intrinsic logic, mutual relations, and historical limitations, is given below.

First, there is the adaptation theory which argues that higher education must adapt to the planned economy. In the early days of the founding of the PRC, China employed a planned economy system, which inevitably came to influence higher education. After the Cultural Revolution, adaptation theory, which had been adapting to a planned economy, then developed into an independent higher education theory. This newfound theory, while still based on the relationship between economic base and superstructure, required higher education to develop steadily, as far as economic growth permitted, and stressed the importance of the balance between internal and external relationships in higher education. When Jiang Nanxiang, former Minister of Education, summarized adaptation theory from the point of view of his experience as an educational administrator, his description bore a distinct resemblance to adaptation theory of the planned economy era.

In January 1979, Jiang Nanxiang was appointed Minister of Education. His administrative program involved resuming the education line that had begun during the seventeen years leading up to the Cultural Revolution. He once said the following:

> Today's foundation of education was laid in the 17 years before the "Cultural Revolution." The "Cultural Revolution" negated the 17 years. In the 17 years, we developed socialist education, which, despite its shortcomings, shall be adhered to rather than negated. The line in the 17 years before the "Cultural Revolution" was in the right direction, and only needs to be gradually perfected in its reform.
>
> (CSHE 2008: 23)

In December 1980, during the National Symposium on Education, Jiang proposed that the reason for higher education reform was to properly deal with two issues regarding proportional relations: (a) the external proportional relations of education, more specifically the proportional relationship between education expansion and economic growth; and (b) the internal proportional relations of education, primarily referring to proportional relations within the higher education system. He pointed out that "in the past three decades, each time the economy advanced rashly, educational spending was cut and education was required to grow faster. This requirement was beyond the realm of possibility. It is proven that if the law of planned and proportional development is not followed, both economic construction and educational development will get into trouble" (Hao & Long 2000: 349). Jiang firmly believed that the state was still in financial difficulty, and determined that educational spending could not be increased and that higher education should be developed further.

However, some policies wound up running contrary to Jiang's adaptation theory when the planned economy system was changed. Jiang's secretary Hao Weiqian recalled that "the years when Mr. Jiang Nanxiang acted as Minister of Education largely overlapped the process of bringing order out of chaos, being a transitional period and a recovering stage. Actually, the state's undertakings did not get on track until 1982. It is like someone has just recovered from a severe illness and needs a period of recovery. However, if you do not get things done quickly, you will look conservative under the slogan of reform and opening-up" (CSHE 2008b: 23). He added that "Mr. Jiang Nanxiang assumed his office right in a transitional stage, which involved a complicated situation that in all aspects was difficult to cope with and control" (CSHE 2008b: 24). Though Minister Jiang Nanxiang faced many difficulties, the contradiction between his adaptation theory with a planned economy and economic reform was the likely cause and aggravator of these difficulties.

Second, there is the adaptation theory which argues that higher education must adapt to the commodity economy. In October 1984, the Central Committee of the CCP passed a decision to reform the economic system, which was a highly centralized planned economy, in order to open up and develop the commodity economy. In the decision made by the Central Committee of the CCP on educational system reform in May 1985, it was stressed that the purpose of higher education system reform was to reduce or eliminate excessive central supervision and control in the planned economy to motivate each party and help China's higher education system grow (Hao & Long 2000: 402).

He Dongchang, the successor to Jiang Nanxiang as Minister of Education, believed that the core issue of higher education system reform remained the continuing adjustment of the internal and external proportional relations of higher education. In May 1983, He argued in a national conference on higher education that "the reform and adjustment of higher education primarily dealt with two relationships. The first is the proportional relation between education and economic construction. We need to increase investment. The second is the internal proportional relations of education. Currently, we mainly need to develop what we lack to adapt to socialist modernization" (Jin 1995: 1439). In an article that he wrote, he said that "education reform cannot have its orientation determined only by figuring out the internal law of education. We must expand our horizons, keep an eye on the situation and trends of students, and identify their requirements on education" (He 1983). If Jiang's adaptation theory stresses that education shall develop as far as economic growth permits, following a top-down model, then He's adaptation theory requires education to prepare for the commodity economy, following a grassroots-based model. These two adjustment theories differ only in that one adapts to the needs of the traditional planned economy and the other to the emerging commodity economy.

Both adjustment theories focus on the function that universities serve for society and neglect their especially important role in knowledge production. The fact that knowledge production is diversified and unpredictable determines the flexibility and hierarchy of talent acquisition and the openness and diversity of social services. However, simply requiring higher education to adapt to modes of economic activity precisely negates the difference between knowledge production and material production and will in turn make adaptation theory only see relationships and neglect people – which is to ignore human resources and social resources – resulting in a situation where the mission of educating people loses ground to other priorities.

Third, there is the adaptation theory which argues that higher education must adapt to the market economy. This adaptation theory variation was established in the mid-1980s and was developed into an authoritative higher education theory in the mid-1990s. It differs from the previously mentioned two adaptation theory variations, in that it is result of the research of Pan Maoyuan, a famous scholar, rather than a theory proposed by a leading educational authority. Higher pedagogy majors in China systematically and thoroughly discuss this theory during the course of their studies.

In 1983, Pan Maoyuan published China's first book on higher pedagogy, *A Lecture on Higher Pedagogy*, in which he theorized the relationship between the so-called "external law" and "internal law" of education. Under the external law, also referred to in the text as the "upper law," "education must be restricted by and serve the politics, economy, culture and science of a society" (Pan 1985: 34). Under the internal law, which the text also refers to as the "lower law," "socialist education must foster well-rounded people development through moral, intellectual and physical education" (Pan 1985: 44). The relationship between these two laws is as follows: "The lower law must be in line with the upper law, which shall be realized through the lower law"; and "the external law of education restricts its internal law, and shall be realized through the external law" (Pan 1985: 32–33). Pan Maoyuan held that higher education has two basic characteristics, arguing that its nature and task are different from those of general education (for it is higher, specialized education) and that the students in HEIs are different from middle and primary school students. The students are generally intellectuals of about 20 years of age who are physiologically and psychologically different from middle and primary school students. They are defined as being "somewhat socially experienced" and "different from grown-ups" (Pan 1985: 13).

Maoyuan's adaptation theory may be easily misunderstood to only be stressing the unilateral adaptation of higher education to the economy. Therefore, Maoyuan pointed out that the "economy, politics and culture can influence higher education both positively and negatively" (Pan 1991: 217). In terms of politics, the formulation that "education serves proletariat politics" is correct. However, "it was wrong when education was later politicized and people were turned into slaves of politics and tools of class struggle, and education [was turned] into a dependency of politics." Regarding the commodity economy (and later the market economy as well), Maoyuan pointed out that "today, we say education shall serve the development of the commodity economy. It is not wrong, either. However, if the negative aspects of the commodity economy control and commercialize our education, we will go astray" (Pan 1991: 217–218). He reiterated that higher education shall actively adapt to the commodity economy or market economy to avoid economic laws replacing the laws of education, or the market operation mechanism replacing the educational operation mechanism. Maoyuan argued that:

> the overall goal of our educational reform and development today shall be the two adaptations, rather than one. One is adapting to the development of the socialist commodity economy, and the other to the needs of the world's new technical revolution and of the twenty-first century. In this way, we can properly integrate long- and short-term goals and make all-round, correct decisions.
>
> (Pan 1991: 223)

Although Pan Maoyuan's Two Adaptations theory is more in line with guidelines espoused by Deng's Three Orientations of Education, it is still chained down by adaptation theory due to the theory of the two laws of higher education being a mere replica of the internal and external relationships theory. No matter how adaptation theory is used, it is still difficult to defy one fundamental historical phenomenon: the basic principle of higher education has not experienced radical change since its origins, despite the fact that society has changed countless times. Higher education naturally embodies knowledge production and will not purposefully change itself to adapt to any external object as long as the mode of knowledge production remains largely unchanged. From the perspective of knowledge production and the social division of labor, Pan's adaptation theory has two critical shortcomings.

First, this theory has not identified the essential characteristics of higher education. Higher education is a series of teaching, scientific research, and service activities surrounding knowledge production, which by default involves critically reflective academic activities made possible through the principle academic autonomy. Critical reflection refers to the unique critical disposition of academics, in which any sort of knowledge is deemed as worthy of further study, verification, and joint exploration. Critical reflection does not need a standard answer, but equal dialogue between academic community members. Knowledge production is undoubtedly based on the classification of specialties, but in a strict sense specialized education is just a facade of higher education, and it exists for its critically reflective nature, rather than for the classification of specialized knowledge. By contrast, the knowledge provided by basic education in general only includes cultural products approved by a social authority or state power. Such knowledge must be strictly basic, authoritative, and normative, and it requires standard answers in a certain form. If higher education provides profound knowledge, then the acquisition of such knowledge is only connected with the nature of knowledge production and not directly with the psychosocial characteristics of knowledge seekers.

Second, this theory is still deduced from the relationship between economic base and superstructure. According to Pan Maoyuan, "to put it simply, education is superstructure ... Now that education (or part of education) is superstructure, it shall be restricted by and serve economic base and therefore politics, which is the concentrated expression of the economy. Specific issues must be handled by following this law" (Pan 1985: 35). All forms of adaptation theories share a common characteristic – they try to justify themselves based on the relationship between economic base and superstructure.

On May 28, 1983, Hu Qiaomu, a member of the Central Committee of the CCP and President of the Chinese Academy of Social Sciences, met with Minister of Education He Dongchang, pointing out that "education is rather complex. It is deemed as productivity and superstructure, but I think this is not the last word. Education shall include what goes beyond productivity and superstructure" (RGHAED 2008: 32). He added: "Marxist oppositions between productive forces and relations of production, and between economic base and superstructure are not all-inclusive. They cannot cover all social phenomena. If all social phenomena are classified in this way, we will get into trouble." Hu Qiaomu's conclusion was that "when studying problems, one cannot absolutize Marxist classical formulations and look at problems in a fixed way. This will easily lead to endless arguments." Unfortunately, some higher education theorists did not pay sufficient attention to such an authoritative viewpoint.

The key to identifying the social attributes of higher education is to look at higher education from the perspective of the social division of labor. Karl Marx elaborated the historical division of intellectual and physical labor, and three stages of the great social division of labor (first between agriculture and herding, and then between agriculture and handicraft, and finally between handicraft and commerce) as well as their relationships with privatization and the rise of nations. However, does the capitalist social division of labor have any other unique characteristics? In answer to this question, Marx argued that increasing specialization may also lead to workers with poorer overall skills and a lack of enthusiasm for their work. Marx described the process as alienation: as workers become increasingly specialized, their work becomes repetitive – a process which leads eventually to workers' complete alienation from the production process. However, Marx and his colleague Friedrich Engels did not delve into another aspect of the capitalist division of labor, namely, the rapidly increasing requirements of capitalist production on the accumulation of knowledge and the production skills of the labor force. The picture behind this issue is actually the social development trend of an increasingly intensified and expanded division of knowledge production and material production. The division of knowledge production and material production fundamentally secures the relative independence of higher education, which is therefore unlikely to be reduced to a dependency on economic activities.

As knowledge production is an institutionalized process with its own specialized market, and as it is increasingly integrated with material production, it has effectively gone beyond the point of traditional mental labor. If this hypothesis is correct, then knowledge production is neither part of the economic base nor part of the superstructure, but a relatively independent academic innovation activity that is primarily supported by institutions of higher education. As the goal of knowledge production is the pursuit of truth, with its principle of action being academic autonomy and its mode of activity being critical reflection, the process knowledge production does not adapt to other activities. Though knowledge production is independent of social activities of any other nature, its products reach all other parts of the social system, including both the economic base and superstructure. Therefore, knowledge production becomes a vital social intermediary between politics, the economy, social communication, and culture. Such a role as a social intermediary is understood in a positive sense, as knowledge production pursues truth and thereby brings hope to human society. Therefore, the most important function of higher education is not to adapt to modes of economic activity, but to lead human society on the way to its future development through the pursuit of truth.

Among the applications of cognitive rationality, economic rationality is a widely used thinking style that is often tied to cognitive rationality. Economic rationality and cognitive rationality are similar in two aspects. First, both the former and the latter are prone to shirk restrictions through social forces such as politics, religion, and cultural tradition in favor of pursuing goals through natural scientific experimentation and reasoning. Second, both economic rationality and cognitive rationality are both useful in market environments – cognitive rationality needs to be recognized by the academic community in the academic market, and economic rationality needs to be verified by production and exchange activities in the economic market. Therefore, under certain historical conditions, especially when both the academic market and the economic market are underdeveloped, many people will easily mix up economic rationality for cognitive rationality and vice versa.

Despite this fact, economic rationality and cognitive rationality differ indisputably in the following three respects.

First, economic rationality and cognitive rationality pursue different goals. Cognitive rationality is the common belief of knowledge producers, and it concerns itself with the pursuit and substantiation of truth. Economic rationality can also be deemed as having a concern for truth, but it pursues the use of truth in economic activities, where truth is required to accommodate economic benefits. Therefore, the concept of "the reasonable man" in economics refers to economic rationality reflected in individual behavior and cannot be arbitrarily applied to other fields, especially to knowledge production.

Second, economic rationality and cognitive rationality have different modes of action. Cognitive rationality looks at knowledge production dialectically, and it values most highly knowledge product innovation, eliminating knowledge products proven to be flawed. Instead, economic rationality looks at commodity production from the perspective of inputs and outputs. Commodity production concerns profit rather than correctness and will continue production as long as it is profitable. If economic rationality dominates cognitive rationality, then cognitive rationality will be forced to adapt to the principles of profit and efficiency, jeopardizing freedom of thought and the spirit of critical reflection.

Third, cognitive and economic rationality have different social functions. Cognitive rationality can be applied in almost any form of social activity, being an intermediary that enables social activities to continue to interact. In principle, economic rationality can only be applied to economic activities, being one of the key indicators of economic success. Economic activities, no matter how significant, shall not edge out or replace other social activities. The development of economic rationality sometimes needs to adapt to a certain basic mode of economic activity, but the development of cognitive rationality essentially does not need to be adaptive as long as it adheres to the pursuit of truth. Therefore, higher education, as an undertaking to develop cognitive rationality, shall undoubtedly be geared toward the needs of modernization, the world, and the future.

The limit of practical rationality: the conflict between goals and measures in building the world's top universities

In Chinese society, administrative activities have a heavy influence on political life and economic life. When higher education development no longer adapts to the transformed economic system and turns to pursue its own goals, such as building the world's top universities, the state-level administration will begin to play a direct and decisive role in the process. Administrative activities are examples of practical activities, emphasizing the principle of administrative efficiency, and are characterized by planning and strategizing activities. Here, the term "practical rationality" is used to identify the rationalization of administrative activities for two reasons: (1) in China, the rationalization of administrative activities once permeated instrumental rationality, political rationality, and economic rationality, typically sharing some common characteristics with practical rationality; and (2) the rationalization of administrative activities is consistent with China's traditional practical rationality.

Max Weber once pointed out that traditional Chinese rationalism is unique in that it pursues not a rationalized world outlook but a rationalized way of practice, that is, it sought "to achieve a specific realistic goal using meticulously devised proper measures in a planned and procedural manner" (Weber 1995: 32). He especially stressed the point that "Confucianism is more rationalist and sober, in the sense of the absence and the rejection of all non-utilitarian yardsticks, than any other ethical system, with the possible exception of Bentham's. Yet Confucianism, in spite of constantly actual and apparent analogies, nevertheless differs extraordinarily from Bentham's as well as from all other Occidental types of practical rationalism" (Weber 1995: 32–33).

After the mid-1990s, the Central Committee of the CCP formulated a strategic plan known as "Invigorating China through Science and Education," which was later approved as a basic national policy. On May 4, 1998, on the one-hundredth anniversary of Peking University, President Jiang Zemin said: "Our universities shall become a strong new force to invigorate China through science and education ... To achieve modernization, China needs a number of the world's top universities" (CSHE 2008a: 504). Later on, the Central Committee of the CCP and the State Council decided to support a number of key colleges and universities, including Peking University and Tsinghua University, in order to build a number of the world's top universities in a period of approximately two decades, thereby officially launching the famous Project 985. If the "Invigorating China through Science and Education" strategy is a systematic project, then Project 985 is at its core because no other project, including Project 211, launched in the same period is comparable to it in terms of investment, duration, and social influence. Though Project 985 only covers some of the key universities, it has boosted the development and change of the entire higher education system.

Two supporting measures were deployed for Project 985. The first measure involved an enormous investment, which since the inception of the project has involved RMB 28 billion from the central government and a roughly equivalent sum from local and other sources. The second measure involved selection and rewarding of outstanding graduates by initiating such projects as "Outstanding Doctoral Dissertations," "Distinguished Professors," "The Yangtze River Scholars," "Trans-Century Outstanding Graduates," and "Outstanding Young Teachers." It is true that some Project 985 universities have nearly caught up with the world's top universities in terms of hardware facilities and the number of published papers. However, in terms of the fostering of outstanding graduates and academic innovation, there is still a wide gap between Project 985 universities and even some universities not considered as among the world's best. More worryingly, under the lure of enormous material benefits, such phenomena as academic fraud and the fabrication of scientific research results persist.

On July 29, 2005, Premier Wen Jiabao paid a visit to world-renowned physicist Qian Xuesen, who regretfully informed the Premier that none of his recent students has been as academically successful as those who studied under him during the period of the ROC. He gave an example that since the establishment of the National Top Science and Technology Award in 2000, fourteen scientists had been crowned, eleven of which had graduated from universities before 1951 (Shen & Rui 2010). In fact, Qian mentioned several times that Chinese universities had failed to produce top-notch graduates. He once pointed out that "up to now, no university in China is run in a mode that helps foster graduates who can invent. They have just been following suit and acting so-so, and have no uniquely innovative things, as they are influenced by feudal ideas" (Tu et al. 2009). On May 4, 2010, Premier Wen Jiabao said to the students of Peking University that "the question raised by Mr. Qian Xuesen is both piercing and encouraging to me" (Gai 2010).

A world-class university can produce top academic graduates because one of the determinants is the capability of producing scholars of international renown. The Southwest Associated University, in the ROC period, fostered such Nobel Prize winners as Yang Zhenning and Li Zhengdao. Before the inception of Project 985, world-famous scientists such as Wang Xuan and Yuan Longping have been recognized, but none have bene recognized since, though there are many outstanding young academics in China. It seems that Chinese society is getting further and further away from developing the world's top universities. Where does the problem lie? From the perspective of engineering construction, if you do not construct a product properly, then the more time you invest, the less satisfactory the results will be. If this is true with Project 985, then besides insufficient investment, the scientific research system may require reform.

The current implementation of Project 985 has two characteristics – external economic incentives and grading. Both are influenced and determined by administrative authority rather than by deliberate academic rigor. Therefore the building of world-class universities is driven by administrative measures, as had been in the past. The only difference now is that in the past, when using an administrative measure to pursue industrialization, political debate, economic development, and other goals, practical rationality indirectly functioned behind instrumental rationality, political rationality, and economic rationality. Today, however, when administratively pursuing the goal of building world-class universities, practical rationality functions without restriction as the guide of the state's thoughts and actions. Under such guidance, the parties involved are less concerned with accumulation and perfection in the process of academic activities and instead attach more importance to the number and efficiency of scientific research results produced. This practice will likely be detrimental to the objective of building and developing world-class universities.

Higher education, as a relatively independent system, should pursue the core goal of developing cognitive rationality, which interrelates with the constituents of knowledge production, and which therefore should be the key factor in maintaining the regular operation of a higher education system. Also, the higher education system needs to exchange information and energy with such external systems as the economic system and the political system, which jointly constitute the external environment of the higher education system. However, the input of social resources works positively only when guided by cognitive rationality, or, to put it another way, when the internal environment of the higher education system remains stable.

Since the launch of Project 985, the relevant parties (i.e. government departments and HEIs) have made great efforts to improve the external environment of the higher education system and to increase the input of social resources. However, these parties have not effectively improved the internal environment and the efficiency with which social resources are used. Some current practices, including the hierarchy of universities, the talent appraisal system, and he bureaucratization of academic power, though they may provide short-term incentives, may increasingly impede the building of world-class universities and in the end lead to alienation, as such practices are not guided by cognitive rationality.

First, the hierarchy of HEIs is under question. Since the founding of the PRC, HEIs have been built and developed under the hierarchy of "key" and "regular" universities. Chinese HEIs were further classified into several ranks after the inception of Project 985, with the aim of positively promoting a diversity of educational tracks. However, there are a few problems with this project. Universities are excessively hierarchized; the process of hierarchization is administratively planned, which has not been a standard practice in the history of development of world-class universities. We need to carefully analyze and discuss the issue of whether or not such hierarchization of universities actually helps build world-class universities.

Project 985 was implemented in two phases. Universities chosen in the first phase were classified into two ranks. The first rank included nine universities, including Peking University, and the second rank included twenty-five universities. In terms of spending distribution, since the inception of Project 985, shortlisted universities have been hierarchized (as we have just discussed). Peking University and Tsinghua University were among the most highly financed, each receiving RMB 1.8 billion in three years, and each of the other universities receiving roughly RMB 100 million to RMB 600 million. Being more financially secure, Peking University and Tsinghua University have been provided with far better facilities than any other university in over a decade. In addition, hierarchization was expanded among Project 985 universities, between Project 985 universities and Project 211 universities not covered by Project 985, and between Project 211 universities and ordinary universities. The rank of a university is more or less connected with the amount of state funding it receives.

Given the fact that China's financial strength was limited, it is realistic that its higher education development strategy involved preferentially developing a group of high-level colleges and universities to drive the development of other universities over time. However, if this strategy should become set in stone, it will have a clear negative effect on the higher education system. Most worryingly, in the past fifty to sixty years, some local colleges and universities could by their own efforts have become national key universities. However, after the launch of Project 985, the Matthew effect has been seen among universities, making it impossible for other HEIs to overtake Peking University and Tsinghua University in academic excellence. Moreover, without being challenged by strong domestic rivals, Peking University and Tsinghua University will not likely become world-class universities themselves.

The production of world-class universities depends on the design of a competitive system rather than a highly hierarchized system as noted above. The US has about thirty high-level research universities at the top of its higher education system pyramid that consists of over two thousand HEIs. However, US universities operate according to the principle of academic freedom and compete with one another for funding. The higher education system in the US is therefore a floating one, in which no HEI can be preferentially treated or be provided an exclusive opportunity for development. European countries such as France and Germany adopt a flat higher education system, in which generally hierarchical and differentiated development is not allowed among universities. The UK is a somewhat special case, as Oxford and Cambridge have for a long time been leading world-class universities; other universities somewhat differ, and the government has taken measures to prevent further differentiation. However, Oxford and Cambridge are actually two universities consisting of a number of individual colleges, each of which is a traditionally classified teaching and scientific research unit rather than a strictly discipline- or specialty-based organization. Some of these institutions share some of the same disciplines and majors. Therefore, it is more accurate to say that these colleges are similar to independent universities and that Oxford and Cambridge are academic unions uniting some of these "independent universities."

The above-mentioned examples demonstrate that countries with developed higher education in general maintain a certain level of competition between their top universities for more routine forms of academic development. The US as a great power can afford to hierarchize higher education while managing to maintain the quality and number of its world-class universities, but it still has a strict system in which hierarchy is eliminated. Medium-sized countries such as France and Germany can only choose a flat higher education policy. The UK's practice falls somewhere in between, but roughly achieves the same (or a similar) effect. In general, an academic unit can only support the development of up to two academic schools. If other academic schools are not treated equally, so-called "academic contention and innovation" will easily become formalistic. In summary, in any country, world-class universities can only exist in the form where they are continuously competing with each other.

Second, more attention should be paid to the way in which outstanding graduates are chosen. Since the launch of Project 985, outstanding graduates have been habitually chosen through experts' evaluation of their work. Candidates first submit application reports, and experts then organize to review these reports. The results of the reviews decide the granting of outstanding graduate titles. This practice has an obvious flaw, in that such titles are not granted after recognition by the academic community, but are instead granted by several authoritative scholars, whose appraisal cannot match or replace the critical reflection offered by the academic community as a whole. When the academic community is administratively subordinate, the chosen outstanding graduates will appear to be administrative officials whose academic ability usually does not match those of the expert reviewers.

It is difficult to substantially change habits in any field. Therefore, when the fostering of outstanding graduates does not achieve the expected result, the relevant parties do not try to reform the method of graduate selection but instead continue to expand the scope of selection and increase the number and value of the incentives. For example, the 1,000 Scholars Plan, designed to introduce overseas graduates in the later phase of Project 985, is provided with a far wider scope of selection and far stronger financial support than previous programs such as Trans-Century Outstanding Graduates and Outstanding Young Teachers. However, the problem remains that most award-winners have to act as administrative leaders and few of them have become internationally renowned scholars and scientists in their respective academic communities. It seems that China has not yet found the solution to Qian Xuesen's question, discussed above, of why Chinese universities have failed to produce top-notch graduates.

Zhang Youshui, an official from the Science and Technology Division of the Ministry of Education said the following:

> A problem in such appraisals is that expert appraisal tends to choose old disciplines, because in old disciplines there are more old professors, many of whom are very famous; in those emerging disciplines there are fewer professors and many of them are not well-known, and therefore not likely to be chosen. However, from the perspective of long-term development, we attach greater importance to those emerging disciplines, which, however, find it difficult to be chosen. For example, in appraising the discipline of computer science, I attended the group meeting, and the members present ended up choosing Wang Xuan from Peking University.
>
> (CSHE 2008b: 181)

His doubt about Trans-Century Outstanding Graduates was that "the reason why quite a lot of the winners of this Trans-Century Outstanding Graduates fund act as leaders may be connected with the policy of the personnel department," and so he had "no clear idea about the eventual effect of the Trans-Century Outstanding Graduates Plan, because I have not sufficiently studied its outcome, but I'm sure it has taken a positive effect" (CSHE 2008b: 190).

Any system of evaluation is by default an external incentive system based on an administrative plan, the legitimacy of which lies in the innovation, instead of the efficiency, of the related activities. The contradiction between efficiency and innovation in knowledge production can be illustrated in the following three ways.

First, knowledge production is by default a process to pursue truth, which can be either true or false without substantial connection to efficiency. Jean-François Lyotard once pointed this out:

> When the efficiency of knowledge production becomes the sole criterion for university management to classify and screen scientific research activities, those research activities that look irrelevant to capital growth, such as the activities of great thinkers such as Descartes, Spinoza, Marx and Darwin, will be inevitably excluded in universities; under the guidance of a value of pursuing knowledge production efficiency, all

activities of a university will turn into technical ones, inevitably losing reflection, justice and artistry and the like that decisively make human thinking sound and healthy.

(Lyotard 1984: 50)

Second, the efficiency criterion depresses knowledge innovation. Knowledge production has two primary modes: the first is the application and promotion of existing knowledge production paradigms; and the second is the creation and experimentation of new knowledge production paradigms. People have already recognized the former mode, so it tends to be highly productive and more efficient, and it is more lucrative to the producer; the latter mode is challenging and risky, and it is usually suppressed by prevailing theoretical paradigms. Its success is only dependent on the constant critical reflection of the academic community. Therefore, three factors play key roles in knowledge innovation: knowledge producers' firm belief in the values of cognitive rationality, the spirit of critical reflection espoused by the academic community, and sufficient degree of academic autonomy. External incentives are necessary but have their limitations. Finally, the efficiency criterion stifles imagination, which cannot be evaluated but only used and appreciated, being an indispensable part of the dynamic of knowledge innovation. Knowledge innovation is not purely rational, but it is the dialectical unity of rational and irrational activities. In general, academic appraisal can only be used to evaluate quantifiable and procedural processes, but imagination is neither quantifiable nor procedural. However, without such a key factor as imagination, knowledge production will largely remain mediocre, making the making of outstanding graduates and knowledge innovation all but impossible.

Third, administrative power has been increasingly infiltrating academia. The power to allocate resources in the academy is referred to as "academic power," which is generally characterized by the unequal capacity of scholars with different levels of prestige and different qualifications to control social resources. Academic power is granted in two ways. It is granted by the administrative organization or by the academic community, the latter being more fundamental and authoritative. The division of academic power should be flexible; otherwise, academics and administrators will be indiscriminate, and this would threaten the order of teaching and scientific research. For example, in US universities scholars generally include assistant professors, associate professors, and professors. Most other titles are honorary and not necessarily linked with specific qualifications. By contrast, in a country or region that is academically underdeveloped, academic power will more likely operate in the way administrative power does.

In most cases, the academic community recognizes academic reputation largely without involving administrative power. However, a strange practice slipped into the Chinese academic community: each organization either pushes people with qualifications into leadership roles or recommends leadership roles for its so-called "outstanding graduates," making higher education increasingly administrative. Though such a practice advantageously facilitates solicitation, the rewarding of research projects, and the maximization of individual and small-group benefits, it had its disadvantages. The normal academic research order is spoiled, semi-public academic cronyism and attachment is favored, relationships in the academic community are undermined, and the academic lives of a large number of promising young scholars are sacrificed. When academic power turns administrative, academic officials may be produced, but greatly influential outstanding graduates in the international academic community are not.

Still more incredibly, the titles of university teachers are increasingly being subdivided. In particular, a so-called "first grade professor" generally acts as an academician while at the same time enjoying the lifetime power to initiate major scientific research projects. Such a practice is substantially jeopardizing the living environment of the academic community and bureaucratizing academic organizations. An academic community has two basic characteristics that should be honored. First, academic rights should be shared equally. While academic degrees or professional titles may differ, they should not influence the fundamental equality and equity in academic activities. Second, an academic community has the spirit of critical reflection without the hindrance of academic authorities. As knowledge production is often varied and unpredictable, knowledge innovation may make breakthroughs on the edge of the knowledge system. One can imagine that Isaac Newton's disciples were not likely to criticize classical mechanics and that Einstein's students were not likely to question the theory of relativity. China has no Newton and no Einstein, but the academicians have far greater power to allocate social resources than either Newton or Einstein could have ever imagined. Just as unrestrained power can inevitably be abused, so academic power can be taken too far.

Premier Wen Jiabao once argued that "university reform shall create an environment for students to think independently and innovate boldly. Universities still need to be run by those who know education well. Educationists shall be engaged in education for a lifetime rather than a moment. Universities shall gradually cease to be administrative and be run educationally" (Gai 2010). To this, we add that the key to disentangling universities from the infiltration of administrative power is not to separate teaching and scientific research from administrative activities, but to restore the "balance of academic power." That is to say, administrative power should be weakened, or it should be isolated from academic power. Even an educationist, if addicted to the pursuit of administrative power or even restrained by it, cannot be expected to help achieve substantial progress within higher education.

We do not oppose building world-class universities, but the measures used to achieve this goal must be chosen based on the awareness of the contradictions and conflicts between cognitive rationality and practical rationality. The following ideas can help the state, administrators, and academics achieve such awareness.

First, cognitive rationality and practical rationality belong to different fields. Cognitive rationality is primarily involved in the field of knowledge production, and practical rationality is primarily involved with politics and culture. In traditional society, practical rationality often restricts and suppresses – and seldom protects and promotes – the development of cognitive rationality. The "feudal tradition" mentioned by Qian Xuesen is still extraordinarily culturally influential in the building of Chinese HEIs.

Second, cognitive rationality and practical rationality perceive academic law differently. Cognitive rationality deems academic freedom as a prerequisite for academics because it profoundly realizes the diversity, persistence, and unpredictability of academics, and therefore opposes the interference of politics or administrative power with academics. Practical rationality, instead, views academic activities as linear, interim, and predictable, and is therefore inevitably characterized in its implementation by administrative power.

Third, cognitive rationality and practical rationality lead to different modes of action. Cognitive rationality is neither individual nor collective thinking, but the basic consensus reached and shared by each member in an equal, open, and interactive academic community. Critical reflection between academic community members is both the normalcy of academics and the basic mode of the formation and development of cognitive rationality. Practical rationality, instead, obviously reflects the ideology of bureaucracy, and it therefore habitually hierarchizes scholars and universities in an administrative manner and tries to artificially foster outstanding graduates and world-class universities through the unequal allocation of academic resources. The conjunction of administrative power and academic power is the root cause why academics turn administrative.

Getting back to cognitive rationality: promoting knowledge innovation and fostering outstanding graduates through the academic market

The development of cognitive rationality requires some social and historical conditions, most important of which its protection by certain academic rules and institutions (academics represent the highest level of cognitive activity). During the Middle Ages, though cognitive rationality was governed by religion, academic freedom laid the foundation for its future development. The reform at Berlin University in the nineteenth century added something new to the principle of academic freedom based on the development of modern science, including the separation of academics from politics, the spirit to pursue science, and the integration of teaching and research activities. In modern society, as cognitive rationality continues to mature, it requires increasingly complicated academic rules and institutions. As can be seen from the internal relations of academic activities, prerequisites to rationalizing cognitive activities include academic evaluation criteria, relations between academic schools, and the value commitment of the academic community. As can be seen from the external relations of academic activities, whether academics meet the needs of material production and social life is indicative of whether social resources can sufficiently support the development of cognitive rationality. Only when these issues are comprehensively considered and corresponding measures taken is it possible for proper institutions to be created to help develop cognitive rationality and drive higher education forward in a positive way.

Adaptation theory fundamentally negates the independent value of cognitive rationality. Therefore, though it has been trying to solve the conflicts between higher education and social needs, it neglects the internal conditions of academic activities that underlie higher education. In solving these conflicts, relatively simple measures have been taken: adaptation theory tends to use one social need to replace others, thereby restricting the direction of higher education. It simplifies the relationship between higher education and social needs as the former having to "adapt to" the latter. Such "adaptation" has caused the entire higher education system to go off-track. One scholar has argued that although domestic higher education reform "made higher education again adapted to social development, it might hinder the development of higher education itself (especially in the long run)" (Hu 2001: 289). The root cause of this phenomenon is as much about the ignorance of the differences between higher education development and social, political, and economic development as it is about the autonomy of knowledge production. Higher education did adapt to various external objects, but it failed to consciously adapt to the objective requirements of cognitive rationality development regarding the academic system and its rules.

Modern academia can be seen in recent years to have acquired two main characteristics. The first is that academia has been increasingly normalized, which is indicated by the increasingly regular frequency of knowledge production, increasingly objective and just academic evaluation, and increasingly open and transparent academic discussion. The second characteristic is that people more widely recognize the mobility, variability, and unpredictability of academia. These characteristics have been seen in China's building of world-class universities. We believe the rules of modern academia are more like those of the market economy and much less like those of the planned economy. In this study, we have introduced a sociological concept to explain these rules, which we refer to as the "academic market."

We believe that the academic market is a market mechanism promoting the free exchange and flow of knowledge production factors (primarily including human resources, knowledge, and academic reputation), and that its operation can secure the best allocation of knowledge production factors. Knowledge products, although sharing some properties of commodities, still have independent characteristics, such as creativeness, public awareness, and critical reflection. Therefore, knowledge production cannot be simply identified with commodity production. The academic market and the economic market have their respective, independent operating systems with almost completely different operating rules.

Regarding the concept of the academic market, Neil J. Smelser, Joseph Ben-David, and Eric Ashby have discussed it from a variety of different perspectives. Ben-David pointed out that, in modern history, only Britain, France, Germany, and the US are or once were global centers of learning and therefore established rather independent and sound academic markets. The academic activities of other countries and regions are, to varying degrees, dependent on these centers of learning, and their academic products generally need to be tested by one of these "academic markets" before being recognized (Ben-David 1977: 5). In the present study, we do not simply repeat and endorse their viewpoints. Our perception of the academic market is as follows: (a) the academic market, no matter where it is, is always based on the academic community; (b) the continuance of academic community activities forms the so-called "academic system"; (c) the academic system can tolerate different academic schools; and (d) all academic schools shall be consciously guided by the values of cognitive rationality. We will now discuss this multifold understanding of the academic market.

First, there needs to be a standard measure for the values espoused by an academic community. The first prerequisite to the existence of any type of market is a certain medium of exchange; otherwise, no exchange will be possible. The academic market does not directly use currency as the medium of exchange; instead, the evaluation by and the recognition of the academic community acts as the medium of exchange. As the academic community measures the value of all academic activities through evaluation, such evaluation actually serves as the measure of value of the academic market. The academic community will generally not recognize the value of all academic activities without this measure, including knowledge production, knowledge transmission, and knowledge storage. Regarding knowledge production, each of its three basic factors, educated people, knowledge, and social prestige, enters the spheres of exchange and circulation only after recognition by the academic community. If the role of the academic community is weakened or simply replaced by administrative power or economic levers, knowledge products will be subject to a divergence between price and value, and the operation of the academic market will collapse into chaos.

As a measure of value, evaluation by the academic community must be objective and just. The academic community's evaluation is produced through equal dialogue, and therefore has two basic characteristics. First, the academic community denies the existence of absolute truth, and it only accepts the existence of relative truth. It will not grant anyone the right to promulgate truth, but will only grant the right to put forward an idea or hypothesis and demonstrate it. An idea or hypothesis will be deemed valid only after the academic community has recognized it as such. Second, the academic community's evaluation is critically reflective. Any proposition or theory will be highly appreciated in the academic community only after it is questioned and most questioners can be convinced of its validity from both a logical and experiential standpoint. It is true that practice is the sole criterion for testing truth, but in academics practice will be qualified to ascertain truth or falsehood only through interpretation and evaluation by members of the academic community. Academic communities are classified based on discipline and specialty, their structure is open and changeable, and the academic evaluation criterion will gradually change with the development of academia itself.

In a sense, the role of money and power represents the influence and restraint of social forces on the activities of the academic community. Money and power should not directly influence or interfere with the evaluation of a given theory or work by the academic community. Moreover, the evaluation of the academic community is always accompanied by academic contention and it usually takes a rather long time before members of the academic community reach a consensus. Therefore, people should be patient enough to wait for the conclusion of the academic evaluation process without attempting to seek instant success and instant benefits from their research. Furthermore, evaluation by the academic community cannot tolerate the monopolizing of academic power. If such was to happen, it would inevitably alienate the academic market into an academic power rent-seeking market and give rise to moral bankruptcy and the stagnation of academic activities.

Second, it is important to keep the higher education system both internally and externally balanced. The operation of the academic system needs to meet both the internal demand of this system for knowledge growth and the demand of other social systems, especially the economic system, for knowledge application. This causes a dilemma: which demand should knowledge production meet first? Ben-David identified the four centers of learning as the UK, France, Germany, and the US, pointing out that these centers share a common characteristic: their academics first meet the needs of the academic system before meeting various needs raised by external systems (Ben-David 1977: 110). By contrast, most other countries and regions stress the application value of academics, which means that knowledge products are primarily used to meet the needs of social systems. The practice of Ben-David's centers of learning facilitates the balance between the input and output of the academic system, and higher education will therefore more likely achieve a sustainable level of development; otherwise, if an opposite practice is adopted, either the output of knowledge products will be insufficient, or the academic system will be compelled to remain unbalanced or even chaotic.

For the academic system, knowledge production and application are a basic contradiction. Knowledge production is not possible without knowledge application; and without knowledge application, knowledge production lacks the momentum for lasting development. However, knowledge production remains the primary aspect of this contradiction, and knowledge application the second. Knowledge production may sometimes result in a large number of knowledge products that are inapplicable. However, as knowledge is a whole, some knowledge, even if not applicable for a time, can indirectly help knowledge application, as long as it contributes to knowledge as a whole. The dialectical relationship between knowledge production and knowledge application is input before output. Haste brings no success; and seeking petty advantages will make the whole knowledge enterprise unsuccessful.

By means of academic power, the academic market can significantly guide and normalize the development of higher education in the following three ways. First, the academic market can maintain the persistence of specialized training to secure the growth of specialized knowledge. As social needs are ever-changing, temporarily "popular" specialties formulated just to meet social needs will someday turn into unpopular ones and be partly eliminated and/or replaced with more up-to-date specialties with the advancement of science and technology. The academic market, if it were to exist, could help higher education formulate specialties based on the categories of knowledge production, so that the provision of specialties remains persistent without being excessively affected by changing social needs.

Second, the academic market can improve the efficiency and quality of teaching. As required by the specialized division of labor in the academic market, HEIs should transmit systematic and theoretical specialized knowledge and exclude purely experiential or methodical knowledge. This can maximally improve teaching efficiency and lay a solid foundation of the transmission of specialized knowledge to students who will be able maintain an adequate level of adaptability and flexibility. Otherwise, teaching will lose its independence and continuance and be downgraded to vocational training for enterprises or other entities. Furthermore, such a process will safeguard the independent value of science and normalize scientific research. Scientific research projects most favored by the economic market are mainly well-established, technologically mature, short-cycle and fruitful projects, while those pioneering, technologically immature, and long-cycle projects whose yields are not fully identified are overlooked. In addition, most of these "blue-chip" projects are not logically continuous; one is followed by another which is distantly related or quite similar. This is not likely to boost knowledge production or improve the level of academic research. One thing the academic system can do to assure its own well-being is to safeguard the independent value of scientific research to prevent it from being restrained and misled by the economic market.

Third, fostering free competition among academic schools will benefit the entire higher education system. Knowledge production is inherited and continues through academic schools, which emerge because of critical reflection. When different academic viewpoints are respectively systematized through competition, academic schools naturally come into being. Academics cannot live without competition, which in turn gives birth to academic schools. The academic market is necessary in that it provides the best institutional environment for the separation of academic schools. Weber therefore argued that the emergence of academic schools is related to the difference in scholars' values. He argued, for example, that it is possible for an anarchist law professor to become an outstanding legal scholar, despite the fact that he negates the validity of general laws. Instead, his anarchist values can help him identify some disputable issues that are covered up by common sense (Weber 2006: 85). Therefore, Weber held that different types of values could become

Archimedean points in academics that will continuously enrich and breathe new life into academics. The academic market only becomes a market inasmuch as it tolerates different beliefs and values than the economic market does.

The natural sciences have evolved from theories to hypotheses, and vice versa. Therefore, the natural sciences involve negations, affirmations, and negations of negations that are characterized by divergence, competitiveness, and unpredictability. Lyotard (1997: 131) pointed out the following:

> Returning to the description of scientific pragmatics, it is now dissension that must be emphasized. Consensus is a horizon that is never reached. Research that takes place under the aegis of a paradigm tends to stabilize; it is like the exploitation of a technological, economic, or artistic "idea." It cannot be discounted. However, what is striking is that someone always comes along to disturb the order of "reason." It is necessary to posit the existence of a power that destabilizes the capacity for explanation, manifested in the promulgation of new norms for understanding or, if one prefers, in a proposal to establish new rules circumscribing a new field of research. Applied to scientific discussion and placed in a temporal framework, this property implies that "discoveries" are unpredictable.

The development of the natural sciences does not differ substantially from that of humanistic studies and the social sciences. They are equally caused by the dialectical nature of academic activities and must equally present themselves through the separation of academic schools.

In the 1930s, Qian Xuesen studied at the Massachusetts Institute of Technology (MIT) and later transferred to the California Institute of Technology (Caltech), where he was under the supervision of aerodynamicist Theodore von Karman. Qian recalled that when he came to Caltech, he "felt it was quite different from MIT. It was overwhelmed by academic innovation, which could be called its spirit. Here you needed to think about things that others had not imagined and say what others had not said" (Tu et al. 2009). Von Karman told him that the key to academic innovation was to "have very good academic ideas." Caltech "provided these scholars, professors, and also young students and postgraduates, with adequate academic power and democracy. Different academic viewpoints, even from different schools, could be fully expressed. Students could fully express academic ideas and challenge authorities" (Tu et al. 2009). In his later years, von Karman said: "I'm home for many years. I feel we have no such university. All of ours are average. They just say what others have said and dare not to say what was not said. No top-notch talent could be fostered in this way. This problem shall not be solved in our country" (Tu et al. 2009).

Fourth, cognitive rationality should be properly guided within the higher education framework. A value is a cultural object, which becomes a characteristic of an individual through internalization or of a group through institutionalization. A value is by definition normative in its significance for action by defining what is desirable; it is also a factor in the organization of a system of action, notably a social system, because it favors the development of some possibilities and discourages the development of others. In modern society, with the differentiation of social spheres, people's values are also differentiated: different social spheres have their own independent values; the values of different social spheres constitute a complete value system. Generally, in the value system, values of different social spheres could be interconverted – actions shall be taken in accordance with the type of values of a specific social sphere one enters into; otherwise, the entire value system will be functionally disordered. Different value systems both differ from and oppose one another, but they also share some things in common.

Cognitive rationality is also a type of value system. According to Platt and Parsons:

> the cognitive complex, the subject of this chapter, is such an institutionalized complex. It embodies the value-component of cognitive rationality. The term "cognitive" has a cultural reference whereas that of the term "rational" is primarily social. Cognitive rationality is a value-pattern linking the cultural and the social levels which are not reducible to one another.
> (Platt & Parsons 1973: 38)

They added that "cognitive rationality addresses intellectual problems which are different from questions of the desirable patterns of behavior such as between parents and their adolescent children" (Platt & Parsons 1973: 39). Cognitive rationality is connotatively the unremitting pursuit of truth, during which an individual belief-based commitment to such ideas as academic freedom, critical reflection, and objectivity and justice is made. Cognitive rationality's value-pattern must both be the common belief of members of the academic community and be institutionalized in knowledge production. In higher education, the cognitive rationality value-pattern is a core idea. That is, it can be applied to other value-related activities, but does not allow other values to be applied to its own activities. In the academic market, the cognitive rationality value-pattern must permeate any and all activity; otherwise, the academic market will cease to be normative and may be downgraded to a place where academic integrity can be traded for money or power. Therefore, the maturity of an academic market is indicated not by the completeness of its rules and regulations, but by whether cognitive rationality is well recognized and becomes a common academic criterion.

If the role of cognitive rationality as a mainstay in higher education is negated, an undertaking to pursue truth will turn into one to pursue the utilitarian use of knowledge, and academic development will therefore lose its spiritual impetus – this might be the most dreadful gap between the world's top universities and Chinese universities. The goals of constructing a sound academic market in China are both to redesign the academic system and to revolutionize the ideology of higher education.

Higher education can serve a number of goals, but never a single internal or external goal. In this sense, the critical reflection on the adaptation theory of higher education in the present study is intended not to completely negate its historical effect, but to provide another way of thinking from another perspective, namely, the relationship between cognitive rationality and practical rationality. We are convinced that in terms of the so-called "internal law" and "external law" of higher education, the most important thing is not that one of them adapts to the other, but that each country or region has several choices based on their own political, economic, and cultural conditions. If, in the past sixty years, adaptation theory has been our helpless historical choice, then it is necessary to shake it off and go beyond it in the name of China's higher education development and social progress. Cognitive rationality is actually a thinking style that organically incorporates various forms of practical rationality (and even some forms of irrationality); it is necessarily deemed as an object differing from instrumental rationality, political rationality, and practical rationality only because it is dominant in cognitive, or, as we may say, academic, activities. Academic market construction is absolutely not a social development objective that higher education shall adapt to, but a reformation of the relations of production to be carried out in order to emancipate the productive forces of knowledge production, eliminate academic monopoly, encourage academic competition, and establish sounder organizational and managerial systems for higher education in China. Looking ahead, when China's domestic academic market matures, China can realize a future with many world-class universities.

References

Ben-David, J. 1977. *Centers of Learning: Britain, France, Germany, United States.* San Francisco, CA and New York: The Maple Press.

Chinese Society of Higher Education (CSHE). 2008a. *A Special Study of the Experience in the Development of China's Higher Education in Its 30 Years of Reform and Opening-Up.* Beijing: Education Science Press.

Chinese Society of Higher Education (CSHE). 2008b. *Oral Accounts of the Witnesses of China's Higher Education Reform in Its 30 Years of Reform and Opening-Up.* Beijing: Education Science Press.

Du, Q. & X. Sui. 2000. *A History of the Educational System of Peking University 1949–1998.* Beijing: Peking University Press.

Gai, C. 2010. "Wen Jiabao Went to Peking University to Celebrate the May 4th Youth Day with Students, Emphasizing Science and Democracy." *People's Daily.* Available from: http://cq.people.com.cn.

Hao, W. & Z. Long. 2000. *The History of Higher Education in the People's Republic of China.* Haikou: Hainan Press.

He, D. 1983. "Education Reform Shall Be Based on China's Reality." *China Education Daily.*

Hu, J. 2001. *The Origin of China's Modern University System: University Reform in the Early 1950s.* Nanjing: Nanjing Normal University Press.

Jiang, N. 1998. *Collected Works of Jiang Nanxiang (Book 2)*. Beijing: Tsinghua University Press.
Jin, T. 1995. *Memorabilia of the Education of the People's Republic of China (Volume 2)*. Jinan: Shandong Education Press.
Liu, B. 2008. "The Hard Times: Tsinghua during 1964–1976." *Contemporary China Press* 3: 27, 40.
Liu, G. 1990. *Memorabilia of the Higher Education of the New China 1949–1987*. Changchun: Northeast China Normal University Press.
Lyotard, J.-F. 1984. *The Postmodern Condition: A Report on Knowledge*. Minneapolis, MN: University of Minnesota Press.
Lyotard, J.-F. 1997. *The Postmodern Condition: A Report on Knowledge*. Beijing: SDX Joint Publishing Company.
Northeast China Normal University & Shaanxi Normal University (NCNU/SNU). 1982. *Memorabilia of the Higher Education of the People's Republic of China 1949–1981*. Changchun: University Cadres Class for Advanced Studies of Northeast China Normal University and Shaanxi Normal University.
Pan, M. 1985. *A Lecture on Higher Education*. Beijing: People's Education Press.
Pan, M. 1991. *Collected Works of Pan Maoyuan on Higher Education*. Beijing: Xinhua Press.
Party Literature Research Center of the CPC Central Committee (PLRC). 1992. *Collected Works of Mao Zedong (Book 7)*. Beijing: Central Party Literature Press.
Party Literature Research Center of the CPC Central Committee (PLRC). 1996. *Collected Works of Mao Zedong (Volume 7)*. Beijing: People's Press.
Platt, G. M. & T. Parsons. 1973. *The American University*. Cambridge, MA: Harvard University Press.
Qian, W. 1957. "Educational Objectives of Higher Industrial Schools." *People's Daily*.
Research Group on Historical Achievements and Educational Development (RGHAED). 2008. *Major Historical Education Events in China in Its 30 Years of Reform and Opening-Up*. Beijing: Education Science Press.
Shanghai Higher Education Bureau. 1979. *Selected Important Documents about Higher Education since the Founding of the People's Republic of China (Volume One)*. Shanghai: East China Normal University.
Shen, Z. & B. Rui. 2010. "A Century Topic: 'Qian Xuesen's Question'." Beijing: Resource Center of National Outstanding Courses. Available from: http://news.jingpinke.com/details?uuid=ee12b734-127b-1000-bce6-3db61f9ef985. Accessed on January 21, 2014.
Su, Y. 2000. *Tsinghua University before the War of Resistance against Japan: A Study of China's Higher Education between 1928–1927*. Taipei: Institute of Modern History.
Teng, X. 2003. *A History of the Harbin Institute of Engineering (Book Two)*. Changsha: Hunan Science and Technology Press.
Tu, Y., J. Gu & M. Li. 2009. "The Final Systematic Talk of Qian Xuesen – About the Fostering of College Graduates in Technical Fields." *People's Daily*.
Weber, M. 1995. *The Religion of China: Confucianism and Taoism*. Beijing: The Commercial Press.
Weber, M. 2005. *The Methodology of the Social Sciences*. Beijing: Central Compilation & Translation Press.
Weber, M. 2006. *Max Weber on Universities*. Nanjing: Jiangsu People's Press.
Zhou, X. 2004. *Mission: The Century Legend of Renmin University of China*. Beijing: People's Press.

12 Donor behavior, donation income, and Chinese higher education institutions

Chen Xiaoyu and Feng Qianqian

Among the appropriations for higher education in many countries, donation income is another important source of income for higher education institutions (HEIs) following government grants, tuition revenue, and social service income. Over the past thirty years, the expansion of higher education and increased training costs have resulted in a sharp increase in the funding demands of HEIs. To make up for a lack of funds, HEIs worldwide have continued to seek further government investment and have striven to find other sources of funding support. In light of global cost-sharing reform, the significance and value of donations to HEIs by enterprises, social organizations, and individuals has become more significant. Donors have become major contributors to higher education cost-sharing following governments, individual students and families, and HEIs themselves.

In 1993, the Central Committee of the Chinese Communist Party (CCP) and the State Council jointly promulgated the *Outline for China's Education Reform and Development*, which stated that "China welcomes the education-aid donations of compatriots from Hong Kong, Macao and Taiwan, overseas Chinese, and foreign friendly people." The *Higher Education Law* of the People's Republic of China (PRC), promulgated in 1998, also explicitly stipulates that "the state encourages the investment in higher education by enterprises, institutions, social groups, other social organizations, and individuals." Since the 1990s, Chinese HEIs have gradually launched fundraising campaigns for higher education through multiple channels. In the mid-1990s, HEIs, including Peking University, Tsinghua University, and Zhejiang University, registered and established education foundations as independent legal entities, whose primary responsibility was to collect donations to support the teaching and research development at their respective universities. In the past ten years, many HEIs have established alumni associations, development committees, school boards, foundations, and other organizations related to the raising of funds. Over ninety foundations and over two hundred school boards raised a great deal of funds, enhanced the financial management functions of HEIs, and promoted the comprehensive development of HEIs. HEI fundraising efforts help ease the financial burden on higher education development and encourage HEIs to widen their social networks and promote the sustainable development of higher education in China. However, the proportion of donated funds in the incomes of HEIs is significantly low and has not reached the level of social donations owed for several reasons: (a) the initial stage of fundraising work by Chinese HEIs; (b) insufficient attention to some aspects; (c) the insufficient fundraising experience of HEIs; (d) insufficient management standardization across programs; and (e) difficulties in implementing the preferential tax policy for education donation (see Table 12.1). This situation shows that Chinese HEIs must improve their fundraising efforts and that they have many sources and options available to them when seeking out donations.

Relevant research literature on social donation behaviors

Donation to HEIs can be regarded as a private behavior consisting of the voluntary provision of public goods. According to existing studies, the motivation for donation can be generally divided into three categories: pure altruism, rationalism, and mixed altruism. Donation based on pure altruism is the most ethical category and is the most ethical form of donation behavior; it represents a personal choice to support group interests rather than to gain immediate personal benefits. Donation based on rationalism involves donating personal funds to public welfare establishments to obtain maximum personal returns, including tangible and intangible rewards such as a boost in reputation, an increase in social prestige, moral satisfaction, and a sense of accomplishment. However, many empirical studies carried out by Western scholars show that real donation behaviors often have more complex motives that cannot be explained through the models of pure altruism or rationalism. While admitting that free donation behaviors embody altruistic motives, we should also notice the more complex motives behind donation, including, but not limited to, self-interest (Steinberg 1987). These are donation behaviors that fall into the category of mixed altruism.

The analyses and studies on donation motives have theoretical significance when explaining donation behaviors, but they also help reveal the behavioral characteristics of different donors. Additionally, these analyses and studies help provide useful reference information to the government when the latter formulates relevant educational policies; they also help HEIs identify potential donors and carry out the important work of fundraising. Recent foreign studies show that many factors influence the donation behaviors of alumni, thus affecting the amounts their alma maters can bring in. Such factors include graduates' gender, living and working conditions, degree of involvement on campus, satisfaction with education received, income level, education quality, and the fundraising efforts of their respective alma maters (Harrison 1995; Clotfelter 2003; Thomas & Smart 2005; Holmes 2009).

In recent years, Chinese scholars have also begun to realize the significance of social donation to the development of HEIs and have researched fundraising organizations, donors, and donors' behavioral characteristics (Cai 2006). After studying the donation behaviors of the enterprises (not just those

Table 12.1 Total incomes and donated and raised incomes of Chinese HEIs from 1993 to 2006

Year	1993	1994	1995	1996	1997	1998	1999	2000	2001	2002	2003	2004	2005	2006
Total incomes of HEIs	168.4	221.4	262.3	310.7	375.6	544.8	704.2	904.4	1145.2	1446.7	1683.1	2000.2	2341.8	2699.8
Social funds donated and raised	1.2	2.9	4.2	5.1	8.6	11.5	16.2	15.2	17.3	27.8	25.6	21.5	21.1	19.3
Percentage	0.71	1.31	1.60	1.64	2.29	2.10	2.30	1.68	1.51	1.92	1.52	1.08	0.90	0.72

Source: China Educational Finance Statistical Yearbook

Note: Unit = RMB 100 million

involved in education) in Fujian Province in 2004, Cao Hongbin (2006) found that enterprises with more advertising expenditures, a lower asset-liability ratio, and more employees had more donations; the donation amount had nothing to do with corporate profits, but it had a significantly positive correlation with taxes. After conducting a statistical analysis of the donations received by the Tsinghua University Education Foundation from 1994 to 2005, Huang et al. (2006) found that the donations from outside the Chinese mainland accounted for over 70% of the total donations received and that most donations received were being used for specific purposes. Only alumni and school-affiliated enterprises provided non-directional funds. In addition, some studies suggest that donation tends to go to HEIs of superior academic renown. Comparatively speaking, major HEIs, especially the renowned Tsinghua University and Peking University, are more attractive to donors (Zheng 2008).

So far, the data and research literature regarding donations to Chinese HEIs are relatively sparse. The limited literature and data that we have is mainly about the introduction of foreign experience, summaries of fundraising experiences and the lessons that HEI employees have learned. There is almost no literature containing an empirical analysis using certain types of representative data. However, the literature we do have has important reference value and has significant relevance for the fundraising work carried out by HEIs.

Based on the survey data on the fundraising conditions of HEIs in China that the China Charity and Donation Information Center (CCDIC) and the China Education Development Foundation (CEDF) conducted in 2009, the present study analyzes the characteristics of the funds donated to HEIs, the main features of donation income, and the behavioral characteristics of donors. It aims to provide advice for HEIs in the form of specific fundraising strategies and plans and reference data that the state can use to formulate relevant policies to encourage education-based donations.

Data description

The sample data herein is about the donation income of 109 HEIs subordinate to central departments and 743 local HEIs from 2005 to 2008, and 21,958 donations received by local HEIs from 2005 to 2008. The frequency distribution of sample HEIs and the total donation income amounts of various HEIs from 2005 to 2008 are presented in Table 12.2.

The data in Table 12.2 shows that among the 852 HEIs that reported donation income, comprehensive universities ranked first in total donation income received from 2005 to 2008, with an average donation income of RMB 38,446,338. Meanwhile, the average donation income of nationalities and science and engineering HEIs were RMB 24,539,522 and RMB 14,892,636, respectively (based on the nature of the HEI). The average donation income was RMB 35,788,976 for universities, RMB 5,929,351 for undergraduate colleges, and RMB 2,339,025 for higher vocational and professional colleges (based on administration type). Lastly, the average donation

Table 12.2 Frequency distribution of sample HEIs and total donation income of various HEIs from 2005 to 2008

Nature	N	Proportion (%)	Mean donation income	Standard deviation
Comprehensive universities	162	19.0	3,844.6338	14,416.38439
Science and engineering universities	297	34.9	1,489.2636	8,007.87007
Agricultural and forestry universities	40	4.7	542.6774	630.99638
Forestry HEIs	10	1.2	1289.4550	2829.39290
Medical HEIs	75	8.8	479.2916	1261.39552
Normal HEIs	125	14.7	691.3709	1,774.98865
Language HEIs	14	1.6	773.8243	842.87296
Finance and economics HEIs	58	6.8	645.0981	1,597.13015
Politics and law HEIs	21	2.5	550.7186	1,066.95677
Sports HEIs	12	1.4	179.8083	231.63523
Art HEIs	29	3.4	535.5751	1,172.31782
Nationalities HEIs	9	1.1	2,453.9522	5,734.45221
Administration type	**N**	**Proportion (%)**	**Mean**	**Standard deviation**
Universities	307	36.0	3,578.8976	13,055.02685
Undergraduate colleges	266	31.2	592.9351	1,392.15184
Higher vocational and professional colleges	279	32.7	233.9025	505.17301
Projects 211/985	**N**	**Proportion (%)**	**Mean**	**Standard deviation**
Non-Project 211/985 HEIs	743	87.2	715.8606	2,618.61977
Project 211/985 HEIs	109	12.8	7,246.0248	20,544.99280
Total	852	100	1,551.2924	8,019.35879

Note: Unit = RMB 10,000

income of Project 211/985 HEIs was RMB 72,460,248 from 2005 to 2008, and for the non-Project 211/985 HEIs it was RMB 7,158,606.

Statistical data on HEI donation income shows that different types of HEIs are quite different when it comes to the level of donation income they receive, and that big differences exist between Project 211/985 and non-Project 211/985 HEIs, among universities, undergraduate colleges and higher vocational and professional colleges, and among HEIs with different discipline specializations. In order to more accurately and intuitively measure the differences between HEIs when it comes to donation income distribution, the present study will analyze the distribution of donation income of Chinese HEIs from 2005 to 2008 by using the Lorenz curve and the Gini coefficient. Figure 12.1 shows the Lorenz curve, in which the horizontal coordinate denotes the cumulative percentage of HEIs and the vertical coordinate denotes the cumulative proportion of donation income of each university or college to total HEI donation income. In Figure 12.1, the donation incomes of all HEIs (under the central government or local governments) from 2005 to 2008 are arranged in order from lowest to highest.

Figure 12.1 shows that the distribution of HEI donation income in China is not even. According to the Lorenz curve, the Gini coefficient calculated is 86.7%, and donated funds show an obvious concentration tendency. Eighty percent of the total donation income comes from donations made to the top 10% of the HEIs with the most donations. Fifty percent of the reported 852 HEIs with little donation income only account for 1.53% of total donation income. The donated funds of a few HEIs account for a large proportion of the

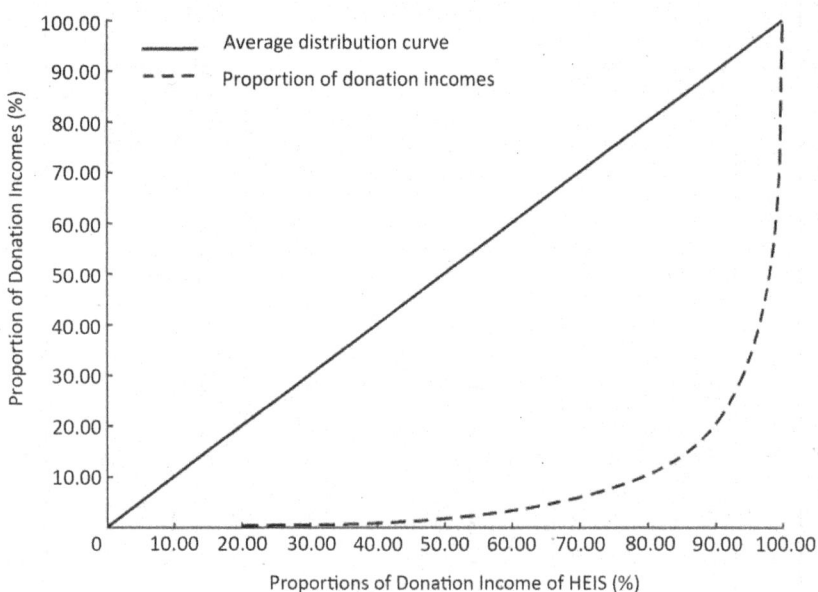

Figure 12.1 Lorenz curve on distribution of HEI donation income

donated funds of all sample HEIs. Except for very few special circumstances, those HEIs with the most donations are well-known institutions with a great deal of social prestige and are leaders in teaching and scientific research. For example, the total donation income of Peking University, Tsinghua University, and Zhejiang University from 2005 to 2008 exceeded RMB 3 billion, accounting for over one-quarter of total donation income of all 852 sample HEIs during the same period. The distribution of HEI donation income shows the presence of the Matthew effect (also Pareto principle). Overall, donations to HEIs are an income source that supports the strong instead of the weak.

Single donations of local HEIs from 2005 to 2008 come from six types of donors: enterprises, public institutions, social organizations (excluding foundations), foundations, individuals, and governmental organizations. Donations are used in six categories: scholarships and grants, faculty scholarships, scientific research and disciplinary development, infrastructure construction, other specified uses, and non-specified uses. The distribution of various donations and average amounts are shown in Table 12.3.

Table 12.3 shows that the donations received by local HEIs from 2005 to 2008 share the following characteristics: (a) among the different types of donors, enterprises and individuals rank first in the number of donations, which respectively account for 36.3% and 28.9% of 21,958 total donations; (b) on average, the single donation amounts of foundations and individuals are relatively large, at RMB 772,238 and RMB 391,398, respectively; (c) the donations for non-specified uses and scholarships and grants predominate, at 38.9% and 28.9%, respectively; and (d) donations for infrastructure construction and scientific research and disciplinary development have the largest mean amounts, at RMB 881,278 and RMB 535,069, respectively.

Further analysis and research results show that different donors have different purposes for and tendencies toward donating to different types of educational institutions (see Supplementary Table 12.S1 and Supplementary Table 12.S2 below). Overall, the number of donations to universities (46.2% of all donations) and academies (35.4% of all donations) are much higher than the number of donations made to higher vocational and professional colleges (18.5% of all donations). The donations of foundations are most concentrated in universities (70.8%), social organizations (52.8%), and enterprises (47.9%), which prefer donations to universities. For different types of HEIs, the lists of donors who have donated most frequently are very different. Donation purposes of different types of donors are obviously different: most donations from enterprises, social organizations, and foundations are used for scholarships and grants, while most donations from individuals, governments, and public institutions are for non-specified uses.

Factors influencing the donation income of local HEIs

In accordance with existing research literature and data, the present study assumes that the following factors influence the donation income of local HEIs:

Table 12.3 Frequency distribution of donations received by local HEIs from 2005 to 2008 and donation amounts

Type of donor	N	Proportion (%)	Mean amount	Standard deviation
Enterprises	7,979	36.3	13.6263	64.54359
Public institutions	2,794	12.7	7.0794	71.72789
Social organizations (excluding foundations)	986	4.5	14.6403	38.97016
Foundations	1,563	7.1	77.2238	432.94153
Individuals	6,348	28.9	39.1398	201.57464
Governmental organizations	1,605	7.3	8.5010	32.53463
Total	21,275	96.9	24.7118	169.25939
Loss	683	3.1		
Donation use	N	Proportion (%)	Mean amount	Standard deviation
Scholarship and grants	6,344	28.9	13.1684	140.20588
Faculty scholarship	236	1.1	36.2100	129.71570
Scientific research and disciplinary development	865	3.9	53.5069	309.39331
Infrastructure construction	1,847	8.4	88.1278	343.82157
Other specified uses	3,323	15.1	17.6740	122.89921
Non-specified uses	8,550	38.9	17.5909	98.97943
Total	21,165	96.4	24.1094	164.55879
Loss	793	3.6		
Total	21,958	100.0	25.2449	169.17698

Note: Unit = RMB 10,000

Teaching and scientific research level and social reputation: the latest rankings of China's 800 universities released in the 2010 Report on Evaluation and Study of China's Universities by the University Evaluation Research Group of the China Alumni Network is used as an indicator.[1]

Disciplinary nature: a set of dummy variables is constructed according to the disciplinary nature codes of HEIs in order to distinguish the comprehensive universities, science and engineering HEIs, normal HEIs, medical HEIs, and other HEIs from one another.

Administration type: a set of dummy variables is constructed according to different administration types (universities, undergraduate colleges, higher vocational and professional colleges).

Location: a set of dummy variables is constructed according to regions (eastern, central, and western) where the HEIs are located.

Fundraising efforts: whether the university or college has established a foundation that is independently responsible for fundraising is used as an indicator.

First, the variance analysis of donation income was carried out by using the above variables, and the impacts of the factors (ranking, type, nature, region, and the establishing foundation) on HEI donation income were respectively checked. The results of multi-factor variance analysis are shown in Supplementary Table 12.S3, which demonstrate that except for disciplinary nature, the significance probabilities of all other factors after the variance analysis are less than 0.05. Therefore, the original hypothesis is rejected, and it is proven that with different rankings, different administration types, different locations, and different situations regarding the establishment of a foundation, the average donation income of HEIs will be significantly different.

The stepwise regression was conducted with the donation income logarithm as the dependent variable and with universities, academies (different from higher vocational and professional colleges), university or college ranking, central regions, western regions, foundations, comprehensive universities, science and engineering HEIs, normal universities, and medical HEIs (different from other HEIs) as the independent variables. The regression results are presented in Table 12.4.

The regression results presented above show that foundation (established or not), ranking, and geographical location of the university or college significantly influence the donation income that the university or college will receive. On average, the donation income of HEIs with foundations is 10.36 times greater than HEIs without foundations (e2.338 = 10.36). A rise of one ranking means the average donation income increases by 0.3%. The average donation income of HEIs in central regions is less than the donation income of HEIs in other regions.

On the one hand, the quantitative relationship between donation income and the establishment of a foundation shows that the specialized fundraising organizations of HEIs can facilitate fundraising efforts. On the other hand, it is necessary for those HEIs with more donation income to establish an independent foundation to fundraise and manage donations. This is because an independent organization itself needs certain resources to support its operations. In addition, China's relevant national and local regulations have made corresponding stipulations regarding the original fund limits required for the registration of foundations.[2]

Table 12.4 Regression coefficients of factors influencing HEI donation income

Model	Non-standardized coefficients		Standard coefficients	t	Sig.
	B	Standard error			
(Constant)	6.283	0.191		32.915	0.000
Having foundations or not (1 = having)	2.338	0.244	0.413	9.581	0.000
Rankings	-0.003	0.001	-0.256	-5.972	0.000
Central regions	-0.530	0.168	-0.135	-3.157	0.002
R squared = 0.291					

Note: Dependent variable = donation income logarithm

However, these explanations prove the significance of an independent fundraising organization in fundraising work. HEIs with upper rankings can obtain more donations, which is consistent with the conclusion in the foreign empirical research literature that education quality and students' satisfaction with their alma mater education affect the likelihood of their alma mater receiving donations. On the one hand, the university or college with the higher academic ranking and the better social reputation is likely to obtain more social recognition and attention, thus being more likely to attract more donors. On the other hand, it is generally believed that graduates from HEIs with higher teaching levels and higher levels of scientific research will perhaps earn higher incomes and therefore be better able to repay their alma maters. Graduates of universities or colleges with higher a higher ranking should have a higher degree of satisfaction with their alma mater education, so they will likely be more willing to donate to their alma mater. The donations to HEIs in central regions are less than those in other regions primarily because (a) eastern regions of China have a higher level of social and economic development; (b) donors have more abundant resources, making the potential for donation greater; (c) western regions have a special attraction for donors inasmuch as they contain many poverty-stricken areas; and (d) there has existed a "western development strategy" for some time now. However, the same resources and conditions that have been referred to above are simply not available to HEIs in the central regions of China.

Donation behavioral characteristics of different types of donors

The present study analyzes the donation motives and behavioral characteristics of different types of donors. From the perspective of the donors' nature category, the donation behaviors of enterprises should be rational if they belong to organizations that pursue maximum profits. Enterprises will usually select the donation objects and items that maximize publicity, their social influence, and their corporate image, or that promote cooperation between enterprises and HEIs. Nonprofit organizations, including social organizations and foundations, have as their mission the promotion of the development of corresponding public welfare undertakings, so their donation behaviors perhaps show more signs of altruism. Public institutions and governmental organizations belong to the public sector, which means that the allocation and use of their financial resources are restrained by public selection processes and administrative procedures. The objectives of individual donations tend to vary. For example, alumni tend to donate to their alma maters, while non-alumni tend to donate due to a sense of altruism or in pursuit of bettering their social image and garnering public opinion in their favor. It may be likely that the donation motives of public institutions, governments, and individuals are combined with altruism.

The present study discusses how HEIs are receiving their donations as well as the behavioral differences of different donation subjects according to ranking, type, and nature through the multivariate logistic regression method and according to donation frequency. The data used is the detailed data on the single donations received by local HEIs. For easy analysis, the present study classifies local HEIs into five groups according to their ranking: (a) comprehensive universities; (b) science and engineering HEIs; (c) medical HEIs; (d) normal HEIs; and (e) other HEIs (according to their disciplinary natures). These categories are further divided into universities, undergraduate colleges, and higher vocational and professional colleges (according to their administration types). The independent variable "donation subjects" is introduced in a form of classified variable, and donation subjects are divided into enterprises, public institutions and governments, nonprofit organizations (including social organizations and foundations), and individuals. With "donation subjects" as the independent variable and with ranking, discipline category, and administration type as the dependent variables, we conducted a multivariate logistic regression analysis, the results of which are shown in the following table.

Table 12.5 shows that the probability of HEIs in Group 3 and Group 4 obtaining donations is lower than that of HEIs in Group 5, which is the benchmark group of the "ranking" category. The regression coefficients on enterprises' donations to HEIs in Groups 2–4 are all negative, indicating a lower frequency in donations to HEIs in Groups 2–4 than in donations to HEIs in Group 5, which is the benchmark. The frequency of donations to HEIs in Group 1 is slightly lower than the frequency of donations to HEIs in Group 5.

This data indicates that enterprises tend to donate to the HEIs with the upper or lower rankings, rather than the HEIs with middle rankings. The frequency with which public institutions and governments (including governmental organizations) donate to the HEIs in Groups 1–4 is much lower than the donations to the HEIs in Group 5. This data also indicates that public institutions and governments prefer donating to the HEIs with lower donation rankings. The nonprofit organizations obviously prefer donating to the HEIs with upper donation rankings. Donation preferences of individuals are relatively scattered, and the groups with the highest to lowest donation frequency are Group 1, Group 5, Group 3, Group 2, and Group 4.

From the perspective of discipline category, the frequency with which public institutions and governments donate to comprehensive universities is lower than the frequency with which they donate to "other HEIs," which is the benchmark group. The frequency of donating to comprehensive universities by nonprofit organizations is higher than that of donating to "other HEIs," and the probability of science and engineering HEIs obtaining donations is higher than the probability of "other HEIs" obtaining donations. From the perspective of administration type, the probability of universities and undergraduate colleges obtaining donations is higher than the probability of higher vocational and professional colleges obtaining donations.

With donation subjects as the independent variable, and with donation use as the dependent variable, we conducted a multivariate logistic regression, results of which are shown in Table 12.6.

Table 12.5 Logistic regression results on tendencies of donations to different HEIs by different types of donors

	Ranking					Discipline category				Administration type		
	Group 1	Group 2	Group 3	Group 4		Comprehensive universities	Science and engineering HEIs	Medical HEIs	Normal HEIs	Universities	Undergraduate colleges
Enterprises	−0.055	−0.517	−0.435	−1.140		0.002*	0.614	−0.922	−0.797	0.719	0.209
Public institutions and governments	−0.549	−0.616	−0.788	−1.237		−0.548	0.126	−0.254	−0.196	0.410	0.339
Nonprofit organizations	0.991	0.257	−0.122	−0.489		0.556	0.080*	−0.480	0.103*	1.823	0.917
Individuals	0.062	−0.782	−0.136	−0.812		0.018*	0.250	−1.509	−1.309	1.367	1.481
	Group 5 of "ranking" as the benchmark					"Other HEIs" as the benchmark				"Higher vocational and professional colleges" as the benchmark	

Note: p of "*" > 0.10, p < 0.10 on average

Table 12.6 shows that, comparatively speaking, enterprises prefer donations for scholarships and grants, and non-specified uses; public institutions and governments prefer donations for non-specified uses and other specified uses, including international exchange and academic activities; nonprofit organizations prefer donations for scholarships and grants and non-specified uses; and individuals prefer donations for non-specified uses and infrastructure construction. Enterprises and nonprofit organizations prefer donations for scholarships and grants, while the probability of them donating for other specified uses is lower than that for non-specified uses. The probability of donating for faculty scholarships is the lowest of them all. Table 12.7 summarizes the donation preferences of various donors (i.e. donation subjects).

After analyzing the various categories and the nature of the donors, we can see that the data indicates that enterprises are rationally motivated to donate and that nonprofit organizations donate out of altruism. Meanwhile, enterprises prefer donating to the HEIs with the upper or lower rankings. Thus, science and engineering HEIs and scholarship projects and grant programs can perhaps secure a relatively large amount of social influence, actively publicize their image, and have priority when it comes to cooperating in scientific research activities, the application of the results of those research activities, and the recruitment of future researchers (students). However, nonprofit organizations prefer donating to universities with upper rankings, comprehensive universities, and scholarship and grant projects to improve their levels of teaching and scientific research.

It is noteworthy that, to some extent, the personal preferences of decision-makers at organizations affect the donation behaviors of various organizational donors. Different donors belonging to the same organization may have

Table 12.6 Logistic regression results on use tendencies of donations by different donors

	Scholarships and grants	Faculty scholarships	Scientific research and disciplinary development	Infrastructure construction	Other specified uses
Enterprises	0.176	−3.125	−2.097	−2.315	−0.731
Public institutions and governments	−1.450	−4.964	−2.239	−3.693	−0.638
Nonprofit organizations	1.718	−1.802	−1.350	−0.850	−0.149
Individuals	−1.286	−4.112	−2.749	−0.865	−1.748

Non-specified uses as the benchmark

Note: $p < 0.10$ on average

Table 12.7 Summary of relative behavioral preferences of donation subjects

Donation subjects	Ranking	Administration type	Nature	Use of funds
Enterprises	Lower and upper	Science and engineering HEIs	Universities	Scholarships and grants, non-specified uses
Public institutions and governments	Lower	Science and engineering HEIs	Universities	Non-specified uses, other specified uses
Nonprofit organizations	Upper	Comprehensive universities	Universities	Scholarships and grants, non-specified uses
Individuals	Relatively scattered	Science and engineering HEIs	Undergraduate colleges	Non-specified uses, infrastructure construction

different donation motives, and the donation behavior of one single donor is perhaps the result of complex motives. Therefore, the donation motives of various types of donors should be relatively different. Strictly speaking, the most significant characteristic of various types of donations is perhaps that they are the result of various mixed factors.

Conclusions and reflections

After analyzing the data on the donation income of HEIs from 2005 to 2008 and the data on donations to local HEIs over the same period, we have reached the following conclusions.

The distribution of the donation income of different HEIs in China is quite uneven: donation income is extremely concentrated in few well-known HEIs. The Gini coefficient on donation income distribution is at 86.7%, showing a significant Matthew effect or Pareto phenomenon. Overall, donations to HEIs are an income source that supports the strong rather than the weak.

Whether an institution has established a foundation, its ranking, and its geographical location have a significant impact on a university or college's donation income. Ranking as well has a significant impact on the donation income of a university or college. If all other conditions are the same, the rise of one ranking level could mean a 0.3% increase in donations. Compared to the local university or college without a foundation, the local university or college with a foundation is likely to obtain more donation income, indicating the important role of a foundation during fundraising work. In addition, compared to HEIs in the eastern regions and western regions in China, local HEIs in the central regions obtain less donation income, and the donation income distribution shows the characteristic of "less in central regions, and more in eastern regions and western regions."

Different donation subjects have different donation preferences. After analyzing the donor behaviors of donations to local HEIs from the perspectives of ranking, type, nature, and fund use, it was found that different types of donation subjects have different behavior preferences. Enterprises prefer donating to the HEIs with upper or lower rankings, such as science and engineering HEIs and universities for scholarships and grants and non-specified uses. Public institutions and governmental organizations prefer donating to the HEIs with lower rankings, science and engineering HEIs, and universities for non-specified uses and other specified uses, including international exchange and student activities. Nonprofit organizations prefer donating to HEIs with upper rankings, comprehensive universities, and universities for scholarships and grants and non-specified uses. Individuals prefer donating to science and engineering HEIs and undergraduate colleges for non-specified uses and infrastructure construction. Donations of individuals are relatively scattered among HEIs with different rankings.

The reference significance of the above study results to the realistic thinking and fundraising practices of HEIs is understood from four aspects:

The distribution of donation income of Chinese HEIs is quite uneven, and the incomes of HEIs with less donation income are significantly low. Fifty percent of the reported 852 HEIs with low donation income only account for 1.53% of total donation income. In addition, the majority of HEIs, without reporting their donation incomes, have very low or no donation income. Therefore, although many HEIs have started fundraising efforts, a considerable number of HEIs have not yet launched fundraising efforts, which means that there is considerable development space for donations to Chinese HEIs. These HEIs have only achieved preliminary results in their fundraising efforts, and they all have a lot of potential donation resources that they can develop.

Donations are highly concentrated in a few well-known HEIs with upper rankings that have received more donations, which means that donors do not focus on helping HEIs solve their funding issues, but rather focus on supporting improvement and development, and creating new projects such as the establishment of buildings, research centers, and colleges, and the provision of scholarships and grants for student development. Therefore, in the long term, the improvement of HEIs' core specialties is what will help them obtain the resources they need and create favorable conditions for receiving donation income. In the short term, potential donors are more attracted to the advantageous projects of HEIs rather than the weaker projects. The projects with better foundations, higher teaching and research levels, and greater strengths are more likely to attract donations. Some universities state that they are too poor to raise money. On the contrary, if a professor with one university is likely to win the Nobel Prize in the future, he or she must be able to collect donations. Therefore, in order to raise a lot of money the university must first have an ambitious plan and convince donors of the university's significant achievements that were made possible through donated funds (Cheng 2005).

The donation income of the university or college with an independent foundation is much higher than the university or college without an independent foundation, indicating the important role of the foundation during fundraising efforts. Because of the operating cost of an independent fundraising organization and the restrictions placed on the establishment of such a foundation, it is not necessary that the university or college with little donation income establish an independent fundraising organization. However, for the university or college with a fundraising foundation and scaled donation income, the establishment of that foundation (and/or a school board, alumni association, or some other fundraising and management organization) is important, for it plays an active role in carrying out specialized fundraising work and in improving the level of donation planning and the management of donation income.

Donation motives and behavioral characteristics of different donation groups are varied. Analysis of behavioral characteristics of different types of donors and the targeted design of appropriate donation projects will be conducive to developing potential donation resources and promoting the fundraising work of HEIs. For example, the donation behaviors of enterprises are relatively more rational; enterprises pay more attention to the social influence of their donation projects, project-naming situation, and the possibility of having priority to cooperate with HEIs in science and technology projects and talent recruitment. Nonprofit organizations pay more attention to the effect of using the donated funds and the quality of the project's management. Alumni are loyal in their donation behaviors. In order to develop alumni donation resources, the university or college must strengthen their alumni outreach programs and design projects to include and be targeted toward alumni. However, the study results presented herein show that the donation behaviors of various types of donors are mainly the results of mixed motives. Different donors belonging to the same category may have different donation motives, while the donation behavior of one single donor may be the result of various complex motives. Therefore, while realizing the common characteristics of donation behaviors of various types of potential donors, HEIs should analyze potential donors and design fundraising projects that are many different potential donors may find appealing. This will surely advance their fundraising efforts.

Supplementary Table 12.S1 Donations by administrative type of institution

Type of donor		Administration type			Total
		Universities	Undergraduate colleges	Higher vocational and professional colleges	
Enterprises	Quantity	3,823.0	2,293.0	1,863.0	7,979.0
	Donors' natures (%)	47.9	28.7	23.3	100.0
	Administration types (%)	38.9	30.5	47.4	37.5
Public institutions	Quantity	1,112.0	1,057.0	625.0	2,794.0
	Donors' natures (%)	39.8	37.8	22.4	100.0
	Administration types (%)	11.3	14.0	15.9	13.1
Social organizations (excluding foundations)	Quantity	521.0	272.0	193.0	986.0
	Donors' natures (%)	52.8	27.6	19.6	100.0
	Administration types (%)	5.3	3.6	4.9	4.6
Foundations	Quantity	1,107.0	386.0	70.0	1,563.0
	Donors' natures (%)	70.8	24.7	4.5	100.0
	Administration types (%)	11.3	5.1	1.8	7.3
Individuals	Quantity	2,672.0	2,995.0	681.0	6,348.0
	Donors' natures (%)	42.1	47.2	10.7	100.0
	Administration types (%)	27.2	39.8	17.3	29.8
Governmental organizations	Quantity	584.0	521.0	500.0	1605.0
	Donors' natures (%)	36.4	32.5	31.2	100.0
	Administration types (%)	5.9	6.9	12.7	7.5
Total	Quantity	9,819.0	7,524.0	3,932.0	21,275.0
	Donors' natures (%)	46.2	35.4	18.5	100.0
	Administration types (%)	100.0	100.0	100.0	100.0

Supplementary Table 12.S2 Cross-tabulation for donors' natures and donation uses

Type of donor		Scholarships and grants	Faculty scholarship	Donation uses Scientific research and disciplinary development	Infrastructure construction	Other specified uses	Non-specified uses	Total
Enterprises	Quantity	3,174.0	117.0	327.0	263.0	1,282.0	2,661.0	7,824.0
	Donors' natures (%)	40.6	1.5	4.2	3.4	16.4	34.0	100.0
	Donation uses (%)	50.7	49.8	38.2	14.5	39.0	31.4	37.4
Public institutions	Quantity	288.0	7.0	153.0	38.0	827.0	1448.0	2,761.0
	Donors' natures (%)	10.4	0.3	5.5	1.4	30.0	52.4	100.0
	Donation uses (%)	4.6	3.0	17.9	2.1	25.1	17.1	13.2
Social organization (excluding foundations)	Quantity	501.0	12.0	26.0	21.0	147.0	262.0	969.0
	Donors' natures (%)	51.7	1.2	2.7	2.2	15.2	27.0	100.0
	Donation uses (%)	8.0	5.1	3.0	1.2	4.5	3.1	4.6
Foundations	Quantity	1155.0	37.0	51.0	106.0	109.0	35.0	1493.0
	Donors' natures (%)	77.4	2.5	3.4	7.1	7.3	2.3	100.0
	Donation uses (%)	18.4	15.7	6.0	5.9	3.3	0.4	7.1
Individuals	Quantity	894.0	53.0	207.0	1,363.0	541.0	3,236.0	6,294.0
	Donors' natures (%)	14.2	0.8	3.3	21.7	8.6	51.4	100.0
	Donation uses (%)	14.3	22.6	24.2	75.3	16.4	38.1	30.1
Governmental organizations	Quantity	249.0	9.0	91.0	19.0	383.0	841.0	1,592.0
	Donors' natures (%)	15.6	0.6	5.7	1.2	24.1	52.8	100.0
	Donation uses (%)	4.0	3.8	10.6	1.0	11.6	9.9	7.6
Total	Quantity	6,261.0	235.0	855.0	1,810.0	3,289.0	8,483.0	20,933.0
	Donors' natures (%)	29.9	1.1	4.1	8.6	15.7	40.5	100.0
	Donation uses (%)	100.0	100.0	100.0	100.0	100.0	100.0	100.0

Supplementary Table 12.S3 Results of variance analysis of donation income logarithm ANOVAa, b, c

Donation income		Sole method				
		Quadratic sum	df	Mean square	F	Significance
Main effects	(Combined %)	1.249E9	20	6.244E7	10.722	0.000
	Foundation (established or not) (1 = established)	7.329E8	1	7.329E8	125.868	0.000
	Administration type	1.005E8	2	5.023E7	8.627	0.000
	Nature code	7.930E7	11	7209302.945	1.238	0.258
	Region code	7.908E7	2	3.954E7	6.790	0.001
	Ranking group	6.084E7	4	1.521E7	2.612	0.034
Model		1.249E9	20	6.244E7	10.722	0.000
Residual error		3.756E9	645	5823009.559		
Total		5.005E9	665	7525679.127		

Note: Tincome_sum by foundation (established or not) (1 = established), administration type, nature code, region code, and ranking group. All effects were inputted simultaneously. Due to the existence of empty cells or a singular matrix, a higher level of interaction has been canceled.

Notes

1 The rankings were obtained by weighting and sorting the scores of universities and colleges, which are given according to scientific research, personnel training, and social reputation.
2 The *Regulations for the Management of Foundations* implemented in 2008 stipulate that the original funds of a national fundraising foundation not be less than RMB 8 million, that the original funds of a local fundraising foundation not be less than RMB 4 million, and that the original funds of a non-fundraising foundation not be less than RMB 2 million.

References

Cai, K. 2006. "Social Donation: An Untapped Gold Mine – An Important Fundraising Channel for Higher Education Institutions." *Private Education Research* 3: 13–18.

Cao, H. 2006. *Public Economic Analysis of Donations in China*. PhD dissertation. Xiamen University.

Cheng, J. 2005. "Fundraising and Donation Culture of Universities." *Shanghai Education* 7A: 33.

Clotfelter, C. T. 2003. "Alumni Giving to Elite Private Colleges and Universities." *Economics of Education Review* 22(2): 109–120.

Harrison, W. B. 1995. "College Relations and Fundraising Expenditures: Influencing the Probability of Alumni Giving to Higher Education." *Economics of Education Review* 114(1): 73–84.

Holmes, J. 2009. "Prestige, Charitable Deductions and Other Determinants of Alumni Giving: Evidence from a Highly Selective Liberal Arts College." *Economics of Education Review* 28(1): 18–28.

Huang, J., R. You, J. Jing & J. Chi. 2006. "Analysis and Thinking about Donations Received by the Tsinghua University Education Foundation." *Tsinghua Journal of Education* 11: 118–123.

Steinberg, R. S. 1987. "Voluntary Donations and Public Expenditures in a Federalist System." *The American Economic Review* 77(1): 24–36.

Supplementary Table 12.S1. "Cross Tabulation for Donors' Natures and School-Running Types."

Thomas, J. A. & J. Smart. 2005. "The Relationship between Personal and Social Growth and Involvement in College and Subsequent Alumni Giving." Paper presented at the Annual Forum of the Association for Institutional Research, San Diego, California, in May 2015.

University Evaluation Research Group of the China Alumni Network (UERG). 2010. *Report on the Evaluation and Study of China's Universities*. Jiangsu: 21st Century Talent Report.

Zheng, Q. 2008. "An Analysis of Motives and Incentives of Social Donations to China's Higher Education Institutions." *Research in Higher Education of Engineering* 3: 107–111.

13 Changes in knowledge production and diversified models of academic research within world-class universities

Ma Wanhua

Knowledge production changes within research universities

Under normal circumstances, the concept of discipline is used as an approach to classify specific areas of knowledge (e.g. in the natural sciences, you have physics, biology, and mathematics, and in the humanities and social sciences you have history, literature, and education science). Based on this model of knowledge classification, higher education institutions (HEIs) establish different departments and colleges which have their own teaching and research organizations, modes of talent cultivation, and research management techniques. However, this method of knowledge production in research universities has experienced monumental change over the last few decades. Some world-class research universities, including the California Institute of Technology (Caltech) and Princeton University, are taking the lead in teaching and scientific research. Neither of these institutions is large, and both differ from each other in school type and style, but they both boast enduring leadership in their respective teaching and research fields. The key to their durable reputation is that they are both able to maintain the development of leading disciplines while adapting this development with current changes in knowledge production.

Scott (2003) points out that curiosity-driven scientific research in universities has undergone fundamental change and believes that contemporary knowledge production has evolved from involving traditional social values, classical analysis, and purely rational or critical thinking to involving knowledge reform and knowledge innovation. This knowledge revolution has spurred universities to transform their knowledge production activities from traditional basic scientific research to a combination of basic and applied scientific research. Multiple factors have affected this "knowledge production transition," including government involvement in university research, an infiltration of commercial influence on university research, and universities struggling to meet their financial needs while accommodating social demands. Etzkowitz et al. (1998) employed "entrepreneurial science" to describe the changes to knowledge production currently at work at universities. The term "entrepreneurial" has definitions involving both business operations and innovation, and its application to higher education is that knowledge production in universities should be pursued with innovation in mind. The fact that scientific and technological innovation facilitates the regional economic development of North America and Asia has played a pivotal role in this knowledge production transition. The quest for innovation within economic development, combined with university funding shortages, has compelled research universities to take greater initiative in relying more heavily on society to help with academic discoveries and technological innovations. By so doing, knowledge production in universities has become more connected with politics, the economy, culture, and society, forcing traditional research concepts of "seeking the truth" to make place for problem-solving-oriented knowledge production. For instance, cancer treatment and hereditary disease analysis and control have become two focal issues for many university researchers. In the case of biological research, university researchers do not only focus on the theoretical basis of this subject area, but on the technology that could eventually engineer the market application of the outcome of this research. For this purpose, Pau (2003) designed a modern biological research process that shows continual progression from one stage to another:

Biology	Biotechnology	Technology Innovation
Description	Control	Treatment
Knowledge	Adjustment	Market

Based on Pau's explanation of this process, among the nine elements above, biology is considered basic research, which is associated with the construction of disciplinary theory. While conventional university research is centered on the pursuit of knowledge itself, such as in the construction of disciplinary theory in biology, current research not only focuses on biological knowledge accumulation, but on market and social demands as well (e.g. achieving a technical application for biological knowledge, shaping biological knowledge into technological innovation, and introducing innovative products to the social market). This knowledge production process cannot be realized through individual endeavors of critical and abstract thinking alone. Nowadays, scientific research is best carried out through team cooperation, cross-disciplinary research, and even global collaboration. A good example of this trend is recent research carried out on bird flu. In the process of researching on the bird flu virus, scientists were expected to both identify the virus and discover how to destroy it. The regional divergence of the bird flu virus sparked cross-border and cross-regional cooperation in search for a cure. This case shows that scientific research is not only about seeking knowledge, but about applying knowledge for the benefit of society (i.e. improving people's lives and well-being). Considering this new feature of knowledge production, some scholars have employed a double-integration concept. The double-integration concept of knowledge production has brought about new applied professional disciplines. Applied professional disciplines have experienced rapid growth over the past century, despite there being only a slight change in the number of basic theoretical disciplines in universities.

Research discipline classification and the development of applied professional disciplines

The changes in knowledge production have prompted the differentiation and integration of academic knowledge, stimulating the development of applied professional disciplines. In the construction of academic disciplines in research universities, numerous applied professional disciplines deserve our particular attention. During the Sixth International Conference on the Conceptions of Library and Information Science in a talk entitled "Featuring the Future," Bates (2007) systematically analyzed the composition of modern disciplinary knowledge in terms of the relationship between traditional research disciplines and applied professional disciplines. Bates believes that applied professional disciplines, founded as they are on the basic theories of traditional research disciplines, represent in several ways the relationships between disciplinary knowledge and society. She also believes that they can develop on their own relying on the theoretical basis of traditional disciplines. Table 13.1 lists Bates' "spectrum of traditional academic research disciplines."

Many aspects of Bates' classification warrant further discussion and debate. For instance, in Table 13.2 why is industrial engineering listed under law instead of civil engineering? Furthermore, the number of applied professional disciplines that exist far exceeds the number provided in Table 13.2. Bioengineering, genetic engineering, and environmental protection are research fields and professional disciplines at many universities. However, in her analysis of two academic discipline spectrums, Bates doesn't provide the traditional list of these academic disciplines (Table 13.1) and the interrelationship between applied professional disciplines that correspond to this traditional list.

As illustrated above in Tables 13.1 and 13.2, it is clear that knowledge manifests itself as part of a group of disciplines rather than as a sole discipline, and that the development and maturity of these disciplines benefit from the existence of research universities. Besides dispensing knowledge, researchers and professors at research universities undertake extensive theoretical studies by writing and then publishing books and papers. Under normal circumstances, basic theoretical disciplines take a very long time to develop. Kuhn (1964), in his book *The Structure of Scientific Revolutions*, argued for an episodic model in which revolutionary science interrupts periods of conceptual continuity in "ordinary" science. The discovery of "anomalies" during revolutions in science leads to paradigm shifts. When scientific research gathers enough experience and knowledge, it will typically make changes to previous theories and then produce new paradigms.

Nevertheless, the development process of applied professional disciplines differs from that of traditional research disciplines. For instance, information science (IS) was once considered a marginalized discipline, as nobody

Table 13.1 Spectrum of traditional academic research disciplines

Arts	Humanities	Social and behavioral sciences			Natural sciences and mathematics		
Painting	Literature	History	Economics	Psychology	Biology	Geology	Mathematics
Sculpture	Languages	Archaeology	Political science	Anthropology	Chemistry	Physics	Logic
Music	Linguistics	Sociology	Geography		Biochemistry	Astronomy	Computer science
Dance	Philosophy					Oceanography	
Theater	Religion						

Table 13.2 Spectrum of applied professional disciplines corresponding to the research disciplines

Commercial art	Writing	Law	Business	Clinic psychology	Medicine	Agriculture	Geo-engineering	Accounting
Musical performance	Translating	Genealogy	Public administration	Social welfare	Dentistry	Horticulture	Aeronautical engineering	Finance
Dancing	Minister	Criminal justice	Public health	Pharmacy	Forestry	Civil engineering	Computer engineering	
Acting		Industrial engineering		Family science	Nursing		Wildlife migration	
Architectural design						Applied chemistry		

Note: The nine columns in Table 13.2 expand upon the applied professional disciplines that coincide with the traditional spectrum described in Table 13.1 (Bates 2007).

recognized its academic value. People equated it with library science, which was limited to book selection according to bibliography, cataloguing, the formulation of lending rules, classification, and the preservation of books of various editions. However, the extensive application of computer technology at the end of the twentieth century impelled the rapid development of IS. Information has since evolved to become a valuable part of many commercial applications, including online material searching, borrowing and purchasing, and local and global information exchange. Meanwhile, IS has become a focal point of venture capital, stock markets, and government funding, turning the once shelved discipline of IS into the academic center of many research universities. Furthermore, network information management and exchange have become the key components of library science, resulting in fundamental changes in this field as well. Information technology (IT) has provided library science with new approaches to disciplinary knowledge. From this perspective, applied professional disciplines and basic theoretical disciplines are vastly different due to their diverse development models.

Applied professional disciplines have resorted to building their own research methods and academic standards grounded on corresponding basic theoretical disciplines. For instance, Ridley (2008), at the University of Tasmania, Australia, outlined how information science is based on scientific design and pragmatism.

Zmud et al. (1988) echoed Ridley's views on the framework of the future of IS during their formation study of IS in the United States. In the 1970s, there were few IS faculty members in the United States and just two or three recently established IS doctoral programs. In the United States today, IS has become one of the most prevalent disciplines at research universities. It is well known that IS is a rapidly changing discipline, as its growth and development accompany technological improvement and social demands. IS develops much quicker than most basic theoretical disciplines do, which be explained in part by its social service function and its close link to knowledge production. With the development of applied professional disciplines, various forms of degrees for applied professional disciplines have emerged in universities across the world.

Development mode of applied professional disciplines in research Universities

In the research explaining the development of new disciplines, Messier (2004) believes that for a certain period of time, applied professional disciplines – especially those involved with business, chemical, and information technologies – have witnessed more rapid growth than their disciplinary counterparts. However, these disciplines will likely reach saturation after having developed to a certain stage, or they will even face stagnation or vanish altogether. For example, before the arrival of television, radio was the best tool for people to acquire information and receive entertainment programs; however, radio's

Table 13.3 Example of possible change for each component of the framework

Level 1 component	Level 2 component	Example of change (IS)
Mechanisms of control		Introduction of new publication outlets for IS; change to the administrative placement of IS schools in Australian universities with changing enrollments
Core body of knowledge (theoretical knowledge of basic disciplines)	Research and teaching methods and standards	Introduction of new methods of IS research, or teaching, or standards
	Unique symbol set	Reaching agreement on a unique symbol set for the IS community
	Key research and teaching IS topics	Introduction of new IS topics for research or teaching
	Laws, rules and evidenced guidelines	Development of new theory and its publication
Impact of local contingencies		Local contingencies impacting on the degree of professionalism, such as recent IS staffing retrenchments in universities reducing the degree of specialization in collaborative research teams
Degree of professionalism		Linked through an inverse relationship

Source: http://epress.anu.edu.au/info_systems_aus/mobile_devices/ch03s06.html

popularity severely diminished with the onset of black and white television sets, which became obsolete in the wake of color television sets. Now, increasingly powerful smartphones are challenging the fashionable flat screen and plasma televisions. This examples illustrate the idea that one discipline must undergo constant and sustained knowledge renewal in order to maintain relevance and vibrancy. Messier put forward an S-curve model for discipline development to illustrate the development and change process of many applied professional disciplines.

Figure 13.1 indicates that changes to external environment influence the development of applied professional disciplines. To adapt to external changes, the various disciplines will require a constant supply of new information, as the driving force for a discipline's sustainable development is new information from other disciplines. University discipline integration and healthy discipline development requires an upgraded discipline management system and the establishment of a disciplinary evaluation system.

Using Messier's S-curve model as illustrated in Figure 13.1, the early phase of the development and change process may require a longer period of time for individuals to recognize and accept a new discipline. However, once through the first phase, the new discipline will increase and reach maturity quickly. As resources are depleted or market demands are met, the growth of the discipline flattens or even fades away. Messier uses biochemistry as an example to more clearly demonstrate his S-shaped discipline growth model. Chemical engineering is a relatively new discipline, having only been developed in the last one hundred years or so. In the 1920s, for example, many sectors in the United States – such as the food and beverage industry, agriculture, and the healthcare industry – began seeking chemical materials and technologies to support their development. However, chemists did not yet have the experience

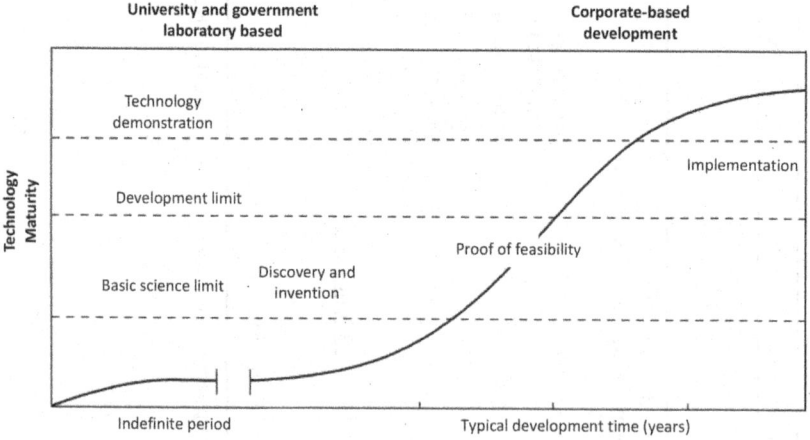

Figure 13.1 Messier's S-curve model.
Source: Adapted from Messier (2004: 45)

of turning knowledge into technological applications, so the level of theoretical knowledge during this period was not yet high enough to able to meet large-scale industrial demand, let alone engineering design. Thus, chemical engineering attracted the participation of scientists of then marginal disciplines, like civil engineering, mechanical engineering, and electrical engineering, which served as catalysts for the development of chemical engineering. The development of chemical engineering first involved basic chemistry and included the power, thermal, and conduction fields. For a period of over twenty years after its inception, the field of chemical engineering grew at a steady pace since the developing food-processing and pharmaceutical industries required it to do so.

However, the discipline of chemical engineering reached saturation in the 1980s and thereafter began to decline. The largest contributing factor to this decline was the ever-rigorous regulation and supervision by the US federal government on the pharmaceutical and food-processing industries. At the same time, the profit-driven pharmaceutical and food-processing industries were expanding international trade and they began importing significant quantities of chemical materials and products, resulting in a decline in business-oriented research and development funding for universities. Messier (2004) believes that discipline adjustment and integration with other disciplines (e.g. merging the chemical engineering discipline with the promising biochemistry and bio-catalysis disciplines) is required to tackle the stagnation of chemical engineering.

For instance, in 2002 the University of California, Berkeley evaluated its physics department, and the results shocked University administrators – the University had lost its leading position in this discipline. Although administrators were very aware that new breakthroughs and discoveries in disciplinary study were essential to regain the department's pre-eminence, it was a daunting challenge to restore the University's leadership role in the field of physics. Administrators were facing a fundamental shift in US federal government research funding as well as the phenomenon of "brain drain," as a few young teachers were enticed away prior to the department's evaluation. Therefore, the University's president decided to raise US$300 million to reorganize the physics department. This situation illustrates that discipline development requires the support of multiple platforms, a theoretical foundation of traditional research disciplines, updated technology, a disciplinary development system, and financial backing.

Diversified models of academic research within research universities

In the footsteps of the changes to knowledge production, and emerging in a large number of applied professional disciplines, a recent trend has seen research universities turn to diversified models of academic development. First, the advent of large comprehensive laboratories, especially those funded by governments, is exerting a direct influence on the development and integration of applied professional disciplines. These laboratories aid in scientists' academic and scientific research and in engineering development, and their ultimate goal is to ensure national security and to respond to scientific issues of national importance.

For example, in just over fifty years, the Lawrence Livermore National Laboratory and Radiation Laboratory (also known as "Rad Lab") located at the Massachusetts Institute of Technology (MIT) were formed, as well as numerous comprehensive labs at research university campuses worldwide. These laboratories have become indispensable knowledge production tools. Additionally, the Jet Propulsion Laboratory (JPL) at Caltech has conducted significant scientific research in the areas of aerospace, outer-space exploration, gravity recovery and climate experiments, and lunar radiometer experiments through multidisciplinary team efforts. In 2003, after five years of construction and an initial investment of US$300 million, the Comprehensive Biology Research Center at the University of California, Berkeley was put into operation.

Along with these large-scale research and development centers, it is also interesting to note the formation of interdisciplinary or cross-disciplinary research centers and institutes. The creation of interdisciplinary or cross-disciplinary research centers and institutes transcends the boundaries of traditional academic research while tackling scientific problems that singular disciplines cannot resolve on their own. When professors, scientists, and researchers across disciplines conduct joint research, disciplinary boundaries becomes blurred and approaches that students employ to judge issues also change, as students are able to gain insights from multiple perspectives and hone their research and critical thinking skills under the guidance of teachers from several disciplines. In other words, the emergence of interdisciplinary or cross-disciplinary research centers and institutes liberates academic research from the confinement of disciplinary knowledge; interdisciplinary cooperation injects dynamism and vitality into university-level scientific research while facilitating the reform of university human resource management. In research centers and institutes, the organizational tasks and missions vary in response to the changing nature of research topics and research projects. In order to adapt to the ever-changing nature of research problems, most researchers are contractors or part-time employees. For example, at the Center for Studies in Higher Education (CSHE) at the University of California, Berkeley, all staff members, including CSHE core research fellows, are contractors. However, the research topics being conducted at the CSHE run the gamut from higher education reform in California to global education issues. CSHE academic activities include expert seminars, publications, collaborative research, and hosting international conferences. The key factors of vitality that these contracted professional researchers bring to the CSHE are their disciplinary (and cross-disciplinary) expertise and their mobility. With regard to this second factor, it is the fact that so many visiting scholars and postdoctoral research fellows from all over the world come to the Berkeley campus that has propelled the CSHE to international eminence and that has given it a leadership role in discussing higher education policy issues.

Another factor in enhancing academic vitality is the formation of a variety of applied professional colleges or departments, breaking free of the traditional academic degree system. The monopoly of PhD degrees was dismantled in the 1950s in the United States, as the emergence of professional degrees (such as the Juris Doctor and Doctor of Engineering) demonstrates the diversity of high-level talent opportunities. This diversity of degree education has provided various professional leaders with the opportunity to advance in post-industrial society. Meanwhile, in the course of applied professional disciplines' knowledge production and teaching, the introduction of the case study model and the formation of teaching and practice systems have made disciplinary teaching more applicable to real-life situations and issues.

In conclusion, academic development and disciplinary construction in research universities have exhibited such features as diversity and variety, which is in line with the changing nature of knowledge production. From this study on the trajectory of research universities' academic development, the following areas can serve as positive models for China to build its own world-class universities. First, knowledge production in universities should attend to theory-building while stressing the real issues facing economic and social development. While knowledge has no national borders, its transformation into productivity in China will help bring the country a much-needed increase in economic growth. This is perhaps a very obvious conclusion, but in the current academic research climate, people often only go after quantity (e.g. number of publications, amount of research funds received). Converting these publications and funds into the ability to tackle significant issues facing China today deserves deep consideration.

Second, academic organizations in China's universities are still classified by discipline and are pronounced in their insularity. Limited disciplinary knowledge means that universities' capacity for knowledge integration remains weak. This disciplinary isolation often weakens the vitality of academic research; therefore, in the process of disciplinary development, we should enhance the linkages between basic disciplines and applied professional disciplines to integrate theoretical research and practical applications. Over the past twenty years, China has reorganized many single-discipline colleges into comprehensive universities, but discipline growth and development cannot be ultimately achieved by merging alone. Instead, universities should encourage further integration based on the transition currently underway in knowledge production.

Third, China's universities lack large comprehensive laboratories. The scarcity of such laboratories contributes to the deficient research capacity of our universities to study certain critical issues. In order to change this situation, we need to initiate systematic innovation, upgrade university-based research and development centers' comprehensive research competence, and establish cooperative partnerships with external laboratories.

References

Bates, M. J. 2007. "Defining the Information Disciplines in Encyclopedia Development." *Information Research* 12(4). Available from: http://www.informationr.net/ir/12-4/colis/colis29.html.

Etzkowitz, H., A. Webster & P. Healey. 1998. *Capitalizing Knowledge: New Intersections of Industry and Academia.* Albany, NY: State University of New York Press.

Kuhn, T. 1964. *The Structure of Scientific Revolutions.* Chicago, IL: University of Chicago Press.

Messier, R. 2004. "Growth of a New Discipline." *Materials Today*, March, 44–47.

Pau, B. 2003. "From Knowledge to Innovation: Remodeling Creative and Knowledge Diffusion Processes." In G. Breton and M. Lambert, eds, *Universities and Globalization: Private Linkages, Public Trust*, 119–125. Paris: UNESCO Publishing.

Ridley, G. 2008. "Characterising Academic Information Systems in Australia: Developing and Evaluating a Theoretical Framework." In G. G. Gable et al., eds, *The Information Systems Academic Discipline in Australia*, 109–150. Canberra: ANU E Press. Available from: http://epress.anu.edu.au/info_systems_aus/mobile_devices/ch03s06.html.

Scott, P. 2003. "Changing Players in a Knowledge Society." In G. Breton and M. Lambert, eds, *Universities and Globalization: Private Linkages, Public Trust*, 211–222. Paris: UNESCO Publishing.

Zmud, R., J. J. Elam, M. J. Ginzberg & P. G. W. Keen. 1988. *Transforming the IS Organization: The Mission, the Framework, the Transition.* Washington, DC: ICIT Press.

14 Loan financing behaviors and financial operation characteristics of Chinese higher education institutions after enrollment expansion

Bao Wei

If we admit that the introduction of a cost-sharing mechanism in the early 1990s broke the single mode of government-funded financing in China, then we must admit that bank loans have successfully diversified the financing channels for Chinese HEIs after enrollment expansion. Bank loans have become the third major financing channel for Chinese HEIs following government funding, tuition, and fees. Thus, the capital market became another major capital supplier for higher education following the government, student families, and corporations, through providing loans to higher education students and HEIs. An increasing dependence on the capital market may be seen as another major characteristic of China's higher education financing system in recent years. In terms of studying the financing of China's HEIs, one must clearly learn about the loan situation at these HEIs, analyze the factors determining the size of the loans they receive, and determine how HEI loans are assessed for risk.

On this basis, this study first introduces the characteristics of HEI financing and specifies the analytical framework that it will follow. It will then, on the basis of this framework, make a deep empirical analysis with regard to the financing selection mechanism of Chinese HEIs, their loan situation, their financial operation characteristics, and the correlation between the size of HEI loans and HEIs' financial operation characteristics. Finally, this study will consider the policy implications of its conclusions on HEI financing, which it will have drawn from its research results.

Study background and analysis framework

In order to clearly understand HEI financial operation characteristics and financing behaviors, this section will examine the macro-level development trend of China's higher education financing after enrollment expansion. In so doing, it will try to establish an analytical framework for the present study.

Background: Macro-level development trend of China's higher education financing after enrollment expansion

The change in the higher education financial system is one of the key factors impacting the decisions of Chinese HEIs. Looking into the macro-level development trend of the Chinese higher education financial system, we can see the importance of the following four major issues.

Financing of higher education: false impression of diversification

In the 1990s, due to limitations in the ability of the state to fully finance public education, the Chinese government put forward the policy goal of a government-funding-based diversified financing mechanism, following the principle of construction by the beneficiary, through the expansion of management autonomy and the introduction of a cost-sharing mechanism for HEIs. In reality, however, after the expansion of student enrollment, the total amount of government-funded financing in education, which is the key funding source for HEIs, has continued to rise. But the growth rate lags far behind the speed with which the higher education system has expanded. In 2007, fiscal funding dropped to 48% of total higher education expenditure, a decrease of 44% from 1993. By contrast, the extent of HEI self-financing, in particular via tuition and other fees, rose sharply during this same period so that this method became the second key financing source following state funding. In terms of building a diversified financing mechanism, HEIs have made vigorous attempts to explore new financing channels and expand their current financing channels, examples of which are scientific project cooperation, technological transfers, equipment leasing, educational funds, and social donations. All of these channels were once expected to widen the financing sources for HEIs. However, these channels ended up exposing some severe limitations in HEI financing. After enrollment expansion, Chinese HEIs turned more homogeneous in their financing practices – the core status of government was gradually weakening, while the importance of individuals (i.e. students and their families) was rising. And so in the end, HEIs failed to widen their financing channels (Bao 2007).

Capital allocation for higher education: special investment mechanism

How do we utilize limited financial resources to boost higher education? It is a policy challenge that every country across the world faces. The Chinese government decided to invest its limited resources in several core HEIs. That is to say, China offers special public funding for the key HEIs represented by those under the direct administration of the Ministry of Education. Concretely speaking, the central government has raised the special fund for higher education since the 1990s. The two most important and largest projects in the higher education sector since the founding of the People's Republic of China

(PRC) are Project 211 and Project 985. Project 211 is aimed at one hundred HEIs under the direct administration of the Ministry of Education. Project 985 is aimed at the key universities under the direct administration of the Ministry of Education, like Peking University and Tsinghua University. In addition, from the state's allocation of funds to HEIs, we can see that the proportion of research investment continues to increase, which doesn't include the increase in special funding for educational construction. Competition-oriented funding for scientific research helps to further intensify the special investment mechanism of higher education financing, widening the funding gap among different HEIs.

The funding gap in higher education: it's only getting wider

The funding gap in higher education is being widened at an increasing rate. It is the result of the reform of China's higher education financial system after enrollment expansion. This gap not only exists among HEIs in general, but also among different regions and among different higher education departments due to imbalanced regional economic development and the different financing capabilities of higher education departments. Studies show that, since 2003, the Gini coefficient of educational funding allocated per higher education student across China has risen slightly. The budgetary funding per higher education student has risen remarkably since 1998, with the Gini coefficient far higher than the figure of extra-budgetary funding per higher education student (Bao & Liu 2009). This means that, after enrollment expansion, the gap in educational expenditure per higher education student has widened in different regions across China. The gap in budgetary funding per higher education student, that is, the gap in the financial allocation per student to institutions of higher education in different regions is the key factor widening this regional gap. The widening funding gap indicates an increasing imbalance of resource allocation in the higher education sector. This not only poses a threat to the overall coordination and sustainable development of China's higher education system, but it also prevents the realization of a fair and equitable higher education system in China.

Rise of HEIs' debt crisis

In the countries where HEIs enjoy high management autonomy but face severe market pressure, it is necessary for the HEIs to diversify their financing channels and seek the best possible balance between higher education activities, capital, and academic performance. Thus, the Organisation for Economic Co-operation and Development (OECD) pointed out in 2004 that it is necessary for HEIs to adopt a series of strategic initiatives with regard to their financial operations and their financing channels in order to improve their financial sustainability (OECD 2004). Admittedly, in a special period that has seen and is seeing the rapid expansion of higher education, bank financing is an effective means of relaxing the funding supply-demand contradiction, especially as governments at various levels cannot offer enough funds to fill the capital gap caused by enrollment expansion. However, as special entities, HEIs are limited in their ability to repay debt. Whether HEIs are operating appropriately with the loans is not only related to the stable and long-term development of higher education, but it is also directly related to the smooth implementation of public fiscal reform. According to the document entitled *Analysis and Prediction on China's Social Situation for Year 2006* issued by the Chinese Academy of Social Sciences in China, the total amount of bank loans made to public HEIs was between RMB 150 billion and RMB 200 billion, and almost every HEI borrowed money from the bank (Ru et al. 2005). Some HEIs took out loans that far exceeded their debt-paying capabilities. And what is worse, when the state raised the banking interest rate, they were even unable to pay the interest and slipped into a vicious circle:

> enrollment expansion → increasing loans → increased debt → further enrollment expansion

Analytical framework and research problems

Amid the fundamental change in the fiscal system of higher education, what on earth caused HEIs to borrow money? What is the correlation between HEI financing decisions and HEI financial operation characteristics? What factors determined the financing amounts? The present study analyzes and discusses these three key questions through financial information investigations performed at and interview-based surveys administered at participating HEIs.

In reality, why HEIs select loan financing is not simply determined by the HEIs themselves. In fact, it is a result of the interaction between several stakeholders pursuing their individual interests. And this is why it is important to examine what factors affect HEIs' selection of financing channels on the basis of the concept of "stakeholders" and to discusses stakeholders' motivations and return expectations in HEIs' selection of loans as a tool to obtain much needed funds. It is also paramount to look at stakeholders' influence upon loan financing decisions. In terms of specifying the stakeholders of higher education institutional loan financing, in accordance with Mitchell's (1997) classification, the present study is focused on the deterministic stakeholders, namely, the banks, HEIs and governments involved in financing decision-making. All three parties have a legal status that gives them a great deal of influence. In terms of analyzing the factors affecting the size of higher education institutional financing, the present study examines the correlation between financial operation characteristics and the financing amounts, and considers the institutional characteristics and the social and economic development level of the regions where the relevant HEIs are located. In terms of surveying HEIs' financial operation characteristics, the present study examines the current financial situation of the HEIs through a ratio analysis method. On the basis of a special financial ratio, the ratio analysis method is a basic financial analysis technique that is widely used to determine the key factors behind HEIs' operating efficiency. Financial ratio analysis may be also applied to identify the signs of poor financial management among HEIs, such as a single financing channel and a reduced capacity to repay debt. By using these techniques, this study may help higher education administrators and government administrators better understand HEIs' current financial predicament and learn from the mistakes that some HEIs have made in dealing with financial crisis.

Figure 14.1 (below) shows the analytical framework used by the present study. On the basis of this framework, and with reference to the financial survey data and field investigation data (obtained from HEIs under the direct

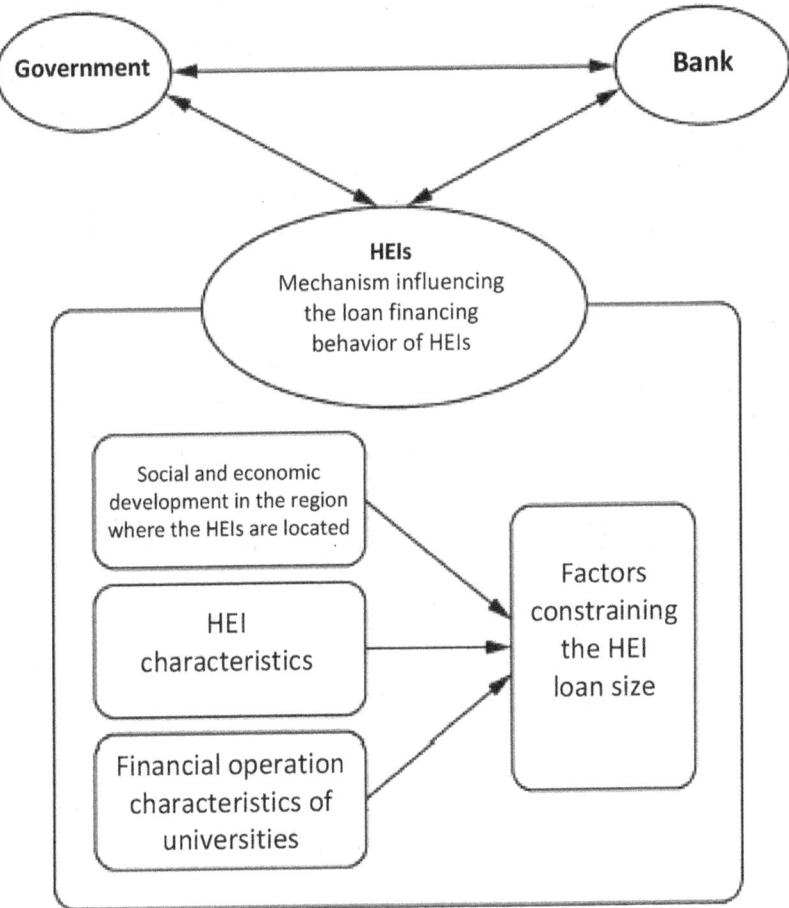

Figure 14.1 Analytical framework

administration of the Ministry of Education), this study also covers the following three issues: (1) why Chinese HEIs decided to borrow money from banks; (2) HEI financial operation characteristics; and (3) the correlation between the size of the financing and HEI financial operation characteristics. Due to the limited number of data sources, the analysis is only targeted at seventy-six HEIs under the direct administration of the Ministry of Education, with the data up to the year 2005.

The reasons why HEIs sought loan financing after enrollment expansion

From the perspective of government: HEIs' borrowing due to top-down guidance

The Chinese government had already recognized educational institutions' financing decisions in the capital market in 1993, when the State Council released *China's Educational Reform and Development Guidelines*, and in 1995, when it released the *Law of Education*. However, at that time, before enrollment expansion, loan financing was not a major financing channel for the majority of HEIs.

The situation has fundamentally changed since the expansion of higher education enrollment in 1999. State Council Vice-Premier Li Lanqing pointed out the following in the *Report to the Third National Education Work Conference* in 1999: "Proceeding from local conditions, we must guide social forces to invest in education and encourage social forces to run schools and make contributions to education through positive fiscal, financial and tax policies." After the Third National Education Work Conference, the "bank–higher-education cooperation model" was widely adopted by HEIs across China. In 2002, the People's Bank of China and the Ministry of Education issued *Opinions Concerned to Further Enhance Construction Capital for Student Apartments, Logistical Services and Facilities of Universities and Colleges*, which stated that "commercial banks shall further improve the relevant regulations and rules inside the system to enhance the credit support for student apartments, logistical services and facilities of higher education institutions." It accelerated loan financing among HEIs. Obviously, the policy guidance from the central government promoted the popularization of loan financing operations among HEIs.

Special attention should also be paid to the special role that local government plays in the promotion of loan financing among HEIs. After the implementation of tax reform, especially since 1999, land transfer revenue has become a key source of extra-budgetary funds for local governments. Being driven by their own interests, after the implementation of enrollment expansion policies, a number of local governments spared no expense in developing higher education park and university zones in a bid to achieve comprehensive urban planning reform that would help advance science and technology, education, and society as a whole. On the other hand, it helped raise land transfer revenue and expand extra-budgetary capital. Unfortunately, under such an interest-driven mechanism, the implemented policies posed a big risk to the future well-being of HEIs – loans would soon get out of control. Some local governments began to offer subsidiary funding for higher education loans. This lowered the interest burden for HEIs and encouraged financial institutions to be more enthusiastic about offering loans. However, it also led to the rapid rise of higher education institutional obligations.

But it was not just explicit guidance from the government that promoted loan financing for HEIs through policy formulation, as mentioned above. There were also some tacit forms of guidance: governmental financial investment in higher education lagged far behind demand after enrollment expansion, and higher education teaching assessment standards were constantly being upgraded. These factors also prompted HEIs to borrow money from banks.

Concretely speaking, as the HEIs enrolled more and more students, they needed more infrastructure and facilities. The resulting funding shortage placed a great deal of pressure on the HEIs' financial operations. It is the main reason why a number of HEIs selected loan financing.

The Chinese government has made several upgrades to the assessment standards for higher education teaching in order to ensure a high level of teaching quality and provide sound learning and living conditions for new higher education students. In 2004, the Ministry of Education specified basic running standards for ordinary HEIs in a teaching assessment regulation. According to these standards, HEIs should add RMB 40,000–50,000 worth of fixed assets for every student enrolled, among which infrastructure investment should account for about RMB 40,000 (Jiang 2006). Admittedly, it is both necessary and important to make assessment systems for HEIs to ensure their teaching quality. However, current unified assessment indicators give no consideration to the individual differences in capital situations and higher education objectives of different types of HEIs. This mismatch and subsequent discounting of some HEIs' financial strength is another factor that has driven these same HEIs to seek funds from banks in the form of loans.

From the perspective of the bank: to cooperate with HEIs is a reasonable option for financial institutions to expand business scope and improve capital flow

Since the middle of the 1990s, deposits have been increasingly higher than loans in China's commercial banks. By the end of June 2004, the total amount of deposits in Chinese financial institutions was approximately RMB 6 trillion higher than the total amount of loans, while the total deposit amount of commercial banks was approximately RMB 5 trillion higher than the total loan amount (Li & Chen 2004: 4–7). Several factors prompted financial institutions to slow their lending. In terms of external conditions, most Chinese companies proceeded slowly when it came to the transformation of ownership. They were engaged in lower-level industries, with poor technological capacity and an unsound inner management mechanism. They were weak due to the competition they faced in an oversupplied market, and they were therefore unable to meet the lending requirements imposed on them by the financial institutions. On the one hand, the rising gap between deposits and loans exposed the obstacle standing in the way of the transfer of savings to investment, while the financial system as a whole was far from functioning a full when it came to resource allocation. On the other hand, this situation reflected how weak the financial institutions were when it came to innovation: their capacity to approve loans and their efficiency in so doing was quite low. And this prevented the funds from being used in society. As banks transferred to a new running system in which they were to be responsible for their own profits and losses, they were faced with a new challenge – to come up with new ideas, seek more high-quality credit customers, and raise valid credit investment.

Amid such a background, the cooperation between banks and HEIs guided by the government was a favorable change for Chinese financial institutions. At that time, China was trying to improve its higher education system. Financial institutions in China regard HEIs as a huge potential market that can be developed due to high potential returns and powerful support from governmental departments. Banks could adjust the credit structure and smooth the deposit-loan gap through making loans to HEIs. Loans to HEIs were seen as high-quality incremental credit assets incurring low risk. Meanwhile, financial institutions could, through cooperation with the HEIs, attract the attention of high-quality faculty members and students, turning them into customers or potential customers.

Of course, in order to mitigate risk, banks were tendentious in selecting HEIs with which to do business. According to relevant analyses and reports, banks adopted different credit policies for different HEIs. More specifically, banks offered credit with a view to vigorously supporting the large-scale, high-quality HEIs that had the best facilities. Credit to HEIs was determined on the basis of several indicators, such as social reputation, cash flow, financial investment, stability of student population, standard tuition rate, employment rate, and management level (Bank of China 2006). Bank selection has had a huge impact on the structural difference in the size of the loans taken out by different HEIs. This is discussed further below.

From the perspective of HEIs: to operate on borrowed funds is a realistic choice given the financial difficulties that ensued after enrollment expansion

As organizational decision-making bodies, HEIs decided to select the channel of loan financing for the following three reasons. First, government financial input fell far short of their funding requirements for enrollment expansion. In particular, the infrastructure fund supplied by the State Development and Reform Commission was so low that HEIs were faced with funding crises after enrollment expansion.

Second, there is limited room for raising the standard tuition rate, so it is difficult for HEIs to increase self-generated revenue. In recent years, the government has, quite remarkably, transferred a great deal of higher education costs to the individual over a short period of time, following as it did the "burden on beneficiaries" principle for investing higher education funds. According to calculations,[1] one higher education student needed to pay on average RMB 25 for tuition and fees in 1990. The figure rose to RMB 2,145 in 1998. As HEIs charged higher tuition fees after enrollment expansion, the figure jumped to RMB 4,857 in 2004. It has now far exceeded the level that people can reasonably be expected to meet, leaving little room for further increases.

In addition, some HEIs have had few external financing channels. It is another important factor motivating them to raise money from banks. As pointed out above, government financial support fell far short of HEI requirements, and universities had limited financing channels for scientific research and social services. Local ordinary universities, especially those located in undeveloped regions, faced severe funding crises. It comes as no surprise, then, that they chose to borrow money from banks.

Factors affecting financing channel selection and the rise of the debt crisis

Above, we have discussed why HEIs select various loan financing channels from the perspectives of the government, banks, and HEIs. Results have shown that there are several factors that lead Chinese HEIs to operate through loan financing channels (see Figure 14.2). It is in the mutual interest of HEIs and of financial institutions, under the direction of government

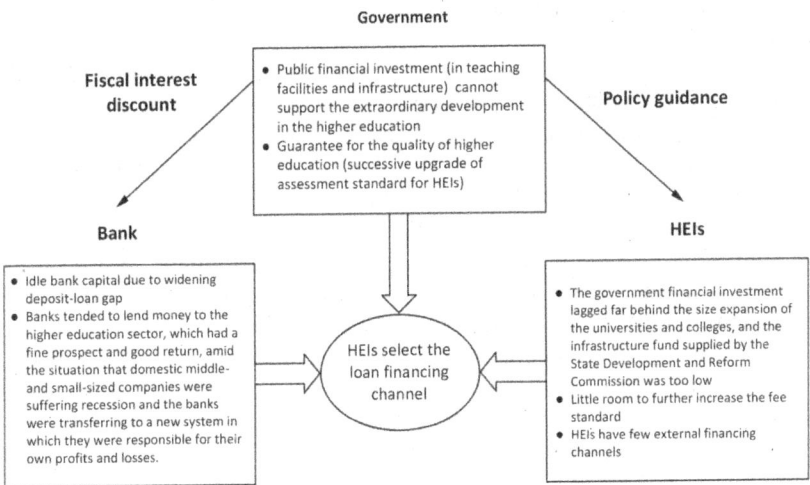

Figure 14.2 Factors that led HEIs to borrow money from banks

policies, due to the dual pressures of declining support from government funding and the sharp increase of operational expenses caused by enrollment expansion.

In the former system, loan financing acted as a strong financial support mechanism for HEIs to use in order to make much-needed infrastructure improvements could not have otherwise been made (due to decreasing financial support from the government). This special financing channel offset the funding shortage for higher education well for a significant period of time. However, as loan size and the loan growth rate spiraled out of control, the ensuing debt crisis has become a severe challenge that HEIs face in their financial operations. This has drawn a great deal of attention from government decision-makers and from society as a whole. The source of the higher education debt crisis may be explained with regard to the following four issues.

First, there were no effective loan monitoring systems and risk prevention mechanisms in place. In 1999, the Ministry of Education stipulated clear requirements in the *No.10 Document* that every HEI should be responsible for the loans that it borrowed. It emphasized that, as an independent legal entity established independently in society, the HEI should "enjoy civil rights and assume civil obligations in accordance with the law." In 2004, the Ministry of Education and the Ministry of Finance issued *Opinions on Further Strengthening Capital Safety Management for Higher Education Institutions under the Direct Administration of the Ministry of Education*. By virtue of the stipulations in this document, higher education loans were largely regulated and controlled. It must be pointed out that the present loan monitoring system and risk prevention mechanism are only followed at the level of the central government. By contrast, as far as higher education loans are concerned, some local governments have overemphasized the need to boost the local economy and social development, and this has resulted in loan sizes getting out of control.

Second, HEIs showed a lack of awareness of the debt crisis and of debt management more generally. They also did not possess strong financial management capabilities. Some higher education administrators were simply not aware of the debt crisis and about HEIs' civic duty to manage and be responsible for independent loans. As their financial funds decreased and the market pressure increased day after day, many HEIs failed to develop a strategic financial plan that took their long-term development prospects into account. They also failed to conduct a careful analysis of the initiation and repayment plan for their loan financing programs. So the following questions must be asked: How can we improve the management efficiency of HEIs? How do we improve the cost recovery mechanism? How do we boost resource use efficiency? How do we increase revenue and the value of funding? Higher education administrators and financial personnel did not attach enough importance to these questions. On the contrary, some HEIs made blind investments without careful consideration of the financial consequences they could have.

Third, since the second half of 2003, the Chinese government has adjusted its monetary policy, which tightened the rules concerning loan release and recovery. This was another factor that led to the rise of the higher education debt crisis. In the second half of 2003, the People's Bank of China adjusted the state's monetary policy and raised the deposit reserve rate. This lowered the capital liquidity of commercial banks, tightening short-term capital while raising the inter-bank offering rate. This adjustment to macro-financial policies changed the supply-demand relations in the capital market, and it became more difficult for HEIs to borrow money from banks. The debt crisis therefore got a lot worse for those HEIs that took out new loans to pay off old debts.

Finally, since 2005 HEIs have slowed their rate of expansion. It is another factor we should not ignore in discussions about the rise of the higher education debt crisis. The Chinese government began to slow higher education expansion in 2005. The adjustment of the development trend for higher education heavily impacted those HEIs that primarily relied on self-funding (i.e. tuition and other fees) because the adjustment decreased the funds available for repaying loans.

The current situation with regard to HEI debt

Growth trend of loan size in recent years

Higher education loans have experienced rapid growth since 1999. The total amount of banking loans to HEIs under the direct administration of the Ministry of Education was only RMB 500 million in 1998. The figure soared to RMB 8.8 billion by the end of 2002, to RMB 14.1 billion in 2003, and to RMB 23.7 billion in 2004.[2] The higher education loan growth rate has exceeded the HEI revenue growth rate. HEIs have obtained the following types of loans: credit loans, mortgages, equipment loans, project loans, liquidity loans, and institutional loans. They have received these loans from a variety of sources, including state banks, credit unions, joint-stock banks, other financial institutions, and other non-traditional funding channels.

HEIs have repaid loans through the following means: support service operations, logistics services to the public, sale and lease of faculty member and/or student apartments, land replacement, and tuition fees. Tuition and accommodation fees are the two significant revenue sources for HEIs. Tuition fees accounted for 60% of the repayment in the Chongqing case (Zheng 2007).

Since 2004, government education administration departments have strengthened their monitoring of higher education debts. However, the monitoring was only effective relative to explicit debts. There is no effective monitoring of those tacit debts which have resulted from unconventional means of financing. At present, higher education tacit debts may be classified into three categories. First there are payable fees for finished or unfinished projects – since HEIs have adopted the cash-basis financial accounting system, such debt-related data was seldom shown in the HEIs' financial statements. Second, HEIs have raised funds from faculty members and higher education employees. Third, HEIs have misappropriated idle funds, and this as well does not get recorded on HEI financial statements. If these tacit debts were monitored by the state, the higher education loan size of HEIs would be much larger and the current debt crisis would be seen to be far worse.

Difference in HEI loan amounts

In 2005, the total outstanding loans of seventy-six target HEIs reached RMB 33.58 billion, with the outstanding loan principal being RMB 30.04 billion. On average, each HEI assumed a loan amount of RMB 442 million. In the same year, these seventy-six HEIs achieved total revenues of RMB 65.666 billion. On average, each HEI had revenue of RMB 864 million. From this, we can calculate that, at present, loans account for 51.1% of total revenue. Conceivably, the pressure to repay these loans has been one of the key factors affecting Chinese HEIs' normal operations.

Of course, not every HEI is plagued by excessive debt. Among the HEIs visited, five did not borrow any money from the bank: two foreign language universities and two technology universities. This means that higher education institutional borrowing behavior may be closely related to the institution's disciplines. Through a Box Plot, Figure 14.3 illustrates intuitively the distribution information of the loan amount per student in different types of HEIs. We can see that the loan per student in comprehensive HEIs is highest, with the median being RMB 17,388. What is more, the distribution spans a wide range. That is to say, there is a huge difference in the loan amount even among the same types of HEIs. The second-largest borrowers are agricultural and forestry HEIs (with the median being RMB 16,224) followed by economics and law HEIs (with the median being RMB 13,801), normal universities (with the median being RMB 12,359), and technology universities (with the median being RMB 11,909). The smallest borrowers are art HEIs and foreign language HEIs.

Loan amounts are not only related to higher education disciplines, but they also have a close correlation with higher education revenues, faculty member performance, and number of students.

The size of the higher education institutional loan varied, depending on the HEIs' positions in the higher education system. In the study, HEIs listed in Project 985 are seen as excellent. The target HEIs are classified into three levels: core HEIs listed in Project 985 (2+7), other HEIs listed in Project 985, and HEIs not listed in Project 985. The loan amount per student in the core HEIs listed in Project 985 is RMB 13,839 (median). The figure for ordinary HEIs listed in Project 985 is RMB 12,707, and the amount is RMB 11,355 for HEIs not listed in Project 985. As shown in Figure 14.3, the loan amount per student maintains a growth trend in those HEIs with higher revenues and larger numbers of students.

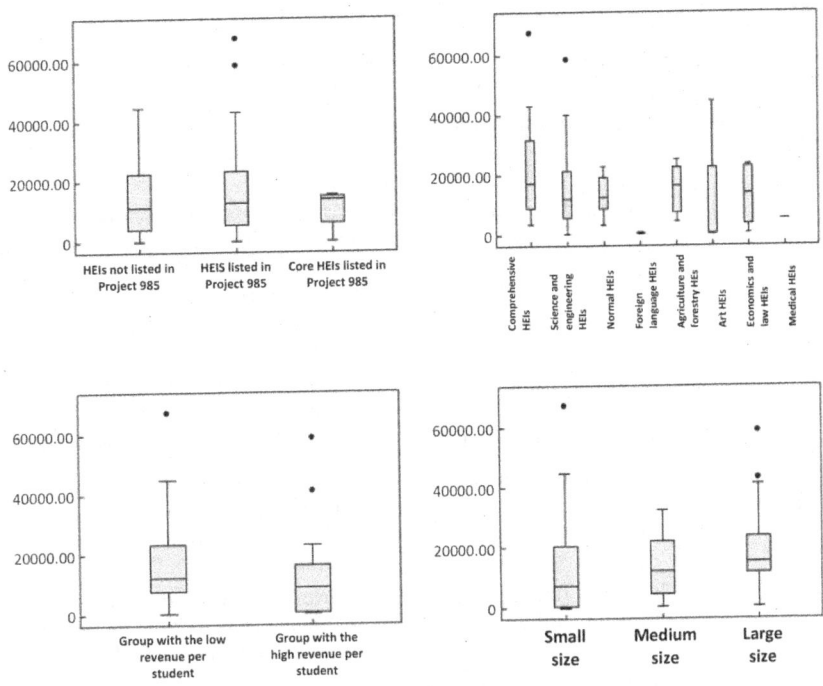

Figure 14.3 Average loan per student for different types of HEIs (Unit: RMB)

Financial operation characteristics of HEIs

The present section discusses the financial operation characteristics of HEIs through the ratio analysis method. Of course, in terms of the assessment and analysis of the HEI's financial situation, it is vital to select appropriate indicators and to construct a proper indicator system, which will directly determine whether the research conclusion is scientific, objective, accurate, and reliable. It is vital that the research conclusion be sound for it will then be able to be used by decision-makers in their policymaking activities. In order to show the higher education institutional financial situation scientifically, fairly, objectively, and completely, Table 14.1 specifies financial analysis indicators by referencing the research achievements of Tang et al. (2006), INUF (2006), and Nonaka et al. (2001). This approach may better reflect how positive and how sound the HEIs' financial situations are. A systemic analysis is performed with regard to the following four factors: (1) besides governmental financial allocation and tuition fees, whether the HEIs manage to expand new financing channels, to diversify their fund sources for sustainable and long-term operations (namely, through the diversification of funding sources); (2) as an independent legal entity, whether the HEIs have formed a sustainable financial operations on the basis of sustainable funds, (namely,

Table 14.1 Specification for analysis indicators of higher education financial operations

Analysis items	Analysis indicators	Definition
Diversification of fund sources	Dependence on tuition fees (-)	(Tuition fee – accommodation fee) Total revenue x 100
	External financing ability (+)	(Training revenue, research revenue, operating revenue, construction from auxiliary units, other revenue) Total revenue x 100
Fund stability	Public financial support (+)	(Government funding for education, government funding for scientific research, other funding) Total revenue x 100
	Asset-liability ratio (-)	Total liabilities/Total assets x 100
Fund sufficiency	Expenditures per student (+)	Total annual expenditures (junior college students x 0.8 + undergraduate students x 1 + graduate students x 2.5)
	Research funding per faculty member (-)	(Governmental funding for scientific research + research revenue)/number of full-time faculty members
Fund use efficiency	Ratio of water, electricity, and heating fees (-)	(Water, electricity, and heating fees)/ public expenditure
	Turnover of fixed assets (+)	Total revenue/fixed assets

fund stability); (3) whether various sorts of financial resources are sufficient for the improvement of teaching quality and research (namely, fund sufficiency); and (4) on the basis of a guarantee for the smooth operation of educational services, whether various sorts of financial resources are used effectively (namely, fund use efficiency). For more details about the indicators, please refer to Table 14.1.

From the above analysis of the loan amounts for different types of HEIs, we can clearly see that different types of HEIs adopt different financial models. To further understand the financial operation characteristics of HEIs, one must investigate the financial situation of different types of HEIs from a micro-level perspective by taking into account their institutional characteristics. Here, HEIs are interactively classified into four types on the basis of the number of students enrolled and the average revenue per student (Figure 14.4).

Type I represents the large-size, high-revenue HEIs. All ten universities of this type are comprehensive universities or technology universities and are on the Project 985 list, with an average history of seventy-eight years. During the enrollment expansion period, 80% of Type I institutions were merged, with student numbers soaring remarkably. In addition, Type I institutions are all

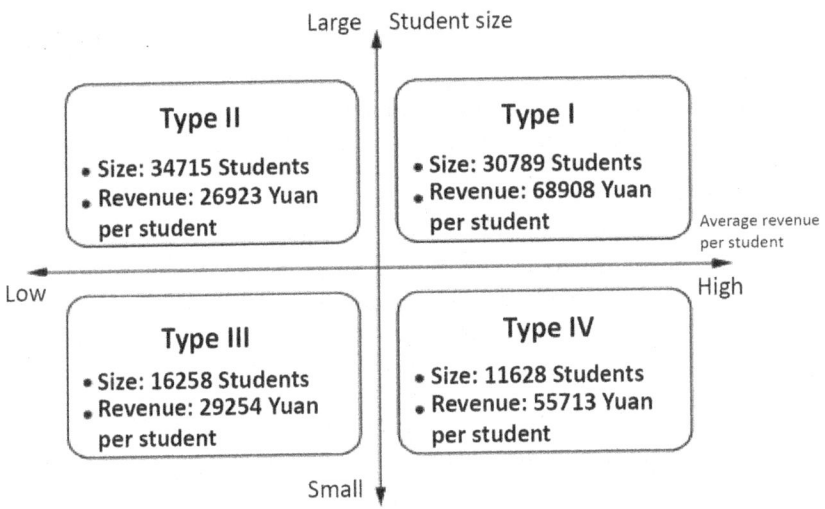

Figure 14.4 Classification for HEIs

located in economically developed regions. Type II represents those large-size, low-revenue HEIs. There are twenty-three HEIs of this type, most of which are comprehensive universities or technology universities, with an average history of fifty-nine years. Differing from Type I institutions, only 56% of Type II institutions are on the Project 985 list of HEIs, and only 30% of them are located in economically developed regions. Type III represents small-size, low-revenue HEIs. Most HEIs of this type are agriculture and forestry HEIs or normal universities. Only 11% of Type III institutions are on the Project 985 list, and 19% of them were once merged during the enrollment expansion period. Type IV represents small-size, high-revenue HEIs. Like Type III institutions, HEIs of this type were founded not long ago. But in contrast to Type III institutions, most Type IV institutions are foreign language HEIs, art HEIs, and medical HEIs, and they are all located in economically developed regions.

Diversification of funding sources

Government funding, which has long been the core financial source for HEIs, lagged far behind the growth rate of higher education during the period of enrollment expansion. This is a serious problem for HEIs, including those under the direct administration of the Ministry of Education, with regard to their financial operations. However, due to the rapid expansion of student enrollments, the increasing demand for investment in teaching and infrastructure also imposed a great deal of pressure on the financial operations of HEIs. Thus, on the one hand, to a certain degree, HEIs need to raise their fees for students. On the other hand, however, they should introduce a market mechanism to expand financing channels so as to lay a diversified capital foundation upon which they can build future sustainable development.

The section analyzes the diversification of funding sources for HEIs through two indicators: dependence on tuition fees and external financing. An overdependence on tuition fees indicates that the HEIs manage to boost revenues through expanding their student enrollment or increasing their tuition fees. However, such a revenue structure is easily affected by fluctuations in student enrollment demand. Any change in government policies on higher education enrollment may directly affect the stability of HEIs' financial operations. External financing reveals the ratio of other funds (with the exception of tuition fees) to HEI total revenue. A high external financing ratio indicates closer relations between the HEI and corporations and/or society at large. It also indicates that the HEI has formed a diversified financing mechanism through extending its teaching and research services outward beyond it walls.

As shown in Figure 14.5, the HEIs under the direct administration of the Ministry of Education raise 32% of their funds from external channels, which is more than ten percentage points higher than the figure from tuition fees (tuition fees account for 20% of the total). That is to say, at present the HEIs under the direct administration of the Ministry of Education do not boost revenue merely through expanding student enrollment and increasing tuition fees. Instead, these HEIs have successfully diversified their financing channels through providing training services, through research cooperation with other HEIs, and through higher-education-run corporations. Different types of

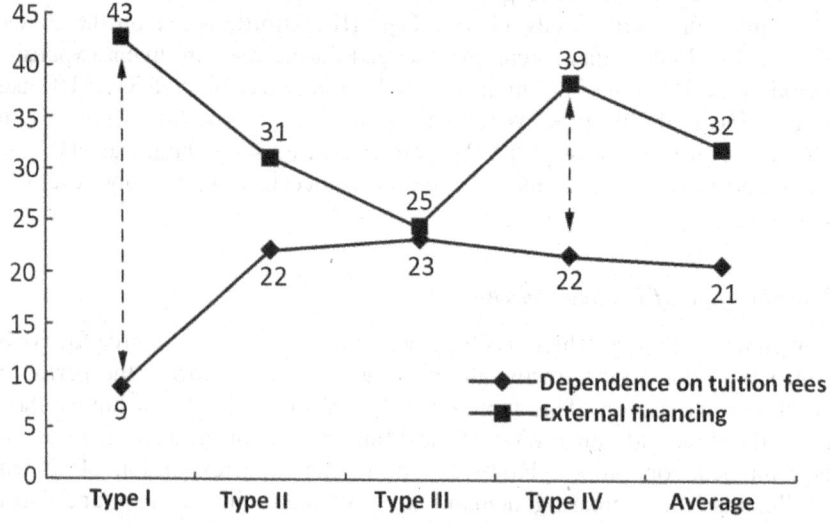

Figure 14.5 Diversification of funding sources for different types of HEIs (Unit: %)

HEIs have different structural characteristics. The average revenue per student of Type I and Type IV HEIs is higher than that of Type II and Type III. Type I and Type IV HEIs depend, on average, more on external financing than their Type II and Type III counterparts. Type I HEIs are able to raise more funds externally, with this figure being 34 percentage points higher than the figure for tuition fees. Type IV HEIs are also able to raise funds externally, with this figure being 17 percentage points higher than the figure for tuition fees. By comparison, Type II and Type III HEIs are relatively weak when it comes to external financing.

In terms of specific external financing channels, Type I HEIs mainly rely on scientific research revenues (17%), non-formal education revenues (11%), social donations (13%). This indicates that these HEIs have reached a certain level of scientific research cooperation income and social donation income by means of their social reputation (and all this has to do with the strengths of their scientific research). By contrast, non-formal education accounts for 18% of total revenue obtained through external financing channels for Type IV HEIs. That is to say, Type IV HEIs obtain external revenues depending on their teaching strengths through the provision of teaching training to unconventional students and the expansion of target customers. By comparison, Type III HEIs obtain only 7% of total revenue from scientific research, a low figure compared with the other three HEIs types.

Fund stability

Along with the decrease of the ratio of government funding to total HEI revenues, HEIs are faced with new risks and challenges with regard to their financial operations due to their decision to seek out new financing channels, the most notable of which are bank loans. Of course, achieving a stable financial position does not necessarily entail the prevention or avoidance of all risks. But HEIs must ensure consistency between assumed risk assumed and expected return (OECD 2004). Below, fund stability will be looked at from two financial indicators – public financial support and asset-liability ratio. Stronger public financial support indicates stronger government funding support. Such a funding structure enables HEIs to conduct various activities on a sustainable basis. Asset-liability ratio reflects how capable an HEI is in carrying out activities on the basis of the funding provided by the lending organization. Asset-liability ratio reveals how well the debt is managed. The ratio must be controlled within a reasonable range. If the ratio goes too high, it may lead to a financial crisis; if it goes too low, the HEI cannot use the funds for their intended purpose. Since the HEI's assets belong to the state and to society as a whole, they generate an intuitively social benefit in addition to a purely economic one. Thus, the asset-liability ratio for HEIs shall not generally be higher than 50% and must be under the safety threshold of 60%. The lower the ratio, the more sufficient HEI assets are to cover HEI debt.

278 *HEI loan financing and financial operation*

Figure 14.6 (below) shows the public financial support and asset-liability ratio indicators for different types of HEIs. It should be noted that, according to the *Accounting System for Universities and Colleges*, the fixed assets of Chinese HEIs are free from depreciation. Instead, the HEIs collect "maintenance and purchase funds" at a certain rate from service and operation revenue to cover fixed asset maintenance and update expenses. In this sense, maintenance and purchase funds are not value transfers of fixed assets. Accounted for at their original value, the actual value of an asset deviates from its book value, and this generates a distortion in the asset information (Chen 2002). Thus, we should keep in mind that the asset-liability ratio below may be underestimated. Average public financial support accounts for 48%, nearly half, of total revenue of the seventy-six HEIs under the direct

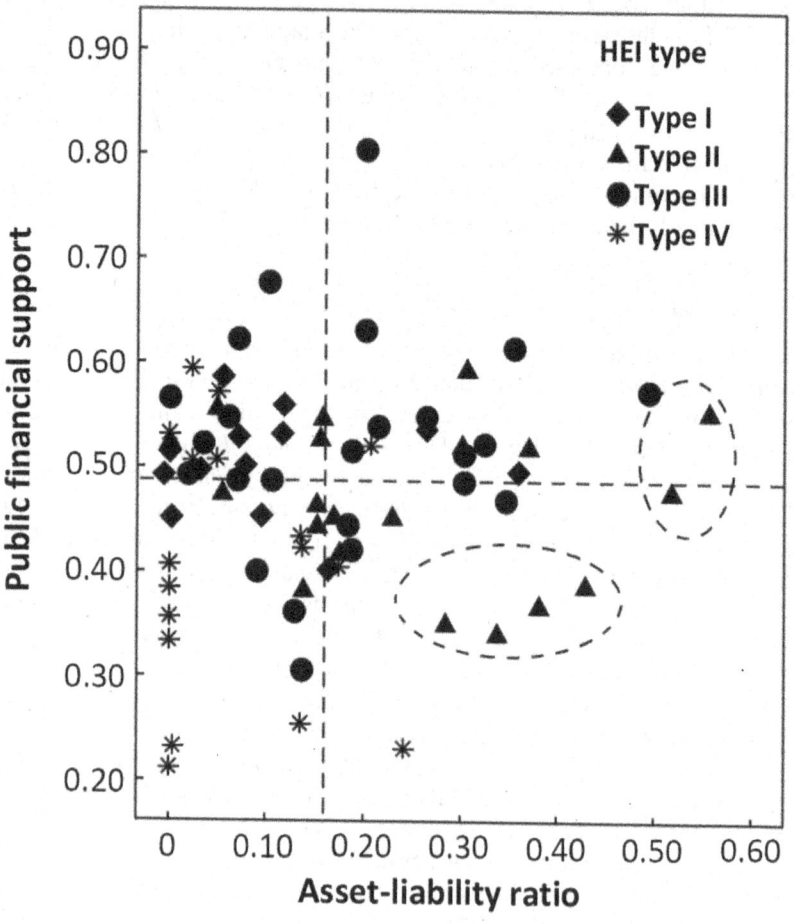

Figure 14.6 Financial stability of different types of HEIs

administration of the Ministry of Education. Even so, there are still thirty-one HEIs whose public financial support is lower than this level. Most of them are Type II and Type IV HEIs, with an average asset-liability ratio of 16%, a moderate figure. Those assuming no liability are mostly foreign language and art HEIs.

At present, in terms of the asset-liability ratio, two Type II HEIs have exceeded 50% and are facing a serious financial crisis. In addition, attention should be also paid to the HEIs that fall into the fourth quadrant (with an asset-liability ratio higher than the average level and public financial support lower than the average level). Due to the lack of powerful and sustainable support from the public purse, these HEIs have to repay their debt based on tuition fees and external financing. Such debt repayment mechanisms will be inevitably affected by market fluctuation and other external factors. From Figure 14.6, we can see that most HEIs in the fourth quadrant are Type II institutions.

Fund sufficiency

Can the HEIs obtain sufficient income to fund their operations? The core functions of HEIs can be divided into three categories: teaching, research, and community service. Community service is provided on the basis of the first two functions. In other words, community service is provided through the implementation of the first two functions. It is difficult to clearly distinguish these three functions in cost accounting terms. The present study focuses mainly on the first two functions – teaching and research. Expenditure per higher education student is a substitutive indicator for training cost per student. A high indicator level means that the HEI can offer more funding for teaching activities. Scientific research funding per faculty member refers to the average amount of scientific research funding provided to the faculty member. A higher figure indicates that the higher education faculty members enjoy a higher level of funding for scientific research activities.

Figure 14.7 shows that the high-revenue Type I and Type IV HEIs have a higher average expenditure per student than the other types. One of the reasons why Type IV HEIs have a higher average expenditure per student is that Type IV foreign language HEIs and art HEIs usually have only 5,000 students, far lower than the average figure for the seventy-six HEIs (22,719 students). As for the average scientific research funding per faculty member, the figures for Type I HEIs are two to three times those of the other types, fully revealing their dominant status as research HEIs.

Fund use efficiency

The HEIs would not be able to truly focus on decreasing their operating costs without the emergence of a crisis. Today, in the face of increasing financial pressure, they must manage to expand their external financing channels. On the other hand, how do they improve the use efficiency of existing higher

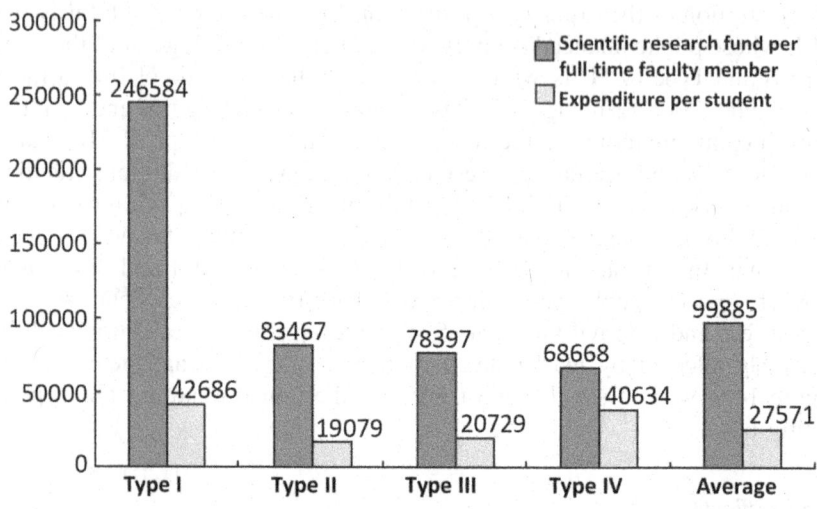

Figure 14.7 Fund sufficiency of different types of HEIs (Unit: RMB)

education institutional resources? How do they reasonably lower and control their operating costs? These have been important questions that HEIs should no longer neglect when it comes to financial management. The water, electricity and heating fee ratio reflects the proportion of those fees to the total public expenditure. A high water, electricity, and heating fee ratio translates to a high level of consumption of water, electricity, and heating (and vice versa). Since teaching and research activities in different disciplines have different consumption structures, the differences between disciplines should be taken into account. The turnover of fixed assets reveals the use efficiency of fixed assets, such as buildings, teaching facilities, and land. Strictly speaking, the denominator refers to net fixed assets (namely, the balance of fixed assets after depreciation). However, the denominator is substituted by fixed assets due to the limitations of the present accounting system.

Table 14.2 shows the average figure of 6.9% for the water, electricity and heating fee ratio. The water, electricity and heating fee ratio is relatively low

Table 14.2 Fund use efficiency of different types of HEIs

	Ratio of water, electricity and heating fees	Turnover of fixed assets
Type I	4.4	7.0
Type II	7.0	5.7
Type III	7.5	5.6
Type IV	7.3	7.8
Average	6.9	6.3

in Type I HEIs. That is to say, they have made some progress in lowering water, electricity and heating fees and energy consumption levels. The turnover of fixed assets for the low-revenue HEIs of Type II and Type III is lower than average. That is to say, these two types of HEIs are relatively weak when it comes to fund use efficiency.

Comprehensive and sound level of financial operation for HEIs

Above, this study analyzed the financial operation characteristics of the HEIs under the direct administration of the Ministry of Education with regard to four factors: diversification of fund sources, fund stability, fund sufficiency, and fund use efficiency. Here, an attempt is made to comprehensively analyze the level of soundness of the financial operations for the HEIs with regard to these four factors. It is calculated on the basis of the characteristics of financial analysis indicators. In the case of a positive analysis indicator, it queues from high to low, scoring 4 for the sample HEIs between 100% and 75%, scoring 3 for those between 74% and 50%, scoring 2 for those between 49% and 25%, and scoring 1 for those between 24% and 0%. In the case of converse analysis indicators, they are scored conversely. On the basis of this schema, every analysis aspect is scored and a comprehensive score is given for how soundly and comprehensively HEI finances are managed, as shown below in Table 14.3.

From the financial operation characteristics of the four different HEI types, we can see that Type I HEIs are in the best financial situation, particularly with respect to fund sufficiency and fund source diversification. By comparison, the large-sized, Type II HEIs are relatively weaker when it comes to fund stability and fund sufficiency. That is to say, the biggest challenge that this type of HEI faces is how to avoid financial crises and how to improve fund sufficiency in its financial operations. Type III HEIs are relatively weaker when it comes to fund source diversification, fund use efficiency, and fund sufficiency. In other words, the biggest problems faced by this type of HEI are shortage of funds, lack of effective external financing channels, and low resource use efficiency. Type IV HEIs are in a relatively better financial

Table 14.3 Score for the sound level of financial operation for different types of HEIs

Type	Diversification	Stability	Sufficiency	Efficiency	Total score
Type I	23.8	17.9	24.4	20.6	86.7
Type II	18.8	13.0	12.6	14.7	59.1
Type III	16.2	15.8	13.6	13.5	59.1
Type IV	20.2	17.4	17.7	17.3	72.6
Average	18.9	15.6	15.6	15.6	65.7

situation. However, there is room for improvement in fund stability, fund sufficiency, and how efficiently funds are used.

The correlation between loan size and financial operation characteristics of HEIs

In the analysis model, it is supposed that the size of the loan is limited by three factors: (1) the level of economic and social development of the target region, (2) the institutional characteristics of the HEI, and (3) the financial characteristics of the HEI. Before looking at the results, it is perhaps instructive to briefly describe the variables (i.e. the factors). First, the level of economic and social development in the target region is represented with per capita GDP. Second, the institutional characteristics of the HEI are represented by HEI type with a comprehensive HEI dummy variable, social reputation with HEI level, and the size of the HEI with number of students enrolled. Third, the financial operation characteristics of the HEI are represented according to the above analysis of the level of soundness of HEI financial operations. Therefore, the following financial operating funding characteristics are represented: prospects with external funding dependence; fund sufficiency with expenditure per student; and fund use efficiency with the water, electricity, and heating fee ratio.

Table 14.4 shows the results of an analysis of the factors affecting HEI loan size. Model 1 reveals that loan size has little connection to the level of economic and social development of the region where the HEI is located. This means that the gap in the size of the loan among HEIs in different regions is mainly caused by the HEIs' own respective characteristics. However, it should be noted that the analysis is only targeted at the HEIs under the direct administration of the Ministry of Education. Such HEIs are mainly funded by the central government instead of the local government. This is the main reason why their loan size has little connection to the level of economic and social development of their local region. Model 1 also reveals that, in terms of the HEIs' organizational characteristics, the comprehensive HEIs borrow more money from banks than non-comprehensive HEIs, while the HEIs with a strong social reputation borrow less money from banks than those with a weaker social reputation (with all other variables remaining unchanged). In addition, an increase in HEI size largely led to a corresponding growth in loan size.

As for the correlation between the HEIs' financial operation characteristics and loan size, on the supposition of no change in institutional characteristics, the study discovers that, although the indicator of external financing doesn't pass the significance test, the results show that those HEIs depending more heavily on external financing borrow less money from banks. That is to say, the HEIs with advanced diversified financing channels borrow less money from banks. Compared with the indicator of dependence on external financing, the expenditure per student and water, electricity, and heating fee ratio

Table 14.4 Multiple linear regression analysis on the factors affecting HEI loan size

		Model 1	Model 2
(Constant)			
Level of economic and social development of the region	Per capita GDP in 2005	0.034	0.306***
Institutional characteristics of the HEI	Higher education discipline	0.287	
	Comprehensive HEI virtual		
	Three levels	-0.428 ****	-0.554 ****
	Social reputation		
	Size of the HEI		
	Student enrollment number	0.880 ****	0.906 ****
Financial characteristics of the HEI	Diversification of fund source		
	Ratio of external funds	-0.041	-0.042
	Fund sufficiency	0.171 *	0.060
	Expenditure per student		
	Fund use efficiency	0.157 *	0.224***
	Water, electricity, and heating fee ratio		
Institutional type	Type IV: High revenue and small size	—	-0.272**
	Type II: low revenue and large size	—	-0.431 ***
	Type III: low revenue and small size		-0.358*
	R squared after adjustment	0.578	0.609
	F value	15.679 ****	13.994 ****

Note: Dependent variable = total outstanding loan. Type of sample HEI: Type < high revenue and large size. Significance level: *p<.10, **p<<.05, ***p<.01, ****p<.001

have passed a 0.1 significance test, and all are of positive effect. With all other variables remaining unchanged, the HEIs that have higher fund sufficiency and lower fund use efficiency borrow more money from banks.

Model 2 explains the relation between HEI size and loan size without considering the institutional characteristics and financial operation characteristics of the HEI. The results of the analysis show that Type I HEIs have a higher incremental effect of loan size than the other three types.

Conclusion

This study has carried out an in-depth analysis of the roots of the emergence of the higher education debt crisis and of Chinese HEIs' selection of loan financing as a major source of funding after enrollment expansion. This study explained the correlation between the amount of debt and the financial operation characteristics of the HEIs under the direct administration of the Ministry of Education using information and data obtained from a field survey. And it has come to the following conclusions.

First, there are several factors compelling Chinese HEIs to obtain funds from the capital market. Loan financing reflects the mutual interest of HEIs and financial institutions, under the direction of government policies, due to the dual pressures of declining support from government funding and sharp growth in operational funding needs caused by enrollment expansion. This special financing channel helps offset HEI funding shortages during difficult times. On the other hand, offering loans to HEIs helps financial institutions adjust their credit structure and improve their capital flows. However, HEIs have been hit hard by the central government's adjustment of its financial policies and higher education expansion policies – an adjustment that came about as a result of a lack of effective monitoring and risk prevention mechanisms for higher education loans. In addition, higher education administrators have a general lack of awareness about issues related to debt responsibility. The higher education debt crisis has therefore gotten worse.

Second, higher education loan financing polarizes the higher education system and widens the financing gap among educational institutions. Table 14.5 shows the financial operation characteristics and financing behaviors of different types of HEIs. The majority of Type I, high-revenue, large-size HEIs have a long history and a strong social reputation and are on the Project 985 list. They were merged with other HEIs during the period of enrollment expansion, and they have a large number of students. This type of HEI has special financial support from the government and has successfully diversified its financing channels. Thus, they have sufficient funds for scientific research and have therefore laid a firm foundation for future sustainable development. Financial institutions regard them as high-quality credit customers. It is easy for them to borrow a lot of money from banks because of their capacity to repay debt. There is no financial risk for such loans, due to the low asset-liability ratio.

Table 14.5 Financial operation characteristics and financing behavior for different types of HEIs

Type	Proportion	Institutional characteristics	Financial operation characteristics	Financing behavior
Type I (High revenue, large size)	13%	• High academic performance • Mainly of comprehensive universities and technology universities • With long history • In economically developed regions • Most of them were merged with other HEIs	• High financial support and effective external financing channel • Sufficient funds for teaching and scientific research • High fund stability	Financial institutions see them as high-quality credit customers. And it is easy to borrow a lot of money from the bank.
Type II (Low revenue, large size)	30%	• High academic performance • Mainly of comprehensive universities and technology universities • Most of them were merged with other HEIs • More than half of those HEIs are located in economically undeveloped regions • Most of them were jointly founded by the central government and local government	• Poor financial support • No effective external financing channel • Serious shortage of funds for teaching and scientific research • Low fund stability	Vigorous financing to increase fund
Type III (Low revenue, small size)	34%	• Low academic performance • Mainly of agriculture and forestry HEIs and normal HEIs • Half of those HEIs are located in economically undeveloped regions • Never merged with other HEIs	• Poor financial support • Dependence on tuition fees and weak external financing • Shortage of funds for teaching and scientific research	Hard to conduct effective financing, though they are very short on funds, since they are seen as high-risk customers by banks
Type IV (High revenue, small size)	22%	• Low academic performance • Mainly of foreign language and medical HEIs • In economically developed regions • Not merged with other HEIs	• Low ratio of tuition fee • Obtain external funds through non-formal education • Sufficient funds for teaching and scientific research • Moderate fund stability	No active financing behavior

Compared with the former type, the Type II, low-revenue, large-size HEIs have a weaker social reputation. The biggest difference between these two types is that the latter are located in economically undeveloped regions, and that it is a negative factor for the HEIs to expand external financing channels. Generally, they fall short of funds for teaching and scientific research. In order to increase these funds, they manage to borrow funds from banks. And this may lead to severe financial risks and a high asset-liability ratio. At present, Type II HEIs account for 30% of all HEIs under the direct administration of the Ministry of Education, nearly twice the percentage of Type I HEIs.

Type III HEIs are mainly located in economically undeveloped regions. They usually run just one discipline. Most of them are small, low-revenue agriculture and forestry HEIs and normal HEIs. They depend heavily on governmental financial support and tuition fees, and have low external financing capabilities. Although they are short of funds, they cannot easily borrow money from banks, since the latter regard them as high-risk credit customers. This type accounts for up to 34% of the total HEIs under the direct administration of the Ministry of Education.

Type IV, high-revenue, small-size HEIs are mainly located in economically developed regions. Most of them specialize in foreign languages, art, and medicine. This type accounts for 22% of the total HEIs under the direct administration of the Ministry of Education. Since they have never been merged with other HEIs, they have a relatively small number of students. In terms of funding sources, the main financial operation characteristic of this HEI type is to vigorously carry out external financing through non-formal education activities. At the same time, in terms of tuition revenue, they charge relatively higher fees in order to offset their low student enrollments. If HEIs of this type have sufficient funds, there is no need for them to resort to loan financing.

From the above analysis, we can see that there are limitations to the ability of loan financing to offset the funding shortage experienced by HEIs. In implementation of loan financing, the selection adjustment made by financial institutions produces an indirect result: the imbalanced development of the higher education system is further intensified as bank capital flows toward the powerful HEIs of Type I. Although Type II HEIs are recognized by banks and may borrow money from them, they are steeped in financial crisis due to excessive loans and their heavy interest burden. The weak HEIs, most of them of Type III, find it difficult to borrow money from banks due to refusal by the latter to lend them money, thus partly falling into an even worse financial situation.

Third, through an analysis of the factors determining higher education loan amounts, it was found that the loan amount is not only related to HEI type, social reputation, and student body size, but that it also has a close connection with the financial situation of each HEI.

Interestingly, the results of this analysis indicate that the HEIs that take out large loans have sufficient funds, but they use them at a low level of efficiency.

The trend is worsening. High fund sufficiency indicates debt crisis is not merely limited to poor HEIs. Low fund use efficiency indicates that some HEIs suffering severe debt crisis use financial resources inefficiently and that they fail to make the necessary efforts to lower fund expenditure and control business costs.

In according with the analysis presented above, the authors of the present study would like to offer the following advice to Chinese HEIs with regard to financial operation management. First, with regard to the HEI financial burden mechanism, the responsibilities of government and the HEIs should be clearly defined so as to further increase governmental financial investment in higher education. The government should increase its investment in higher education as soon as possible. It is of the utmost importance that the government solve the debt crisis that HEIs currently face. Second, financial operation management should play an important role in resource reallocation so as to narrow the gap among different types of HEIs. Third, social accountability mechanisms must be strengthened and a financial monitoring and risk prevention mechanism for HEIs must be established. Finally, in order to solve the higher education debt crisis, HEIs should establish a mechanism for overseeing higher education management and strategic financial operations. On the one hand, they should make vigorous efforts to expand financing channels. On the other hand, they should improve the efficiency of their existing resources and lower their energy consumption levels and operating costs.

Notes

1 Tuition fees per student is calculated on the basis of the total number of university and college students of that year as well as the total amount of tuition and fees charged by universities and colleges, which is shown in the *Statistical Yearbook of Education Funding*.
2 The data source for the years 1998 and 2002 is Zhang (2004). The data source of years 2003 and 2004 is Zheng (2005).

References

Bank of China. 2006. *Analysis of the College Credit Risk (Internal Data)*. Beijing: Strategic Planning Department, Bank of China.
Bao, W. 2007. "Study on the Financing Mechanism for China's Higher Education System after Enrollment Expansion." *Education Development Research* Z1: 69–74.
Bao, W. & Y. H. Liu. 2009. "Regional Differences in the Resource Allocation to China's Higher Education Institutions from the Perspective of Fairness." *Education Development Research* 23: 37–43.
Chen, D. 2002. "Indicator Analysis on Higher Education Institution Moderate Debt." *Economist* 10: 110–111.
Institute for National University Financial Analysis (INUF). 2006. *Financing Report of National Universities in 2005*. Tokyo: Center for National University Finance and Management.

Jiang, X. H. 2006. "Discussion about Public Policies Concerned with Loan Repayment for State-Run Higher Education Institutions." *Chinese Public Administration* 10: 72–74.

Li, D. & Y. W. Chen. 2004. "Analysis on the Gap between Deposit and Loan in Chinese Banks as well as Countermeasures." *Regional Financial Research* 12: 4–7.

Mitchell, A. & D. Wood. 1997. "Toward a Theory of Stakeholder Identification and Salience: Defining the Principle of Whom and What Really Counts." *Academy of Management Review* 22(4): 853–886.

Nonaka, I., F. Yamaguchi & M. Umeda. 2001. *Financial Analysis of Private Universities*. Tokyo: Otsuki Shoten.

Organisation for Economic Co-operation in Europe (OECD). 2004. *On the Edge: Securing a Sustainable Future for Higher Education*. IMHE-HEFCE Conference. January 8–9. Paris.

Reed, W. S. 2001. *Financial Responsibilities of Governing Boards*. Washington, DC: Association of Governing Boards of Universities and Colleges.

Ru, X., X. Y. Lu & P. L. Li. 2005. *Analysis and Prediction on China's Social Situation for the Year 2006*. Beijing: Social Science Literature Publishing.

Tang, Y., Q. H. Cheng & M. Z. Yang. 2006. *University Governance: Finance, R&D and Personnel*. Taipei: Psychology Press.

Wang, C. F. 2005. "Discussion about Reform of the Accounting System of Chinese Higher Education Institutions." *China Audit Newspaper*, May 19, T00.

Zhang, Q. L. 2004 "Analysis Higher Education Institutions' Credit Capital Situation." *Accounting Communications* 9: 94–96.

Zheng, E. 2005. "Preventing of Higher Education Institution Loan Risk." *Journal of Beijing Normal University* 5: 117–121.

Zheng, J. 2007. "The 'Black Hole' of Higher Education Institutional Loans Contains a Deep Crisis and Increases the Costs of Housing." *Economic Information*. Available from: http://u.shnu.edu.cn/Default.aspx?tabid=10491&ctl=Details&mid=22369&ItemID=1496&SkinSrc=%5BL%5DSkins/texxmh1/twxxmh1&language=zh-CN.

15 An examination of the "engineer of human souls" metaphor

Liu Yunshan

The questions

There are all kinds of metaphors for education and for teachers. Among them, the metaphors of growth, molding, and sculpture used by Israel Scheffler have been widely discussed (Scheffler 2004).[1] This study begins with the metaphor of the teacher as "engineer" and asks three main questions: how do teachers in the material world connect with human souls? What strategies and mechanisms are adopted to mold new generations of students? How are these strategies and mechanisms presented in modern Chinese education?

According to an investigation by Chen (1997), the term "engineer of human souls" originated from a talk between Russian leader Joseph Stalin and Russian writer Maxim Gorky. Stalin called Gorky and other writers "engineers of human souls." Later, Mikhail Kalinin, an educationist in the Soviet era, emphasized the importance of education in shaping a student's character and morality. He said: "Many teachers always forget that they should be an educationist, while the educationists are engineers of the human soul." In China, this metaphor first appeared in an editorial published in the *People's Daily* in 1951. "As the engineers of the human soul, teachers must be strict with themselves and remold thoughts carefully, in order to deserve the honorable title of 'People's Teacher'." In the same year, an editorial entitled "People's Teachers Must Be Marxists" published in *People Education* stated that "the People's teachers and educationists are the engineers of the souls of children and youths in new China. They assist the working class in leading the country. To a great extent, teachers decide the nation's future." In June 1957, Zhou Enlai said at the fourth session of the 1st National People's Congress that "teachers are soul engineers to educate the younger generation. Based on previous thought-remolding, they shall continuously conduct self-education and self-transformation on a voluntary basis" (Chen 1997: 407–409). This statement contains three keywords: "engineer," "soul," and "human."

Engineer

This is the most fundamental profession in an industrial society. Engineers are authoritative in professional and technical areas and they rely on their vast instrumental knowledge. Engineers adopt the factory model, which emphasizes extrinsic standards. The formulation of such standards is subject to governmental regulations or is controlled by the market. When the concept of "engineer" is implanted in education, humans are treated as raw material and become laborers waiting to be processed. Then, the "products" are classified as either "safe products" or "dangerous products," or as "high-class products," "qualified products," or "inferior-quality products." Education and schools are likened to factories producing talents. Administrators and the public are generally concerned about the direct input and output of education rather than its processing details, which as a whole are likened to a black box. The black box is not transparent because such transparency is not needed. Smooth operations and high economic returns are enough.

Soul

Does education need to touch the soul? How does it touch the soul? In the evolution of educational and philosophical concepts, different scholars have offered up different answers to these questions (Dupuis & Cordon 1977). Classical and philosophical views on education represented by Plato and Aristotle focused on the duality of human beings. Human beings consisted of body, soul, and mind, with the soul being the most important of the three. The soul was the essence of human beings. The soul controlled the human body. As far as the ultimate purpose for human beings was concerned, soul healing and peace of mind were the most relevant objectives to pursue. Religious activity became a core part of school education. School and church were closely related. The history of Western education is a history of communication between religion and education. Over the last one hundred years, liberalist educational philosophy has dominated educational practice. Liberalists doubt that humans are super-empiricist and supernatural. They deny the separation of body and soul. Education teaches that they are sons of nature, rather than sons of God. The body is liberated in school education. Daily living skills are what is trained in schools. With the expanding of liberalist educational curricula, the education of soul and spirit was insufficient. Instead, school education focused on cultivating personal emotion, physical development, and vocational skills, as well as social adaptability. In such an education scheme, students lose their identities because they are overly concerned with skill training. Meanwhile, teaching becomes a profession limited to certain areas, with teachers becoming transformed into "masters of certain specialties."

Human

"Human being" is a collective and abstract term. In educational practice, teachers face individual students, rather than abstract and holistic "human beings." People are different. At the macro-level, people vary with respect to state, nationality, traditions, and culture. At the micro-level, people are different with regard to gender, stature, motivation, and interests. The object and product of education should not be average people without individualities. Such abstract "human beings" become objects of education or the "results" of education. Students are treated as average people being deprived of distinctive personalities as well as people predicated by laws and regulations. Students are developed into a new type of "people" through normalized training and they become the result of normality shaped by statistical politics. However, the objects of education are not "blank slates."[2] The dynamics of human nature rest in its diversity and great potential, as well as in its situationality and its mystery.

This paper focused on the following questions, namely: how individuality is replaced with normality, how norms become the core of education, what is the origin of the political philosophy in remolding a new generation, and how powerful the forces are in shaping a new generation in Chinese socialist education. In other words, this paper intends to discuss the conceptual basis for the concept of "the engineer of human soul" and how human soul is shaped in the context of Chinese society.

"Normal" and teachers

"Normal" is a term closely associated with teaching. This term has two main meanings: (1) conforming to a standard, and (2) the state of being usual.

Normal school (teachers' college) is an institute for the training of teachers and a place to cultivate a teacher's spirit and culture. The term "normal" is derived from the Latin *normalis*, which had the meaning of "conforming to common and/or usual standards." In the Chinese language, normal is interpreted as "those who have more knowledge can be teachers, those who have integrity can be models." This is a pursuit for teachers, namely, to be normal.[3]

Teachers are the carriers of various norms. In the framework of Foucault's (1998) Panopticon, the exercise of power is introduced, offering an important interpretation. On the surface of the educational power matrix, teachers act as executors of discipline, while students are the recipients of discipline. More deeply, teachers are both bearers and heirs of discipline.[4] Teachers are not only executors of but also products of the exercise of power. The process of training teachers is disciplined. It should be noted that whether teachers are there "to be disciplined" or "to discipline," when they exert power, their power functions as a structure beyond their control and beyond the control of individual actors. Actors have to obey the structure and integrate themselves into the structure. Teachers follow the logic of "to be disciplined" and the reproduction of "discipline." Thus, the exercise of power is more than a teacher's power. If "the teacher's power" functions as the leading actor in the theater of "the exercise of power," the exercise of state power, cultural power, and educational power constitutes the structure of this theater.

In modern democratic society, "normal" receives its new meaning – a normal state. In statistics, normal refers to a curve of normal distribution. Chi-Jeng Yeh (2003) analyzed two key statistical concepts – the mean and variance from the perspective of the sociology of knowledge. According to the empirical methods, in particular, the quantitative method and individuals are classified into different types (Foucault (1998) pointed out that Europeans presented facts via tables in the seventeenth and eighteenth centuries. In terms of the presentation of knowledge, quantitative methods started to become popular at this time). Such a method was applied to the classification of social groups. According to majority principle, the normal state of individuals is defined by the normal state of groups.

The term "statistics" is derived from the term "state." In the sixteenth century, some nations created a set of statistical theories and techniques in order to effectively control their citizens in general and their homeless populations in particular. Statistics combines science and politics. Statistics becomes a ruling tool under state authority thanks to its scientific rationality. In the UK, this technique was called "political arithmetic." During the Enlightenment in Western Europe in the eighteenth century, moral science was merged with the introduction of the scientific way of thinking about human and social phenomena. Once moral normalization was linked to the facts described by statistics, biased normalization was justified by "objective facts." In the nineteenth century, the concept of "normal distribution" created new social groups. People believed in the existence of general rules due to the concept of probability. The general rules were established based on the majority. The majority referred to specific and operable variables rather than to different individuals. Thus, through mathematics the average became representative of social groups above (or outside of) individuals. Individuals were classified. People received scientific training according to such classification.

"Normal state" and "abnormal state" are distinguished by the concepts of mean and variance. To decide the standard deviation, it is assumed that $-1.96 \sim +1.96$ is a standard range with which to draw a line between a normal state and an abnormal state. Within this range, anything is normal (e.g. normal intelligence), while the values outside of this range are abnormal (e.g. superior intelligence or low intelligence). Thus, the "quantitative" representation of a normal distribution curve transfers to "qualitative" differences. The majority within the boundary (central tendency) constitutes basic or universal characteristics. The minority outside the boundary becomes the heterogeneity that the society intends to control and is also a target to be transformed by education.

Moral science views society as a holistic unit. Normal men (or average men, more accurately) are merged under the normal distribution. Normal men (average men, in particular), the concept of "the people" as defined in the French Revolution, and mass society challenge the concepts of rationality and rational men. Maybe, with an emphasis on personal choice, rational men do exist (making choices requires rationality). However, rational men cannot control public life. The mystery of rationality is that will of the majority is above rational judgment. It is normally irrational. For individuals, each process and detail is rational; however, as a whole they may turn out to be irrational. As a social order, public life must be collective in form and must be above individuality. Statistics is considered as an effective way to seek such rationality in order to build social order. Thus, the average in mathematics expands to become a moral mean. The average is used to normalize moral man and normal man in a society. Take the fitness standard as an example. The fitness standard is a scientific health standard used to assess whether people are overweight or underweight (a height-to-weight ratio calculated by a mathematical formula). Unfortunately, according to this standard 50% or even more than 50% of people are overweight in our society. However, such a majority cannot change the standard. "Fat" and "thin", these neutral biological terms become value-biased moral judgments based on aesthetic and health concepts valuing fitness. "Fat" signifies "lazy," "overeating," and/or "poor." Even weight-loss is called "building lean muscle." The negative term "fat" is replaced with the positive term "lean." To this extent, social life is dominated by normalized values represented by average people without individualities.

In the majority-based definition of human nature, individualism is swallowed up by collectivism. According to the majority principle, more and more people become such individuals, more and more are close to the average, and more and more will disappear in the collective image. The hero (elite) worship that emphasized minority, specialty, stability, consistency, and deviation (unconventionalism) in the past has disappeared in mass society. The concept of the "average man" implies the elimination of intrinsic personal characteristics. Only public characters are shown. The observable, measurable, assessable indicators are the most important. The author of the present study participated in editing *History and Society* – a high school textbook. The theme of Volume I is "Individuality and Society." The editing logic is self-centered, from near to far, from small to large. Starting from daily life, there are five units in total: "Self-Perception," "My Family," "My School," "My Community," and "My Country." We made several changes to Unit 1, "Self-Perception." Initially, a psychologist proposed a process of self-understanding from physiological characteristics extending to psychological characteristics, and then to a behavioral model and style of thinking. Students are asked to fill in their personal information (i.e. height, weight, blood type, and appearance) as well as their psychological characteristics (i.e. extrovert, introvert, health status, and mood). This proposal was amiable because it was close to students' lives and their perceptions of themselves. This design, however, was first questioned by educationists: how can we use appearance and changeable indicators, such as height and weight, to recognize ourselves? Self-cognition cannot be based on such superficial variables. Education cares about a unique self with dignity, which has different experiences and which is part of different cultures. How could such a "self" disappear in a normal indicator system? Finally, philosophers were selected to edit this part because the psychologists' proposal failed to pass administrative review. The textbook's discourse now replaced the individual "I" with the "I" in society: "I am Chinese (historical identity)," "I love our country (political loyalty)," and I am a Chinese youth in the new times (modernity)." Again, correct and normal macro-narration excludes diversified and differentiated individuality.[5]

Modern education originated from a thriving "garden culture." Bauman (2002) pointed out that the development of modernity was a transformative process from "wild culture" to "garden culture." Like wild weeds, wild culture needs no conscious care to reproduce. As a core concept of garden culture, education is thought of as a tool that can be used to maintain a new order (an order different from the past). The origin of modern intellectuals can be found in the overlap between state administrators and educationists, who integrated politics, economics, and society into an overarching hegemonic ideology of culture. Bauman (2002: 262) quoted the following from Ernest Gellner: "At the base of the modern social order stands not the executioner but the professor. Not the guillotine, but the (aptly named) *doctorat d'état* is the main tool and symbol of state power. The monopoly of legitimate education is now more important, more central than is the monopoly of legitimate violence."

Education designs society according to rational voices and transforms society based on the public interest and rationality. So, education becomes a means by which human society can be shaped. The state has the power and is obligated to remold its citizens and guide its citizens' behaviors. In educational practice, average men or regulators are considered as the standard recipients of education, both for students and teachers in the educational structure. Average men are the representatives of social norms. It is a social fact; more importantly, it is a moral fact. All variances outside the standard deviation are flaws, a result of errors. Average men define difference as deviation. The purpose of education is to correct deviation, so as to maintain the "normal" in statistical terms and the moral norms behind normality. Thus, to create the "new man" is to shape the average man by eliminating differences. Both education and teachers are devoted to cultivating a new generation adaptable to the new order. This new order is a normalized world. Personalities are defined as wild seeds that are uncultivated, and they therefore need to be eliminated. Educators play the role of legislators of social life in youth education.[6]

Creating the new man

How do the legislators in this educational society shape the new generation of students? There is a lesson in a primary school textbook, which is called "A Little Blue Stone." This text vividly illustrates the process of remolding a new generation. It is surprising that this text has been kept in this textbook for so long, surviving several editions and revisions and influencing several generations of students, because China has undergone great changes and textbook contents have also been changed dramatically. Here is the text:

A Little Blue Stone

There is a little blue stone and a black stone in a mountain. The little blue stone says, "Here, it's too quiet! I am fed up with everything here. It's too boring to live here. It will be great that I can go freely like a butterfly or locust."

After thinking for a moment, the little black stone replies slowly, "Don't talk nonsense. We are born to be immobile."

"That's not good. In our hometown – on the mountain, there are many crystals and agates. Now, they go to cities. Some of them become hairpins, some of them become buttons. They travel all around and see new stuff. That's great. I have lovely colors too. Maybe, I will become hairpins or buttons if I go to cities."

A group of workers come to the shore. They scoop up stones with large shovels and put them into the trolley. Workers ship stones to the cities by trucks.

Little blue stone is pleased, "I am going to the city and may meet my old friends – crystals and agates. Will I become hairpins or buttons? Whatever, it's better than staying on the shore. Hey, pick me up quickly."

Little blue stone and his peers are placed on the wide road. They are scooped up and mixed with sands, cements and water, and then repeatedly stirred.

Little blue stone is dizzy and wet all over. He is very angry, "What on earth is going on? Why are we mixed? They are really out of line. Shouldn't we be sent to the jewelry shop?"

Stones are strongly stirred by the shovels. Little blue stone cannot breathe, being mixed in sands and cements. Finally, stones are spread out on the road. After they are flattened, the stones are covered with a mat.

Little blue stone is very tired and has to keep quiet. Suddenly, it's amazing that his body becomes stronger. He becomes a hard stone. Now, he feels much stronger than previously. Such rigidity is different.

"It's strange. What am I now?" little blue stone is wondering. He looks at himself. Now, he becomes a part of the concrete. "What, this is me?" He seems lost and confused.

Year after year, tens of thousands of people step on this little blue stone. Sometimes, cloth shoes jump over it. Sometimes, straw shoes run on it. Sometimes, leather shoes walk on it. Sometimes, bare feet step on it. Little blue stone sees many feet and feels very happy.

To become a road and serve the pedestrians is the happiest thing. Now, he neither belongs to Mr. Zhang nor Mr. Li. Instead, he serves the public. With his peers, he supports the feet of the public. Now, he no longer envies crystals or agates. He thinks, "This is the most meaningful life."

The purpose of shaping the new man is a process to reshape the natural state of "I" (little blue stone in the mountain) into "We" in the political state (concrete on the road). The term "We" means an aggregate beyond the individual. How is "I" replaced with "We"? How do we make the transition from self-welfare to public interest? What price do "I" pay for this? What logic is behind creating the new man? These concepts and practices are derived from the work of Jean-Jacques Rousseau.

According to Rousseau, the process of transferring from the natural state to the political state is built on "agreement" (Bloom 2003). Human rationality requires "I want" to be replaced by "We want" – this is a normal choice for rational people (also the only choice for average men). If people have the same demands, it is possible for them to establish a common community sharing the same will and responsibility (Bloom 2003). That "We" is above "I" indicates strong social connections. When "I" is replaced with "We," we become more powerful and receive more support. "We" controls "I." Social groups are therefore worshipped as "God." This is the origin of why we teach children that a drop of water must flow into the sea.[7]

In *The Social Contract*, Rousseau stated that "each of us puts his person and all his power in common under the supreme direction of the general will, and, in our corporate capacity, we receive each member as an indivisible part of the whole." He pointed out that:

> He who dares to undertake the making of a people's institutions ought to feel himself capable, so to speak, of changing human nature, of transforming each individual, who is by himself a complete and solitary person, into part of a greater wholesomeness from which he in a manner receives his life and being; of altering man's constitution for the purpose of strengthening it; and of substituting a partial and moral existence for the physical and independent existence nature has conferred on us all. He must, in a word, take away from man his own resources and give him instead new ones alien to him, and incapable of being made use of without the help of other men. The more completely these natural resources are annihilated, the greater and the more lasting are those which he acquires, and the more stable and better the new institutions.
>
> (Zhu 2003: 54)

How are human strengths to be accumulated? How is independent physiological life replaced with moral life? The answer involves the transferring of all individual powers to the social and moral state, forming a transparent and identical moral sector without impurity. The key strategy of the public will is to politicize daily life and to publicize private life.[8] Through revolutions, private life is expelled from the public arena and thus the boundary between public and private is blurred. Private morality is equivalent to public political behavior.

Rousseau's concepts had been tried in reality. Creating the new man for the People's Republic of China (PRC) was an important measure in rebuilding civil society. Le Perretiere, from the Jacobins, proposed a uniform education reform:

> All children are taken from their father and the state takes charge of their education. Education is free. All boys from five to eleven and girls from five to twelve receive the universal training. They wear the same uniform and receive the same education. Schools have strict requirements on food. Wine and meat are prohibited. They must cut the linkage with the family and become a new race of men ... Civic education first comes from transparent order of supervised equality and of pure and lasting mores.

Thanks to strict disciplinary measures, there are no unregulated places and behaviors in modern schools. The purpose is that "a new, strong, industrious, orderly and disciplined race [will be created] separated by an impenetrable wall from all impure contact with the prejudices of our ancient species."

Maximilien Robespierre revised Le Perretiere's plan and submitted it to the National Convention. He said: "Education is related to everyone and benefits the public. Before we establish a system, we need to decide the basis of such a system. A system only benefits the few, while education can benefit all. Therefore, it is necessary to establish a complete educational scheme. The gist of this scheme is comprehensively upgrading, namely, creating a new man!"[9]

The gist of shaping the new man is to transform individuals into carriers of the public will. At the individual level, the public will is built upon self-control. Self-control is the essence of moral experience. For a moral and respectful individual, the most important thing is to truly and freely obey the public interest, rather to than to satisfy his or her desires like an animal. This is the dignity of individuals and the basis for a good society.

Through continuously mixing with sand and cement, little blue stone begins to think from the perspective of "We." It says: "They are really out of line," breaking out of expectations of self-identity and role. "Shouldn't we be sent to the jewelry shop?" The stone was flattened, could not breathe, and was finally covered with a mat. The stone lost its "self-identity" without any choice. Now, little blue stone does not exist and becomes part of the concrete used to build a road. "What, this is me?"

In a short period of time, such a combination creates a moral common community, representing individual covenanters. The number of common community members equals all voters in the community. Thus, the common community gains its uniformity, collective public identity, and its life through such behavior. This is the "public personality," which comprises all its members (Zhu 2003).

The emergence of this public personality is the transformative process of a society in Rousseau's revolution. A new substance is created in chemical combination, namely, a "public personality" or a "moral common community." Educational tasks are "social chemical" reactions that transform a secular society into a moral society: "As long as private will conforms to public will, each person is moral" (Zhu 2003).

The public will is higher than, and may even be opposite to, the common will. But, why are the masses willing to accept the public will? (Zhu 2003). A mysterious force is needed to realize this transformation. Who can provide such a mysterious force? This is not a technical problem. Instead, it needs, according to Rousseau, an endowed divinity, at least a prophet or a demigod. Such a figure gazes at the public and only listens to the inner heart calling. The inner voice is magnified throughout the square, generating an implied hypnotic effect throughout the crowd, so that the masses become numb all together. As Rousseau said, this is "a moral state ignorant of morals" – Rousseau's inner heart ruling law (Zhu 2003).

Rousseau added a fourth kind of law, after political laws, civil laws, and criminal laws (which prevailed in the eighteenth century), namely, the governing law of inner life. This law is engraved on the hearts of the citizens: "This forms the real constitution of the State. When other laws decay or die out, it restores them or takes their place ... I am speaking of morality, of custom, above all of public opinion" (Zhu 2003: 245).

Due to the governing law of inner life, the governing authority no longer limits itself to regulating citizens' extrinsic behavior. Instead, the inner hearts of citizens are governed and moral activities are controlled. The scope of legitimate governance is expanded. The rulers' legitimacy is first built on approving citizens' consciences: the jurisdiction that is ruled is expanded from citizens' extrinsic behaviors to their inner states. "Political ruling" changes to "moral ruling" (Zhu 2003). Through moral politics, which are different from behavioral politics, inner ruling replaces extrinsic normalization. Rousseau's state is no longer a social keeper, but a social reformer. Such a state is like a secular temple. In this temple, individuals own nothing, while the state controls everything. The state controls education, belief, ideology, and all things in the spiritual world. By virtue of the inner ruling law, the state takes over the jurisdiction of Pope and churches and rebuilds a church without the instruments of *kasaya* or bishops (Zhu 2003).

Education is an important part of the state machine, while teachers are the extension of state power. New men are the subjects of such a society and state, as well as the physical carriers of public personality.

Moral precept or role model?

In Chinese educational practice, the governing law of inner life plays a dual role, namely, as an extrinsic precept (Foucault's "Calling") and as a role model to remodel the new man. Through moral education, Chinese society functions both as a precept society and a role model society.[10]

Chinese society once had strong collective social characteristics. It was totally under the control of state political power. The masses were highly dependent on the state. People were fully controlled by society. In such a society, the boundary between the public arena and the private arena was blurred. Individuals were gathered under the umbrella of a shared authority[11] instead of being allowed to establish direct connections in a mutually dependent community. Such "atomization" of the masses was not only for securing political governance, but for ensuring the mobilization of the people. In such a context, teachers are given high expectations and are called "People's Teachers."

"People"[12] in "People's Teacher" has two meanings. First, it refers to teachers serving the people. Here, people are the objects of teaching.[13] Second, it means people's teacher. "People" is an attributive concept, referring to teachers who serve people. For the first meaning, "People's Teacher" is a populist term. "People" in "People's Teacher" raises the social status of the unprivileged population. "Shoemakers always rebel against the masters. It's never seen that the masters rebel for being shoemakers. But, it happens now" (Liu 1998: 212). The government has asked intellectuals to step outside the reading room: utopian ideology was being transferred to utopian actions.

"Go to the people" became a new spiritual mantra and action strategy for intellectuals.[14] For the second meaning, "People" is an abstract attribute. "People" refers to the public personality and transparent and moralized public will. "People's Teachers" has a strong revolutionary connotation. Teachers are responsible for social enlightenment and liberation.[15] Such "People's Teachers" occupy a commanding position. They lose identity and stance and also act as a "mouthpiece" and "megaphone."[16] In educational practice, they act as the public personality, serving to shape public morals.

First, teachers becoming a part of the people (public personality) is a process of continuously being sermonized. They pursue the embodiment of political belief.

Political belief is integral – its adherents must wholehcartedly spread such belief. In other words, ideological members consider belief as moral characteristic, rather than as an object of recognition and understanding. Therefore, they consider that their only identity is as carriers of thoughts, rather than as individuals with personalities. The final result of such an orientation implies deeper meanings: thoughts and beliefs are therefore "personalized," while distinctive individuals are "ideologicalized" (Walder 1996: 140–141).

People's Teachers consider themselves as a tool for the cause of the people. Although schools are not directly involved in distributing key resources (such as property, professional titles, and salaries) in the economic system, schools are responsible for classification, recruitment, and the provision of targeted training to national elites. The school is characterized as a closed space featuring a high degree of mobility and time discontinuity. Students are required to perform excellently in a short period of time so as to accumulate various valuable assets and obtain good opportunities and resources. The school is organized into an educating place with a unified environment, distinctive rhythm, strict discipline, complex rituals, and endless training. New men are produced here and are depersonalized, even to the extent of having to efface their lives as individuals. To some extent, a core part of school-based education involves "self-effacing," disciplinary techniques that aim to produce "tamed bodies," "correct thoughts," and/or a "tamed souls."

It is necessary here to correct a certain kind of misunderstanding, namely that the tamed body is produced by the military camp and that tamed thoughts are produced by schools. Actually, Foucault's analysis reveals that the "tamed body" and "tamed thoughts" are inseparable. Therefore, such disciplinary techniques are spread quickly between military camps and schools (Foucault 1998: 157). We have many reasons to group schools and military camps under the same governing framework. Passive members hardly survive in either military camps or schools. From this perspective, people in schools or military camps are only different in terms of whether they are pursuing a normalized mind or a normalized body.

In her book *Children of Mao*, Chan (1988: 12) classified the four categories of activists as follows: the conforming activist and purist activist by value dependency, and the rebellious activist and pragmatic activist by behavioral consistency.

In *Communist Neo-Traditionalism: Work and Authority in Chinese Industry*, Walder (1996) carefully investigated how disciplinary techniques are present as performance in Chinese organizations – "impression decoration" under a pair of eyes (eyes could be secret and abstract personal records, or serve as a specific, visible, and ubiquitous form of supervision): daily life in a politicized reward system requires the development of a conscious and calculative "presentation of the self" – one must speak, act, and think in such a way as to express loyalty according to different roles in different scenarios.

Organizational hierarchy is also engraved in school education. For example, student cadres – how a position to serve classmates and class changes to a special status, even a privilege. This tiny thing reflects the hierarchical status system in education, which entails the grabbing and monopolizing of limited resources. Individual living space, discursive power, and even expanded free space is built on invading or oppressing others' space. This is why people compete for a civil service position: in such a system, a few elites enjoy major privileges, while the majority of people are robbed of such privileges – maybe, this is due to the influence of administrative logic in past eras.

Role-model education works well with the concept of discipline. As was mentioned above, Chinese society is not only a moral precept society, but also a role model society. The moral precept society focuses on human behavior and emphasizes behavioral norms. The role model society focuses on spirit and focused on the pursuit of inner spirituality. The former has to do with passive control by laws and regulations, while the latter has to do with an active inducement encouraging you to accept good advice. Punishment dominates the moral precept society, while praise is the most important tool in the role model society. The moral precept society relies on hard power (i.e. state authorities, such as the courts, the military, and prisons) to deter the majority through punishing the minority, so as to govern the society. By contrast, soft cultural powers such as customs, education, art, and culture permeate the role model society. Social control is realized through self-discipline and internalized norms. In Foucault's Orwellian control, humans are objects that need to be supervised and corrected at all times. In the role model society, humans are active and are even actors. They actively participate in social activities and understand social rules. Even personal sacrifice is considered as self-fulfillment and the peak of personal morality, rather than as a kind of self-negation. In the role model society, social control transfers to social connection based on the concept and sense of internal common community. By contrast, the moral precept society is controlled by an external "Big Brother." Therefore, morality is transformed from a binding force to a constructive force. Borge Bakken (2000: 86) explained the Chinese character 德 ("morality") and its connotation. The character on the left-hand side shows a diagram of a crossroads, which means "to go" or "to move," indicating transformation. On the top right of the character 德 ("morality") are the dual components 眼 ("eye") and 心 ("heart"), referring to seeing and thinking, respectively. In Chinese socialization theory, the term "heart" denotes an intrinsic aspect of socialization, while "eye" denotes an extrinsic aspect of socialization. Morality is about observing appropriate behaviors with the eyes, and then internalizing them with the heart. In the role model society, setting a good example is an important educational practice. Then, the behavior of the role model is adopted throughout society through imitation and praise. The initially small number of role models will transform into a great deal of role models who will have moral characters and who will perform moral deeds.

Shaping the role model

A role model not only represents norms, but also an important means to maintain social order. The role model is not only a kind of social construction, but it is also a kind of social memory. The shaping of the role model concept in Chinese educational practice is an interesting research area. The history of establishing role models experienced a process of transformation from moral embodiment to functional hero (from sage to expert), from hero to representative, from elite role model to group role model, from the deed system (sacrifice) to a representative system,[17] and from a function-diffusive role model to function-specific role model. The former is related to a main social theme, while the latter engages with a certain area, from heroic deeds to good deeds in daily life. The purpose of establishing role models is to connect social worship (worshipping of society) to daily life, that is, to promote good deeds for all people. What is the basis for the role model? Is the process of producing a role model based on a top-down approach or a bottom-up approach? Shaping a living role model should be a top-down process. If role models are not real or contextually related, or weak in social connection and cultural foundation, they will not be convincing.

After establishing a role model, imitation and repetition are important strategies for moral education. For individuals, imitation means growth. For groups, imitation means increasing social cohesion. Therefore, imitation takes on dual responsibilities: education and governance. Imitation supports special social connection and order, devoting itself to social integration. Learning from role models is neither a simple teaching method, nor just copying or repetitive imitation of social exemplars (simple copying and imitation are animal instincts). The power behind the role model deserves our attention. Let us end with a look at two educational techniques.

Role-playing. Role-playing can be oral or behavioral, automatically extending role models – similar to activists' deeds. Role-playing not only reinforces roles, but also emphasizes the formation of character. Role-playing brings actors through the process of socialization a subtle manner. "To do something" is more important than "what this is" in moral practice. "To be a man" is to act according to social expectation – with self-discipline, loyalty, and obedience; such classical terms are keywords for "being a man." It is interesting that the term "make" is closely related to the terms "drama" and "theater." However, in Chinese society, "performance" and "acting in a play" do not occur among strangers. Instead, they take place in rigid social structure built on strict rules and norms. People's attachment to society is integrated into social hierarchy and norms, defining different social statuses. In Chinese society, human perception focuses on the relationship between men and society, rather than non-relational personal characters. Therefore, adapting to external norms is important for "being a man." In short, extrinsic morality is far more important than intrinsic morality, and "to do something" is more important than "what this is."

Praise. "Praise" is also an important educational technique. Through praise, the typical actions of role models are affirmed and rewarded. Also, praise must take place publicly. The more people participating in it, the higher the level of praise will be. Or, the higher the level of the place receiving praise, the more valuable the praise. In the role model society, we need to further explore a key question: what is the role of praise in human growth and in shaping diversified personal character? Praise always encourages ambition and encourages us to stand out in the group. Such praise becomes a kind of privilege and advantage. For example, the debate on eliminating a top student award represents such a tendency. Is this debate about award standards being too limited or about this award not being suitable for education?

The eye of power, role model guidance, imitation and repetition, role-playing, and praise incentives are not only different strategies for shaping the new man, but also levers with which to achieve the transcendence of souls. They are moral practices under the theme of enlightenment and soul salvation in the context of modernity. More importantly, in the period of postmodernity, this theme still exists: the wine bottle has changed, not the wine. Foucault's "eye of power" (the minority supervised by the majority) changes to Bauman's "active showing" (the minority attracts public attention). The role models are transferred from the carriers of worshipped value and behavior to the normal state and average man in social statistics (excluding internal characteristics and statistical average temperament). Through mass media, fashion becomes an important mechanism to decide young people's behavioral orientation and aesthetic standards. Fashion also shapes the new generation in a haphazard manner.[18] Social collective connection is formed with people flocking to fashion. This is the significance for reviewing the old metaphor of the "engineer of human soul."

Notes

1 Behind different metaphors, social structures, economic forms, and cultural concepts vary. Thus, educational concepts and cultures are quite different. Accordingly, students' outlooks, teachers' outlooks, and teaching outlooks are different. For the growth metaphor, children are likened to plants, while teachers are likened to gardeners. This is an agricultural metaphor of education emphasizing that children are like plants, different seeds growing up in different shapes. Teachers serve as gardeners, indirectly facilitating the child's growth. Teachers must respect the natural rules and intrinsic characteristics of seeds, providing favorable conditions for their development. This metaphor emphasizes the prior life experience. Education is a reasonable process, rather than a continuous building process. Teachers play a passive role as caretakers. Alexander Sutherland Neill's Summerhill School well illustrates such a metaphor. The "molding" metaphor likens the child to clay, and the teacher to a potter. The teacher's task is to put clay into molds to produce unique shapes. This is a well-known metaphor of education. Teachers are engineers. Such a metaphor emphasizes teachers' initiative and responsibility, while ignoring intrinsic principles of student growth. The molds' standards and models are extrinsically established. It is a kind of invasion and transformation of personal growth and mindset by culture, society, and power. The "sculpture" metaphor likens students to sculptured works, and teachers to sculptors. This is an artistic metaphor of education. It emphasizes teaching students in accordance with their aptitudes. Or, education is an ongoing process in which students and teachers continuously communicate and inspire one another. As sculptors, teachers cultivate students according to students' characteristics, rather than allowing students to develop by themselves like gardeners do or treating students as raw materials like engineers do. Through dialogue, students are inspired to make their own decisions; students and teachers make positive progress together.
2 Previous educational ideology has a basic assumption – a child's mindset was a *tabula rasa* on which people could draw all kinds of beautiful pictures. This is an important basis for the authority of teaching as a profession.
3 "Learn to be an Excellent Teacher; Act as an Exemplary Person" is the motto of Beijing Normal University, one of the earliest normal universities in China.
4 A similar syntax structure is: individuals are both producers and products of history.
5 See *A Civic Reader for the Young Americans*, Lesson I: You, Chapter 1: "You: A Person" (a healthy person; you have your personality; getting along with others is necessary to be a good citizen); Chapter 2: "You: A Student" (having different study capabilities, improve your study and think clearly); Chapter 3: "You: A Family Member" (families are different, family problems, to be a good family member); and Chapter 4 "You: A Citizen" (government in your life and reasons for the existence of government). See D. Lin, "*U.S. A Civic Reader for the Young American*. Lesson I: You." *The Beijing News*, August 7, 2005.
6 *Chinese Language Textbook Volume X*, for Six-Year Primary School Education in Nine-Year Compulsory Education published by the People's Education Press.
7 In Chinese educational practice, collectivism has become a powerful constructive force. To explore this topic further, we need to know whether collectivism is

derived from Chinese agricultural production or traditional culture, or from communist political practices, or from a localization of communist culture. Benjamin Schwartz believed that Chinese ideologies tended to be public-oriented, emphasizing collectivism and average life, along with the Great Unity valued in Chinese traditional culture. In traditional Chinese society, family and clan were social units. Individuals depended on family. Social communication followed a from-close-to-far approach. After the People's Republic of China was founded, the model of dependent individuality was retained and even reinforced. Organizations became family. In children's textbooks, the homeland was referred to as "mother," while state leaders were often called "fathers."

8 Such concepts and strategies had been implemented in the Cultural Revolution and in the French Revolution.
9 See Gérard Walter (1983), *Robespierre*, p. 378. Beijing: Commercial Press.
10 Borge Bakken (2000) uses the concept of "the exemplary society" to summarize modern Chinese moral education and moral construction.
11 The lesson of "To be Chairman Mao's Good Children" in a primary school textbook published by People's Education Press: "To be Chairman Mao's Good Children Chairman Mao, Chairman Mao, Your photo is hung on our classroom wall. I seem to see you when I see your photo. One time, I drew a chicken on the book. When I saw you, I seemed to hear your voice, 'Why do you scribble in your book?' I quickly stopped it. One time, I played ball in class. When I looked at your photo, you seemed to say, 'Why don't you study?' I quickly put the ball into my bag. When I achieve good results in study or perform excellently on my duty day. When I looked at your picture, you seemed to say, 'Well done.' Chairman Mao, Chairman Mao, I want to be your good kid."
12 David Bloom (2003) argued that Rousseau made the term "people" problematic.
13 Mao Zedong wrote an inscription in *Teachers on the Border Area* (Spring 1938) to motivate teachers: "Make an effort to educate new generations."
14 "Bourgeois educational authority finds ways to exploit the people. Hired scholars try their best to seek legitimacy for political power. They raise the status of academics and lock people in the dark hell forever." Therefore, "The academic status shall be placed into the mass and return their true face with civil spirits. Fight against all noble scholars" (see Liu Xiaofeng [1998], Anarchism in China, in *Introduction to the Modernity Social Theory*, Shanghai SDX Joint Publishing Company, p. 213).
15 Mao Zedong emphasized the following in 1957: "To build socialism, the working class must have its own army of technical cadres and of professors, teachers, scientists, journalists, writers, artists and Marxist theorists. This is a task that should be basically accomplished in the next ten to fifteen years. The tasks after that will be to make further efforts to develop the productive forces and expand the army of working-class intellectuals" (*Selected Works of Mao Zedong, Volume 5* [1977], 462–463, Shanghai: People's Press).
16 Could our education system convert teachers back to the masses? Can teachers have their own voices in education and bring their personal experiences, memories, and stances to their teaching? Unfortunately, several years ago the author of the present study wrote an article entitled "How Has the True Voice Disappeared?" Doubts were raised about this article. Teachers are responsible for transmitting knowledge. Do we need their voices? The correct and scientific voices are the most important in education.
17 When we select role models, all aspects are considered, such as province, gender, age, nationality, and different behavioral characteristics.
18 In his investigation of the origin of fascism in Germany, Marcuse pointed out that the influence of young generation was one of origins of the emergency of fascist in Germany due to the decline of family as an agency of socialization, while family

authority replaced with state authority. In the Soviet era, the state took over many family functions. Children were passionate about the state. People worshipped party leaders and the Communist Party. In post-industrial and democratic society, the father's authority in the family was reduced. Young people found authority in their peers and mass culture. David Riesman called this new social figure "other-directedness." Today, the behavior and norms of idols and fans replace the father's authority. The fever of "Super-Girl" that erupted in the end of the spring of 2005 is a good example of such a social and cultural phenomenon.

References

Bakken, B. 2000. *The Exemplary Society: Human Improvement, Social Control, and the Dangers of Modernity in China.* New York: Oxford University Press.

Bauman, Z. 2000. *Legislators and Interpreters.* Shanghai: Shanghai People's Press.

Bauman, Z. 2002. *Life in Fragments: Essays in Postmodern Morality.* Shanghai: Academia Press.

Bloom, D. 2003. *Rousseau: The Turning Point, Giants and Dwarfs.* Beijing: Huaxia Press.

Chan, A. 1988. *Children of Mao: Personality Development and Political Activism in the Red Guard Generation.* Tianjin: Bohai Bay Press.

Chen, G. 1997. *An Analysis of Education's "Pedagogic Vision".* Shanghai: East China Normal University Press.

Dupuis, A. M. & R. L. Cordon. 1977. *Philosophy of Education in Historical Perspective* (2nd Edition). Lanham, MD: University Press of America.

Foucault, M. 1998. *Discipline and Punish.* Translated by LiuBeiching. Beijing: SDX Joint Publishing Company.

Liu, X. 1998. *Introduction to Modern Social Theory.* Shanghai: Shanghai SDX Joint Publishing Company.

Scheffler, I. 1994. *The Language of Education.* Translated by L. Fenqi. Taipei: Laureate Books.

Walder, Andrew G. 1996. Translated by GongXiaoxia. *Communist Neo-Traditionalism: Work and Authority in Chinese Industry.* Oxford: Oxford University Press.

Yeh, C. 2003. *The Tower of Babel of the Average Man/Dispersive Man: Two Key Concepts in Statistical Sociology.* Shanghai: Shanghai People's Press.

Zhu, X. 2003. *The Collapse of Moral Utopia.* Shanghai: Shanghai SDX Joint Publishing Company.

Index

Australia 3, 52, 254–5

Beijing 1, 3, 9–10, 38, 40, 42, 74, 89, 97, 148, 161, 205, 303
Beijing Normal University 303
brain drain 257
Brazil 3, 4, 5
BRICs 3, 5, 6, 145
Bush, George W. 149

Canada 3, 52
California Institute of Technology 225, 250
Chinese Communist Party (CCP) 8, 37, 38, 40, 42–6, 48–9, 187, 195, 196, 198, 200–02, 205, 207, 210, 212–13, 229
Copernicus 142–3, 153
Cultural Revolution 193, 195–6, 198, 199–204, 205–6, 304

Deng, Xiaoping 202–3, 205,

ethics 139, 212, 230
ethnic minority/ies 1–2, 38
Europe 52, 63, 110, 132, 134, 140–1, 143, 146, 152, 157, 216, 292
  Erasmus Programme 52
  European Union 34
  Socrates Programme 52
faculty 2, 9–11, 158–9, 172, 235–6, 242, 247, 254, 268, 271–2, 274, 279,
France 3, 141, 164, 167, 216, 222–3, 292–3, 304

Galileo 142–3, 153
Gaokao 1, 5
gender 1, 20–21, 35–8, 43, 67, 72, 74–8, 80–1, 84, 230, 291, 304
geography 3, 253

Germany 107, 141, 165, 197, 216, 222–3, 304
Global financial crisis 162
globalization 1, 6, 51–2
governance 6, 107, 112–13, 117, 119, 149, 158–9, 186–7, 298–9, 301–2
Great Leap Forward 196, 198, 200, 202
Guangzhou 1, 3

higher education
  debt 14, 263, 264–5, 269–70, 271–2, 277, 279, 284, 287
  financing 13–14, 261–88
  rankings 3, 5, 6, 13, 236–44, 248, 249
Hong Kong 3, 4, 15, 75, 133, 172, 229

India 3, 5–6, 110
Indonesia 3
Industry 17, 20–1, 26, 30, 36, 38–40, 42, 44–8, 153, 159–61, 165, 181, 193–5, 256, 300
internationalization 9, 51–66
Italy 167, 110, 141

Japan 3–4, 15, 34, 52, 111, 146, 156, 165, 167–8

Kazakhstan 3

leadership 8, 44, 45, 49, 72, 113, 195–6, 198, 218, 250, 257, 259

Macao 4, 229
Mao, Zedong 195–6, 200, 202, 304
Marx, Karl 113, 200, 210, 217, 289, 304
Massachusetts Institute of Technology 157, 225, 258
migrant children 3, 15, 184
migrant workers 3, 15, 174, 184

Ministry of Education 166, 217, 262–3, 266–7, 270–1, 275–6, 278–9, 281–2, 284, 286
Mongolia 111

Obama, Barack 149
Organization for Economic Co-operation and Development (OECD) 161, 185, 263

Pakistan 3
Peking University 7, 8, 15, 35–6, 48, 53–7, 61, 63–5, 70, 74, 102, 152, 161, 172, 175–7, 181–2, 202–3, 213, 215, 217, 229, 232, 235, 263
Popper, Karl 126, 142
Programme for International Student Assessment (PISA) 3–4
Project 211 36, 39, 43, 45, 47–8, 213, 215, 233–4, 263,
Project 985 36, 162, 213–17, 233–4, 263, 272, 274–5, 284

Quacquarelli Symonds World University Rankings 5

rural 1, 3, 11, 72, 159, 162, 169–191
Russia 3–6, 194, 197, 289

Saudi Arabia 105
Shanghai 1, 3–5, 15, 38, 40, 42, 148
Shanghai Jiao Tong University's Academic Ranking of World Universities 5, 15
Singapore 3, 54
South Africa 3, 5
South Korea 3, 15, 54, 167
study abroad 3, 5, 6, 51–66

Taiwan 4, 229
technology 7–8, 10–11, 30, 42, 54, 64, 85, 100, 114, 123–53, 156–7, 159–61, 168, 196, 205, 213, 224, 245, 251, 254, 257, 266, 272, 274–5, 285
Thailand 3
Tianjin 38, 40, 42
Times Higher Education World University Rankings 5
trends
 enrollment 2–3, 13, 14, 32, 165, 170, 172, 175, 198, 255, 261–87
 basic/primary education 1, 2, 17–31, 86, 88, 179, 185–7, 209
 higher education 1, 2, 3, 6–7, 9, 11–12, 17–31, 32–50, 51–66, 67–85, 105, 112–14, 117, 135, 151, 157–8, 160, 162, 164, 166–7, 176, 180, 183, 185, 190, 192–228, 229–249, 250–260, 261–288
 secondary education 1, 2, 17–31, 78, 183, 185
Tsinghua University 15, 172, 175–7, 181–2, 198, 202, 204, 213, 215, 229, 232, 235, 263

United Kingdom (UK) 3, 34, 223, 292
United States (US) 3, 6, 15, 52, 100–01, 161, 165, 167, 183, 223, 254, 256, 259
University of California, Berkeley 161, 257–8
urban 1, 3, 7, 15, 17–31, 72, 74, 77, 150, 162, 171, 174, 182, 185, 202, 266
U.S. News & World Report 52

Vietnam 4

Wen, Jiabao 166, 213, 219
World-class universities 213–16, 219–20, 227, 250–9

Zhejiang University 229, 235
Zhou, Enlai 202, 289